Institutional Games and the U.S. Supreme Court

Constitutionalism and Democracy

GREGG IVERS AND
KEVIN T. MCGUIRE,
EDITORS

Institutional Games and the U.S. Supreme Court

EDITED BY
James R. Rogers, Roy B. Flemming, and Jon R. Bond

UNIVERSITY OF VIRGINIA PRESS   CHARLOTTESVILLE AND LONDON

University of Virginia Press
Printed in the United States of America on acid-free paper

First published 2006

9 8 7 6 5 4 3 2 1

LIBRARY OF CONGRESS CATALOGING-IN-PUBLICATION DATA

Institutional games and the U.S. Supreme Court / edited by James R. Rogers, Roy B. Flemming, and Jon R. Bond.

    p.   cm. — (Constitutionalism and democracy)
  Includes bibliographical references and index.
  ISBN 0-8139-2527-4 (cloth : alk. paper)
  1. United States. Supreme Court. 2. United States. Congress—Powers and duties. 3. Separation of powers—United States. 4. Political questions and judicial power—United States. I. Title: Institutional games and the US Supreme Court. II. Rogers, James R., 1960– III. Flemming, Roy B. IV. Bond, Jon R. V. Series.
KF8742.A5I57 2006
347.73'26—dc22

                           2005029109

CONTENTS

PREFACE

How do the governmental institutions enmeshed in America's system of separated power and federalism interact, and with what consequences? Or, to rephrase the question to fit the concerns addressed by this book, how can we better understand the interaction between the Supreme Court and its institutional environment? This book reflects a recent and refreshing return of enthusiasm among law and politics scholars for deciphering how interactions between the Supreme Court, the lower courts, political branches, and the states mutually shape their decisions and behavior. This book squarely centers on developing new ways of understanding the complexity and consequences of these interactions. Game theory and formal modeling establish the book's leitmotif, but these approaches do not obscure the substantive contributions of the chapters that emerge from empirical tests of specific theories or models. The book's touchstone is that theory must be tested by data to yield new insights.

Games are puzzles abstracted from complicated patterns of human behavior. Game theory and formal modeling provide solutions to these puzzles or at least that is their promise. The United States Supreme Court confronts law and politics scholars with tough puzzles in institutional dynamics. Some of these puzzles deal with the Court's internal decision processes. Close observers compare the Court to the Vatican in Rome in terms of trying to decipher the Court's behavior. Its ethos of secrecy, relative inaccessibility to scholars, and the enduring, legitimizing myths enveloping its decisions add to the difficulties of solving these puzzles. Equally challenging puzzles emerge from the Supreme Court's external relationships. With neither the power of the purse nor the sword at its disposal, the Court must often navigate its way through roiling political seas as it follows John Marshall's famous declaration in *Marbury v. Madison* (5 U.S. 137 [1803]) that it is the Supreme Court's responsibility to decide what the law is.

This book offers game theoretic solutions to several of these puzzles. It adds a distinctive voice to the revival of interest in how the Supreme Court affects and is affected by its institutional relationships. Not too long ago, law and politics scholars busied themselves primarily with the internal decision processes of the Supreme Court. The so-called "attitudinal model," with its assumption that individual justices vote in cases on a "sincere" basis according to their personal policy preferences, encapsulated their concerns. That is to say, the justices, because of life tenure, no ambition to seek other offices, and no real prospect of being impeached, are free to act as single-minded policymakers. This perspective, a fundamental building block of the modern behavioral study of the Supreme Court for the past fifty years, originated with C. Hermann Pritchett's *The Roosevelt Court,* which was published in 1948 and which focused on the voting behavior of the justices. A decade later, Glendon Schubert, in *Quantitative Analysis of Judicial Behavior,* introduced greater sophistication to the measurement of judicial attitudes and decisions. With his second book in 1965, *The Judicial Mind: The Attitudes and Ideologies of Supreme Court Justices, 1946–1963,* and then its follow-up in 1974, *The Judicial Mind Revisited: A Psychometric Analysis of Supreme Court Ideology,* Schubert refined and honed the precision with which law and politics scholarship could be performed.

It would be misleading and a mistake to say the Court's position within American federalism and its system of separated powers was ignored as the modern era of judicial research evolved. Still, the attitudinal model, because of its emphasis on sincere voting behavior by the justices, could not be adapted easily to studying the Court's institutional interactions. The pioneers in the field of judicial politics, however, certainly recognized the importance of these relationships. As criticism of the Warren Court built up during the 1950s, for example, they turned to the Court's relations with Congress. Pritchett published *Congress versus the Supreme Court, 1957–1960* in 1961. A year later, in 1962, another pioneer of the modern era, Walter F. Murphy, released *Congress and the Court: A Case Study in the American Political Process.* In the preface to this book, Murphy (1962, vii) remarked that "relatively little literature . . . actually explores the reactions of other branches to Court decisions" and that he wanted to "shed some light on Court-congressional relationships" that would create "steppingstones to a more complete theory of American politics." Since the publication of these books, many scholars have picked up the challenge of understanding these relationships, but much of this otherwise fine work is legal or historical, as exemplified by the research of Louis Fisher (1992, 1988).

During the past ten years or so, two major changes occurred in the behavioral study of the Supreme Court that shape the orientation of this book. These shifts in perspective have prompted scholars to focus more intently on constructing what Epstein and Knight (1998) call the "strategic account." The first shift reconsidered whether justices behave in a "sophisticated" fashion as they pursue their goals. In contrast to the attitudinal model, this view portrays the justices as interdependent actors, whose attainment of their policy ends requires them to vote or to decide differently than they otherwise would have if they were free of these interdependent constraints. To simplify considerably the story behind the emergence of the strategic account, we should recognize that Walter Murphy's book, *Elements of Judicial Strategy*, released in 1964, while not a rigorous exercise in model building, laid out an intuitively appealing framework that, with some notable exceptions, failed to spark sustained interest in this account. More than thirty years later, as enthusiasm for the strategic account spread among law and politics scholars, Forrest Maltzman, James Spriggs, and Paul Wahlback (2000), in *Crafting Law on the Supreme Court: The Collegial Game*, revealed both the potential and the limits of analyzing the justices' decisions as the product of sophisticated calculations. The position of the strategic account, when applied to the internal dynamics of the Supreme Court, seems reasonably secure. Its position with respect to the Court's institutional interactions, however, appears more problematic.

The second shift reemphasized the Supreme Court's place within its institutional environment and underscored the Court's interdependence with this environment. Coincident with this shift was the implication that justices would be more likely to behave like sophisticated decision makers when confronted with unfavorable alignments of policy preferences among their institutional competitors. The number of works considering how the executive and legislative branches constrain the judiciary has grown rapidly. One important impetus for this boom in strategic accounts of the Court's external relationships was Brian Marks's (1989) study of the congressional response to (or lack thereof) to the Supreme Court's *Grove City* decision (*Grove City College v. Bell* 465 U.S. 555 [1984]). A second impetus occurred when William Eskridge (1991a, 1991b) published two law review articles on what he called the "civil rights game" in which he analyzed the interplay between the Supreme

Court, Congress, and the president in the evolution of civil rights statutes, their interpretation, and revision. These articles, employing simple spatial models, went some distance toward boosting academic interest among behavioral social scientists in what came to be called the "separation of powers game." Eskridge's models, however, functioned more as illustrations for his stories than as predictive models capable of being tested with empirical data.

Jeffery Segal (1997), a proponent of the attitudinal model, subsequently challenged Eskridge's assumptions and empirical foundation of his model. He showed that, with more careful measurement of the policy positions of the major actors over a larger number of cases, the justices rarely were politically compelled to act in sophisticated ways to achieve their policy goals. While Segal's article did not close off the argument or slow efforts to develop more sophisticated formal models of the separation-of-powers game, his work points to the importance of combining careful construction of game-theoretic models with appropriate empirical tests. We also would note that, while this game has received considerable attention, the puzzles that proliferate within judicial hierarchies, by comparison, remain relatively unexplored.

This book is intended to continue the dialogue over the utility of formal models and to extend them to other aspects of the Supreme Court's institutional interactions. The first half of this book thus includes chapters that deal with the Court's "horizontal" relationships with Congress and the states. In the first essay, Andrew Martin argues that the strategic account applies only to constitutional cases, while the attitudinal model works best when the justices interpret statutes. The separation-of-power model implicitly conveys the notion of a zero-sum game between courts and legislatures. James Rogers's essay, however, reveals a different aspect to this game by showing why a court would defer to a legislature even if the judges want the law to reflect, as in the attitudinal model, their views. A further complicating facet to relations between courts and legislatures is the role of interest groups as links between the two institutions, as Christopher Zorn explains in the third essay. Because courts, even the U.S. Supreme Court, have few means at hand to assure compliance with their decisions, the puzzle arises as to why compliance ever occurs. Georg Vanberg in the fourth essay offers a solution to this puzzle by emphasizing how transparency, when combined with public support, makes compliance the rule and not the exception. The last essay in section 1, by Cliff Carrubba and James Rogers, makes what for many readers may be a counterintuitive argument: the Supreme Court's review of how states regulate trade among themselves reflects not an "ascendant" court dominating the states but a weak court that strategically uses the dormant Commerce Clause to achieve its ends.

The second half of the book turns to the "vertical" interactions within the judicial hierarchy of the federal court system. Precedent is a way of bringing uniformity to judicial decisions. Thomas Hammond, Chris Bonneau, and Reginald Sheehan, in the sixth essay argue the appearance of noncompliance when a lower court fails to follow precedent may be deceiving, because it creates an opportunity for the Supreme Court to modify rulings it no longer supports because of changes in the composition or views of the Supreme Court justices. The next essay, by Charles Cameron and Lewis Kornhauser, explores the notion of "errors" more broadly within judicial hierarchies and develops models that include litigant decisions to appeal in order to determine which one is likely to minimize errors. Precedent and accurate decision making also are the focus of Ethan Bueno de Mesquita and Matthew Stephenson, whose essay works though the ramifications of an information-based model that challenges the attitudinal model's dismissal of the "legalist" features of courts. The final and concluding essay by Stefanie Lindquist and Susan Haire, uses a "principal-agent" approach to examine the environmental decisions of the U.S. Courts of Appeals. Their results reveal these courts have "multiple principals," not just the Supreme Court, adding to the complexity of unraveling the puzzle of how the judicial hierarchy operates.

Versions of these essays were first presented as papers at a conference entitled "Institutional Games and the U.S. Supreme Court" at Texas A&M University on November 1–3, 2001, at the Bush Presidential Library Conference Center. The editors express their gratitude for the generous financial support, without which the conference would not have been possible, provided by the Department of Political Science at Texas A&M University and the George Bush School of Government and Public Service. Professor Kenneth J. Meier also offered indispensable support and guidance from the first time we discussed with him the idea of a conference with this orientation, through its planning stages, and to its ultimate completion. We also want to thank Dick Holway, our editor at the University of Virginia Press, as well as its editorial adviser, Kevin McGuire, University of North Carolina, for their encouragement and useful advice on revising the conference papers for publication.

We believe this book will appeal to those readers with some familiarity with game theory as well as to readers for whom game theory at first glance looks more like a puzzle than a solution. Indeed, it is our intention that this book not be seen as just for specialists or practitioners of the "black art" of game theory but also as a series of nonintimidating conversations about how to think about various aspects of the Supreme Court that will introduce readers to how game theory contributes to a better understanding of the interaction of the Supreme Court and its institutional environment.

To that end, we've taken steps we think will assist readers who are not trained in game theory. To help readers orient themselves to the book's perspective, we invited two eminent scholars, Kenneth Shepsle and Lawrence Baum, each of whom has a different approach to law and politics, to prepare a foreword and an afterword respectively to place the contributors' papers into a broader intellectual context. In addition, Jim Rogers prepared a primer on game theory as an appendix to this book that introduces the basic ideas of formal modeling and the game-theoretic approach to solving puzzles. Each chapter includes an abstract summarizing the chapter that also links it to the chapters that precede and follow it to enhance the continuity and cohesiveness of the book. Finally, we edited the chapters with the aim of striking a balance between accessibility and sophistication, while remaining true to the authors' intentions.

FOREWORD

KENNETH A. SHEPSLE

In his splendid "Afterword" to this volume, Lawrence Baum offers an important observation, one that resonates with those of us who have been deploying models or using quantitative methods in various institutional vineyards lo these many years. If told as a fable, it would go something like this: Once upon a time, a tribe of modelers (or methodologists) invaded a substantive field, believing (perhaps a bit too confidently) they had something to contribute to making sense of extant empirical patterns, practices, and regularities there. Their arrival was not greeted with uniform enthusiasm by the local tribes living in the field. The modelers thought of themselves as hail fellows well met. (If truth be told, some of their number harbored a view of themselves as heroes or saviors.) Whatever! These modelers were regarded by many of the locals as an occupying force. Over time, however, the modelers began to acquire and appreciate the local knowledge of substantive specialists who worked in this field, while substantive scholars began to see some virtue in the tools and techniques brought in from the outside. New intellectual crops were harvested, yields of both the old and the new were up, *arbitrage* replaced *conquest* as the operative endeavor, and tensions declined as modelers and substantive scholars sat at the same table and broke bread together—in subsequent generations, at least, if not in the first. The fable is ongoing, and, alas, it is too early to conclude that these tribes will live together happily ever after. Hostility on the one side, and hubris on the other, have not dissipated entirely; but it is fair to report that respectful dialogue and productive collaboration have become dominant modes of interaction.

This is a story of one path of intellectual development. Let me be clear, all is not sweetness and light; it is a fable after all. In reality, there are downs as well as ups. There are bumps in the road. Yet the essays in the present book, written mostly by younger scholars (with a grizzled veteran here and there) who have mastered both theoretical tools and substantive

knowledge, are an affirmation of this developmental pattern. The essays
are analytical without being pedantic; they are not mere exercises in technical virtuosity. They tackle questions easily recognized as substantively
central and fundamental. They place considerable weight on the *structure*
of the judiciary—a single court, an entire court system, or the environment occupied by other institutions—as the context in which judicial
performance (strategic, attitudinal) occurs. They focus on puzzles:

- Are judges generally strategic? Or is strategic behavior more evident in
  one sector (constitutional pronouncements) or another (statutory in-
  terpretation), in one court or another, or perhaps not at all?
- Why would (intelligent) judges defer (even) to (relatively ignorant)
  legislators?
- Why an autonomous judiciary? Will it not usurp legislative power?
- How are declarations of the court enforced—by lower courts? by legislatures and executives? Why are they honored at all? Indeed, are they?
- Does a judicial hierarchy with an appellate system correct mistakes?
- Why do judges adhere to precedent as a matter of principle, even
  when adhering to it sometimes produces holdings they do not prefer?
- In a world of many principals, for whom are judges actually agents? To
  whom do they listen? Are they agents at all?

Just listing the puzzles should whet the reader's appetite. The essays
develop arguments and resolve puzzles in a systematic way, so I will not
give away any of the surprises found in them. I will instead spend a few
moments on some thorny issues with which models of courts and judges
must grapple. (Some of these are revisited by Baum in the concluding
essay.) I should be clear here that this does not put modeling at a disadvantage, because these very same issues also haunt nearly every other
approach to courts and judges—at least those that place explanatory
weight on the political structure of the judiciary and the role of judges and
justices. Indeed, because the modeling tradition places so large a premium
on transparency and consistency in arguments, it makes these problems
more apparent than other approaches do, even though they lurk in the in-
terstices of nearly all these other approaches as well.

Judicial Preferences

At a conference some years ago on the new institutional economics, I
asked Judge Richard Posner, "What do judges maximize?" I prefaced the
question by suggesting to him that political scientists were reasonably

confident about the objectives of legislators (reelection, chamber influence, good public policy) and bureaucrats (budgets, authority, slack), but had always been, and remain, puzzled by judges—especially those with life tenure. The usually loquacious and articulate founder of the law and economics tradition was rendered mute by my question—but not for long. In a paper published less than a year after my question had stumped him, he put the puzzle thus:

> At the heart of economic analysis of law is a mystery that is also an embarrassment: how to explain judicial behavior in [rational] terms, when almost the whole thrust of the rules governing compensation and other terms and conditions of judicial employment is to divorce judicial action from incentives—to take away the carrots and sticks, the different benefits and costs associated with different behaviors, that determine human action in an economic model. . . . The economic analyst has a model for how criminals and contract parties, injurers and accident victims, parents and spouses—even legislators, and executive officials such as prosecutors—act, but falters when asked to produce a model of how judges act. (Posner 1993, 2)

He went on to reason that just as politicians generally are not thought to be extraordinary or superhuman—even though the history books are dominated by the few who made their marks—so it must be with judges and justices:

> Politics, personal friendships, ideology, and pure serendipity play too large a role in the appointment of federal judges to warrant treating the judiciary as a collection of genius-saints miraculously immune to the tug of self-interest. By treating judges and Justices as ordinary people, my approach makes them fit subjects for economic analysis; for economists have no theory of genius. It is fortunate for economic analysis, therefore, that most law is made not by the tiny handful of great judges but by the great mass of ordinary ones. (Posner 1993, 3–4)

Posner goes on to examine various objectives that he believes animate the actions of "ordinary" judges. I will not detail his argument here. (It may be found in the original article, of course, as well as in Shepsle and Bonchek 1996, 405–31). Suffice it to say that Posner pushes the employment relation (using the analogy of working in a nonprofit organization) and the idea of on-the-job consumption.

In contrast, most of the essays in the present collection—and most work in the modeling of courts and judges more generally—employ what I call the "legislator in robes" view of judges. Accordingly, the perspective on legislator objectives made famous by Richard Fenno (1973) and David Mayhew (1974) more than a quarter of a century ago applies. Judges, like politicians more generally, seek reelection (reappointment), good public policy, and institutional influence. To this we may add career advancement (see below) for those who are not at the pinnacle of a judicial career. In those cases where appointment is for life, and in which institutional influence is a less-significant attraction, judges are animated by their conception of good public policy.

This, in fact, is the conception most commonly adopted in the literature, and in the essays of this volume. With most of the work in this area committed to judges with policy preferences, the issue of paramount concern is whether they act directly on their preferences, as in the attitudinal model, or behave strategically, as in many game-theoretic formulations. (In some circumstances, these approaches are observationally equivalent, with strategic actors behaving in equilibrium in "sincere" accord with their preferences.)

The problem in my view is that the contexts in which judges engage in judicial behavior are not identical. Indeed, the fact that we employ a common label for such a variety of judicial circumstances may mislead us. Justices of the peace are not the same as justices of the U.S. Supreme Court. The issues, opportunities, and constraints facing an administrative law judge differ from those presiding in other jurisdictions. Elected state courts differ in important ways from the life-tenured federal bench. (To the untutored eye of someone like me not trained as a judicial scholar, the class of politicians we call "judges" appears far more heterogeneous than the class we call "legislators.") We risk being too facile in homogenizing judicial objectives if the heterogeneous political circumstances judges face shape their objectives. But even if they do not—that is, even if objectives are exogenous—political circumstances may nevertheless *sort* and *select* different "types." It is my view, a sentiment echoed and elaborated in Baum's afterword, that attention must be given, theoretical as well as empirical, to the connections between context, selection, objectives, and ambitions.

Judicial Information

The opening sentence of any brief history of formal theory in political science is something like: "In the beginning there was Arrow." Kenneth Arrow did not *invent* formal political theory—and there were many precursors (recounted in McLean and Urken 1995) of whom the marquis de Condorcet is perhaps the most eminent. The significance of this "first sentence" is to underscore the central place in formal political theory of problems of *social choice*—the aggregation of preferences and the institutional arrangements by which this is facilitated. Many of the models reported in the essays of this volume follow in this tradition—with multiperson courts, like multiperson legislatures, arriving at decisions through some sort of preference aggregation in accord with exogenously established procedures.

The present collection of essays, however, reflects two significant theoretical transformations in the social choice theoretic foundations of positive political theory. The first is the move to game theory. Social contexts and institutional settings are not merely the places in which preferences, exogenously arrived at, are faithfully revealed. The institutional setting constitutes a "game form," a process or structure that transforms (strategically considered) actions into social outcomes. Preference revelation is, itself, a matter of calculation, premised on personal objectives to be sure, but undertaken with an eye to what others are up to and how procedures and arrangements "manufacture" social outcomes.

The second theoretical transformation is informational, and several essays in this volume make this a major focus of their analysis. Institutional actors, in the courts themselves and in the larger political environment, operate behind a veil of uncertainty. Even if an actor knows what he or she wants, there still may be uncertainty about what to do, what others want, what others know, or what others do. Rational agents take this on board. So, from James Rogers we learn that there are circumstances in which even knowledgeable judges may defer to legislators because the aggregation of information from which a legislative decision was taken will be informative to the judges. From Charles Cameron and Lewis Kornhauser we learn that appeals processes often give prominence to those with an informational advantage (litigants), so that the very choice by a losing litigant to appeal transmits valuable information to informationally challenged appeals judges. From Ethan Bueno de Mesquita and Matthew Stephenson we are given a novel interpretation of precedent as a mechanism by which higher courts communicate doctrine clearly to lower courts in a world otherwise fraught with interpretive uncertainty.

Informational models, of which the essays above are instances, have elicited growing interest among institutional modelers. There was a tendency in the literature on legislatures of the 1980s and 1990s to partition explanations into those that are information based and those that are preference based (Shepsle and Weingast 1995, chap. 1). Possibly because the technology was more primitive a decade or more ago, modelers felt compelled to choose one approach or the other, and even to advocate the superiority of one or the other. Increasingly, it has been possible to blend the two approaches, and students of courts seem better equipped than some of their forebears to skip over the intermediate position of advocating exclusivity for one approach or the other.

It is clearly important to focus on both preferences and beliefs. Institutions aggregate *both* preferences and information. Strategic actors make use of the latter in participating in the former. A situation is an *equilibrium* when an actor's beliefs are fulfilled—so that he or she has no incentive to alter beliefs—and, in light of these fulfilled beliefs, he or she cannot, by modifying behavior, improve the outcome vis-à-vis personal preferences. The difficulty is in exactly how to specify the mechanisms by which information is transmitted and processed, and thus how beliefs are updated. We tend to treat these issues in a fairly primitive manner. We have moved away from early social choice and game-theoretic formulations that assumed complete and perfect information. But we still lack a very general formulation of the kinds of uncertainty that judicial agents encounter.

Let me briefly take up two additional topics that will continue to attract the attention of those modeling judicial phenomena.

Agency Models

Many of the essays in this volume make use of an agency metaphor—specified in a huge variety of ways. Lower courts are agents for courts higher in the judicial hierarchy. Courts are agents for legislatures. Legislatures and executives are agents of courts (implementing their policies, or not). Judges are agents of an enacting legislative coalition and, indirectly, of interest groups (enforcing their intentions). Sometimes the metaphor illuminates, but sometimes it obscures. The terms are slippery in many contexts, at least in part because an institutional environment consists of a complex of connections, and a particular analysis tends to isolate only some of them.

I have no problem with an agency-theoretic approach that abstracts from some of this complexity in order to shine the light brightly on a specific feature. I simply urge some self-awareness on this score. The identity of "principal" and "agent" in some of the original theoretical developments of this model (Jensen and Meckling 1976, Fama 1980, Grossman and Hart 1983) derived from one of two considerations. In the theory of the firm—and especially in the debate over the separation of ownership and control—the principal is the "residual claimant" and the agents are factors employed by the principal to maximize this residual. In the contract-theoretic literature, the principal is the designer of the contract—in effect, the creator of a game form—and the agents are those who can accept or reject whatever is on offer. These and other principles may be employed to sort out who is whom in the principal-agent metaphor. Typically, the principal is a proactive first mover, whereas agents are reactive last movers, making their choices in light of earlier moves. In a complex setting, like a separation-of-powers institutional arrangement, different actors assume different roles, the games in which they are engaged are intertwined, and most analyses are partial equilibrium at best. This is the nature of the beast—and awareness of this should modify interpretations and temper conclusions.

Judicial Careers

Part of the ambiguity over judicial preferences to which I alluded earlier is, in my view, derived from ambiguity about judicial ambition and sense of career. In a static analysis of a particular decision or class of phenomena, judicial preferences may be *stipulated,* often without doing much damage to the analysis. But judges, like politicians generally and even scholars, presumably think ahead—how will this action now affect me then? how far down the road is "then"? how much do I discount the benefit "then" relative to the costs I bear now? Myopic maximizing in accord with a stipulated objective function and subject to a variety of possibly binding constraints, fails to take this intertemporal dimension into account. Fenno (1978) writes about legislators in the *expansionist* and *protectionist* phases of their careers. Joseph Schlesinger (1966) and David Rohde (1979) write about *static* and *progressive* ambition. Judges have careers, too, and coming to terms with their ambitions is, perhaps, the single largest issue in terms of its likely spillover effects on the theoretical questions entertained in this collection. I expect that deep inside the judicial field, out of the view of interlopers like me, empirical work on just these issues is proceeding apace. It would benefit theoretical work immensely to bring empirical insights to bear on the issues of career and ambition.

The essays of this volume are fresh and exciting. They begin interesting theoretical conversations about the institutional world that judges and their courts find themselves in. They are not the last word—and this is part of what makes them so good.

Strategic Games with Congress and the States | 1

Statutory Battles and Constitutional Wars

Congress and the Supreme Court

ANDREW D. MARTIN

How does the separation of powers influence Supreme Court justices when they vote on the merits of cases? The standard claim is that if justices do vote strategically, they are most likely to do so when interpreting statutes. This paper challenges this view. It demonstrates that strategic judicial behavior occurs in constitutional cases. Evidence from a large sample of civil rights and civil liberties cases shows that when prescribing constitutional standards, Supreme Court justices respond strategically to the separation of-powers system. Thus, while the attitudinal model underlying the conventional view seems to hold for statutory interpretation, the strategic explanation holds in constitutional decisions. This institutional structure, designed by the Founders, anticipates the possibility of differences in preferences between the separated powers, thereby producing a check on each while creating at the same time institutional incentives for the Supreme Court to diminish the antidemocratic effects of its decisions when Court preferences differ from the other branches.

Congressmen have an impressive array of weapons which can be used against judicial power. They can impeach and remove the justices, increase the number of Justices to any level whatever, regulate court procedure, abolish any tier of courts, confer or withdraw federal jurisdiction almost at will, cut off the money that is necessary to run the courts or to carry out a specific decision or set of decisions, pass laws to reverse statutory interpretation, and propose constitutional amendments either to reverse particular decisions or to curtail directly judicial power. . . . [A]s Chief Executive, the President may order executive officials from marshals on up to the Attorney General or the Secretary of Defense to refuse to enforce Supreme Court decisions, pardon persons convicted of criminal contempt of court, . . . influence the future course of judicial power . . . [through the appointment process, and] persuade congressmen.
—Walter Murphy, Elements of Judicial Strategy

After the *Brown v. Board of Education* (347 U.S. 483 [1954]) decision, many political pundits were concerned about the power of the Supreme Court and its ability to enact seemingly countermajoritarian public policy. Yet, the Founders created a separation-of-powers system whereby no single institution could enact policy unilaterally. Indeed, it is precisely this institutional interdependence that allows for the possibility that the Court might remain a legitimate policymaking institution without producing public policy that is antidemocratic. And, as Murphy (1964) explains, both Congress and the president have a myriad of tools they can use to check what Hamilton called "the weakest branch." While the empirical study of judicial decision making in the separation-of-powers system has grown dramatically, little attention has been paid to the checks on the justices in constitutional cases.

While the empirical evidence of strategic adoption of Supreme Court justices with respect to the separation-of-powers system is mixed, nearly all scholars are in agreement that if such a constraint exists, it most likely does (or, perhaps exclusively does) for cases when the Court interprets a law rather than for those when the Court determines the constitutionality of a law (some notable exceptions include Rosenberg 1992, Meernik and Ignagni 1997, Epstein et al. 2001). The reasoning is seemingly obvious: Congress can overturn statutory decisions by amending or changing a statute but must pursue a more arduous process to overturn constitutional decisions. Because Congress has rarely pursued this latter strategy, many scholars conclude the justices need not pay attention to the preferences and likely responses of other government actors in constitutional disputes. In this essay, I take issue with this conventional wisdom. I argue instead, based on a cost-benefit analysis, that justices are *more* likely to pay attention to separation of powers concerns in constitutional interpretation cases than in statutory interpretation cases (a similar argument is developed by Epstein et al. 2001). To complete the case, I also present evidence from a large-sample study of Supreme Court decision making on civil rights and civil liberties cases.

A key tenet of the modern study of Supreme Court decision making is that justices are policy-seeking political actors, but the manner in which Supreme Court justices pursue their policy goals remains hotly debated. The attitudinal model (Segal and Spaeth 1993) asserts that because of institutional features such as life tenure and institutional privacy, Supreme Court justices decide cases by sincerely translating their policy preferences into votes. This explanation, however, seems incomplete and is at odds with the notion that the Court operates within an interinstitutional context. As noted by numerous scholars (e.g., Murphy 1964, Marks 1989, Eskridge 1991b, Epstein and Knight 1998), if justices are *truly* interested in policy, they should anticipate reactions to their decisions by the "political" branches of government. By this account, justices not only decide cases to achieve their policy goals on the Court, but also to further their policy goals in a larger system characterized by the separation of powers. John Ferejohn (1999, 355) notes that "the federal judiciary is institutionally dependent on Congress and the president, for jurisdiction, rules, and execution of judicial orders." While judges themselves are independent actors, the judiciary is dependent on the other branches to enact policy. This interdependence is one mechanism that protects us from excessive judicial power.

The Argument

My theoretical argument proceeds in three steps. First, I review the literature on strategic decision making by the Supreme Court and summarize extant empirical findings. I then present a simple spatial model that yields predictions about when we should observe more or less sophisticated behavior on the Court. Finally, I draw a distinction between statutory and constitutional interpretation cases, using a cost-benefit argument suggesting that constraints on the justices should be most apparent in constitutional interpretation decisions.

STRATEGIC DECISION MAKING ON THE SUPREME COURT

The attitudinal model of Supreme Court decision making has perhaps the broadest empirical support. It takes its contemporary form in Jeffery Segal and Harold Spaeth's *The Supreme Court and the Attitudinal Model,* who describe it as follows:

> [The attitudinal model] holds that the Supreme Court decides disputes in light of the facts of the case vis-à-vis the ideological attitudes and values of the justices. Simply put, Rehnquist votes the way he does because he is extremely conservative; Marshall voted the way he did because he is extremely liberal. (Segal and Spaeth 1993, 65)

This model asserts that because of a number of factors, justices can sincerely pursue their policy goals. In other words, justices are not strategic when voting on the merits. An alternative explanation is that Supreme Court justices are, in fact, strategic. These explanations of Supreme Court behavior can be traced to Walter Murphy's *Elements of Judicial Strategy*

(1964). Murphy begins with the same axiom as the attitudinal model: that judges are policy-driven actors, who use their resources to pursue preferred policies given political constraints. He stresses that the Supreme Court is not the final word in the policy process; through legislation, implementation, and the veto power, Congress and the president can undermine or overturn decisions made by the Court.

By the late 1980s, scholars began to incorporate Murphy's theory into positive analyses of judicial decision making. Although the progenitor of separation-of-powers models (Marks 1989) treats the Court as nonstrategic and exogenous, scholars quickly picked up on his approach to explain policy outcomes in separation-of-powers games. Many of these researchers applied these models to cases of statutory interpretation. The first analysts who treated the Supreme Court as endogenous in a separation-of-powers game were Rafael Gely and Pablo Spiller (1990), who use a formal model to explain policy outcomes in two statutory decisions. William Eskridge (1991) uses a similar model to explain policy outcomes in various statutory civil rights cases. Spiller and Gely (1992) use a sophisticated econometric model to demonstrate constraints on the Court in cases related to the National Labor Relations Board (NLRB). Gely and Spiller (1992) use a two-dimensional model to explain Franklin D. Roosevelt's Court-packing plan and find that the "switch in time that saved nine" was not a reaction to Roosevelt's threat to pack the Court, but rather a rational response to changes in the legislative branch. While these case studies are persuasive, Segal's (1997) elaborate large-sample test of statutory civil rights decisions shows justices behave overwhelmingly sincerely, results that are consistent with the attitudinal model. In essence, his conclusion is that the Court is rarely constrained by actors in other institutions.

Nonetheless, Lee Epstein and Jack Knight (1998, 147) demonstrate that attorneys convey to the justices information about the other institutions in their briefs. In their random sample of cases during 1990 term, in 75 percent of constitutional cases and 80.8 percent of nonconstitutional cases, attorneys highlighted the issue preferences of other actors in the separation-of-powers system. This information about the other branches, obtained through legal briefs and from other media outlets, also enters into conference discussions about particular case. For a set of cases from the 1983 term, Epstein and Knight (1998, 149) further show that in 46.4 percent of constitutional cases and 69.8 percent of nonconstitutional cases, these issues were raised at the conference. The outstanding empirical question is whether these concerns manifest themselves in the data.

The development of more sophisticated theoretical models has also taken place. James Rogers (2001b) develops an informational model of bargaining between Congress and the Court (see also Hettinger and Zorn 2001). His model is a dramatic shift from the essentially distributive models used throughout the literature. He shows that the Court's response to legislation may inform the legislative branch about potential policy outcomes and develops a set of testable propositions about congressional and judicial behavior. What is clear from the literature is that many questions about judicial strategy remain unanswered. While explanations of strategic judicial behavior on the merits abound, there is little empirical support (besides a handful of oft recycled anecdotes) for the notion that justices anticipate reactions to their decisions by Congress and the president.

PREDICTING SOPHISTICATED BEHAVIOR: A SIMPLE MODEL

To glean empirical expectations, I posit a simple (perhaps trivial) theoretical model. The model makes explicit predictions about the behavior of individual Supreme Court justices. As is the case with all formal models, one makes simplifying assumptions to gain insight into the interaction under study. The game I posit here is played on a unidimensional policy space by three actors: a Supreme Court justice, the pivotal member of Congress, and the president. The sequence of the game is simple. First the Court moves, by choosing between exogenously fixed policies L and C. L represents a liberal policy alternative, and C represents the conservative status quo. The pivotal member of Congress acts to either override the decision and locate policy at its ideal point or let the decision stand. If Congress overrides the Court, the president can veto the bill or sign it. If the veto is exercised, the member of Congress has the last action by overriding the veto or acquiescing to the Court. After the game is finished, the policy outcome is determined and payoffs are assigned to each actor using quadratic utility functions. This model captures the decision problem faced constantly by Supreme Court justices: How should I best pursue my policy goals through my decision, given political constraints on my behavior coming from the president and Congress? Models of this sort (typically with a larger number of actors, including congressional committees and executive agencies) can be found in Marks (1989), Eskridge (1991), and Segal (1997).

If it were the case that we could measure the ideal points of all of relative actors on the same metric with certainty, it would be straightforward to test the predictions of such a model. Indeed, one would have to com-

FIGURE 1 Hypothetical separation-of-power games

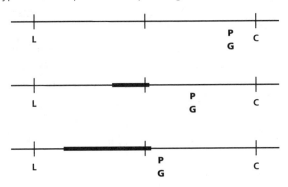

NOTE: *P* is the president's ideal point, *G* is Congress's ideal point, and the dark line represents the range of Supreme Court ideal points where sophisticated judicial behavior is possible.

pute the equilibrium and compare it (in some principled manner) to the observed data. Measurement of this sort is difficult, and moreover, testing the predictions of formal models with oftentimes knife-edge results, using statistical models, is fraught with difficulties. To avoid these problems, I adopt an approach developed by Andrew Martin (2001). Instead of generating predictions about individual behavior, one generates predictions about the *net amount* of sophisticated behavior by averaging over a distribution of preferences. As discussed below, these types of propositions are easily tested using existing methods.

I derive the equilibrium of a similar game using backward induction elsewhere (Martin 1998). There I use simulation to generate predictions about changes in the net amount of sophisticated judicial behavior, given changes in decision context, where sophisticated behavior is defined as choosing a less-than-preferred alternative early in a game to obtain better results in the end (Farquharson 1969). The two key predictions of the model are: (1) holding all else constant, as Congress gets more conservative, we should observe less-sophisticated judicial behavior; (2) holding all else constant, as the president gets more conservative, we should observe less-sophisticated judicial behavior.[1]

To illustrate these hypotheses, see figure 1, where three hypothetical configurations of preferences are depicted. The ideal point of the president is denoted *P*, and the ideal point of the Congress is denoted *G*. For the sake of illustration, I assume that the Congress and the president have homogeneous preferences. The small tick mark in the middle of the line segment is the indifference point between the liberal alternative and the conservative status quo. In the first case, all justices can vote sincerely, because regardless of their behavior, the case will be overturned. In the second case, the president and Congress are both more liberal. Here there exists a small range of ideal points, depicted with a dark line, where the justices could vote in a sophisticated fashion for the status quo and obtain a more preferred policy in the end. In the final case, this range of sophisticated behavior increases. This illustration in no way represents all possibilities, but it does show how the amount of possible sophisticated behavior is decreasing as the president or Congress gets more conservative. This simple model merely provides a directional hypothesis about when we should observe more or less sophisticated behavior *if the Court is paying attention to the other institutions.* Should the Court pay attention? The answer to this question is the final part of my theoretical argument.

STATUTORY BATTLES AND CONSTITUTIONAL WARS

In its policymaking role, the Supreme Court decides two different types of cases: those involving statutory interpretation and those over constitutional questions. Before I highlight the debate in the literature and offer an explanation, it is important to distinguish between statutory interpretation and constitutional cases.[2] Statutory interpretation decisions are those when the Court interprets the meaning of a statute, treaty, executive order, or administrative ruling. In these cases, the Court is charged with determining the meaning of a particular law as it affects the parties in the case. Congress and the president can overturn a statutory interpretation decision by passing a different statute. If, for example, the Supreme Court interpreted a congressional act in a manner not acceptable to a congressional majority, Congress could simply repeal the previous law and pass a new, more clearly worded one. *Grove City College v. Bell* (465 U.S. 555 [1984])—where the Court was determining the meaning of Title IX of the Education Amendments of 1972—is an example of a statutory interpretation decision. While this decision did not sit well with many members of Congress, for seven years Congress was unable to overturn the decision (until the Civil Rights Act of 1991) because of an important congressional gatekeeper (Marks 1989).

Constitutional cases place a very different type of question before the justices. In these cases of judicial review, the Court is deciding whether a particular law or administrative action violates a constitutional provision. These decisions are quite difficult for Congress and the president to overturn, although it is possible (Murphy 1964, Rosenberg 1992, Epstein and Knight 1998). In the civil rights domain, *Brown v. Board of Education* is an example of a case where the Court found that segregation in public schools violated the Fourteenth Amendment of the Constitution. In this decision, the Court reversed its earlier constitutional doctrine of separate but equal and found that segregation violated the Constitution. In so doing, the Court made a bold policy prescription, enforced by President Dwight D. Eisenhower and written into statutory law ten years later by the Civil Rights Act of 1964.

A debate rages in the literature about how the Court behaves in both of these decision-making roles. Much of the empirical separation-of-powers literature includes an explicit assumption that the Court is primarily constrained in statutory cases. Epstein and Knight claim that "[w]hile we believe that the separation of powers system operates across a range of substantive issues, we also believe that it imposes a more significant constraint on cases involving statutory questions than on constitutional questions" (1998, 140). This follows from the ease in which Congress can overturn a statutory decision. Conversely, "[t]he infrequency of congressional responses to constitutional decisions, coupled with the difficulty involved in overturning them, means that the justices may be less attentive to the preferences and likely actions of other governmental actors." (Epstein and Knight 1998, 141). The literature thus suggests that in these statutory battles, justices should anticipate repercussions.

On the other side of the debate are those who assert that Supreme Court justices should strategically respond to the other branches of government in constitutional cases. Rosenberg lists the attacks Congress and the president can launch against the Supreme Court after an objectionable constitutional decision:

> (1) [U]sing the Senate's confirmation power to select certain types of judges; (2) enacting constitutional amendments to reverse decisions or change Court structure or procedure; (3) impeachment; (4) withdrawing Court jurisdiction over certain subjects; (5) altering the selection and removal process; (6) requiring extraordinary majorities for declarations of unconstitutionality; (7) allowing appeal from the Supreme Court to a more "representative" tribunal; (8) removing the power of judicial review; (9) slashing the budget; (10) altering the size of the Court. (Rosenberg 1992, 377)

While these actions are quite rare, Murphy (1962) notes that by the end of John Marshall's chief justiceship, all of these basic measures had been attempted. Louis Fisher (2001, 28) makes this point when he writes, "If the Court decides that a government action is unconstitutional, it is usually more difficult for Congress and the President to contest the judiciary. . . . But even in this category, there are examples of effective legislative and executive actions in response to court ruling." For example, Rosenberg (1992) argues that in 1803–1804, the finding in *Marbury v. Madison* (5 U.S. 137 [1803]) was affected by an anticipated congressional response. Additionally, during the Civil War era, Congress enacted an 1862 law prohibiting slavery in the territories that was designed to "repudiate the main tenets" of *Scott v. Sandford* (19 How. 393 [1856]). During the New Deal era, the Fair Labor Standards Act of 1938 outlawed child labor even though the Supreme Court upheld it in *United States v. Darby Lumber* (312 U.S. 100 [1941]) on constitutional grounds (Fisher 2001).

As recently as the early 1990s, there was talk in Congress of removing jurisdiction and passing constitutional amendments in response to unpopular abortion and flag-burning decisions. Attacks on constitutional courts are not unique to the American case. Georg Vanberg (2000, 333) highlights the curtailment of powers of Spain's constitutional court in 1985 as well as the abolition of courts in Cyprus in 1964 and Austria 1932 as salient examples. The findings of James Meernik and Joseph Ignagni (1997) are consistent with the historical examples. They show that while congressional response to the Court does not happen frequently, there are recurring cases of coordinate construction when Congress responds to the constitutional decisions of the Court. Epstein and colleagues (2001) also demonstrate, using aggregate data, systematic constraint in constitutional cases.

Should justices care about Congress and the president when making statutory decisions? Do justices take into account highly unlikely congressional and presidential reactions to their constitutional decisions? Do the checks and balances cause justices to behave in a strategic manner? Perhaps justices respond differently in those cases when they are merely interpreting civil rights statutes as opposed to when they are testing the constitutionality of governmental actions. The argument I make, outlined in figure 2, is that justices feel more compelled to consider the separation of powers in constitutional cases than in statutory ones. This argument follows from a consideration of the institutional costs and policy benefits of both types of decisions.

I begin with the benefits. Assuming that Congress does not respond adversely to a statutory interpretation decision, the Court accrues a policy benefit: it is able to read its policy preferences into law and, perhaps, fundamentally change the course of public policy. But that impact may only be transitory, because it is possible that future presidents and Congresses will amend the statute in question, thus overriding the Court's interpre-

FIGURE 2 Costs and benefits of Supreme Court statutory and constititutional interpretation decisions

	Benefits	Possible congressional response	Cost of unsuccessful congressional response	Cost of successful congressional response
Statutory interpretation decision	Policy benefit / read policy preferences into existing law	New statute	None	Harm legitimacy of the court
Constitutional decision	Policy benefit / policy prescriptions	Attack on the court*	Harm legitimacy of the court	∞

tation. In so doing, the other actors may render the Court's decision meaningless. In contrast, owing to the difficulty of altering them both in the short and long terms, constitutional decisions are less permeable. Accordingly, they have greater policy value to the justices, because they also have a prescriptive benefit that statutory decisions do not. When the Court finds a constitutional basis, its decision does not merely hold for the particular law under analysis but also is binding on all future action. Constitutional decisions set the parameters with which the contemporaneous Congress and president—as well as their successors—must comply.

What costs do the justices bear if the president and Congress have an adverse reaction to their decision? If the other institutions are unsuccessful in their attempt to override an opinion interpreting a law, then no harm comes to the Court. If, however, they succeed by overriding the Court's decision, the Court will certainly pay a policy price: its interpretation of the statute no longer stands, thereby robbing it of the opportunity to affect public policy. It also may bear a cost in terms of its institutional legitimacy, which every successful override degrades (if even marginally so). Given that the justices' ability to achieve their policy goals hinges on their legitimacy, any erosion should be a nontrivial concern.

But the large policy payoff is in constitutional cases. What does the ability of the president and Congress to attack—through overrides or other means—constitutional court decisions imply in terms of the costs the justices bear? If an attack succeeds and the Court does not back down, it effectively removes the Court from the policy game and may seriously or, even, irrevocably harm its reputation, credibility, and legitimacy. Indeed, such an attack would effectively remove the Court from policy-making, thus incurring an infinite cost.[3] With no constitutional prescription for judicial review, this power is vulnerable, and would be severely damaged if Congress and the president were effective in an attack on the Court. But even if the attack attempt is unsuccessful, the integrity of the Court may be damaged, for the assault may compromise its ability to make future constitutional decisions and, thus, more long-lasting policy.

To make predictions about constraints on the Court, these costs and benefits must simply be compared. When weighing the policy benefit with the negligible institutional cost of being overturned in statutory cases, the justices need not pay attention to the other branches of government. This is because statutory decisions are comparatively fleeting. Constitutional decisions, however, are a different issue. In these decisions, the justices are motivated by a large policy benefit, because constitutional decisions are those that can affect larger policy change. At the same time, these decisions can cost the Court as an institution if Congress and the president launch an attack. While the probability of such an attack is minuscule, a successful attack would effectively remove the Court from the separation-of-powers system. We would therefore expect justices to temper their unfettered policy preferences in response to the separation of powers in constitutional cases.

DESIGN

To test these hypotheses, I turn to data on Supreme Court decisions on the merits in civil rights cases. I choose civil rights as a substantive focus, because it (1) contains a substantial amount of litigation, (2) contains a substantial amount of legislation in response to Court decisions, and (3) is politically contentious, thus producing interinstitutional conflict. In addition, the major empirical nonfinding (using a different empirical operationalization) focused on civil rights statutory interpretation decisions (Segal 1997).

STATISTICAL MODELS

I include both statutory and constitutional decisions in my sample and fit four statistical models to test the hypotheses. First, to serve as a baseline, I estimate a model that corresponds to the attitudinal model. In this case, I estimate a pooled probit model with only judicial preferences as the explanatory variables. The attitudinal model suggests that it is appropriate to pool votes across decision contexts because preferences alone are determinative.

The theoretical argument, conversely, suggests that justices behave in profoundly different ways, depending on the context of their decision. By this account, it is inappropriate to pool all observations, because as decision context changes, so too does the net amount of sophisticated judicial behavior. This implies that the structural relationship between preferences and behavior should vary across contexts; in certain circumstances, preferences should be strongly related to behavior, and other times the relationship should weaken. To model these changes, I employ a two-level hierarchical probit model (detailed in the appendix to this essay). This is a model of a set of dichotomous decisions $y_{i,k}$, where $i = 1, \ldots, n_k$ indexes the decisions in contexts $k = 1, \ldots, K$. Each vote is coded as one for the conservative policy and zero for the liberal policy. At the first level of the hierarchy, I assume the observed data is generated from:

$$y_{i,k} = \begin{cases} 1 & if \quad z_{i,k} > 0 \\ 0 & if \quad z_{i,k} \leq 0 \end{cases} \qquad (1)$$

Where $z_{i,k} = x'_{i,k}\beta_k + \varepsilon_{i,k}$ and $\varepsilon_{i,k} \sim N(0, 1)$, which is the standard latent utility specification of a probit model. $x'_{i,k}$ is a row vector of explanatory variables—in this case a constant and a preference measure. The magnitude of the preference to behavior relationship $\beta_{2,k}$ is expected to covary systematically with the congressional and presidential ideal points. Thus, at the second level of the hierarchy, I model the first-level parameters with explanatory variables A_k that vary by decision context:

$$\beta_k = A_k \alpha + v_k \quad v_k \sim N_p(0, \Omega) \qquad (2)$$

Note that this formulation is hierarchical, with the first level relating preferences to decisions, and the second level incorporating decision context by explaining variation in the β_k parameters.

To test the strategic accounts, I begin by fitting a two-level hierarchical probit model to the entire dataset. At the second level of the hierarchy, measures of political context are used to assess changes in the preference to behavior relationship. The key comparison of the strategic and attitudinal approaches lies in the sign of the α hyperparameters. The theoretical model suggests that the net amount of sophisticated judicial behavior is decreasing in the ideal point of Congress and the president. This implies that as Congress or the president gets more conservative, then the β_k parameters should get bigger. Therefore, the α-Congress and α-president measures should both be positive. I also employ Bayes factors to compare the two models (Kass and Raftery 1995). For both of these models, I perform Bayesian inference by generating draws from posterior distribution of each model, using the Gibbs sampling algorithm (see Martin 2001, and the essay appendix).[4]

This comparison, however, only provides information about the first component of the argument. It remains to be seen whether there are systematic differences between statutory and constitutional decisions. To wit, I then subset the data and estimate separate hierarchical probit models to see whether the hypothesized constraints manifest themselves in the data. The cost-benefit argument predicts that the justices act as if they are unconstrained in statutory interpretation cases—which is the finding of Segal (1997)—yet constrained in constitutional cases. The magnitudes of the α-Congress and α-president coefficients in each of these models compose the evidence.

DATA AND MEASUREMENT

The data necessary to test the hypotheses derived above are: a set of judicial decisions across terms (to provide variance in judicial preferences and in decision contexts), a measure of judicial preferences, and measures of political decision context—in this case, measures of presidential and congressional preferences. The dependent variable in this analysis is the vote of each justice in all civil rights cases between 1953 and 1992. I obtain the data from the Supreme Court Database (Spaeth 1997).[5]

To explain votes of individual justices, I require a measure of judicial preferences independent of voting behavior. Jeffery Segal and Albert Cover (1989) provide an exogenous measure of judicial preferences, which they calculate using content analysis of newspaper editorials during the nomination hearings of each justice. These scores predict aggregate judicial votes for each justice quite well (Segal et al. 1995), especially in the civil liberties domain (Epstein and Mershon 1996). I transform the Segal and Cover scores so that they range from 0 (liberal) to 1 (conservative).

The first measure of decision context I require is the location of the Congress. I use the Nominate Common Space Dimension One (Poole and Rosenthal 1997) measure of congressional preferences. To measure the pivotal member of Congress, I compute the median member of the House and Senate and calculate the midpoint between these two members. The second measure is that of presidential policy preferences. Segal and colleagues (2000) construct a measure by surveying one hundred presidency scholars. They asked these scholars to place each post–World War II president on a liberal to conservative scale for both social and economic issues. I adopt the scores for each president on the social dimension as a measure of presidential policy preferences in civil rights cases. To keep all measures pointing in the same direction, these scores are rescaled between 0 (liberal) and 1 (conservative).[6]

Finally, I must define the decision contexts in which the Supreme Court acts. By definition, each term of the Court is a new decision context; the makeup of Congress may change, and the president may also change. As presented in table 5 (in essay appendix), I define each term of the Court as a separate decision context. In all thirty-nine of these decision contexts, the Supreme Court decided at least one civil rights case. I therefore estimate α parameters for each decision context in the hierarchical models presented below.

The Evidence

The evidence begins with a simple probit model with data pooled across all decision contexts. I estimate this model using the Gibbs sampling algorithm of James Albert and Siddhartha Chib (1993). I report the posterior means, medians, and standard deviations for the attitudinal model in table 1. Note that the posterior mean or median can be interpreted just as a point estimate in frequentist statistics can be interpreted, and the posterior standard deviation can be interpreted just as the standard error is. The results show judicial preferences are strongly related to judicial behavior. The posterior mean of the slope coefficient is 1.23, with a small standard deviation. Indeed, 100 percent of the posterior density sample falls above zero, implying that the coefficient is positive at nearly the level of certainty. This is an intuitive finding that comports with the work of Segal and Spaeth (1993), among others.

The next step is to estimate a hierarchical probit model. The results are reported in table 2. For the hierarchical probit models below, the measure

TABLE 1 Pooled probit estimates of Supreme Court decision making in civil rights cases, 1953–1992

VARIABLE	POSTERIOR MEAN	POSTERIOR MEDIAN	POSTERIOR STD. DEV.
β_1 – Constant	−0.83590	−0.83578	0.02264
β_2 – Preferences	1.23369	1.23329	0.03841

Ln(marginal likelihood) = −6299.42556 Clusters = 39
Burn-in iterations = 500 n = 10135
Gibbs iterations = 5000

TABLE 2 Hierarchical probit estimates of Supreme Court decision making, 1953–1992

VARIABLE	POSTERIOR MEAN	POSTERIOR MEDIAN	POSTERIOR STD. DEV.
α_1 – Constant β_1	−0.71320	−0.72523	0.37537
α_2 – Constant β_2	0.62776	0.62294	0.45212
α_3 – Constant β_3	0.08981	0.09750	0.97320
α_4 – President β_4	0.74516	0.75565	0.70024
Ω_{11} – Error	0.30038	0.21831	0.26076
Ω_{12} – Error	−0.10344	−0.11502	0.13944
Ω_{22} – Error	0.49671	0.46210	0.19077

Ln(marginal likelihood) = −6187.44449   Clusters = 39
Burn-in iterations = 500   n = 10135
Gibbs iterations = 5000

of decision context (with G_k representing the Congress measure and P_k representing the presidency measure in context k) is:

$$A_k = \begin{bmatrix} 1 & 0 & 0 & 0 \\ 0 & 1 & G_k & P_k \end{bmatrix}$$

Since the signs and magnitudes of the α parameters are the key test of the strategic account, I only report the estimates from the second level of the hierarchy. Note that the sampler simultaneously generates draws from the posterior density of the β_k parameters.

In table 2, note that the posterior mean on the α-Congress measure is near zero and has a large standard deviation, implying that the net amount of sophisticated judicial behavior does not covary with congressional preferences. The results for the president are stronger; the posterior mean of α-president is 0.75, with a posterior standard deviation of 0.77. In fact, 85.1 percent of the posterior density sample lies above zero.[7] This means that with 85.1 percent certainty α-president is positive, which is a weak result. In addition to interpreting coefficient values, the Bayesian model comparison tools can also be used to determine which model is a better explanatory model of the data. With an equal prior probability that each model is the true data generating mechanism, the Bayes factor is simply the ratio of marginal likelihoods. The Bayes factor can be interpreted on the scale of probability that Model j is the true data generating mechanism compared to Model k. For these two models, the Bayes factor $B_{j,k} = -6187.44 - (-6229.42) = 41.98$, which is *very strong* evidence that model j, the hierarchical probit model, is the data generating mechanism

TABLE 3 Hierarchical probit estimates of Supreme Court decision making in statutory interpretation cases, 1953–1992

VARIABLE	POSTERIOR MEAN	POSTERIOR MEDIAN	POSTERIOR STD DEV.
α_1 – Constant β_1	–0.69885	–0.70836	0.32665
α_2 – Constant β_2	0.69081	0.69222	0.44513
α_3 – Constant β_3	0.07769	0.08384	0.96375
α_4 President β_4	0.57995	0.57876	0.69287
Ω_{11} – Error	0.32995	0.27270	0.19933
Ω_{12} – Error	–0.13233	–0.13377	0.12814
Ω_{22} – Error	0.57125	0.53994	0.19790

Ln(marginal likelihood) = –3888.34176   Clusters = 39
Burn-in iterations = 500   n = 6409
Gibbs iterations = 5000

(Kass and Raftery 1995, 777). Indeed, the cutoff on the Bayes factor scale for very strong evidence is five, which is greatly exceeded by $B_{j,k} = 41.98$. This is an exceptionally strong result, because the Bayes factor is biased against the nonparsimonious hierarchical probit model.

Yet these results only speak to the first part of the theoretical argument. To assess the impact of the separation-of-powers system with respect to different types of cases, I divide the data into statutory interpretation decisions and constitutional decisions.[8] In table 3 I present hierarchical probit results for statutory decisions. The results of this model are quite similar to the results in table 2. The variance in the β_k parameters is not explained by the measures of decision context: α-Congress is indistinguishable from zero, and while α-president is positive, its posterior standard deviation is greater than the parameter value. Here only 79.4 percent of the posterior density sample is positive, implying only a three in four chance that the coefficient is positive. The weak result in table 2 has gotten weaker. These results lead me to reach the same conclusion as Segal: "[T]he empirical results cast doubt on whether the justices vote other than sincerely with regard to congressional preferences, except on the rarest of cases" (Segal 1997, 42). This conclusion requires an obvious caveat—in statutory interpretation decisions.

The tale is quite different when looking at constitutional decisions. I present the hierarchical probit results for constitutional decisions in table 4. The results here look quite similar to those in the previous table except for the presidency parameter. In this subset, the α-president parameter has a posterior mean of 1.35, with a standard deviation of 0.69. In this case,

TABLE 4 Hierarchical probit estimates of Supreme Court decision making in constitutional cases, 1953–1992

VARIABLE	POSTERIOR MEAN	POSTERIOR MEDIAN	POSTERIOR STD. DEV.
α_1 – Constant β_1	−0.96744	−0.97455	0.27780
α_2 – Constant β_2	0.50408	0.50312	0.43756
α_3 – Constant β_3	0.12482	0.12594	0.96739
α_4 – President β_4	1.35086	1.35272	0.69110
Ω_{11} – Error	0.41402	0.37945	0.17258
Ω_{12} – Error	−0.17206	−0.16363	0.14475
Ω_{22} – Error	0.70351	0.65541	0.26183

Ln(marginal likelihood) = −2134.53759   Clusters = 39
Burn-in iterations = 500   n = 3726
Gibbs iterations = 5000

97.6 percent of the posterior density sample falls above zero. Thus, with a probability of 97.6 percent, one can state that α-president is positive. This implies that the president systematically and significantly affects judicial behavior in constitutional civil rights cases, thus demonstrating that justices are strategic actors who respond to changes in their decision context. This conclusion also requires an obvious caveat– in constitutional cases.[9]

Implications and Extensions

During the ratification debates, one concern of the Anti-Federalists was unfettered judicial power. Yet, as Ferejohn (1999) discusses, the Founders developed two mechanisms that Congress and the president could use to control the judiciary: the selection of justices, and explicit checks that could be employed. Robert Dahl (1957) argues that the former mechanism is determinative and that the replacement of justices is what keeps the Supreme Court in line with the ruling regime. The analysis presented here, as well as the work of Meernik and Ignagni (1997) and Epstein and colleagues (2001), show that the latter mechanism is also important, especially for constitutional interpretation cases.

This essay begins with a simple question: How does the separation of powers influence Supreme Court justices when voting on the merits? The results presented above provide an answer to that question and challenge pure attitudinal explanations of judicial behavior. The results demonstrate that the president is the primary constraint on the justices. Why is Congress not constraining the Court? Perhaps the justices do not have enough information to anticipate congressional responses to their decisions. Perhaps this is the case because the pivotal member of Congress remained relatively stable ideologically from 1953 to 1992. Perhaps it is the case that the president is most salient in the judicial mind. The results nonetheless imply that the context in which decisions are made must be taken into account when trying to understand judicial behavior. While the attitudinal model has enjoyed strong empirical support, the results presented here suggest that justices anticipate the reaction to their decisions by the other branches of government. These reactions thus should be incorporated into empirical studies. The conclusions fit well with other literature that demonstrates that justices are strategic when voting on *cert* (Boucher and Segal 1995), during opinion assignment (Maltzman and Wahlbeck 1996), and when bargaining over policy (Epstein and Knight 1998).

Yet, the story is not that simple. The Supreme Court plays very different policymaking roles when deciding constitutional versus statutory cases. I posit an argument that suggests justices strategically respond to the separation of powers in constitutional cases but not in statutory cases. Not only is this argument consistent with past statistical work (Meernik and Ignagni 1997, Segal 1997, Epstein et al. 2001), but it also provides insight into judicial behavior in times of constitutional crisis. These results demonstrate strategic judicial behavior *only* in constitutional cases; when prescribing constitutional standards for civil rights policy, Supreme Court justices strategically respond to the separation-of-powers system. Thus, while the attitudinal model seems to hold in statutory cases, the strategic explanation holds in constitutional decisions. These findings, however, should only be taken as suggestive. First, the theoretical model is crude at best and can perhaps be viewed as trivial. Better theoretical models are needed and will provide a much more subtle look at judicial decision making. The work of Rogers (2001b), among others, seems very promising in this regard. Similarly, the empirical analysis is limited and should be extended in numerous ways—to other issue areas, a longer time period, and with better measures.

At the end of the day, this research provides some (admittedly limited) empirical evidence that Supreme Court justices are sometimes strategic when deciding cases on the merits. It is clear that the separation-of-powers scheme created by the Founders established an institutional interdependence among the branches that allows for the possibility that the Court might be a protector of the rules of the game without producing a substantial countermajoritarian effect. This institutional structure anticipates the possibility of differences in preferences, thereby producing a

TABLE 5 Supreme Court decision contexts, 1953–1992

CONTEXT	TERM	CONGRESS	PRESIDENT	PRESIDENCY MEASURE	CONGRESS MEASURE
1	1953	83	Eisenhower	0.631	0.108
2	1954	84			0.086
3	1955	84			0.086
4	1956	85			0.088
5	1957	85			0.088
6	1958	86			−0.079
7	1959	86	Kennedy	0.336	−0.079
8	1960	87			−0.025
9	1961	87			−0.025
10	1962	88	Johnson	0.165	−0.084
11	1963	88			−0.084
12	1964	89			−0.149
13	1965	89			−0.149
14	1966	90			−0.053
15	1967	90	Nixon	0.551	−0.053
16	1968	91			−0.029
17	1969	91			−0.029
18	1970	92			−0.043
19	1971	92			−0.043
20	1972	93			−0.061
21	1973	93	Ford	0.607	−0.061
22	1974	94			−0.148
23	1975	94	Carter	0.330	−0.148
24	1976	95			−0.134
25	1977	95			−0.134
26	1978	96			−0.097
27	1979	96	Reagan	0.820	−0.097
28	1980	97			−0.014
29	1981	97			−0.014
30	1982	98			−0.031
31	1983	98			−0.031
32	1984	99			−0.041
33	1985	99			−0.041
34	1986	100			−0.073
35	1987	100			−0.073
36	1988	101	Bush	0.672	−0.073
37	1989	101			−0.073
38	1990	102			−0.102
39	1991	102			−0.102

NOTE: The presidency measure is the Segal et al. (2000) measure of social conservatism. The Congress measure is the Nominate Common Space Dimension One, from Poole and Rosenthal (1997).

check on elected officials, but creates institutional incentives to diminish the antidemocratic effects of those differences.

Appendix: Methods and Data

The statistical model used in the paper is a two-level hierarchical probit model (Martin 2001). I am modeling a set of dichotomous decisions $y_{i,k}$:

$$y_{i,k} \sim Bernoulli(\pi_{i,k}) \tag{3}$$

Assuming a probit link function:

$$\pi_{i,k} = \Phi(x'_{i,k} \beta_k) \tag{4}$$

Where $x'_{i,k}$ is a $(1 \times p)$ row vector of covariates, β_k is a $(p \times 1)$ column vector of parameters, and $\Phi(\cdot)$ is the cumulative density function of the standard Gaussian distribution. To facilitate estimation, I adapt the data augmentation approach to estimate the standard probit model (Albert and Chib 1993). For each decision context k, I introduce n_k latent variables $z_{i,k}, \ldots, z_{n_i,k}$. This implies that the observed data are generated from:

$$y_{i,k} = \begin{cases} 1 & if \quad z_{i,k} > 0 \\ 0 & if \quad z_{i,k} \leq 0 \end{cases} \tag{5}$$

This reduces the estimation of β_k to a standard regression model:

$$z_{i,k} = x'_{i,k} \beta_k + \varepsilon_{i,k} \quad \varepsilon_{i,k} \sim N(0, 1) \tag{6}$$

At the second level of the hierarchy, I model the distribution of β_k with a seemingly unrelated regression (SUR) model, which allows the errors to be correlated across elements of the β_k vector. Thus:

$$\beta_k = A_k \alpha + v_k \tag{7}$$

Where $v_k \sim N_p(0, \Omega)$, Ω is a $(p \times p)$ matrix, A_k is a $(p \times q)$ matrix of covariates, and α is a $(q \times 1)$ vector of parameters. I assume a multivariate Normal prior on the α parameter: $\alpha \sim N_q(\mu_0, \Sigma_0)$. For the variance-covariance matrix Ω, I assume a Wishart prior, $\Omega^{-1} \sim W(v_0, R_0)$. Table 5 contains the definition of the decision contexts and the explanatory variables used in the second level of the hierarchy.

Notes

Many thanks to Sid Chib, Lee Epstein, Tim Johnson, Jack Knight, Carla Molette-Ogden, Kevin Quinn, Gary Miller, Alastair Smith, John Sprague, Steve Van Winkle,

Christina Wolbrecht, and conference participants at Texas A & M University for commenting on various aspects of this project. All errors are my sole responsibility.

1. These hypotheses are directional (instead of symmetric) because of the assumption that L < C, and because of two substantively motivated modeling assumptions: (1) that the pivotal member of Congress is never to the right of the conservative status quo, and (2) the median member of Congress and the president are "close" relative to the distance between the status quo and the alternative.

2. Justices oftentimes decide the basis for their particular decision. Sometimes they decide cases on narrow statutory grounds, and other times they decide cases on broad constitutional principles. Spiller and Spitzer (1992) provide a strategic account of judicial choice of their basis for decision.

3. It is important to note that this argument holds even if the cost is not infinite. As long as the cost to the Court of a successful congressional attack is greater than the discounted sum of future policy outcomes (which it surely is), then the theoretical prediction holds.

4. For all of the models presented in this paper, I have performed posterior analysis to assure convergence of the sampler, checked for prior sensitivity, and tested alternative model specifications. All of the substantive conclusions are robust to the selection of alternative priors, or changes in model specification. The models were estimated with a prior mean of zero and variance-covariance matrix equal to an identity matrix on the α parameters (and the β parameters for the probit model), and $v_0 = p + 1$ and R_0 equal to an identity matrix for the variance parameters.

5. To select all civil rights decisions, I include all cases in my analysis where the variable VALUE = 2.

6. This measure of presidential social conservatism correlates above $r = .90$ ($n = 8$) with the Nominate Common Space Dimension One measure of presidential preferences (Poole and Rosenthal 1997).

7. For all of these models, I report posterior summary statistics in the tables. In the text, I also use the entire posterior density sample to compute the posterior probability that a coefficient differs from zero.

8. To create subsets, I use the authority for decision variable in the Supreme Court Data Base (Spaeth 1997). Following Epstein and Segal (2000), constitutional interpretation decisions are those that arrive to the court under the power of judicial review. I thus select the cases when AUTHDEC1 = 1 or AUTHDEC1 = 2. Statutory interpretation decisions are those that require the Court to interpret laws of various forms. Statutory interpretation decisions are thus those when AUTHDEC1 = 3 or AUTHDEC1 = 4 or AUTHDEC1 = 5 or AUTHDEC1 = 6 or AUTHDEC1 = 7.

9. There is an alternative explanation for these findings. Namely, that the Supreme Court does not grant *cert* in statutory cases when the justices are constrained by the other institutions of government. By this account, here also must exist a norm that the justices grant *cert* in constitutional cases, even when they are constrained by Congress and the president. However, numerous constitutional cases are filed for review, only a small percentage of which are actually taken. Thus, if the justices avoid constraint in their *cert* granting in statutory cases, why would they not behave the same way in constitutional cases?

Why Expert Judges Defer to (Almost) Ignorant Legislators

Accounting for the Puzzle of Judicial Deference

JAMES R. ROGERS

> The preceding essay argued that Supreme Court justices behave strategically, depending on whether they are resolving constitutional or statutory questions. This essay addresses a court's relationship with the elected branches from a different angle, one that considers when judges who want the law to reflect their views nevertheless will defer to legislatures. A strong reason for judicial deference is anchored in the institutional characteristics of legislatures, courts, and their interaction. Policy-oriented judges, it is argued, will rationally defer to legislative decisions even if the judges have greater expertise than any individual legislator, because legislatures can aggregate *information* as well as aggregate preferences. The implications of this argument also are consistent with "two-tiered" judicial review in which courts sometimes review legislation deferentially and sometimes review legislation with heightened scrutiny.

Strategic behavior by judges is one way they can pursue their policy preferences in constitutional cases. Justices take into account the competing preferences of the elected branches to make feasible policy gains consistent with judicial views. So why, instead, would judges ever *defer* to legislatures? Judges often apply a deferential "rationality" standard to review the constitutionality of challenged legislation. Under this standard, judges do not directly decide whether they think legislation is constitutional or not. Rather, as Justice Stephen Breyer put it, judges review the constitutionality of legislation "at one remove" (*United States v. Lopez* 514 U.S. 549 [1995], 617).

Under deferential review, judges do not ask whether they believe legislation is constitutional; they instead ask whether legislators could rationally have believed that the legislation is constitutional. Consider the difference between the two questions in a context less rarefied than constitutional law. There is a difference between whether you believe it will rain tomorrow and whether a rational person could believe that it will rain tomorrow. It is very easy to imagine a circumstance in which you do not believe it will rain tomorrow, yet you would fairly admit that a perfectly rational person could come to the opposite conclusion. In constitutional law, under the rationality standard, if a judge believes *legislators* could have a rational basis for believing the statute is constitutional, then the judge will affirm the law's constitutionality. Hence, under this standard, judges affirm the constitutionality of a challenged law even if, as an original matter, the judge believes the legislation is actually *un*constitutional. This standard requires that judges give legislatures the benefit of the doubt regarding the constitutionality of their enactments.

This essay advances two claims regarding deferential judicial review. First, I argue that extant theories of judicial deference do not really explain the phenomenon. Secondly, I provide a possible explanation for the puzzle anchored in the institutional characteristics of legislatures, courts, and their interaction. Specifically, I argue that policy-oriented judges will rationally defer to legislative decisions made by plural legislatures even when those judges have greater expertise than any individual legislator, because legislatures are mechanisms that can aggregate information as well as aggregate preferences. Further, while this essay focuses on the puzzle of judicial deference, the implications of the argument are consistent with "two-tiered" judicial review in which courts sometimes review legislation deferentially and sometimes review legislation with heightened scrutiny (see, e.g., Rogers 1999b). As such, the argument developed here does not justify the broader Frankfurterian position that legislation should always be reviewed deferentially (Levinson 1973, Urofsky 1991).[1]

I should emphasize from the start that the argument is suggestive at best, for both substantive and methodological reasons. The goal of this essay is to sketch the outlines of an argument that accounts for judicial deference that is superior to existing alternative justifications.

Rationality Review in American Constitutional Jurisprudence

Deferential "rationality review" is the default standard of review in the American judiciary's "two-tiered" system of judicial review. In the context of Fourteenth Amendment litigation, Justice Clarence Thomas explained the choice of the standard-of-review this way: "In areas of social and economic policy, a statutory classification that neither proceeds along suspect lines nor infringes fundamental constitutional rights must be upheld against equal protection challenge if there is any reasonably conceivable state of facts that could provide a rational basis for the classification" (*FCC v. Beach Communications, Inc.* 508 U.S. 307 [1993], 313).

There are several implications of rationality review, whether in the context of rights litigation or litigation over governmental structure and relations. First, legislation evaluated under the rationality standard enjoys the presumption of constitutionality. Those challenging laws evaluated under the rationality standard have the affirmative burden of proving the challenged laws unconstitutional. (Under heightened review, whether a form of "intermediate" review or "strict scrutiny," the challenged law comes to the Court with the presumption of *un*constitutionality, so the government bears the burden of affirmatively proving to the Court that the challenged law is, in fact, constitutional.) The standard of review is important for case outcomes, because in constitutional litigation, as in other areas of litigation, "where the burden of proof lies may be decisive of the outcome" (*Speiser v. Randall* 357 U.S. 513 [1958], 525).

Second, the rationality standard does not require the legislature to adduce *any* actual evidence or finding to support its statutory choice. When there are merely "plausible reasons" for the legislative action, the judicial "inquiry is at an end" under the rationality standard (*FCC v. Beach Communications, Inc.* 1993, 313–14). As Justice Thomas explained for the Court:

> [T]he absence of "legislative facts" explaining the distinction "on the record" . . . has no significance in rational-basis analysis. . . . In other words, a legislative choice is not subject to courtroom fact finding and may be based on rational speculation unsupported by evidence or empirical data. (*FCC v. Beach Communications, Inc.,* at 315)

In *United States v. Lopez,* striking down the Gun-Free School Zones Act of 1990 as being beyond Congress's Commerce Clause power, the Court similarly affirmed that "Congress normally is not required to make formal findings as to the substantial burdens that an activity has on interstate commerce" (*United States v. Lopez* 1995, 562).

The "rationality" standard imposes minimal requirements on the legislature, including minimal informational requirements. Under this standard, legislatures need not demonstrate in court that a policy problem actually exists or that the means adopted in the statute to address the problem is likely to solve the policy problem. Under this standard, judges do not second-guess legislative decisions. Even when the trial process produces a careful record of empirical evidence that challenges a law's constitutional reasonability, a judge applying the rationality standard would nonetheless uphold the law, because "a legislative choice is not subject to courtroom fact-finding and may be based on rational speculation unsupported by evidence or empirical data" (*FCC v. Beach Communications, Inc.* 1993, 315).

Why would judges defer to a legislative decision under these conditions? Let me draw out the puzzle. Say we have a record devoid of any legislative fact-finding. No committee report, indeed, no committee hearings at all. No deliberation on the floor of the legislature. No statement of legislative intent. In contrast, the judicial record extends, say, over 3,000 pages, with 148 pages reciting the court's findings of fact (see, e.g., *Southern Pacific Co. v. Arizona* 325 U.S. 761 [1945], 787). Judges applying the rationality doctrine nonetheless would defer to the legislature's decision, unless those attacking the law meet the burden of "negativ[ing] every conceivable basis which might support [the law]" (*FCC v. Beach Communications, Inc.* 1993, 315). Why would judges in a separation-of-power system with an independent judiciary ever choose to adopt such an extremely deferential posture toward legislative enactments? We now turn to consider several major lines of argument that have been forwarded to explain or justify judicial deference.

Arguments Seeking to Justify Judicial Deference

I briefly consider four main arguments often asserted to justify (positively or normatively) deferential judicial review: that courts defer to the more democratic branches of government; that courts defer to legislative informational expertise; the Landes-Posner argument that deferential review promotes legislative bargaining in pluralist political systems; and that courts are deferential when their policy preferences converge with the legislature's. I argue that none of these arguments succeeds in justifying deferential judicial review as represented by the rationality standard. Consider each argument in turn.

DEFERENCE TO DEMOCRATICALLY ACCOUNTABLE DECISION MAKERS

One argument frequently advanced to justify judicial deference to legislative outcomes is that in republican polities, nonelected judges should naturally defer to democratically accountable legislators in policy matters (Ely 1980, cf., Rogers 1999b). The argument has been around for well over one hundred years, being popularized in the nineteenth century by Harvard law professor James Bradley Thayer. Thayer's argument influenced the "Harvard" justices, notably including Oliver Wendell Holmes, Felix Frankfurter, and Louis Brandeis. Yet, there are problems with this argument.

Consider more broadly the relationship between courts and legislatures not only at the national level, but among the states as well. Consider then cases in which judges are elected as well as those in which judges are not elected. First, if judges are elected—as they are in any number of states—then there is no democratic reason for them to humble themselves before the decisions of an elected legislature. Nevertheless, elected judges also apply the rationality standard when reviewing legislative enactments (at least those that do not touch on fundamental rights or suspect classifications). While it is possible that these judges are simply wrong in applying a standard of review predicated on deference to the republican branches of government, most observers, I think, would concede that any adequate justification for judicial deference should apply equally to elected as well as nonelected judges. If so, a different principle must be invoked to justify such deference.

Now consider nonelected judges. I might first note that the notion that judges who are not popularly elected are perforce not a "republican" branch of the government would be a surprise to the framers of the American constitutional regime. For example, in *The Federalist* No. 39, Publius (the nom de plume for Alexander Hamilton, James Madison, and John Jay) affirmed the republican character of the American judiciary (1788/1961).[2] More important, however, is that the articulated purpose of immunizing judges from *direct* electoral pressures is precisely to free them to apply their best independent judgment when reviewing legislation.

If that is true, then it critically undermines the argument that judges should defer to the democratic branches of government. It makes no sense to immunize judges from direct electoral pressures in order to encourage them to exercise their independent judgment when reviewing legislation, and then turn around and argue that *because* they are immune from direct electoral pressures, they therefore should *not* employ their best independent judgment when reviewing legislation but should instead defer to the legislature's policy judgment because legislators *are* elected. So, an adequate justification for judicial deference must not discriminate between elected and nonelected judges and must be consistent with judges applying their best independent judgment.

INFORMATIONAL SUPERIORITY OF LEGISLATORS

Another common argument for judicial deference to legislative decisions is that legislators are better positioned to acquire and use information than are judges. Hence, judges should normally defer to the legislature's informational superiority. While the argument of this essay picks up on an aspect of this, we first consider in what ways the claim is suspect. First, it is certainly easy to doubt that the judgments of individual legislators are informationally superior to those of judges. Louis Lusky advances at least a plausible claim when he writes that "By and large, officeholders are an undistinguished lot. For intellect, insight, and moral courage, few of them compare with most of the Justices" (1993, 2).

Further, it is important to keep in mind that application of the deferential rationality standard is not limited to instances in which the legislature has engaged in a fact-finding process or even deliberated on a law before enacting it. A justification for the rationality standard must be able to justify deference when the record is entirely devoid of information acquisition on the part of the legislature.

It is easy to imagine that judges will often be better informed than legislators. As noted in the previous part, application of the rationality standard is not contingent on the manifest quality of informational inputs into a given piece of legislation. The rationality standard does not require legislatures to have held any hearings on a proposed law or to have made any actual findings of fact supporting the law. In contrast, the judge may have access to reams of pertinent policy information (and would have access to whatever legislative record was created), yet the rationality standard would *still* require that the judge defer to the legislature's judgment. Indeed, if we want to place policymaking decisions into the hands of the best informed and most intelligent people among the three branches of government, it is difficult to argue that judges should be prevented from using their best judgment regarding the constitutional reasonability of legislation rather than mindlessly deferring to legislators who, on average, are likely less intelligent and less well informed than judges are on the policy implications of challenged legislation.

THE LANDES-POSNER ARGUMENT

William Landes and Richard Posner (1975) developed an "interest group" theory of judicial independence that also implics judicial deference to legislative decisions (Zeppos 1993). In this theory, judges aim only to enforce the original conjectures of statutory framers regarding the expected outcome of policies. The legislature maintains judicial independence irrespective of partisan control, because each party derives more benefit from its legislation lasting a long time relative to its being short lived should partisan control of the legislature rotate along with partisan control of the legislature. The model has attracted a lot of attention, particularly in the legal literature. I rehearse one well-known objection to the theory, then advance two additional objections that I haven't stumbled across in the literature interacting with the model. (But I fully admit that I have not mastered the voluminous literature on the model, so my responses might have been anticipated previously.)

One well-known problem with Landes and Posner's model is that it is unclear why judges will be satisfied simply to enforce legislative bargains made long ago, even if their (i.e., the judges') policy preferences diverge from the outcomes of those bargains. Presumably, judges are kept honest by the threat of legislative sanctions should judges cease enforcing legislative bargains. Yet, while that might deter judges from flouting bargains made by a current legislature, it is difficult to imagine that a current legislature controlled, say, by Party D, would seek to discipline a judge also of Party D who sets aside a law enacted years ago by Party R when it controlled the legislature. But if the legislature would not discipline this judge then, as we will see more explicitly in a little bit, the whole deal will unravel.

Further, we can move the Landes-Posner argument back one step. If legislation can be understood as a bargain among interest groups that rely on scrupulous judicial implementation of original purposes, then constitutions may also be understood as commitment devices that depend on judicial implementation. But at the stage of constitutional design, it is plausible that a constitution's framers expected judicial enforcement of constitutional provisions against subsequent legislatures that would attempt to enact bargains that contravened those provisions. But, given the Landes-Posner argument, judges scrupulous to enforce the constitutional bargain would not perforce defer to subsequent legislative bargains. They might instead actively strike down laws that violate constitutional restraints.

Finally, and more important, I would argue that the original Landes-Posner model is underspecified and that this underspecification critically affects their conclusions. Landes and Posner reach their conclusions by comparing two static outcomes: the surplus from legislative bargains with an independent judiciary and the surplus from legislative bargains without an independent judiciary. As noted above, they argue that the legislative surplus from the former will be greater than the legislative surplus from the latter. I am not convinced of this but will grant the claim for the sake of the argument. Given the assumption, however, since the former is greater than the latter, Landes and Posner conclude that legislative majorities of each partisan stripe will coordinate on the efficient outcome.

There is a well-known problem, however, with this type of argument; it neglects that off-equilibrium strategies (i.e., strategies that are played in equilibrium with probability zero) may critically affect equilibrium outcomes. Indeed, the prisoners' dilemma (see book appendix for a discussion of "prisoners' dilemma") is the superlative example of a game in which the players will not realize an efficient outcome because of incentives to defect from playing mutually welfare-maximizing strategies. Setting the Landes-Posner model in a game-theoretic framework shows why their argument for judicial independence and judicial deference may not be particularly plausible.

As above, assume there are two parties, R and D. The parties rotate control of the legislature, during which time they enact the legislation they prefer. Additionally, when each party controls the legislature, it chooses whether to maintain the independence of the judiciary (I) or to subjugate it (S). The strategy set for each party is $S_I = \{I, S\}, i \in \{D, R\}$. If the judiciary is independent, then, following the Landes-Posner assumption, judges will pretty much just neutrally implement the entire set of legislative bargains made in the past, irrespective of which party made those bargains. If the judiciary is subjugated, then it implements only the policy preferences of the party that subjugated it.

Payoffs are, P_i, $i \in \{D, R\}$, and are the discounted future benefits of having your party's laws on the books. Figure 1 presents a simple 2×2 normal form of this game. If both parties choose to maintain an independent judiciary, that is, for strategy profile (I, I), then their net payoff is as follows: $P_D - f(P_R)$ for party D and $P_R - g(P_D)$ for Party R. $f(\cdot)$ and $g(\cdot)$ are functional transformations of the other party's payoffs. With an independent judiciary, each party not only receives the payoff of having its laws remain on the books, but also must pay *some* cost in the form of having the *other* party's laws also on the books. This can be thought of as the tax cost for a policy that a party opposes or the opportunity cost of not being able to legislate in an area because the other party got there first.

Now, if one party pursues a strategy of subjugating the judiciary, while the other party refuses to subjugate the judiciary—these are strategy profiles (S, I) or (I, S)—then the now-partisan judiciary will only affirm

FIGURE 1 A game-theoretic translation of the Landes-Posner model

		PARTY D	
		I	S
PARTY R	I	$P_D - f(P_R)$; $P_R - g(P_D)$	P_D ; $-g(P_D)$
	S	$-f(P_R)$; P_R	$\frac{1}{2}[P_D - f(P_R)]$; $\frac{1}{2}[P_R - g(P_D)]$

the legislation of the subjugating party and strike down the legislation of the nonsubjugating party. So, if Party R subjugates the judiciary, while Party D does not, then it receives a payoff of P_R. The court strikes down Party D's laws now, so R's payoff is no longer net of $f(P_D)$. Party D receives a net payoff of $-g(P_R)$, because the court strikes down its legislation (so it doesn't receive P_D), while sustaining Party R's legislation, which costs Party D a total of $-g(P_R)$.

If both parties subjugate the judiciary, then we have the "one-period" payoffs that Landes and Posner discuss. Assume each party holds a majority in the legislature half the time. When the party controls the legislature, it enacts the legislation it prefers and subjugates the judiciary. The subjugated judiciary strikes down legislation enacted by the previous legislature (which was controlled by the opposite party) and sustains the legislation enacted by this legislature. The payoffs for each party are therefore $\frac{1}{2}[P_D - f(P_R)]$ and $\frac{1}{2}[P_R - g(P_D)]$, respectively.

Note that $U_D(I, I) > U_D(S, S)$ (because $P_D - f(P_R) > \frac{1}{2}[P_D - f(P_R)]$) and $U_R(I, I) > U_R(S, S)$ (because $P_R - g(P_D) > \frac{1}{2}[P_R - g(P_D)]$), which are the relative payoffs identified in Landes and Posner's model. Even though the payoff to strategy profile (I, I) is greater than the payoff to strategy profile (S, S) for both parties, (S, S) is nonetheless the equilibrium outcome to the game because of off-equilibrium incentives for strategy profiles (S, I) and (I, S), respectively. Note also that this game is "played" with neutral judges in the (I, I) strategy profile. That is itself a dubious assumption that would make the Landes-Posner game even easier to unravel.[3] In any event, as solved here, the Landes-Posner model boils down to the implication that courts "strictly" review the other party's laws while deferentially reviewing its own party's legislation. This, in turn, shares the problem discussed, that judicial deference can be accounted for by judicial convergence with the legislature. Thus, the Landes-Posner model fails to provide a persuasive rationale for judicial deference.[4]

CONVERGENT COURTS AND DEFERENTIAL REVIEW

The implications of both the "attitudinal" model (Segal and Spaeth 1993) and traditional forms of the strategic model (see, e.g., Epstein and Knight 1998) are that, when the policy preferences of a court converge with the policy preferences of the legislature (relative to the status quo), the court will not strike down the challenged legislation. This directly implies a theory of two-tiered judicial review. When the Supreme Court anticipates having preferences over subject matter that it expects will consistently diverge from legislative preferences, then it will apply heightened review to laws challenged in those policy areas (e.g., regulation of speech, racial and gender preferences, etc.). So, too, in areas in which the Court anticipates that its policy preferences will more consistently converge with those of the legislature (e.g., regarding economic regulations), it applies deferential standards of review. From this perspective, the respective standards implied by each tier in two-tiered review are proxies for the substantive policy preferences of judges.

The problem with this argument as concerns deferential review is that it assumes that courts have preferences only over legislative *goals* and do not have preferences over legislative *outcomes.* As I show in James Rogers (2001b, see also, Rogers and Vanberg 2002), while convergent preferences are a necessary condition for a court approving a legislative enactment, it is not a sufficient condition. If a court, in fact, has preferences that converge with a legislature's on a policy goal, then the court will still sometimes *want* to veto a law that, ex post, is not accomplishing the purpose the legislature ex ante thought that it would accomplish when it enacted the law. To the extent that deferential judicial review implies that a convergent court would approve laws with outcomes that the legislature did not (probabilistically) expect and would disapprove, then even a convergent court could consistently apply heightened review standards when passing on the constitutional reasonability of legislation. Convergent preferences are not sufficient to justify deferential review.

A related argument is that courts may be deferential to legislatures for strategic reasons, that is, that they fear legislative discipline should they overturn legislative statutes. The puzzle this essay seeks to solve, however, is whether judicial deference and judicial independence are consistent phenomena. That is, is there any substantive reason that a fully independent court—a court that does not fear legislative retribution for the exercise of the judicial veto—would still *choose* to defer to the legislature's judgment?

Information Aggregation in Plural Legislatures and Judicial Deference

This part of the essay seeks to sketch what I believe is a novel account of judicial deference. It accounts for why an independent judiciary will *want* sometimes to defer to legislative decisions, even when the judge has better information than each of the legislators has. The argument I sketch provides a justification for rationality review as it is articulated by modern American courts. While it accounts for the puzzle of deferential judicial review by an independent judiciary, the argument also accounts for when courts will *not* defer to legislative judgments and, hence, for the existence of judicial vetoes in equilibrium.

The trick, such as it is, is to identify legislatures not simply as institutions that aggregate preferences, but as institutions that can aggregate information as well. The argument is discussed within the context of a simple game of judicial review, illustrated in figure 2. The game is similar to the "baseline" game of judicial review used in James Rogers and Georg Vanberg (2002), which is described in detail in the appendix to this essay. There are two important changes relative to that model. First, while the judiciary here is assumed to know its own policy preferences with certainty, unlike Rogers and Vanberg (2002) (and also Rogers, 2001b), the court does not also know the empirical state of the world with certainty. Rather, it has a prior probability q_c regarding whether the state of the world is R or ~R. As a result, the court can update its assessment of the empirical state of the world by observing the legislature's action in enacting a law, L. The second change relative to Rogers and Vanberg (2002) is that the legislature is expressly assumed to be a plural legislature.[5] Each *individual* legislator has an a priori belief regarding the empirical state of the world q_l. I further stipulate that $0.5 < q_l < q_c$. That is, judges have a better assessment of the true empirical state of the world relative to each individual legislator. q_l is to be interpreted this way: prior to voting on a proposed law, legislators receive a private signal regarding the true state of the world. The legislators' signals are independent draws from a state-dependent distribution and are correlated with the true state of the world (see, e.g., Austen-Smith and Banks 1996, 35).

The legislature's preferences over legislation can be thought of in one

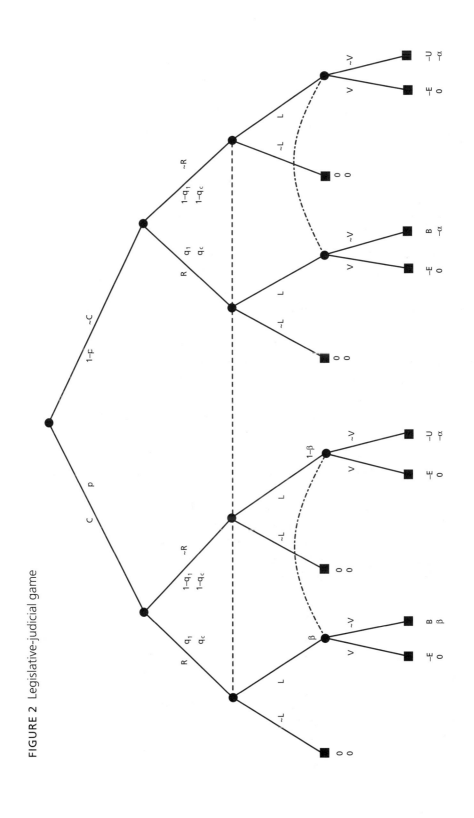

FIGURE 2 Legislative-judicial game

of two ways. First, since we focus on justifying judicial deference in a republican polity, we could posit homogeneous preferences among legislators, with votes pertaining only to the choice of means to achieve an agreed-upon end. While this might sound a bit heroic, I do note that it was a guiding assumption of American republicans during and after the Revolutionary War, and actually has more merit than may appear at first glance. (See, e.g., Rogers 2001a, 136.) But, given that I permit the court to have divergent preferences, it would be rather odd to assume homogeneous preferences among all of the legislators. Secondly, however, one can conceive of the decision to legislate in this fashion. The majority party votes in its caucus whether it desires to enact a proposed law: If the caucus votes in favor of the proposal, then all legislators in the majority party are bound to vote for the proposal on the legislative floor. Since it is the majority party, that means that the caucus vote determines whether a law will be enacted or not. I then further assume that the legislators of the same party share homogenous preferences. In this way we can stipulate that the legislature has two parties in it, yet meet the homogeneity requirement necessary to appeal to the Condorcet jury theorem (see, e.g., Feddersen and Pesendorfer 1999).

First, note that judicial vetoes occur in a proportion of at least $1 - p$, the probability that the court will have divergent preferences. The divergent court will never defer to the legislature, so our focus is on the behavior the convergent court.

Now, in Rogers (2001b) and Rogers and Vanberg (2002), the convergent court knows the empirical state of the world with certainty. Hence, if the empirical state of the world is R, then the convergent court sustains the legislature's enactment. If the empirical state of the world is ~R, then the court vetoes the legislation (an outcome, incidentally, that the policy-oriented legislature prefers). Here, however, the court only knows the true state of the world probabilistically. This is the opening for "true" judicial deference.

First, a definition.

Judicial Deference: A court defers to the legislature's judgment if it votes contrary to its private information regarding the true empirical state of the world.

Recall that the puzzle this paper seeks to answer is why a court might ever apply the rationality standard. This standard requires that a court defer to the legislature's judgment irrespective of the absence of mechanisms to acquire or communicate information (e.g., no committee hearings, no deliberation, no findings-of-fact statement). We have further assumed that each individual legislator is *less* informed regarding the true state of the empirical world than is the judge. A possible solution to this puzzle is suggested by results implied by the Condorcet jury theorem (CJT). There is a burgeoning literature on the CJT that is not my purpose to survey here (see, e.g., Feddersen and Pesendorfer 1999). Rather, with a passing appeal to Andrew McLennan's (1998) demonstration that every "sincere" CJT result can be sustained as a Nash equilibrium (which is not at all to say that it is a unique equilibrium; for a discussion of "Nash equilibrium," see the book appendix), I will simply invoke the result. The point of this essay is simply to suggest an answer to a judicial puzzle that, I argue, has had as yet no adequate answer. For this purpose, I only dip my toe into the CJT literature by way of application and do not at all seek to contribute to the theoretical literature.

In any event, with this result in hand, we can now identify conditions under which a better informed judge will defer to a legislative decision, even though every single legislator is individually less informed than the judge. For concreteness, let there be a legislature of 100 legislators (or majority-party legislators voting in caucus). Each legislator is "almost ignorant." That is, individually, each legislators' private signal is barely correlated with the true state of the world at 0.53. (That is, when there are two states of the world, A or B, a single legislator will identify the true state of the world 53 percent of the time. A completely ignorant person has a 50 percent probability of correctly identifying the true state of the world.) The probability that a majority vote of these legislators will correctly choose whether a proposed piece of legislation is appropriate to solve a given problem will be about 0.70. If the legislators' private signal is correlated with the true state of the world at the 0.56 level, then the probability is 0.87 that a majority vote will identify the correct state of the world (and, hence, choose the most appropriate legislative means to obtain a given end). And if the legislators' private signal is correlated with the true state of the world at the 0.57 level, then the probability is 0.91 that a majority vote will correctly identify the true state of the world.

What's the implication for judicial review? A relatively expert judge might be fairly confident in his or her competence correctly to identify the true state of the world. Let's say the probability for that judge is 0.86, meaning that this judge will correctly identify the correct state of the world three out of ten times *more often* than any individual legislator.

Nonetheless, when this judge considers the legislative enactment, he or she would nonetheless rationally defer to the aggregate judgment of the legislature, even though the judge is more expert individually than each of the legislators.

Now, of course, I do not mean to suggest that judges have anything close to a precise estimate of the level(s) of correlation of the legislators' private signals with the true state of the world. Rather, appeal to the jury theorem might be able to account for the rough intuition that, under reasonable circumstances, judges ought to defer to the collective wisdom of legislatures, because the aggregate legislative decision just might be better than what even a highly informed and expert judge might recommend as an alternative.

The idea that legislatures aggregate information as well as aggregate preferences is potentially able to account for judicial deference in a fashion better than any existing alternative. That being said, it should also be noted that even the convergent judge will not defer under all circumstances. If the judge is certain enough, if a litigant "negatives every reasonable conceivable" justification for a law, then the judge will still set aside the legislature's collective judgment. There might well be any number of circumstances in which a judge would be 90 percent certain of the realization of a given state of the world. In that case, aggregating the court's private information with a legislative recommendation that is correct will less than 90 percent certainty implies that the judge will follow his or her private information and not defer to the legislature.

Conclusion

The argument developed here provides a rationale for why rational, policy-oriented judges will *want* to defer to certain legislative judgments under fairly reasonable circumstances. Further, judicial deference would be rational in these cases even when there is no extrinsic evidence that the legislature has acquired specialized information through the committee system or that it has carefully deliberated on a matter. While the theory developed here is intended to be suggestive and not conclusive, the extant alternative answers to the puzzle are even less persuasive.

Appendix

This appendix is adopted from Rogers and Vanberg (2002) and describes the "baseline" model used there and drawn on for this essay in order to explain the notation used in figure 2.

We begin by developing a model of judicial-legislative interactions in which no advisory opinion is available. This model provides a "baseline" against which we can evaluate the effects of the availability of advisory opinions. The basic legislative-judicial game, depicted by the game tree in figure 2, involves three players: nature, a legislature, and a court. For modeling purposes, we treat the court and the legislature as unitary actors. While both institutions are collegial bodies, the assumption can be justified by the "single-subject requirement" governing most advisory opinions, which limits requests for advice to single issues. As a result, we can think of the "court" or the "legislature" as the median judge or legislator in a unidimensional policy space. The sequence of play in the basic game is as follows. At the outset of the game, nature makes two (independent) moves in selecting the "type" of the court. It first selects the substantive policy preference of the court over the law (more on this below), and then selects a "state of the world" (more on these states below). After nature has selected these two components of the court's type, the legislature decides whether to pass a bill (L) or to maintain the status quo ($\sim L$). The legislature's action set at this stage is given by $A_L^1 = \{L, \sim L\}$. The legislature makes its choice while uncertain of the court's type (i.e., the legislature is uncertain of the court's policy preferences and is uncertain regarding the true state of the world). If the legislature chooses not to pass a bill, the game ends. If it chooses to legislate, the court reviews the constitutionality of the law in the next stage. The court can strike down ("veto") the law (V), or it can sustain it ($\sim V$). The court's action set is given by $A_C^2 = \{V, \sim V\}$. For reasons that will be apparent shortly, the court makes its choice with perfect knowledge of its own type.

As mentioned, the legislature has incomplete information regarding the court's preferences toward the proposed law and the state of the world. Recall the "Frankfurter Objection" that the constitutional reasonability of a statute is, at least in part, a function of empirical consequences that can be observed only after the law has been enacted and implemented. The model captures this by differentiating between two states of the world in the court's type set. In the first state of the world (R), the bill is constitutionally reasonable ex post, that is, it achieves its intended purpose in a reasonable fashion.[6] In the second state ($\sim R$), the law turns out to be unreasonable ex post, that is, it does not achieve its intended purpose in a reasonable manner. Since the legislature cannot know with certainty ex ante whether a law will be empirically reasonable or unreasonable, the legislature does not know the state of the world at the legislative stage. The common prior belief that the law is empirically reasonable is given by $\Pr(R) = q$. Conversely, the prior belief that the law is unreasonable is given by $\Pr(\sim R) = 1 - q$. Since the court reviews the law *after* it has been implemented and in the context of a concrete dispute, the court has access to more information about the state of the world.[7] We capture this fact in the model by assuming that when engaging in ex post judicial review, the court knows with certainty whether or not a law is empirically reasonable in achieving its intended purpose. This modeling choice captures the unique informational advantage enjoyed by courts in the course of ordinary judicial review.

The other component of incomplete information in the court's type set concerns the relation of the court's preferences to the legislature's preferences on the reviewed bill. First, the court may prefer the legislature's bill relative to the status quo. This type of court is designated "convergent" (C). If the bill achieves its intended purpose, the court would like to see the bill implemented. Significantly, however, because the convergent court shares the legislature's policy preference on the bill or law, it also shares the legislature's concern regarding the empirical reasonability of the law. If the law is revealed to be unreasonable ex post, the court would prefer to strike it down rather than uphold it (even though the court agrees with the *intended* purpose of the statute). The convergent court's preferences are therefore be characterized as follows. The court earns a benefit of $\beta > 0$ if the bill is empirically reasonable and is implemented (i.e., it is not struck down by the court). If, however, the bill turns out to be empirically unreasonable but is implemented nevertheless, the court pays a cost of $\alpha > 0$. Finally, if the status quo is maintained (either because the legislature does not pass a bill or because the court vetoes the law), the court's payoff is simply 0.

The court's preferences on a law or bill may also be "nonconvergent" ($\sim C$) with the legislature's preferences (again, relative to the status quo). Specifically, if the statute is enacted and not struck down by the court, the nonconvergent court pays the cost $\alpha > 0$ regardless of the empirical reasonability of the law.[8] It receives a payoff of 0 if the status quo is maintained (either because the legislature does not pass a bill or because the court vetoes the law). The common prior belief that the court is convergent is given by $\Pr(C) = p$, while the prior belief that the court is non-convergent is given by $\Pr(\sim C) = 1 - p$.

Notes

1. At the same time, it should be noted that the argument developed here does not necessarily imply two-tiered review as it has developed since World War II, although it is also not necessarily inconsistent with it.

2. Publius argued that the national judiciary was a republican institution because it was accountable to the elected branches of government for appointment and continuation in office. Hence, judges were "indirectly" subject to the people.

3. Landes and Posner might attempt to argue that the game they model is an iterated prisoners' dilemma rather than a one-shot prisoners' dilemma (PD) game. It must be kept in mind that while achieving the mutually advantageous outcome is an equilibrium in an iterated PD game, so is defection in every period, and everything in between. They would need to explain why they would expect the "cooperative" equilibrium to be the one played. I argue that that equilibrium would be unlikely, for the reasons discussed above, if we permit the judges themselves to be policy oriented. It simply beggars the imagination that a party will discipline a convergent court for striking down legislation enacted by the other party in an earlier period. I might further note that Rogers (2001b) describes a one-shot game that nonetheless accounts for the creation and maintenance of a policy-oriented judiciary by a policy-oriented legislature.

4. It might also be noted that the Landes-Posner model in a sense proves too much. If all the judiciary exists to do is enforce past legislative bargains, then it will never veto legislation. Landes and Posner write vetoes off as the "cost" of judicial independence. But that is unsatisfying. Why would the legislature ever permit a court to veto a legislative enactment? Indeed, Landes and Posner's "independent judiciary" is one that *only* seeks to implement legislative will, irrespective of which legislature it was. But this activity is fully consistent with judiciaries that are not independent, such as the British courts or the Soviet courts, which sought to implement Politburo decrees irrespective of which faction prompted the decree. Landes and Posner actually employ an idiosyncratic definition of judicial independence—that judicial decision making does not change with election results. A more traditional definition of judicial independence is that judges can veto legislation without fear of legislative discipline. By this definition, Landes and Posner do not provide an argument for judicial independence—indeed, they specifically appeal to the threat of legislative discipline to keep judges from exercising their discretion and striking down legislative enactments rather than neutrally implementing them. While they may (or may not) have provided an argument as to why legislatures might want judges who seek only to implement legislative enactments as originally intended by the enacting coalitions, what they do not justified is why a truly independent judiciary would *want* to defer to legislative judgments, and why it would be expected to.

5. This is consistent with Rogers (2001b) and Rogers and Vanberg (2002), who assume a unidimensional policy space in order to treat the legislature as an individual (appealing implicitly to the median voter theorem). I simply note the explicit existence of a plural legislature in order to motivate application of the Condorcet jury theorem.

6. U.S. courts engage in "reasonability" inquiries whenever they weigh the costs and benefits of legislation (Bennett 1979). In many different areas, federal and state courts weigh the significance of the government's purpose and the "fit" between the statutory end and the statutory means in determining whether a challenged statute is constitutionally reasonable. An "unreasonable" law is one in which the realized social cost is greater than the realized social benefit or the costs are imposed on nonbenefited parties (see, e.g., Bennett 1979, and Rogers 1999b, 1103–4). State courts tend to be less deferential toward legislatures than federal courts in reviewing the reasonability of ordinary socioeconomic legislation (Note 1979).

7. See Rogers (2001b, 86–88). Judicial rules, such as the standing doctrine, ensure that litigants before courts have incentives to provide the court concrete ex post information about the reasonability of a statute. Further the doctrine limits access to the judicial forum to plaintiffs with special informational characteristics, for example, to plaintiffs with injuries that are "'actual or imminent,' not 'conjectural' or 'hypothetical'" (*Lujan v. Defenders of Wildlife* 504 U.S. 555 [1992], 560, see also, *Friends of the Earth v. Laidlaw* 528 U.S. 167 [2000], 180–81). Justice Anthony Kennedy, in his concurrence in *Lujan,* lists both an incentive rationale as well as an asymmetric information rationale for the standing doctrine's requirement that plaintiffs must show that the injuries are both concrete and personal (504 U.S. 555, 581 [1992]).

8. In other words, since the nonconvergent court does not agree with the purpose of the bill, the question of reasonability of the means becomes moot. In terms of the two-pronged review that U.S. courts engage in, the bill fails the first "ends" prong. No further inquiry is then needed.

Institutions and Independence in Models of Judicial Review

CHRISTOPHER ZORN

Regardless of whether judges make strategic decisions or choose to defer to the elected branches, two prior and basic questions remain. First, given that an autonomous judiciary runs the risk of usurping legislative power, what are the reasons for the existence of an independent judiciary? Second, given an autonomous judiciary, what accounts for the incidence (or lack thereof) of judicial invalidations of legitimate legislative enactments? These questions can be answered by using a stylized model of Congress-Supreme Court interaction. This model incorporates the seminal argument of William Landes and Richard Posner that interest groups serve as critical links between Congress and the Court. Central to the model is the conviction that groups, acting both in the legislative arena and as intermediaries between the branches of government, play a determining role in the separation-of-powers system.

An enduring, fundamental question in American politics is how to reconcile the existence of an independent, nonaccountable judiciary with a democratically based system of government (e.g., Dahl 1957; Bickel 1962; Casper 1976). In particular, the existence of judicial review, whereby a nonelected Court may overturn laws enacted by a duly elected legislature, seems on its face profoundly threatening to the continued existence of a representative system of government. This "countermajoritarian difficulty" is a subject of continual and ongoing scrutiny among political and legal scholars alike.

At the heart of this difficulty is the relationship between the Congress and the Supreme Court. At least since the landmark case of *Marbury v. Madison* (5 U.S. 137 [1803]), the prerogative of the Court to, in Justice John Marshall's words, "say what the law is" has been generally recognized, if not so generally accepted. Furthermore, the Court is relatively insulated from the political process: judges are appointed for life or good behavior, their salaries may not be reduced while in office, and the institution itself commands a good deal of public support (Caldeira and Gibson 1992). Thus the Court may choose to find any statute brought before it to be against the Constitution without significant fear of reprisal, and the ability of the Congress to remedy such a decision through legislative means is limited, particularly in constitutional cases. These factors have led more than one student of American government to fear the possibility of an "imperial judiciary."

At the same time, other facts suggest that the insularity of the Court is neither as widespread nor as pernicious as these circumstances may suggest. For example, the extent to which the Court has chosen to exercise its authority over legislative enactments has been limited, and instances of direct Congress-Court conflict have been relatively rare. In particular, the Court has only infrequently struck down acts of the Congress as unconstitutional on their face and has upheld many more than it has so overturned. In general, deference to enacted legislation is the rule, and nullification occurs only under extraordinary circumstances (see Baum 1995). Furthermore, recent "neo-institutional" analyses of the judiciary's role within the larger political system suggest that the courts, and especially the Supreme Court, are highly responsive to both the prevailing political climate and to interest groups operating within the political system. These studies further suggest that this responsiveness, rather than stemming from the concordance of beliefs between the Court and the other branches, occurs as a result of the Court's awareness of the ability and propensity of those branches to undo that which the Court has done (see, e.g., Epstein and Walker 1994; Eskridge 1991a; Rodriguez 1994).

These facts pose a double question. First, given that an autonomous judiciary runs the risk of usurping legislative power, what are the reasons for the existence of an independent judiciary? Second, given a judiciary constructed to be largely independent of the more political branches of government, what accounts for the incidence (or lack thereof) of judicial invalidation of otherwise legitimate legislative enactments? This essay seeks to address these questions through the formulation and analysis of a stylized model of Congress-Supreme Court interaction. In particular, it emphasizes the role of organized interests as the critical link between Congress and the Court.

The Landes-Posner Model

In their seminal (1975) article, William Landes and Richard Posner present one theory for the existence of an unaccountable judicial branch in an otherwise representative system of government. They posit an "interest group" model of Supreme Court action, based on a pluralist view of government policymaking. In their theory, legislation that benefits certain groups is created by members of Congress. It is then "sold" to those groups in exchange for campaign contributions, votes, pledges of support, and the like. The distinguishing characteristic of this market, however, is the absence of sanctions, legal or otherwise, for nonperformance on the part of the legislature. That is, a Congress that sells legislation to a particular group may return the following session and enact laws repealing that legislation. While such bad faith on the part of members would doubtlessly reduce the price of legislation, and thus the ability of members to effectively seek reelection, Landes and Posner note that this still may not prevent some members from trading short-term gains for longer-term losses in this manner. And to the extent that votes on many important issues are close and membership turnover is high, the degree of legislative instability is exacerbated.

Landes and Posner argue that two factors serve to offset the potential destabilizing effects of legislative reneging. The first is the institutional inertia of the modern legislature. The second is the presence of an independent judiciary, which, by acting to apply laws consistently and in the manner in which their enacting legislatures intended, serves to bind the parties to legislative contracts to their agreements. This, in turn, makes legislation more desirable to interested groups, and thus facilitates the practice of pluralistic politics.

While independent judges imbue legislation with durability (and therefore serve to increase the benefits of its sale to members of Congress), Landes and Posner also recognize that judicial independence entails costs. They note that in some cases, an independent judiciary will overturn legislation passed by the legislature, and that the gains to members of the legislature from the independent judiciary are reduced as the probability of such a reversal in any given case increases. However, they go on to argue that, historically, the general deference of the judiciary to legislative intentions and the infrequency of such reversals are evidence that the distributive benefits of our independent courts have outweighed their costs in nullified legislative deals. In light of this, they conclude with a number of hypotheses concerning the institutional foundations and performance of the judiciary.

Landes and Posner's analysis is suggestive of the dynamics between the legislative and judicial arms of the government. However, it fails to incorporate one of its central assumptions about the nature of the political system into its analysis of court action. Specifically, in a pluralist political system, courts of any kind do not (indeed, cannot) operate independently of the system of groups involved in legislative policymaking. Because courts are reactive in the way in which they influence the policy process, they must rely on individuals or interests disaffected with existing policies to bring cases before them. At the most basic level, this means that the extent of dependence or independence of the judiciary is a moot issue if the legislation is never challenged. This fact also has implications for the institutional relationships between Congress and the courts, and is suggestive of the importance of interest groups both as actors in the legislative policymaking process and as intermediaries that provide the link between the two branches of government.

My central contention is that in an "interest-group" model of the legislative-judicial relationship, some account must be taken of the role of groups as intermediaries between a purely pluralist Congress and an entirely reactive judiciary. Because the courts are part of and responsive to the larger political system, they must be considered as subject as other policymakers to the constraints that occur as a result of the political environment.

Positive Models of the Judiciary

In the past decade, a substantial amount of work examining the place of the judiciary in the separation-of-powers system has been done by individuals working in the tradition of positive political theory. Early work in this vein focused on the role of courts in the relationship between federal agencies and the Congress (e.g., Ferejohn and Shipan 1990; Ferejohn and Weingast 1992; McCubbins, Noll, and Weingast 1989); more recent research takes the courts themselves as the primary object of study (e.g., Caldeira, Wright, and Zorn 1999; Cameron, Segal, and Songer 2000; Cross and Tiller 1998; Gely and Spiller 1992; Rasmusen 1994; Schwartz 1992; Spiller and Spitzer 1992, 1995; Stearns 2000).

While the application of these models to the courts has done much to enrich their study, there remains one particularly damning criticism of their use to this point. In brief, most positive models treat courts no differently than other political actors in terms of either their motivations or their institutional context and constraints. As a result, positive models tend to portray courts as uncomplicated rational utility maximizers, a portrayal that has important (and potentially misleading) implications for the type of institution we believe courts to be. While there is a substantial body of evidence indicating that ideological and political preferences motivate a good deal of judicial (and particularly Supreme Court) behavior (e.g. Segal and Spaeth 1993), to reduce any theoretical characterization of the judiciary to simple utility maximization is to miss a good deal of what makes courts unique in the political system.

In an important paper, John Ferejohn and Barry Weingast (1992, 265) note this difficulty, and suggest that this need not be the case:

> One of the weaknesses with the PPT models of legislative-judicial interaction is that, as yet, they have not paid much attention to the different ways that courts might resolve particular issues of public law. Models have either taken legal decisions as exogenous or assumed that courts act solely on the basis of their preferences (or ideologies) rather than out of principles. . . . But PPT is not committed to any such realpolitik vision of the judiciary. Judicial preferences need not arise either from private interests or substantive ideologies. They may emerge instead from the institutional position of courts and may be understood as procedurally induced values, according special respect to statutory commands. Judges may prefer one interpretation over another, not because they prefer the policy outcome, but because that interpretation best implements some notion of legislative intention.

The primary insight of Ferejohn and Weingast's discussion is not that positive models are inapplicable to studies of the courts. Rather, it is that such models must account for the unique institutional characteristics of the judiciary in order to be a viable tool in their explanation.

Ferejohn and Weingast examine the implications on policy outcomes of three means by which a court might choose to take up the task of statutory interpretation. They operationalize the distinctive institutional characteristics of the judiciary by placing constraints both on the location of judicial preferences in the policy space and on the means by which those preferences are pursued. Their analysis shows that courts that base their decisions on different institutional rules of interpretation have markedly different effects on the nature of the policies the system produces. Their paper represents an exception to the more common characterization of courts as no different from other actors in the political process.

More generally, models of courts in the political system often address issues that may be profitably considered in light of the insights of Landes and Posner. For example, one of Ferejohn and Weingast's (1992) central concerns is the ability of a sitting legislature to imbue the legislation it passes with some sort of longevity. Their solution lies in the ability of Congress to implement internal controls (e.g., committees with oversight power) so as to insulate legislation from future shifts in the composition of the legislature as a whole. What they do not examine, and what Landes and Posner suggest, is that the judiciary itself may serve as another brake on the ability of future legislative majorities to overturn previously enacted policies.

The representation of the judiciary that emerges from these two modes of analysis lacks synthesis. Landes and Posner's insights regarding the ability of courts to act as benevolent enforcers in a pluralist political system is persuasive, and their notion that a judiciary free from ties to the prevailing political environment enhances the performance of this function is compelling. But their model fails to account for the fact that courts, independent or otherwise, are not entirely divorced from the political environment and must be considered in light of the larger structure of actors and preferences that exist at any given time. Other positive models of courts in the political process do exactly this. By examining courts along with the other actors in the political system, they explicitly model the political circumstances in which the judiciary operates and the implications of its need for responsiveness to that environment. In doing so, however, they most often neglect the aspects of the judiciary that render it to some degree both independent and distinctive from other political entities. What is needed, then, is a means of bringing together these divergent lines of inquiry into a more general model of the judiciary as an institution that is both intrinsically political in its circumstances and atypically apolitical in many facets of its operation.

A Game-Theoretic Model of Congress-Court Interaction

I examine the relationship between Congress and the judiciary in the context of a stylized game. The basic model is a sequential decision game among three actors. The game takes place in one policy dimension and over two periods. We define the policy space as $X = R^1$. The players are the Congress (H), a court (C), and a single organized interest group (G); their ideal points in X are h, g, and c, respectively. For purposes of this paper, all actors are assumed to be adequately represented by a single point in the policy space; this may be thought of as the ideal long-term outcome for the group, and as the position of the median member of both the Congress and the court. Preferences of the actors are assumed to be symmetric and single-peaked over the policy space. All actors possess complete information; equilibria are derived by backwards induction.[1]

Without loss of generality, we normalize such that $h = 0$ and $g > 0$; extensions to the symmetric case of $g < 0$ are straightforward. The game proceeds as follows. In the first stage, Congress sets some policy $x_H \in X$ so as to maximize its overall expected utility. Some cost is assumed to having a policy overturned later in the game, so that all other things being equal, Congress prefers not to have its policies nullified. Nature then draws some $\delta \sim N(0, \sigma_\delta^2)$ and sets the position of the Congress in the second stage equal to that in the first stage plus this disturbance, that is, $h = \delta$.[2] This may be thought of as analogous to an intervening legislative election. Next, the group makes a decision as to whether to challenge the policy x_H in court, based on its information about the position of the court and the policy. A challenge, in this context, amounts to bringing a case before the court, in which the group offers its own ideal point as an alternative to x_H. The groups' strategy set is therefore $x_G \in \{\varnothing, g\}$. Assume that there is some arbitrarily small nonzero cost ε to the group in bringing such a challenge, such that in the case of equality of outcomes with and without action, it will choose not to litigate. If the group decides against litigation (i.e., $x_{II} = \varnothing$), then the game ends and the policy enacted by the legislature becomes the final outcome ($x_C = x_H$). If the group decides in favor of litigation challenging the legislative act (i.e., $x_G = g$), the court hears the case and sets a new policy $x_C \in \{x_H, x_G\}$.[3] Following the ruling of the court, the game ends, and payoffs are calculated.[4]

Equilibria for the game produce a strategy for the Congress's initial policy decision, the group's decision to litigate, and the court's decision, and also serve to illuminate the final outcomes of the entire process under varying assumptions about the positions and natures of the various actors. For our purposes here, we assume that preferences are quadratic in final outcome, so that we may generally write the utility functions (U) for the various actors as:

$$U_H = -(h - x_C)^2$$
$$U_G = -(g - x_C)^2$$
$$U_C = -(c - x_C)^2$$

The players, ideal points, strategy sets, and utility functions for each of the players are specified in table 1.

Results of the game are examined under varying assumptions about the mechanism by which the ideal point of the court is derived. Following the work of Ferejohn and Weingast, the position of the court in the policy space is determined by its "type." The work of Landes and Posner suggests that courts may be of two primary types: "independent" ones, which base their decisions on the intentions of the enacting legislature

TABLE 1 Outline of the game

PLAYER	IDEAL POINT	STRATEGY	PAYOFF
H	$h = 0$	$x_H \in X$	$U_H = -(h - x_C)^2$
G	$g > 0$	$x_G \in \{\emptyset, g\}$	$U_G = -(g - x_C)^2$
C	$c \in X$	$x_C \in \{x_H, x_G\}$	O: $U_C = -(x_H - x_C)^2$
			D: $U_C = -(\delta - x_C)^2$
			I: $U_C = -(c - x_C)^2$

(and that may, on occasion, independently strike down legislative enactments with some positive probability), and "dependent" courts, which serve at the behest of the current legislature. In theory, however, there is no way to determine under what circumstances an independent court will behave in accord with the wishes of the legislature and when it will choose to flout those intentions and strike down a particular legislative "deal." These two characterizations thus prevent one from examining the influence of judicial "independence" in the absence of judicial "originalism," and vice versa. Ferejohn and Weingast identify three types of courts: the "naive textualist," which sincerely interprets legislation as closely as possible to the intention of the enacting legislature, the "politically sophisticated honest agent," which also adheres to original intent, but does so in a sophisticated fashion, and the "unconstrained policy advocate," which seeks to maximize its own utility in a sophisticated manner. Missing from their analysis, however, is the notion of a judiciary that is not insulated from current political circumstances; that is, a "nonindependent" court.

The analysis here, in developing a model of judicial review, incorporates insights from both previous models. For purposes of this essay, I define three types of courts. The first, labeled the "originalist" (or "O"-type) court, represents a court that adheres to the original intent of the legislation in its review of statutes (and subsequent rulings in the cases that come before it).[5] The second type is the "dependent" ("D"-type) court, and represents a stylized version of the judiciary as being tied to the predominant political winds. This type corresponds to Landes and Posner's judges who serve at the pleasure of the current legislature. The final type is the "independent" (or "I"-type) court; this type models a court that acts independently of both the current political situation and the original intention of the legislation; it is thus analogous to Ferejohn and Weingast's "unconstrained policy advocate." We explore results of the game for each type of court.

The Originalist Judiciary

We first examine the model in the case of an originalist court. In this model the interpretations and rulings of the judiciary are based on the "original legislative understanding" of the statute in question. In practical terms, originalist courts will base their rulings in cases challenging legislation on the text of the legislation and on the intention of the enacting legislature (e.g., Berger 1977). Thus, an originalist court can be thought of as one that prefers that the final result of policy pronouncements be as close as possible to the results intentioned by the enacting Congress. This type of jurisprudence may be incorporated into our model by setting the position of the court in the policy space equal to that of policy initially created by the Congress (i.e., $c = x_H$).

We now derive equilibria for the game under the assumption of an "O"-type court. Such a court, when faced with the choice set $\{x_H, x_G\}$ in a case before it, prefers x_H. Proceeding back a step, a group faced with the decision whether or not to litigate will do so only when it expects to win, that is, when the court prefers the position of the group to that of the legislative policy; this occurs with zero probability. Going back yet another step, Congress will choose to set the initial policy x_H equal to its own (first period) ideal point $h = 0$. This last result obtains because the legislature, absent any possibility of a reversal of its initial policy choice by the court, will choose to set policy equal to its preferred point. Thus, because $c = x_H$, it is easy to see that $\max\{U_C(x_H), U_C(x_G)\} = U_C(x_H)$ and thus that $x_C = x_H \forall \{x_H, x_G\} \in X$.

Having established h as an equilibrium, note as well that it is unique. By definition, an originalist court will never deviate from validating the decision of the legislature; neither will the position of any group, regardless of its location, be preferred by the court to that of the initial legislative policy. Finally, the legislature will never implement any policy other than its most preferred, since to do so would be suboptimal.

Proposition 1: When the judiciary construes statutes according to the intention of the enacting legislature:
  1. The Congress will pass legislation corresponding to its preferred policy position.
  2. No litigation challenging that legislation will be forthcoming.
  3. No judicial reversals of that legislation will ensue.

The implications of this result are straightforward. As noted previously, Landes and Posner (1975) note that the presence of an originalist judiciary allows legislators and groups to reap the full multiperiod benefits from the creation of legislation. As in Landes and Posner's analysis, our model shows that the existence of a perfectly originalist judiciary provides maximum effectiveness in enforcing legislative "deals." Provided no effective reversal of a statute is forthcoming from subsequent legislatures (a contingency not explored in this essay), an originalist court allows the full multiperiod benefits of legislation to be reaped by the purchasing groups without risk of reversal by the courts. Conversely, adversely effected groups are left without recourse to the courts in their efforts to secure more favorable final policy outcomes. Also, because the judiciary will always rule in favor of the initial policy x_H, regardless of where that policy is located, Congress may set x_H equal to its preferred position with impunity, secure in the knowledge that it will never be faced with an adverse ruling in the courts. In formal terms, the final utility of legislation for Congress is $-(h-x)^2 = 0$; this represents the best possible outcome for the legislature. Finally, in no instance does the judiciary overturn a congressional statute, nor are any such statutes challenged by disaffected groups in equilibrium. Thus the longevity of congressional "deals" is assured.

The Dependent Judiciary

In the case of a dependent court, we assume that the position of the court on a given issue is linked to the current political context. As initially proposed by Robert Dahl (1957) and implied in earlier work (e.g., Pritchett 1948), research in political science suggests that the decisions of the judiciary, and particularly the U.S. Supreme Court, are responsive to public opinion and political events (e.g., Barnum 1985; Marshall 1989; Mishler and Sheehan 1993, 1994; but see Norpoth and Segal 1994). We operationalize this assumption in our model by setting the position of the court in the policy space equal to that of the current Congress (i.e. $c = \delta$) for "D"-type courts. Thus, a dependent court's position in the policy space mirrors that of the Congress, and shifts to some degree with each passing election.

Under the assumption of judicial dependence, the court will once again decide $x_C \in \{x_H, x_G\}$ by maximizing its utility over its two alternatives. Similarly, a group will undertake costly litigation only if it expects to win; that is, if the court is seen to prefer the policy of the group to that initially set by the legislature. In setting the initial policy, Congress can again, for reasons stated above, maximize its expected utility by selecting a point equal to its first-period ideal point ($x_H = h$). The legislature will

FIGURE 1 Equilibrium policy, dependent judiciary

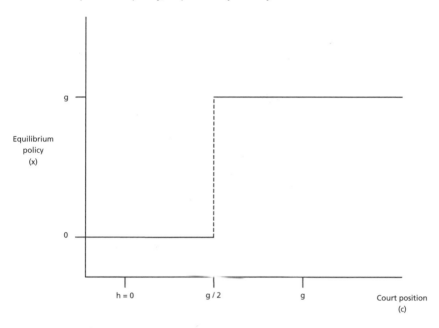

do so because its best expectation about where the court will be in future periods is equal to its current ideal point (i.e., $E(c) = E(\delta) = 0$). Given that initial point, it is clear that the court will prefer the position of the group to that of the initial policy when the value of δ is positive and large enough to place the position of the court closer to the position of the group than to that of the original policy. This occurs when $c = \delta > g/2$, as illustrated in figure 1. Under these conditions, the group will choose to litigate and the court will subsequently set $x_C = x_G$. We may therefore state the following:

Proposition 2: When the judiciary construes statutes in a manner in accordance with the preferences of the current legislature:
1. The legislature will enact policies equal to its initial ideal point.
2. Groups will challenge those policies in court when $c > g/2$.
3. The judiciary will nullify all acts of the legislature which are challenged.

Several characteristics may be noted regarding the outcome of the game under the assumption of a dependent judiciary. First, the Congress will always choose to set the initial policy equal to its first-period ideal point, even though under certain circumstances this policy will be reversed. Such an action, in the absence of better information regarding the policy positions of future legislatures, maximizes the expected benefits of legislation to the Congress, despite the fact that such policies may be subsequently invalidated in the courts.

Second, these results also have implications for the relationship between the political climate and the behavior of the court. We can specify the exact probability of a policy being reversed following an "election" as the probability that $\delta > g/2$. This quantity is a function of both the variance of δ and the position of the group. The relationship between the probability of reversal and the position of the group is negative; that is, holding σ_δ^2 constant, the likelihood of a reversal decreases as g increases. This implies that a broad-based legislature (e.g., one for whom opposition is made up only of relatively extreme groups) will, all else equal, experience fewer nullifications than one opposed by groups closer to it.

Similarly, we note that the relationship is positive in σ_δ^2; that is, holding g constant, the probability of a judicial reversal increases as σ_δ^2 increases. We would therefore expect that, given a "D"-type judiciary and all else being equal, a legislature that exhibits substantial shifts in ideological position from period to period (i.e., a high value of σ_δ^2) will be overturned more frequently than one that remains at a relatively stable ideological position. Likewise, we can see that in a given period, the number of statutory invalidations of legislation from the period immediately prior is closely tied to the amount of legislative "drift" that occurs in the interim. This theoretical result is in line with much of the historical and empirical literature on the Supreme Court and partisan realignments (e.g., Gates 1992). What sets this result off from much of that literature is the fact that these reversals come at the behest of the later legislature, rather than in response to them. That is, the result for a dependent court runs exactly counter to Richard Funston's (1975) hypothesis that, owing to institutional inertia, courts will overturn legislation passed immediately following a realignment.[6]

Finally, note that "D"-type courts represent an overall loss of utility, from the point of view of the legislature, in comparison to originalist ones. This loss is the result of the nonzero probability that a congressional enactment will be subsequently overturned, and mirrors that of Landes and Posner, who note that a perfectly dependent judiciary returns the model to single-period status. Note, however, that the incorporation of an intervening interest group works against this absolute result; while the Landes and Posner model assumes that a dependent court will always have an opportunity to nullify prior legislative deals, our model indicates that the extent to which this is the case is dependent on the position of the group doing the litigating, as well as on the period-to-period congruence of congressional preferences. This fact reinforces our assertion that the inclusion of groups as intermediaries, as well as the placement of the judiciary as one of many actors in the broader political environment, provides a more accurate picture of the implications of different types of the courts in the policy process.

The Independent Judiciary

Finally, we examine the case in which the court is not constrained in its preferences to those of either the enacting or the current legislature. Instead, the position of the court may be anywhere in the policy space and does not change either with the passage of any particular policy or between legislative periods. In this sense, the judiciary is independent of both the intention of the enacting legislature and the contemporary political climate. As such, it is free to rule simply on the basis of its preferred policy. We operationalize the idea of an independent judiciary in our model by allowing the position of the court to take on any value in the policy space (i.e., $c \in X$).

Again, I derive the equilibria for this model by working backward. The court will rule in favor of a group's claim if to do so results in a better outcome for the court than does the policy enacted by Congress. Similarly, a group can only be expected to engage in litigation challenging a statute when it knows it will be successful. Because the positions of both the group and an independent court are fixed and known at the start of the game, however, an enacting legislature will also be aware of what policies will and will not pass judicial muster. And because the Congress prefers to enact a final policy itself rather than be overruled at a later stage, it will also adapt its policies such that they are at the position closest to its own while still preventing the onset of future litigation to overturn them.

Formally, define $p^*(g, c)$ as the set of possible legislative alternatives that will not be subsequently challenged and nullified for particular values of G and C. The goal of the legislature, then, is to maximize $U_H(p^*(g, c))$. Note that we may write $p^*(g, c) = [2c - g, g]$. We may divide the policy space into three regions, on the basis of the position of the court. When $c \leq g/2$, we note that $U_C(x_H) \geq U_C(x_G) \forall x_H < g/2$. We would thus expect the legislature to enact its preferred point $x_H = h$, since in all such cases $\max(U_H(p^*(g, c)))$ is at h. If $c \geq g$, then $U_C(x_G) \geq U_C(x_H) \forall x_H < g$ and $\max(U_H(p^*(g, c)))$ is at g. This implies that the best the legislature can do is $x_H = g$, which the group will not subsequently challenge in court. Finally, for $g/2 < c < g$, we note that $U_C(x_G) \geq U_C(x_H)\forall x_H \geq (2g - c)$ and therefore that $\max(U_H(p^*(g, c)))$ is at $2g - c$. This function represents the point closest to h, which will not be challenged and overturned by the court for a particular value of c in this range. These results may be summarized as follows:

Proposition 3: When the judiciary construes statutes in accordance with its own policy preferences and in a manner independent of the intention of the enacting legislature or of the predominant political sentiments:
1. The legislature will enact policies x_H equal to:
   • Its preferred position, when $c \leq g/2$.
   • $(2c - g)$, when $g/2 \leq c \leq g$.
   • The preferred position of the group, when $c \geq g$.
2. No litigation challenging the initial policy will be forthcoming.
3. No nullifications of legislative enactments will occur.

The combined equilibrium results are displayed graphically in figure 2.[7]

The implications of our results for a model with an independent judiciary are several. First, the result confirms the analysis of Landes and Posner in that it indicates that an independent court will allow legislative deals to remain effective over more than a single period, because that legislation will not be nullified in equilibrium.[8] It also confirms their assumption that such a judiciary will result in costs to the enacting Congress. While Landes and Posner frame this cost in terms of a probability that an independent court will nullify some legislation, the current full-information model results in this potentiality being incorporated into the initial decision calculus of the statute maker. That is, for certain positions of the courts, the Congress will be made to pass policies that are not equal to their preferred ones.[9] As a result, the associated costs are self-imposed at the initial policymaking stage rather than being extracted later by an unconstrained judiciary.

Other results are suggested by a comparison of independent courts with those outlined above. For example, when considering matters of institutional design, Landes and Posner note that legislatures with de facto long tenures will prefer more dependent courts. Our model mirrors this result: legislatures for which σ_δ^2 is small will be expected to benefit more from the gains of not having to incorporate the wishes of a potentially litigious group than they will suffer from the costs of an (unlikely) reversal. Put differently, as the probability of a severe change in legislative preferences decreases, the probability of a reversal by a dependent court also

FIGURE 2 Equilibrium policy, independent judiciary

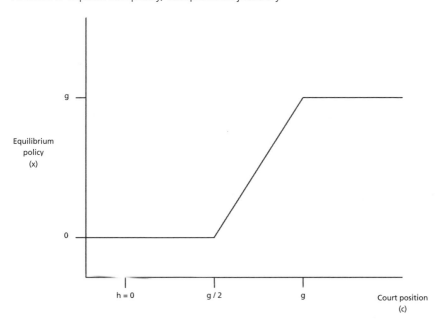

decreases, while that associated with an independent judiciary does not, thus leading such a Congress to favor the former over the latter.

Finally, we note an important result of the model with respect to the influence of courts in the policy process. An independent court, while never overturning enacted legislation or otherwise behaving in a proactive manner, nonetheless has an important impact on the policy outputs of the system. It does so because it forces the legislature to take into account the position of a potentially litigious group in enacting its initial legislation, or else run the risk of a costly override that it could have prevented. In contrast, originalist judiciaries can be counted on to enforce legislation regardless of its position, while dependent courts require, in effect, that a legislature move in the direction of the group first before any judicial policy influence, in the form of a nullification, is manifested. At the same time, these results point out that, regardless of the type of court present, at no point is the court seen to be engaging in activity that appears to re-sult in direct policy influence. Dependent court nullifications necessarily follow a shift in legislative preferences, while the impact of an indepen-dent court occurs in the manner in which the legislature is forced to change its proposals at the policy formulation stage.

More generally, Gerald Rosenberg (1991) has pointed to three primary arguments for a "constrained" view of the ability of the courts to influence social policy: the limited nature of rights claims, the lack of judicial independence, and absence of judicial powers of policy formation and implementation. The model presented here suggests that a fourth factor may also impinge on this ability: the reactive nature of the judiciary. Because the judiciary is forced to rely on the behavior of outside actors to bring matters of policy before it, and because (as our model has shown) these actors may not always choose to do so, the ability of the judiciary to address substantive policy concerns is limited. At the same time, however, this also suggests an argument as to why judicial influence might not be apparent even in those circumstances when it is operative. That is, because earlier actors in the policy process may take the position of the judiciary into account in generating proposals, the apparent inability of the courts to influence policy may instead be an artifact of the stage at which that influence takes place.[10]

Extensions of the Model

The model presented thus far presents the court as being constrained in its choices of outcomes. Specifically, we assume that the court, when faced with a case before it, must select from one of the two positions advocated by the litigants. In formal terms, the court's strategy space is "discrete" and limited to the two points in $\{x_H, x_G\}$. While the dual nature of legal controversies make this a common assumption in models of court behavior (e.g., Schwartz 1992), other authors have assumed a less restricted strategy set. In practice, too, courts often have a good deal of latitude in construing legislation that comes before them. We thus reconsider the model after relaxing this initial assumption in an intuitive way.

In cases at law, competing litigants define their positions according to their own beliefs about what the proper application of the law to their situation is. A court may, then, see the positions of the litigants before it not as all-or-nothing choices, but rather as "endpoints" between which some sort of doctrinal compromise is to be achieved. Considered in this way, the court can be thought of as free to choose any point on the policy dimension between those offered by the litigants as a valid policy outcome. Formally, the strategy set of the court is now $x_C \in [x_H, x_G]$, with any x_C not equal to x_H treated as modifying or striking down the legislation. Given this expansion of the alternatives available to the court, we examine the results of our model for each of the three types of courts.

In the case of an originalist court, the expansion of judicial choices

FIGURE 3 Eqilibrium policy, dependent judiciary (continuous policy placement)

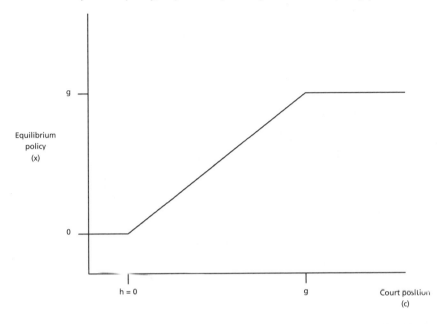

does not change the results presented above. Such a judiciary will still inevitably prefer $x_C = h$ to all alternatives, and all subsequent results follow as before. For the dependent court, there is change when $h < c < g$; because the Congress will still initially enact its own ideal point, a court in this region will be able to implement its own preferred position, which is equivalent to that of the second-stage Congress. As a result, we would find that nullifications would occur in all cases in which $c > h$, or equivalently all instances in which δ is positive and less than $2g$. This represents a strikingly high level of reversals, although in practice we would expect that subsequent legislatures would undertake to modify statutes in accordance with these rulings.[11] Equilibrium policy outcomes for this modified model are presented in figure 3.

Results for an independent court follow those for the dependent court closely in final outcome; policy outcomes for this model with an independent court are also illustrated by figure 3. A critical difference, however, is that, as with the model above, an independent court will never overturn legislation in equilibrium; rather, the potential for such a reversal will be accounted for by Congress in enacting the initial legislation. The results are similar to those above in that the presence of an independent court forces the Congress to take into consideration the preferences of a potentially litigious group in formulating their initial policy. What is different from the case of a court limited to discrete policy choices is the range over which the Congress is forced to adapt its initial response. Because a court limited to setting a policy from among $\{x_H, x_G\}$ has limited options from which it may choose, the Congress does not need to adapt its initial policy to reflect the wishes of the group until the court is at a point closer to *g* than to *h*. In contrast, a court with the power to set policy over a continuous space forces the Congress to adapt, a priori, to the position of the group and the court once $c > h$. This points to an important (and potentially testable) substantive result: as courts are allowed greater latitude to set policy, other policymakers become more constrained in their ability to achieve their optimal outcome without facing a reversal.[12]

An Empirical Test of the Model

The preceding discussion outlines a model of Congress and the courts and presents a number of results that obtain from that model. The extent to which this model accurately reflects the empirical realities it is intended to represent is, however, impossible to determine without the application of real-world tests of the hypotheses it generates. I present results of one such analysis here.

In testing their argument that the role of an independent judiciary is to enforce contracts (in the form of legislation) made between interested groups and legislators, Landes and Posner examine a number of indicators of the reliability of the judiciary in upholding those agreements. Chief among these is the extent to which the U.S. Supreme Court elects to nullify the legislative-interest group contract by ruling enacted legislation invalid. Because, in their model, the multiperiod value of legislation to both Congress and the purchasing groups is an inverse function of the probability that a piece of legislation will be subsequently overturned by the Court, the incidence of such acts on the part of the judiciary provides insight into the relative benefit of judicial independence.

Given the results of the model, it should be possible to differentiate empirically among the various types of courts on the basis of whether or not they are responsive to the political environment in which they exist. More formally, the model suggests that "D"-type courts will be apparent by the presence of nullifications, while neither originalist nor independent courts will have occasion to reverse legislation. Critical to this test, however, is the assumption of complete and perfect information; as noted above, congressional heedlessness of the court's preferences may also result in nullifications, even by independent courts. Because the verity of this assumption cannot be tested, the mere presence of nullifications is not adequate to indicate the degree of political dependence of the judiciary.

At the same time, however, another result of the model allows us to separate among these possibilities. Because the probability of a judicial nullification by "D"-type courts is a function of the amount of electoral drift between legislatures, we would expect that dependent courts would be more likely to nullify a legislative statute as the distance between the enacting legislature and subsequent ones is increased. Recall that the probability of a judicial nullification by a dependent court is simply the probability that the Congress has shifted more than half the distance from its initial position toward that of the affected group. Thus, we may posit that, ceteris paribus, large shifts in the policy position of the Congress will result in higher probabilities of judicial nullifications (and, by implication, greater numbers of such nullifications) by "D"-type courts. In contrast, while independent courts may also reverse some statutes in the circumstances given above, our theory predicts that those nullifications will have no relation to the magnitude of the prior electoral shift. Formulated in this way, an examination of the extent to which nullifications follow shifts in congressional preferences is equivalent to a test of the degree of political dependence of the court examined.

I take as my dependent variable the number of laws enacted by the United States Congress that were overturned by the Supreme Court within eight years of passage. This number was collected for each Congress, beginning with the 5th and continuing to the 100th, for a total of 96 observations. The actual number of such nullifications ranges from zero in many years to nine during the period of the Seventy-fourth Congress (1934–35), with an average of just over 0.7 per Congress. This variable provides some measure, albeit an imperfect one, of the extent to which the judiciary undertakes to overturn the will of the legislature. We limit analysis to bills passed within the previous eight years for two reasons. First, as noted by Landes and Posner, eight years can be considered an adequate amount of time for groups to reap the benefits of the legislative "deals" made with the Congress. Second, from a practical perspective, limiting our analysis to such bills allows for the creation of a measure of the shift in electoral composition, as well as the inclusion of a control for the total number of bills passed during the period under scrutiny.

To measure the degree of congressional shift, we include a variable equal to the absolute value of the difference between the percentage of Democratic Party identifiers in the current congress and the mean of that percentage over the four previous congresses.[13] This serves as a measure of the ideological distance between the current legislature and the average of those legislatures that made up the enacting coalitions of the bills included in our dependent variable. This variable will thus be high during congresses that follow a dramatic change in the party composition of the Congress, and low in those years following little electoral change. Our model would predict that, were the Supreme Court dependent on or influenced by the political environment, this variable would have a significant and positive influence on the number of nullifications of congressional acts passed during the previous eight years. In contrast, where the Court conforms to either the originalist or independent characterizations outlined above, the extent of electoral shift in the Congress should be unrelated to the number of nullifications that occur. This variable can thus be seen as providing an explicit test of the degree of political independence of the U.S. Supreme Court.

Other independent variables in the model include a variable indicating the number of the relevant Congress. Inclusion of this variable controls for systematic changes in the number of nullifications over the past two hundred years; it also allows us to test for the presence of a time trend in nullifications. While the current model says nothing about the long-term trend in nullifications over time, previous research in this vein (e.g., Caldeira and McCrone 1982) suggests that nullifications have become more common over time, particularly in the years following the Civil War. As a result, we would expect that this variable would exhibit a positive relationship to the number of nullifications per Congress. Also included is the natural logarithm of the number of laws passed during the previous eight-year period; this represents an upper bound on the number of possible nullifications (King 1989). This variable also has substantive importance, in that it permits the testing of whether the number of nullifications varies systematically with the overall level of activity in the Congress; all other things being equal, we would expect that this variable would be positively related to the number of nullifications. Following Landes and Posner, I also include a variable that measures the degree of agreement or conflict between the other branches of government. Landes and Posner used a variable on partisan control of the executive and legislature; I opt for a mode direct measure of president-Congress conflict: the number of presidential vetoes occurring during that Congress. General models of separation of powers (e.g., McCubbins et al. 1989) suggest that a Congress and president who are quite divided allow more discretion by other government actors. We therefore expect this variable to be positive in sign, indicating that more reversals occur under widely divided governments. At the same time, the model presented here provides no expectation for either the degree or direction of influence of this variable.

In their initial analysis, Landes and Posner used the mean tenure and age of the justices of the Supreme Court as surrogates for the degree of independence of the Court. As might be expected, the two variables are highly correlated ($r = 0.61$), and the substantive rationales for their inclusion are largely the same. However, the theoretical justification is clearer for the tenure variable. The reasons for inclusion of the age variable are largely based in the idea that older judges are farther along in their careers and are thus less likely to be swayed in their decisions by the possibility of attaining higher office. While this may be true for the lower courts, in fact very few justices leave the Supreme Court for any reason other than retirement or death. In contrast, the influence of tenure can be thought of as a result of the separation between the political coalition responsible for the appointment of a particular justice and the current coalition. Because this rationale is more in line with the concerns of the current model, the mean tenure of the sitting justices of the Court here serves as a surrogate for judicial independence.[14]

Estimation and Results

The phenomenon of interest is the number of Supreme Court nullifications of congressional statutes passed within the previous eight years. Because this count represents an aggregation of a number of discrete binary events, the count itself will be distributed as a Poisson variate under a few minimal assumptions. Because of the potential for correlation among events, however, I estimate the model of Supreme Court nullifications using both Poisson and negative binomial regression models (e.g., Cameron and Trivedi 1998) and using a number of cross-model tests to determine the presence or absence of extra-Poisson variation. These estimates are presented in table 2.[15]

In general, the results of our estimation are consistent with a number of our predictions. The overall fit of the model is quite good; a number of the parameter estimates exhibit statistical significance, and likelihood-ratio statistics indicate that we may reject the null hypothesis that the estimated parameters are jointly zero at the .01 level in both models. Comparing across models, the evidence for overdispersion is mixed. The dispersion parameter is not significantly different from one at traditional levels. This fact is reinforced by the overall similarity in results between

TABLE 2 Event count regression of congressional acts nullified by the Supreme Court within eight years of passage, 1789–1988

VARIABLE	POISSON ESTIMATE	NEGATIVE BINOMIAL ESTIMATE
(Constant)	−8.135	−7.792
	(−3.558)	(−2.969)
ln(bills)	0.588	0.589
	(2.269)	(1.955)
Congress	0.021	0.023
	(3.042)	(2.698)
Court tenure	0.099	0.067
	(1.946)	(1.046)
Presidential vetoes	0.003	0.001
	(1.043)	(0.329)
Congressional shift	4.439	4.031
	(2.742)	(1.926)
(α)		0.500
		(1.065)
Log-likelihood	−96.668	−94.128

NOTE: *T*-ratios are in parentheses. $N = 96$. $-2 \times (\ln L_{\text{Poisson}} - \ln L_{\text{Neg. Binomial}}) = 5.08$ ($p = 0.01$).

the two models. But a likelihood-ratio test indicates a significant improvement in the fit of the negative binomial model, suggesting the possibility of some overdispersion in the data. This would imply that nullifications of this sort result from a contagious process and tend to be positively correlated in their occurrence.

Turning to an examination of our independent variables, our results indicate that the number of nullifications have tended to increase both over time and in relation to the number of bills passed. Likewise, nullifications have tended to be more common as the mean tenure of the sitting justices has increased, although our confidence in this effect is marginal. Taken together, these results generally confirm our previous expectations. Our estimates also indicate that there is no relationship of either substantive or statistical significance between the number of Supreme Court nullifications and the presence of ideological conflict between the executive and legislative branches.

The influence of the congressional shift variable is both statistically significant and substantively large. The effect is also in the direction predicted by a model of a dependent Supreme Court; in general, higher levels of nullifications follow dramatic shifts in the partisan makeup of the Congress. For example, a 15 percent increase in congressional turnover (equal to roughly two standard deviations) is associated with an average increase in the expected number of nullifications of 0.5. These results thus provide support for the proposition that the Supreme Court is, to a substantial degree, subject to influence by the prevailing political environment. While a number of prior analyses have arrived at similar conclusions regarding the behavior of the Court, the results presented here are unique in that they represent an explicit test of the hypothesis of Supreme Court independence as derived from a general model of Congress-Court interaction.

In light of the findings regarding presidential vetoes, this also confirms the intuition of our model that the Supreme Court is largely responsive to, rather than considerate of, the political environment. The variable for congressional shift measures the amount of electoral change between enacting and current legislatures; it is, from the perspective of the Court, an indication of the political tenor of the legislature (and thus a signal as to its utility for recently passed legislation). Conversely, the variable for executive vetoes can be thought of as an indicator of the present amount of ideological "room" in which the Court may operate. That is, the amount of congressional-presidential conflict indicates the climate into which a nullification will pass. To the extent that the Court tends to overrule more federal laws following dramatic changes in the composition of Congress but does not do so when in the presence of division between the Congress and the executive, these results suggest that the Court tends to act largely in concert with the Congress but with little consideration as to the future of its rulings.

Conclusion

I have presented a model of the legislative-judicial relationship. Drawing on insights from positive political theory and pluralist notions of the mechanisms of government, the model sets forth a number of results under varying assumptions about the ideological positions and institutional organizations of legislatures, courts, and organized interests. Central to the model is the conviction that groups, acting both in the legislative arena and as intermediaries between the branches of government, play a determining role in the separation-of-powers system. The model suggests that the extent of legislative-judicial contention, in addition to being a function of the policy wishes of these entities, is also critically linked to the procedural and structural criteria by which courts' decisional mechanisms are constrained.

This model also represents an initial effort to synthesize previously separate modes of inquiry into the role of courts in the political system. Prior analyses have, for the most part, either examined the courts in isolation, divorced from the broader political environment in which they must function, or have failed to account for the distinguishing aspects of courts in their consideration of judicial behavior. By exploring courts within a general political context, while at the same time ensuring the recognition of those institutional factors that make them distinctive, we are able to gain from the insights of this earlier work while at the same time broadening our understanding of the judiciary itself, as well as the context in which it operates.

Finally, my analysis presented results of an empirical test of one of the conclusions the model derives. Most interestingly, and consistent with a model in which the judiciary is, at least to an extent, politically dependent, Supreme Court nullifications of congressional acts are positively related to large shifts in congressional preferences. This result is therefore consistent with the observations of numerous previous scholars (e.g., Dahl 1957) who have made special note of the institutional means by which the Court ought to be expected to be responsive to the political environment. Moreover, these empirical results further suggest that the political dependence of the Court has real consequences for its decision making, particularly in the area of judicial review.

Notes

Data used in this paper are available upon request from the author. I am grateful to Lawrence Baum, Greg Caldeira, Lee Epstein, and Dean Lacy for helpful comments and discussion.

1. In fact, neither perfect information nor a single play are likely to be accurate representations of the process examined. However, similar results obtain under circumstances of imperfect information and repeated play, such that we can make these assumptions for simplicity with no real change in our results.

2. I assume δ to be distributed normally primarily for simplicity and ease of exposition; in fact, these results may be generalized to other distributions for δ as well.

3. To fully specify the set of possible policy outcomes, we assume that in the case where $U_C(x_H) = U_C(x)$, the court defers to the wishes of the enacting legislature and sets $x_C = x_H$.

4. Note that the primary phenomenon of interest regarding the Congress is how the various types of judicial structures affect its ability to conduct the "business" of passing legislation. To this end, it is important that we evaluate the various costs and benefits of

legislative actions from the perspective of the Congress being responsible for making the initial statutory "deals." For this reason, legislative utilities are calculated with respect to the initial (first-period) legislature; thus $U_H = -(h - x_C)^2 = -(-x_C)^2$.

5. Because the court is the final actor in the model presented here, Ferejohn and Weingast's distinction between "naive textualists" and "sophisticated honest agents" is irrelevant to the present analysis.

6. The result of Funston (1975) inheres for a special case of the model presented in the next section, and is examined below.

7. This result is similar in both appearance and intuition to that of Ferejohn and Shipan (1990), who achieve an analogous result in the context of judicial and congressional committee review of agency action under an open rule. Likewise, this result resembles that derived in Ferejohn and Weingast's (1992) model of statutory interpretation in which the court is an "unconstrained policy advocate."

8. The work of Funston (1975) and others, suggesting that nullifications will follow shifts in the position of the legislature because of the institutional inertia of the courts, present an apparent counterexample to the model given here. In fact, however, such theories are consistent with our model of an independent court operating in an environment in which the Congress does not take the position of either the court or the group into account when formulating policy. Under these circumstances, the legislature always chooses its own ideal point for the initial policy, and equilibria are illustrated by figure 1. Separating this result from those in the earlier section, however, is the fact that the position of the court remains independent of the political climate; as a result, the lack of accounting for other actors' preferences by the Congress yields a model that allows for nullifications by an independent court in equilibrium.

9. In this light, we can see that the model of the originalist judiciary outlined above can be thought of as simply the special case of an independent judiciary with $c = x_H$.

10. This is analogous to Weingast and Moran's (1983) point that congressional influence on bureaucracy may not be adequately measured by examinations of instances of overt political interventions into administrative matters.

11. One example of the Supreme Court acting in this manner might be its decision in *Furman v. Georgia* (408 U.S. 238 [1972]), in which the plurality struck down Georgia's law regarding imposition of the death penalty as arbitrary and capricious while at the same time ruling that the death penalty was not per se a violation of the Eighth Amendment prohibition against cruel and unusual punishment. Subsequent modifications of state sentencing guidelines were upheld in *Gregg v. Georgia* (428 U.S. 153 [1976]). See Epstein and Kobylka (1992).

12. Note that the results presented in this section also hold for a court that is truly unconstrained in its policy choices, i.e., one for which $x_C \in X$ (that is, $x_C \in (-\infty, \infty)$). Results are identical to those presented in figure 3 for $h < c < g$; when $c \leq h$, Congress receives its ideal outcome secure that the group will not litigate, and when $c \geq g$, Congress sets $x_H = g$, which the group will not challenge.

13. For purposes of this variable, Jeffersonians were coded as Democrats, and Federalists and Whigs were coded as Republicans.

14. While the main concern of the model is to test for the presence of judicial dependence or independence, we also need to consider that this may manifest itself in a number of ways. For example, a structurally dependent court may be more or less so in relation to how "connected" to the political climate the sitting judges feel themselves to

be. This latter factor can in turn be operationalized via the tenure variable. This control is thus seen to be necessary in order to get an accurate picture of the institutional nature of Supreme Court independence in the absence of individual justice—or court-related factors.

15. King (1989) has derived a generalized event count (GEC) model that allows for flexible estimation of the degree of over- or underdispersion in count data. In addition to the results presented here, I also estimated our model using King's GEC specification, which is equivalent to the negative binomial in the presence of overdispersion, with no significant differences in our results.

"John Marshall Has Made His Decision"

Implementation, Transparency, and Public Support

GEORG VANBERG

Institutional games involve more than how the U.S. Supreme Court makes its decisions and whether it defers to Congress. Supreme Court justices, like judges in other courts, enjoy few means to enforce their decisions. If judicial rulings depend on cooperation from other actors, including legislatures and administrative agencies, for their implementation, courts face a potential compliance problem. This essay presents a simple game-theoretic model to analyze legislative-judicial relations against the backdrop of this problem. It provides a unified theoretical account that explains a number of seemingly contradictory findings on judicial implementation in the United States. The theory provides a basis for understanding prominent examples of noncompliance while explaining why compliance will be the rule rather than the exception. The theory also demonstrates how and when potential enforcement problems will influence judicial behavior, which generates comparative implications about the circumstances under which courts constitute powerful constraints on the other political actors.

The U.S. Supreme Court ranks as one of the most significant and powerful judicial institutions in the world. In other advanced democracies, courts with the power of constitutional review also play an increasingly important role in the policymaking process (See Holland 1991 and Tate and Vallinder 1995). While these courts have successfully established a broad claim to the power of constitutional review,[1] they are curiously "weak" in one important respect: they have few means at their disposal to force compliance with their decisions. Whether President Andrew Jackson's reaction to the U.S. Supreme Court's decision in *Worcester v. Georgia* (31 U.S. 515 [1832]) is apocryphal or not, his retort, "John Marshall has made his decision, now let him enforce it," offers a telling observation of the Court's vulnerability (Smith 1996, 518).

The lack of positive enforcement power is significant, because judicial rulings often require the cooperation of other actors to achieve their intended impact—on many occasions even of the very institutions whose acts the court has just reviewed. As Bradley Canon and Charles Johnson put it in their influential treatment of judicial implementation, "in virtually all instances, courts that formulate policies must rely on other courts or on nonjudicial actors to translate those policies into action" (1999, 1).[2] This need for cooperation from other political actors implies that courts face at least a potential compliance problem. How can a court ensure that its decisions carry weight even if powerful interests whose cooperation is required oppose its rulings?[3] Take, for example, the U.S. Supreme Court's decision in *Immigration and Naturalization Service v. Chadha* (462 U.S. 919 [1983]), which invalidated the one-house legislative veto. To have its full impact, the decision requires Congress to refrain from using the legislative veto in drafting legislation. And yet, Congress has passed more than two hundred statutes containing the legislative veto since the decision was handed down (Fisher 1993). Federal systems, in which national courts may encounter resistance from local policymakers, pose yet another obstacle. Thus, the Supreme Court's desegregation decisions, beginning with *Brown v. Board of Education* (347 U.S. 483 [1954]), encountered "massive resistance" in Southern states and for many years did not result in integrated schools. Similarly, implementation of a decision reviewing actions of an administrative agency may require the agency to change its policies— which policymakers in agencies may be hesitant to do (Spriggs 1996, 1997).[4]

Recognition of the potential enforcement problem has given rise to a substantial literature among scholars of the U.S. Supreme Court on the conditions that affect implementation (see Baum 1976, 1981; Canon and Johnson 1999; Rosenberg 1991). Scholars have concluded that features such as the policy preferences of opposing actors, the clarity of the opinion, and interest group preferences affect whether and how judicial decisions are implemented. At the same time, an important finding is that while prominent counterexamples exist, noncompliance and evasion appear to be relatively rare phenomena. Systematic studies of reactions to U.S. Supreme Court decisions reveal that rulings overwhelmingly result in policy change and compliance (Spriggs 1996, 1997). These findings seem to suggest that despite the lack of direct enforcement powers, the Supreme Court is a powerful political actor that shapes public policy in significant ways in many policy areas (including, sometimes, having a hand in deciding presidential elections).[5]

The implementation literature revolves around the reaction of *other* policymakers to judicial rulings. An interesting question that has received less attention is whether the lack of direct enforcement powers has an anticipatory affect on judicial behavior. Does the expectation that certain decisions are more likely to result in noncompliance than others influence judicial decision making? Such anticipations have been central to interpretations of particular Supreme Court decisions. Thus, Robert Clinton (1994) explains John Marshall's decision in *Marbury v. Madison* (5 U.S. 137 [1803]) in part by assuming that Marshall expected that the Jefferson administration would ignore the Court's decision if it issued a *writ of mandamus* to force delivery of Marbury's commission. Similarly, Jean Edward Smith alludes to anticipations of noncompliance in explaining the Court's seminal decision in *Cohens v. Virginia* (19 U.S. 264 [1821]). At issue was the conviction of two brothers under a Virginia state law prohibiting the sale of out-of-state lottery tickets for selling tickets to a National Lottery authorized by an Act of Congress. In writing the opinion for the Court, John Marshall famously upheld the Supreme Court's authority to hear appeals from state courts, but declined to overturn the Cohens' conviction. Smith concludes that the decision may have been motivated, at least in part, by expectations of noncompliance: "If Virginia defied the Court and persisted in arresting those selling out-of-state ducats, there would be little the justices could do. Marshall was too astute to press an issue that the Court could not win" (Smith 1996, 459). Such anticipatory reactions by judges are potentially important, because they provide an alternative explanation for compliance: Perhaps judges are simply astute at avoiding confrontations.

While explanations of particular decisions that invoke anticipation of noncompliance can often be plausible, they do not constitute a full-fledged theory of judicial behavior and leave important questions unanswered. In other words, the recognition that courts often lack enforcement powers as well as the empirical literature on implementation leave us with several puzzles: Is the enforcement problem merely a theoretical possibility without practical consequence for judicial behavior and judicial power? Or is it a real problem with significant impact? If the latter, how do justices deal with the tension between the power to pass judgment and the lack of power in enforcing those judgments? Under what circumstances will the potential for judicial review impose an important constraint on other policymakers? This essay suggests one approach for thinking about these questions by presenting a simple formal model of the interactions between courts and other policymakers. The theory that emerges accounts for the empirical findings of the implementation literature, provides a basis for understanding prominent examples of noncompliance, demonstrates how and when the potential enforcement problem will influence judicial behavior, and generates comparative implications about the circumstances under which a court like the U.S. Supreme Court will constitute a powerful constraint on other political actors.

Endogenous and Exogenous Enforcement

Two common approaches exist for explaining how courts can come to be powerful actors despite a lack of direct enforcement powers. The first approach seeks to *endogenize* compliance by arguing that, given certain conditions, the actors who are subject to judicial review will have a direct interest in an effective, independent judiciary and that this interest can generate compliance. This approach closely resembles Randall Calvert's (1995) understanding of "institutions as equilibria." Explanations that have been offered in this spirit point to the role of the judiciary in protecting various political interests (especially parties) in an uncertain environment (Landes and Posner 1975; Ramseyer 1994), the informational role that the judiciary can play in the policymaking process (Rogers 2001b), the role of the judiciary as a monitoring device for political competitors (Carrubba 2005), and the benefits of a judiciary that can constrain political antagonists (Whittington 2001). While these studies demonstrate that an independent judiciary is often in the institutional interests of policymakers who are subject to review, they face the difficulty that support for the judiciary as an institution does not *necessarily* translate into a willingness to comply with a specific decision. Unless the maintenance of the system can be made contingent on unwavering compliance in all instances, the enforcement problem remains.

A second theoretical approach, more directly focused on compliance with specific decisions, appeals to an *exogenous* enforcement mechanism. Such explanations point out that the interactions between courts and other policymakers do not occur in a vacuum. Third parties, who take an interest in this interaction, may observe policymaker reactions to judicial rulings. If these outside players value compliance and have means at their disposal to "punish" policymakers who choose to ignore or evade a decision, compliance may be achieved. For instance, in the case of developing nations, international organizations like the International Monetary Fund or the World Bank might threaten suspension of loan programs if judicial rulings are openly flaunted.

More important, arguably, is the role of *political culture,* understood as a widely shared system of beliefs among citizens about what is politically possible and permissible. If citizens generally value judicial independence and regard respect for judicial rulings as important, a decision by other policymakers, especially elected officials, to resist the court may result in a public backlash. The fear of such a backlash can be a powerful inducement to implement judicial decisions faithfully. In other words, public support for an independent court and for the constitutional order can act as an exogenous enforcement mechanism, especially in advanced democracies (e.g., Caldeira 1986; Carrubba 2005; Murphy and Tanenhaus 1990; Gibson, Caldeira, and Baird 1998). Barry Weingast has highlighted the importance of political culture in this sense for democratic stability more generally, concluding that broad citizen agreement that certain "rules of the game" must be respected, coupled with general coordination on what these rules are, can produce powerful constraints on the exercise of political power (Weingast 1997).

While an exogenous enforcement mechanism may be successful in inducing compliance, it relies on two central conditions that are usually left implicit but that must be met:

Condition 1: The sanction that can be imposed by the outside institution/ actors on recalcitrant policymakers must be sufficiently severe to deter noncompliance.

Condition 2: The outside institution/actors that provide exogenous enforcement must be able to monitor policymaker responses to judicial rulings sufficiently effectively and reliably.

If either condition fails, an exogenous sanction cannot act as an effective enforcement mechanism. While both conditions are crucial, the second raises an especially vital issue. The threat of an exogenous sanction will only deter noncompliance if policymakers who attempt to evade a decision are sufficiently likely to be "caught." In other words, *monitoring* of responses to judicial rulings is crucial. But such monitoring is not a trivial task. Under most circumstances, policymakers who attempt to circumvent a decision (especially if they are concerned about being sanctioned) will not oppose a decision openly and publicly, but will circumvent it implicitly. For example, congressional policymakers did not openly attack the *Chadha* decision; instead, they simply ignored it and continued to employ the legislative veto. Similarly, policymakers may change a policy in response to a judicial decision but craft the new policy in such a way as to evade implications of the decision they oppose.

Such implicit evasion appears especially problematic for exogenous enforcement in light of the fact that studies of public opinion generally show that public knowledge on most issues is low (see Zaller 1992). The average citizen is unlikely to be aware of Supreme Court decisions or of the reactions to them by other policymakers—especially if these policy-makers do not openly flaunt their unwillingness to comply. How then can public support for the Court, even if potentially significant, deter non-compliance? The answer lies in the same process that governs the dynam-ics of opinion formation more generally. "Public opinion" is usually formed and mobilized through a two-step process in which information filters down to the mass public via elite opinion (see Zaller 1992; Page, Shapiro, and Dempsey 1987). The question how public support can effectively monitor compliance with judicial rulings thus boils down to the question of the circumstances in which opinion leadership is likely to "activate" or mobilize underlying support for an independent judiciary. This immediately suggests several factors that are likely to be of impor-tance. Highly salient decisions that generate considerable media attention will be more difficult to avoid without notice than relatively obscure cases. Similarly, interest groups that favor the Court's decision and have access to resources can disseminate information about evasion attempts. Such groups can also finance renewed challenges to policies that do not imple-ment the Court's decision fully (Epp 1998, 22). Finally, the less complex an issue is, the easier it will be for citizens to evaluate any claims of non-compliance made by opinion leaders, and thus to monitor compliance. For example, it is presumably easier to decide whether a straightforward decision on criminal procedure has been properly implemented than to monitor a decision on technical regulatory questions. For the present, I will collapse these various components that affect how effectively compli-ance can be monitored and refer to them collectively as the "transparency" of the political environment. The easier it is for the agents that constitute the exogenous enforcement mechanism to monitor compliance with a ju-dicial ruling, the more *transparent* the political environment is.

A Bayesian Model of Constitutional Review

Many prominent accounts of judicial power rely on an exogenous en-forcement mechanism, such as public support for high courts. As pointed out in the previous section, these accounts depend on two conditions whose impact is usually not explored explicitly. In this section, I develop a simple game-theoretic model that investigates the impact of the two conditions on the interaction between justices, legislators, and bureau-crats. Naturally, the model abstracts away from many aspects of what is, in practice, a complex and multifaceted interaction. Along the way, I will attempt to point out precisely how the model simplifies the "real world" interaction and how this simplification may affect the model's results. Nevertheless, in abstracting away from these additional considerations and focusing on essential features of the interaction we are interested in, the model provides valuable insights about the dynamics of constitutional review when judicial decisions must rely on an exogenous enforcement mechanism. To make the discussion more concrete, I will treat "public support" as the exogenous enforcement mechanism. As pointed out in the previous section, however, nothing in the model demands this interpretation. Other mechanisms, such as international agencies, can equally well be substituted wherever the term "public support" appears.

Consider the following incomplete information game, which is played among three players: nature, the "Supreme Court," and an "agent." The agent player can be thought of as any actor whose decisions are subject to review by the Court and who may play a role in implementing the Court's decision, such as a legislature or an administrative agency. The game consists of two stages. In the first stage, nature determines the setting in which the remainder of the game is played by choosing a "policy environment" (more on this below) and a court type (more on these types below). In the second stage, the agent and the Court interact in a policymaking process. First, the agent decides whether to "legislate" (L) or to forego doing so ($\sim L$).[6] The agent must make this decision without perfect information about the policy environment in which it is acting or the court's type. If the agent chooses not to legislate, the game ends. If she legislates, the Court has an opportunity to review the agent's decision. It can choose to deny cert (DC), thus upholding the agent's decision de facto without issuing a decision on the merits. Alternatively, the Court can choose to issue a decision on the merits and either uphold the agent's decision (U) or veto it (V). The Court must do so knowing its own type but being uncertain about its environment. Finally, if the Court decides to veto the agent's action, the agent must implement the Court's ruling and therefore has an opportunity to respond to the decision. She can choose to evade the decision (E), thus sidestepping important aspects of the Court's decision, or she can choose to faithfully implement the ruling ($\sim E$). As will be explained below, the agent is aware of some (but not all) aspects of its environment when deciding whether to evade or to comply.

The first two components of the policy environment capture the impact of the two conditions outlined in the previous section. If the Court enjoys support (PS), an agent's attempt at evading a decision, provided the attempt becomes public, results in a politically costly backlash against the agent. If the Court does not enjoy support ($\sim PS$), evading the Court is not politically costly.[7] I assume that neither Court nor agent can perfectly anticipate whether the Court's ruling will enjoy public support before the ruling is made. Their (common) prior belief that the Court enjoys public support is given by $q \in (0,1)$. Once the decision has been announced, however, the agent can gauge the public reaction to the decision, and so knows whether the Court enjoys support when deciding how to respond to the decision.[8]

The second component of the policy environment concerns transparency. In a transparent environment (T), the agent's response to a decision can be monitored effectively. If the Court enjoys public support, attempts at evasion will become public knowledge and result in a backlash against the agent. In a "nontransparent" environment ($\sim T$), the agent's evasive maneuver remains undetected and therefore does not bring about a backlash. In other words, the various factors that determine how easily a Court decision can be monitored (salience, media coverage, interest group participation, complexity, etc.) are collapsed into this distinction. I assume that neither the agent nor the Court can know with certainty whether potential evasion attempts will be detected before such an attempt has been carried out. The common prior belief that the environment is transparent is given by $r \in (0,1)$.

The final feature of the environment that is determined by nature concerns the Court's preferences, that is, the type of court that the agent must interact with: A *convergent* court (C) or a *nonconvergent* court ($\sim C$). The Court's payoffs are a function of two components. First, the Court has a preference over the policy under review, captured by a policy payoff $A > 0$. The Court reaps this benefit whenever the outcome of the game with respect to the issue under review (whether the statute is implemented or not) comports with its preference for or against the "bill." In addition to caring about the issue under review, the Court also cares about its institutional status. Specifically, a successful evasion is detrimental for the Court, because its position in the political system is challenged. Thus, the Court pays a cost of $I > 0$ if the agent successfully evades the Court. The two court types are differentiated by the interplay of these payoff parameters. A *convergent* court shares the policy preferences of the agent. In other words, the convergent court reaps the benefit A if the policy is implemented. A *nonconvergent* court, conversely, is opposed to the agent's policy preferences and gains A whenever the policy is not implemented.[9]

Finally, I assume that in choosing whether to uphold an agent's decision on the merits or denying cert, the Court cares not only about the practical implications in the current case (the policy is not vetoed) but also considers the impact of a constitutional endorsement it delivers. Thus, a convergent Court pays a cost of $B > 0$ if it denies cert rather than upholding the decision, because in so doing, it does not lend a constitutional basis to the policy if favors. Vice versa, a nonconvergent Court pays the cost B if it chooses to uphold a statute instead of denying cert, because it provides constitutional legitimation to a policy it does not favor. Given these payoffs, the convergent Court will always uphold the agent's action, while a nonconvergent Court will never choose to uphold.[10]

The prior probability that the Court is convergent is given by $p \in (0,1)$. A pure strategy for the Court is a mapping from its type space into its action set. For example, the strategy $s_C = \{U|C; V|\sim C\}$ is a strategy under which the convergent Court will uphold the agent's decision and the nonconvergent Court will veto it. Alternatively, under the strategy $s_C = \{U|C; DC|C\}$, the convergent Court upholds the decision, while the nonconvergent Court denies cert. Given that the convergent Court has a dominant strategy to uphold the agent's action and that the nonconvergent Court will never choose to uphold, these are the only two pure strategies for the Court that we need to consider. Jointly, the three components that determine the environment (transparency, public support, and judicial preferences) create eight different types of environment in which Court and agent can interact.

The utility function for the agent, like judicial preferences, captures policy preferences and institutional concerns. First, the agent earns a policy payoff of $\alpha > 0$ if she can successfully implement the new policy she has proposed (either because the policy is upheld by the Court or because the Court is successfully evaded). Should she be caught in an evasion attempt when the Court enjoys public support, she suffers a cost of $\beta > 0$ (i.e., this "backlash cost" must only be paid if the environment is transparent, the Court enjoys support, and the agent has chosen to evade). Finally, she faces an opportunity cost of $\varepsilon > 0$ to legislate.[11] The agent must (potentially) act at three information sets. Thus, a strategy for the agent specifies whether the agent will legislate and how she will react to a judicial veto, depending on whether the Court enjoys public support. For example, the strategy $s_A = \{L, \sim E|PS, E| \sim PS\}$ is a strategy in which the agent legislates, does not evade a judicial veto if the Court enjoys public support, and chooses to evade if the Court lacks support. The agent has eight possible pure strategies available. For ease of reference, table 1 provides a listing of the parameters.

TABLE 1 The environment of constitutional review

PARAMETER	DESCRIPTION
$q \in (0,1)$	Probability that Court enjoys public support
$r \in (0,1)$	Probability that environment is transparent
$p \in (0,1)$	Probability that Court is convergent
$\alpha \geq 0$	Policy benefit for agent
$\beta \geq 0$	Cost of public backlash for agent
$\varepsilon \geq 0$	Opportunity cost of legislating
$A \geq 0$	Policy benefit for Court
$I \geq 0$	Cost of successful evasion for Court
$B \geq 0$	In choice between upholding on the merits and denying cert, the cost of a "wrong" constitutional endorsement

The appropriate solution concept for this game is Perfect Bayesian Equilibrium (PBE). Loosely speaking, PBE requires that the players' strategies be sequentially rational, given their beliefs at each information set, and that these beliefs be determined (where possible) by Bayes's rule and the players' strategies at information sets on and off the equilibrium path of play. In short, in a PBE, each player's strategy *and* beliefs must constitute an optimal response to the strategy of the other player.

Perfect Bayesian Equilibria

In stating and interpreting the equilibrium results, several definitions will be helpful.

Definition: Define the "agent evasion threshold" as $r^* \equiv (\alpha/\alpha + \beta)$.
Definition: Define the "weak judicial veto threshold" as $q^* \equiv [I/r(I + A)]$.
Definition: Define the "strong judicial veto threshold" as $\tilde{q} \equiv (I/I + A)$.

The significance of these thresholds will become apparent in stating the equilibrium conditions. To anticipate, greater likelihood of transparency as well as greater likelihood of public support for the Court put the Court in a stronger position, while a reduced likelihood of either strengthens the position of the agent. Given this general relationship, the *agent evasion threshold* marks the likelihood of transparency below which the agent will choose to evade a judicial veto even if the Court enjoys public support, because an evasion attempt is unlikely to be "caught."[12] The *weak judicial* *veto threshold* denotes the probability of public support for the Court above which the nonconvergent Court will veto the bill even though it is in a weak position, because the agent evasion threshold is not met and the agent will attempt to evade the ruling.[13] The *strong judicial veto threshold*, conversely, marks the probability of public support above which the nonconvergent Court will veto the bill when it is in a strong position, because the agent evasion threshold is met and the agent will abide by the Court's decision (provided the Court enjoys public support). As is intuitive, $\tilde{q} < q^*$.

There are six pure-strategy, Perfect Bayesian Equilibria (PBE) to this game. In discussing these equilibria, it is most useful to group them into four distinct types.

Agent Self-Censoring Equilibria: In these equilibria, the agent censors her own behavior in anticipation of judicial review and chooses not to legislate. There are two such equilibria:

Equilibrium A: For $r \geq r^*$, $q > \tilde{q}$, and $p < (\varepsilon/\alpha)$, the following strategy profile constitutes a PBE:

Agent: $s_A = \{\sim L, \sim E | PS, E | \sim PS\}$

Court: $s_C = \{U | C; V | \sim C\}$

Equilibrium B: For $r < r^*$, $q > q^*$, and $p < 1 - [(\alpha - \varepsilon)/(\alpha + \beta)qr]$, the following strategy profile constitutes a PBE:

Agent: $s_A = \{\sim L, E | PS, E | \sim PS\}$

Court: $s_C = \{U | C; V | \sim C\}$

The intuition behind these equilibria takes advantage of two facts. First, for a *given* likelihood of transparency, the probability of public support for the Court is so high that the nonconvergent Court (expecting that public backing is likely) chooses to veto the agent's decision if reviewed. In addition, the agent believes the Court is so likely to be hostile to her legislative initiative (p is low) that the opportunity cost of legislating outweighs the expected benefits of passing the bill and engaging in a "showdown" with the nonconvergent Court. The agent censors her own behavior preemptively in anticipation of judicial review by a Court that is highly likely to be hostile. A substantive implication of the analysis is thus that one effect of constitutional review is that congressional majorities or decision makers in administrative agencies may decide not to pursue preferred policy initiatives because of the looming threat of a judicial veto.[14]

This phenomenon has recently received attention among scholars of comparative judicial politics. Alec Stone (1992) has identified important instances in which legislative majorities in the French National Assembly have limited their legislative proposals to guard against a negative decision by the Constitutional Council. Other studies conclude that such "autolimitation" may be a more general phenomenon in Europe (Stone Sweet and Brunnel 1998, Stone Sweet 2000, Vanberg 1998). These equilibria thus suggest that in addition to displays of judicial power through a veto, the substantive impact of constitutional review may also express itself in what does *not* happen, that is, in bills that are not passed but would have enjoyed support in the absence of an anticipated judicial veto. This observation is of direct relevance for judicial scholars, because it implies that the manner in which the possibility of constitutional review shapes the policy process cannot be adequately assessed by considering only instances of judicial intervention.

Judicial Self-Censoring Equilibria: In these equilibria, the nonconvergent Court censors its own behavior in anticipation of the agent's reaction by denying cert and not vetoing the agent's decision despite its preference for seeing the policy invalidated. There are two such equilibria:
Equilibrium C: For $r < r^*$ and $q \leq q^*$, the following strategy profile constitutes a PBE:
Agent: $s_A = \{L, E|PS, E| \sim PS\}$
Court: $s_C = \{U|C; DC| \sim C\}$
Equilibrium D: For $r \geq r^*$ and $q \leq \tilde{q}$, the following strategy profile constitutes a PBE:
Agent: $s_A = \{L, \sim E|PS, E| \sim PS\}$
Court: $s_C = \{U|C; DC| \sim C\}$

In a sense, these equilibria constitute the counterpart to the agent self-censoring equilibria. Their central distinguishing condition is the fact that the probability that the Court will enjoy public support is low (specifically, below either of the two judicial veto thresholds). Because the exogenous enforcement mechanism it must rely on (public backing) is unlikely to be effective, the nonconvergent Court prefers to deny cert to provoking a confrontation with the agent that may well end in a successful evasion attempt. Putting it differently, the nonconvergent Court realizes that, given its political environment, it is in a weak position. Consequently, it chooses to circumvent a confrontation that has the potential to damage the Court's institutional standing by simply denying cert and upholding the agent's decision de facto. Because the agent expects that the Court will not interfere, she chooses to legislate. In other words, an environment that leaves the Court in a weak position creates conditions for "legislative supremacy" in which the Court cannot effectively act as a counterweight to the agent.

Separation-of-Powers Equilibrium: In this equilibrium, the agent legislates. The nonconvergent Court vetoes the decision, and the agent respects that decision (provided the Court enjoys public support).
Equilibrium E: For $r \geq r^*$, $q > \tilde{q}$ and $p \geq (\varepsilon/\alpha)$, the following strategy profile constitutes a PBE:
Agent: $s_A = \{L, \sim E | PS, E | \sim PS\}$
Court: $s_C = \{U | C; V | \sim C\}$

This equilibrium captures what appears, on first thought, to be the "usual" or "expected" interaction between a legislature or administrative agency and the Court in a stable constitutional democracy. Along the path of play, the agent issues a decision. This decision is upheld by a convergent Court and vetoed by the nonconvergent Court. Confronted with a judicial veto, the agent chooses to comply (provided the Court enjoys public support, which I assume to be the case for the following discussion).[15] The sense in which this constitutes a "separation-of-powers" equilibrium is immediate: The agent exercises her powers to initiate policy change, but the nonconvergent Court can effectively prevent the agent's decision from being implemented.

Successful initiation of a new policy thus requires the consent of *both* players—the agent acting as an agenda setter and the Court as a veto player. The conditions that are necessary to sustain this equilibrium are intuitive. First, the probability that the environment is transparent must meet the agent evasion threshold, which induces the agent to respect judicial vetoes when the Court enjoys support, because attempts at evasion are unlikely to succeed. Second, the strong judicial veto threshold must be met so that the nonconvergent Court is sufficiently confident that it will enjoy public backing to veto the agent's decision. Finally, given that the nonconvergent Court can successfully prevent implementation of the policy, the probability that the Court will share the preferences of the agent must be sufficiently high to forestall self-censoring behavior by the agent. The need to satisfy these various conditions already suggests an important conclusion: Successful separation-of-powers arrangements may depend on the presence of external conditions that support mutual respect among the branches without making any branch overbearing (as in the self-censoring equilibria). If these conditions are met, however, the Court is largely unconstrained in pursuing its sincere preferences.[16]

Contentious Equilibrium: In this equilibrium, the agent issues a decision and chooses to evade any judicial veto even if the Court enjoys public support. The nonconvergent Court chooses to veto the agent's decision nevertheless.

Equilibrium F: For $r < r^*$, $q > q^*$, and $p \geq 1 - [(\alpha - \varepsilon)/(\alpha + \beta)qr]$, the following strategy profile constitutes a PBE:

Agent: $s_A = \{L, E | PS, E | \sim PS\}$

Court: $s_C = \{U | C; V | \sim C\}$

This final equilibrium captures an intermediate case. Because the probability that the environment is transparent is below the evasion threshold, the agent feels sufficiently secure in evading a judicial veto to do so, leaving the Court in a fairly weak position. At the same time, the likelihood that the Court will enjoy public support is so high that the weak judicial veto threshold is met and the nonconvergent Court chooses to annul the agent's decision despite the expectation of evasion in hopes of "winning" in a confrontation with the agent. It is crucial to note that of the six equilibria, this is the *only* one in which evasion of a judicial veto occurs even when the Court enjoys public support. This already suggests that the impact of the "evasion problem" on legislative-judicial and administrative-judicial interactions cannot be reduced to (or analyzed by focusing exclusively on) actual attempts at noncompliance. I return to this issue below.

It is noteworthy that the conditions for the six equilibria completely partition the space generated by the exogenous parameters of the game (r, q, and p). For any given combination of these parameters, the model predicts a unique equilibrium. No multiple equilibria problem exists. Moreover, it is possible to "rank" the equilibria according to the degree of "judicial power" in each. For this ranking, we only need to consider the perspective of the nonconvergent Court (since there is no conflict between the agent and the convergent Court). An intuitive way to think about judicial power in this context is to say that the more powerful the Court, the more likely it is to prevent successful implementation of the agent's policy. Given this definition, the Court is most powerful in the Agent Self-Censoring Equilibria (the agent does not even attempt to legislate). It is less powerful in the Separation-of-Powers Equilibrium (the agent can successfully implement the policy when the Court has no support), still less powerful in the Contentious Equilibrium (the agent will successfully evade even if the Court has support when the environment is not transparent), and least powerful in the Judicial Self-Censoring Equilibria (the Court simply upholds the agent's policy). Naturally, the analogous "power ranking" for the agent is given by the reverse order.

Interpretation and Comparative Statics

The discussion and interpretation of these results is organized around a series of observations. These observations draw on table 2, which lays out the comparative statics for the model. Specifically, for each type of equilibrium and each exogenous parameter, the corresponding cell in table 2 shows how an increase in the given parameter may affect the equilibrium prediction of the game. For example, an increase in q (the probability that the Court enjoys public support) may induce a shift from the Judicial Self-Censoring Equilibrium to any of the three other equilibrium types (which implies greater judicial power).

Observation 1: If judicial rulings must rely on an exogenous enforcement mechanism, the extent to which a court can effectively constrain other policymakers (in parliaments or bureaucracies) depends on the political environment surrounding an issue/case.

As the model makes clear, the potential for evasion of judicial rulings has a profound impact on the interaction between the Court and the institutions whose actions the Court is supposed to oversee. Environments that favor effective judicial oversight are those in which transparency is high (thus making monitoring compliance easy) and in which the Court is likely to enjoy sufficient public support (in more general language, environments in which the sanction that can be imposed is likely to be sufficient to deter noncompliance). Conversely, environments in which the Court is not likely to enjoy public support or that are nontransparent hold out little promise for effective judicial oversight. Instead, the agent is largely able to pursue her preferred policies without judicial interference. Since the issues confronting the Court vary both in the degree to which any exogenous sanction for noncompliance is likely to be effective and, perhaps more important, in the transparency surrounding an issue, one major implication of this analysis is the Court does not pose equally effective constraints in all policy areas. The potential enforcement problem implies that judicial power varies not only across Courts and across time, but also for the same Court at the same time across different issue areas.

A concrete example can illustrate these implications. For any given configuration of the exogenous parameters (the players' payoffs and the probabilities of transparency, public support, and the Court's type), the

TABLE 2 Comparative statics predictions

	INCREASE IN q (favors Court)	INCREASE IN p (favors agent)	INCREASE IN r (favors Court)	INCREASE IN α (favors agent)	INCREASE IN β (favors Court)	INCREASE IN A (favors Court)	INCREASE IN l (favors agent)
Agent self-censoring	No change	Contentious separation	No change	Separation contentious judicial S-C	No change	No change	Judicial S-C
Separation of powers	No change	No change	No change	Contentious judicial S-C	No change	No change	Judicial S-C
Contentious	No change	No change	Separation agent S-C	No change	Separation agent S-C	No change	Judicial S-C
Judicial self-censoring	Contentious separation agent S-C	No change	Separation agent S-C	No change	Separation agent S-C	Contentious separation agent S-C	No change

NOTE: The table shows the movement from the equilibrium types listed on the left that can be induced by an increase in the exogenous parameters.

TABLE 3 Monte Carlo simulation results for path of play

	NO LEGISLATION	UPHELD ON MERITS	DENIAL OF CERT	VETO WITH NO EVASION	EVASION WITH NO SUPPORT	SUCCESSFUL EVASION WITH SUPPORT	UNSUCCESSFUL EVASION WITH SUPPORT	TOTAL
$p, q, r \in (0,1)$	0.24	49.89	36.70	8.78	3.56	0.34	0.50	100.00
$p, r \in (0,1)$ $r \in (.5,1)$	0.41	49.88	26.50	16.07	5.43	0.73	0.98	100.00
$p, q \in (0,1)$ $r \in (.5,1)$	0.41	49.89	24.97	16.82	6.75	0.52	0.65	100.00
$p \in (0,1)$ $q, r \in (.9,1)$	0.90	49.88	0.00	46.88	2.33	0.00	0.00	100.00

equilibrium conditions of the model can be used to make a prediction about the path of play, allowing us to answer the question: How likely is each of the various outcomes? Naturally, providing such an answer for a specific set of exogenous parameters is of limited interest, because parameters are usually not given and will vary from issue to issue. One way to deal with this difficulty is to construct a slightly more complicated thought experiment. Imagine that the payoff parameters and exogenous probabilities are randomly drawn from a known distribution (thus mimicking the fact that payoffs and probabilities can vary from issue to issue). Ex ante, how likely would the different outcomes be, given the probability distributions from which the parameters are drawn?

In principle, it is possible (but labor intensive) to answer this question analytically. For our purposes, we can approximate the analytical solution by a series of Monte Carlo simulations. These simulations are constructed as follows. I assume that the two institutional payoff parameters (the cost of a public backlash, β, and the cost of successful evasion, (I) are fixed at 1.[17] The two policy payoffs (α and Λ) are drawn from a uniform distribution on the interval $(0.5, 2)$, implying that policy concerns are, on average, more important than institutional concerns but may well be dominated by institutional considerations on occasion. The probabilities of transparency, public support, and court type are independently drawn from uniform distributions over various subsets of the unit interval. Table 3 reports the results of these experiments, with each row corresponding to a different scenario. Each cell in the table reports the ex ante probability that the corresponding path of play will result.[18]

The results help to make the implications outlined above concrete. The first row corresponds to an environment that is relatively "unfriendly" for the Court. The three exogenous probabilities are drawn from the full unit interval, implying that the Court, on average, enjoys public support in only one-half of the cases and the environment is, on average, equally likely to be nontransparent as to be transparent. As the table shows, the agent is in a powerful position in such an environment. Approximately 85 percent of the cases are expected to end either with the Court upholding the agent's policy or the nonconvergent Court denying cert in anticipation of a confrontation with the agent should it choose to annul. The nonconvergent Court can successfully veto the agent's policy in less than 10 percent of the cases. The picture begins to change as we move to environments that are more favorable for the Court. Row 2 reports results for an environment in which the Court is more likely to enjoy support (on average, in 75 percent of cases), while row 3 reports results for an environment that is more likely to be transparent (about 75 percent of cases).

In either case, we see that the agent is more constrained (although still in a powerful position). She can successfully implement her policy in about 75 percent of cases while the nonconvergent Court can successfully veto in roughly 17 percent of cases. Finally, row 4 reports the results for an environment that favors the Court. The Court is highly likely to enjoy support (about 95 percent of cases) and the environment is highly likely to be transparent (about 95 percent of cases). The nonconvergent Court is now in a strong position vis-à-vis the agent. Only the Agent Self-Censoring and the Separation-of-Powers Equilibria survive, and the nonconvergent Court is able to successfully veto the agent's policy in virtually all cases it confronts.

The variation in outcomes that is reflected in the table powerfully illustrates the message of Observation 1. The potential enforcement problem, coupled with the political environment, significantly affects the interaction between Court and agent. Moreover, this does not imply that actual evasion will occur often. In table 3, successful evasion (when the Court has support) occurs at most in 2 to 3 percent of cases when the Court issues a veto. The results thus suggest that even if evasion is empirically rare, the potential for evasion may yet exercise a powerful effect on judicial and legislative behavior.

Before moving on to the next observation, a separate remark with respect to the transparency variable is appropriate. As we have just seen, transparency is an important resource for the Court and strengthens its position vis-à-vis the agent. As a result, the judges will be expected to have an interest in raising transparency where this is feasible and not prohibitively costly. One means that judges have at their disposal to do so consists of the clarity of their opinion. The more clearly an opinion enunciates the constitutional principles that sustain a decision and its implications for policy, the easier it is to verify whether a response complies with the ruling. This is not a new insight. Previous research has already suggested that opinion specificity has an impact on compliance (e.g., Baum 1981, 50–51; Spriggs 1997). Within the context of the current model, it is impossible to investigate how judges might "manipulate" transparency. But extending the model to incorporate this possibility explicitly provides an avenue for future research.

Observation 2: If judicial rulings must rely on an exogenous enforcement mechanism, the Court becomes more powerful and less deferential as the exogenous sanction that can be imposed for noncompliance increases.

This observation zeroes in on the importance of the first condition: the effectiveness of the exogenous sanction that can be imposed for noncompliance. A natural way to interpret the payoff parameter β is as a measure of the severity of this sanction. As table 2 indicates, increases in the magnitude of this sanction can only induce movements to equilibria that make the Court more powerful. The intuition underlying these results is straightforward; because a more severe sanction raises the expected costs of evasion, the agent will comply with judicial decisions under a wider range of circumstances. Expecting less evasion, the Court is more willing to exercise its powers.

As one would expect, when an exogenously imposed sanction such as public support acts as the major enforcement mechanism for judicial rulings, the Court's power increases as this resource grows and diminishes where it is absent. This result leads to an interesting implication. Where public support is crucial to enforcement, judges on high courts should take an acute interest in the public's support for the Court. This in turn implies that courts may be less insulated against public pressures than is commonly supposed. This implication is consistent with the findings of several studies that conclude that the U.S. Supreme Court is in fact more in line with prevailing public opinion than one might expect of a "counter-majoritarian" institution (e.g., Marshall 1989). Thus, McCloskey (1994, 208) concludes that, "Indeed the facts of the Court's history impellingly suggest a flexible and non-dogmatic institution fully alive to such realities as the drift of public opinion . . . it is hard to find a single historical instance when the Court has stood firm for very long against a really clear wave of public demand."

Observation 3: If judicial rulings must rely on an exogenous enforcement mechanism, courts become more deferential and less powerful in exercising their powers of constitutional review as the political environment becomes less transparent.

This observation focuses on the implications of the second condition for constitutional review: the ease with which responses to judicial decisions can be monitored. In the model, transparency is captured by the parameter r. As r increases, attempts at evasion are more likely to be detected, implying that it is easier to monitor reactions to the Court's decisions. As table 2 makes clear, such increases in transparency strengthen the

Court and can only induce changes to equilibria in which the Court is better able to constrain the agent. Conversely, if the environment becomes less transparent, changes to equilibria in which the Court is less powerful become possible. Substantively, this observation implies that circumstances that limit the ability of outside actors to monitor compliance with decisions will reduce the "bite" of constitutional review. A number of such circumstances are immediate. Courts will be less able to police more complex policy areas than "simple" policy areas in which evasion can easily be spotted. Similarly, the Court's leverage will be reduced on issues that generate little media attention and public interest.

Observation 4: If judicial rulings must rely on an exogenous enforcement mechanism, courts become more deferential and less powerful in exercising their powers of constitutional review as the political importance of the issue under review increases for the policymakers they are supposed to constrain.

Within the context of the model, an increase in α signals that the issue under review is more important to the agent. As table 2 reveals, such an increase can only provoke movement toward equilibria in which the Court is less powerful. For example, if the original equilibrium of the game is the "expected" Separation-of-Powers Equilibrium, an increase in α may lead to a shift to the Contentious Equilibrium or even to judicial self-censoring. In either case, the nonconvergent Court is less powerful in preventing change, because the agent is more eager to evade or because the Court is more deferential in choosing to deny cert in anticipation of an evasive maneuver. Ironically, it is thus precisely in cases in which the *external* constraint on the agent may be particularly important because the agent's preferences are so strong that judicial oversight is least likely to be effective. This implication provides additional theoretical justification for Gerald Rosenberg's contention that the Supreme Court is not likely to be successful in trying to prevent or initiate policy change in opposition to strong preferences by other political players (Rosenberg 1991).

The first four observations call attention to the fact that where judicial rulings acquire force through an exogenous enforcement mechanism, legal and constitutional considerations are not the only variables that shape the interactions between high courts, legislatures, and administrative agencies. The *political* environment within which these institutions act is likely to matter as well. The final observation and corollary spell out methodological implications for the interpretation of observed judicial behavior and for the appropriate empirical approaches for studying the strategic interactions between judges and policymakers.

Observation 5: Because the *anticipation* of potential evasion attempts may exercise an important influence on relations between courts and other policymakers, the impact of the enforcement problem will not necessarily be reflected in actual attempts at evasion.

The potential for evasion may exercise a powerful influence on the interaction between courts and other policymakers. However, as was already pointed out in reviewing the equilibria above, this does not imply that evasion will occur often. When the Court enjoys support, evasion occurs in only one equilibrium along the path of play, even though the potential for evasion still shapes the interaction. The Judicial Self-Censoring Equilibria, in which the nonconvergent Court chooses to deny cert precisely because successful evasion is so likely, provide the most obvious example. The results of the Monte Carlo simulations reported in table 3 point in the same direction: actual evasion may be a rare phenomenon, even though the potential for evasion may powerfully influence equilibrium behavior.[19] As a result, the model reveals that empirical findings that document relatively high rates of compliance with U.S. Supreme Court decisions (e.g., Spriggs 1997) are consistent with the proposition that courts are, in certain circumstances, constrained by the potential for noncompliance. The fact that judicial vetoes are usually respected does not necessarily imply that the enforcement problem is irrelevant to understanding judicial behavior.

Corollary: Empirical investigations of strategic judicial behavior that focus exclusively on decisions on the merits and do not consider judicial decisions on the Court's docket may suffer from a potential selection bias.

This corollary is a direct consequence of the previous observation. If the potential for evasion shapes judicial behavior and, specifically, may lead to "defensive denials of cert"[20] by a Court worried about enforcement of a decision, then the cases in which the Court denies cert take on special significance. If we focus exclusively on cases in which a decision on the merits is issued, we may be missing a crucial stage at which strategic behavior is manifested. Understanding the process of cert denial and its relation to the decision to decide on the merits therefore deserves the attention of scholars interested in judicial behavior (e.g., Perry 1991).[21]

Conclusion

This essay has presented a simple game-theoretic model of the inter-actions between a high court like the U.S. Supreme Court and an agency or legislature whose actions are subject to review by the Court against the backdrop of the potential enforcement problem. The most important contribution of this model is that it provides a unified theoretical account of an issue that has so far been approached from various empirical angles. In so doing, the model allows us to make sense of empirical findings that initially appear to be in conflict within one common framework. Spe-cifically, the model allows us to understand the conditions under which judicial rulings will meet with noncompliance (for example, *Brown* or *Chadha*), but it also explains why such events are likely to be rare. Com-pliance will be the rule rather than the exception in most circumstances. At the same time, the theory demonstrates that this does not imply that the potential enforcement problem is unimportant. Its impact simply does not manifest itself in noncompliance.

A crucial advantage of such a unified account is that it suggests a single theoretical framework that can be fruitfully employed to explain the different degrees of power exercised by different courts in different coun-tries as well as by the same court across time or across different issues. The model allows us to characterize (broadly) the types of environments that favor judicial power and those that hamper it. Variation in these condi-tions can then be used to explain variation in the success with which courts assert their power. Similarly, the model also suggests the conditions under which courts are able to act as unconstrained policymakers (as en-visioned by the attitudinal model) and where the potential for noncom-pliance will constrain justices.

This model constitutes only one contribution to a larger ongoing effort by many scholars to develop a positive political theory of the ju-diciary. To date, these efforts have resulted in considerable conceptual contributions to our understanding of judicial behavior and the inter-actions between courts and other institutions. But much remains to be done. In particular, a crucial future task for this approach will be to sub-ject theoretical models to rigorous empirical testing; that is, to engage in what Roger Myerson has called a "modeling dialogue" (1992). The account offered in this essay invites and facilitates such an evaluation by yielding clear empirical hypotheses. To name only a few, the model pre-dicts:

- that the less transparent the environment in which a court acts, the less likely the court is to pose an effective constraint for other policymakers,
- that courts are less likely to rule successfully against legislative majorities in cases that are particularly important to these policymakers,
- that judges will use their ability to control their agenda to avoid cases that may induce a confrontation.

Are these predictions (and the others that can be derived from the model) borne out? Does the current approach provide a fruitful way for understanding relations between the Supreme Court, Congress, and administrative agencies? Only systematic empirical evaluation will ultimately tell us the answer.

Appendix

This appendix contains the proof for the six Pure-Strategy Perfect Bayesian Equilibria (PBE) of the game.

Tie-breaking assumptions:

If indifferent between evading and not evading, the agent will choose to comply.

If indifferent between upholding and vetoing the bill, the court will choose to uphold.

If indifferent between legislating and not doing so, the agent will choose to legislate.

Lemma 1: In any PBE, if the court has no public support, the agent will choose to evade an annulment. Thus, in equilibrium, the agent's strategy must have the form $s_A = \{*, * | PS, E | \sim PS\}$

Proof: If the agent evades the decision, her payoff is $\alpha - \varepsilon$ for evading compared to $-\varepsilon$ for complying.

Lemma 2: In any PBE, a convergent court will always choose to uphold the statute as constitutional. Thus, in equilibrium, the judicial strategy must have the form $s_C = \{U | C; * | \sim C\}$.

Proof: For the convergent court, upholding the statute yields the highest possible payoff A, and therefore must weakly dominate denying cert or vetoing.

Lemma 3: For the nonconvergent court, denying cert dominates upholding the agent's decision on the merits.

Proof: Upholding the statute yields payoff $-B$, while denying cert yields payoff 0.

Jointly, Lemmata 2 and 3 imply that in equilibrium, only two judicial strategies are possible $s_C = \{U|C; V| \sim C\}$ and $s_C = \{U|C; DC| \sim C\}$.

Proof of the Equilibria:

I. Consider the last stage of the game, in which the agent must react to the court's decision, when the court has public support:

Given that the agent is not certain about transparency, her expected utilities from evading and not evading are given by:

$$EU_A(\sim E) = -\varepsilon$$
$$EU_A(E) = r(-\beta - \varepsilon) + (1 - r)(\alpha - \varepsilon)$$

The agent will choose to evade the decision if and only if:

$$r(-\beta - \varepsilon) + (1 - r)(\alpha - \varepsilon) > -\varepsilon$$
$$\Leftrightarrow$$
$$r < \frac{\alpha}{\alpha + \beta}$$

If this condition holds, the agent evades. Otherwise it complies with the decision.

II. Consider the convergent court at the review stage:
Lemma 2 applies. The convergent court will always uphold.

III. Consider the nonconvergent court at the review stage:
For the nonconvergent court, denying cert dominates upholding the statute. Thus, only the choice between vetoing and denying cert needs to be considered.

Case 1: $r < (\alpha/\alpha + \beta)$ and the agent will evade even if the court has public support.

$$EU_C(DC) = 0$$
$$EU_C(V) = q(rA - (1 - r)I) - (1 - q)I$$

Therefore, the court will choose to veto if and only if:

$$qrA - I + qrI > 0$$
$$\Leftrightarrow$$
$$q > \frac{I}{r(I + A)}$$

If this condition holds, the court vetoes under case 1. Otherwise, it denies cert.

Case 2: $r \geq (\alpha/\alpha + \beta)$ and the agent will comply if the court has public support.

$$EU_C(DC) = 0$$
$$EU_C(V) = qA - (1 - q)I$$

Therefore, the court will choose to veto if and only if:

$$q > \frac{I}{I + A}$$

If this condition holds, the court vetoes under case 2. Otherwise, it denies cert.

IV. Consider the agent at the initial legislative stage:
Case 1: $r < (\alpha/\alpha + \beta)$ and $q > [I/r(I + A)]$. Agent evades and court vetoes.

$$EU_A(\sim L) - 0$$
$$EU_A(L) - p(\alpha \quad \epsilon) + (1 - p)$$
$$[q(r(-\beta - \epsilon) + (1 - r)(\alpha - \epsilon)) + (1 - q)(\alpha - \epsilon)]$$

These imply that the agent will choose to legislate if and only if:

$$qr(1 - p) \leq \frac{\alpha - \epsilon}{\alpha + \beta}$$

If this condition holds, the agent passes the bill under case 1. Otherwise, it chooses not to legislate.

Case 2: $r < (\alpha/\alpha + \beta)$ and $q \leq [I/r(I + A)]$. Agent evades and court denies cert.

$$EU_A(\sim L) = 0$$
$$EU_A(L) = \alpha - \epsilon$$

The agent will always choose to legislate.

Case 3: $r \geq (\alpha/\alpha + \beta)$ and $q > (I/I + A)$. Agent complies and court vetoes.

$$EU_A(\sim L) = 0$$
$$EU_A(L) = p(\alpha - \epsilon) - (1 - p)\epsilon = p\alpha - \epsilon$$

Agent will choose to legislate if and only if:

E) $p \geq \dfrac{\varepsilon}{\alpha}$

If this condition is met, the agent passes the bill under case 3; otherwise, she does not legislate.

Case 4: $r \geq (\alpha/\alpha + \beta)$ and $q \leq (I/I + A)$. Agent complies and court denies cert.

$$EU_L(\sim L) = 0$$
$$EU_L(L) = \alpha - \varepsilon$$

The agent will always choose to legislate.
QED.

Notes

I would like to thank Tatyana Karaman, James Rogers, and participants at the Conference on Institutional Games and the Supreme Court, held at Texas A&M University, November 1–3, 2001, for helpful comments on an earlier version of this paper.

    1. For the U.S. Supreme Court, John Marshall's opinion in *Marbury v. Madison* was, of course, an important milestone in establishing this claim. For a strategic account of the court's ability to establish the power of constitutional review, see Clinton (1994) and Epstein and Knight (1996).

    2. See also McCloskey (1994, 216): "It remains substantially true, as Hamilton suggested in *Federalist 78,* that the Court possesses neither 'purse nor sword' and must depend, therefore, on the willingness of legislative and executive officials to conform their behavior to the judgments announced by the Court."

    3. An issue that is closely related to the "implementation problem" concerns explicit legislative overrides of judicial decisions within a constitutional framework either through statute in statutory decisions or by constitutional amendment (see Ferejohn and Weingast 1992, Segal 1997, Hausegger and Baum 1999, Hettinger and Zorn 2000). The characteristic that distinguishes this phenomenon is that it occurs "within the rules," that is, such responses make use of constitutionally provided means for responding to judicial decisions.

    4. In a certain sense, of course, the lack of direct enforcement powers is no accident. At least for the U.S. Supreme Court, the argument can be made that the Founding Fathers deliberately created a judiciary with few powers of implementation to guard against the danger of "government by judges." Thus, Alexander Hamilton laid out the enforcement problem in *Federalist 78* ("The judiciary . . . has no influence over either the sword or the purse. . . . It may truly be said to have neither Force nor Will but merely judgment; and must ultimately depend upon the aid of the executive arm even for the efficacy of its judgments" [1961, 433]) and called attention to its constraining effect on judicial power in *Federalist 81:* "Particular misconstructions and contraventions of the will of the legislature may now and then happen; but they can never be so extensive as to amount to an inconvenience, or in any sensible degree to affect the order of the political

system. This may be inferred . . . from [the judiciary's] comparative weakness, and from its total incapacity to support its usurpations by force" (1961, 453).

5. For an important dissenting opinion (to which I return below), see Rosenberg (1991), who concludes that the court is severely constrained in being able to shape policy in ways that are opposed by other important actors.

6. Naturally, for administrative agencies, the choice to legislate should be thought of as the choice to issue an administrative decision or ruling.

7. This modeling choice simplifies a much more complex reality. Nevertheless, it captures the fundamental point that political actors must worry about potential back-lashes for noncompliance under some circumstances and that under others, defying the Court may not be politically costly and can even be politically advantageous. In a slight variation on this story in the spirit of Weingast's (1997) framework, the presence of public support can be interpreted as signifying the existence of a citizen consensus that evading a court decision is an action that "triggers" a citizen reaction.

8. Given that public support constitutes the only enforcement mechanism for judicial decisions in this model, this assumption immediately implies that the agent will not comply with judicial decisions when the Court enjoys no public support. This result is tempered if either (a) other enforcement mechanisms exist, or (b) the agent cannot discern with certainty whether the public will tolerate an evasion attempt when choosing how to respond to a decision.

9. Obviously, convergence and nonconvergence of preferences can easily be interpreted as judicial policy preferences. Alternatively, these preferences could be interpreted as signifying a judicial concern with legal criteria that determine constitutionality or unconstitutionality. In other words, the model is open to a legal interpretation as well as the standard interpretation that judges are policy motivated.

10. Upholding the action yields the highest possible payoff (*A*) for the convergent Court without risking an evasion attempt, while denying cert must dominate upholding for the nonconvergent Court. All formal derivations of results are reserved to the appendix. Note that this payoff structure ignores the opportunity cost to the Court of hearing a case, which is surely an important consideration for the justices. Introducing such an opportunity cost would further increase the complexity of the equilibrium conditions without significantly altering the substantive results we are interested in. The primary impact would be that a convergent Court, rather than always upholding a policy would weigh the benefits of providing constitutional legitimation against the opportunity cost of hearing a case. As a result, it might decide to deny cert in certain instances (in essence, the current formulation assumes that the value of a constitutional endorsement of a policy that is favored always outweighs the opportunity cost of hearing the case). A nonconvergent Court never chooses to uphold on the merits, but the introduction of an opportunity cost for hearing a case would further reduce the Court's willingness to make use of its veto.

11. This opportunity cost captures the fact that the agent's time is valuable. Spending time on one bill precludes consideration of other bills. In addition, ensuring passage of a bill through a bureaucracy or a legislature requires gaining sufficient political support, etc., which is costly.

12. Given that the agent knows whether the Court enjoys public support when deciding how to react to a ruling, it is immediate that the agent will always evade the decision if the Court enjoys no support, because there is no enforcement mechanism for the decision other than the threat of a public backlash.

13. As is intuitive (and as can be seen from the formula), given that the agent chooses to evade, this threshold depends on r. Specifically, it decreases in r, because the Court will be more willing to annul the more likely the agent is to be caught in an evasion attempt.

14. Of course, another intriguing possibility, not explored in this model, is that legislative majorities may decide to pass legislation in an effort to "take a position" precisely because they believe that they are isolated against actual implementation through a likely judicial veto (e.g., flag burning).

15. Recall that the information structure of the model is such that the agent can condition her response to a veto on the presence of public support, which means that the agent will never comply when the Court does not have support.

16. As a result, one might expect that the attitudinal model (Segal and Spaeth 1993) would predict judicial behavior under this equilibrium well.

17. This represents a simple normalization of the payoff space that imposes no loss of generality.

18. Each experiment consisted of 20,000 draws from the given distributions, with the corresponding probabilistic assignments of the path of play. Literally, the term "probability" in the text therefore refers to the percentage of cases in which the relevant path of play emerged out of the 20,000 iterations. All experiments were run using STATA 7. The relevant programs are available from the author on request and can easily be amended to allow for different probability distributions and payoff intervals.

19. This, of course, is a conclusion that is common to many strategic theories in which the potential for (and anticipation of) certain outcomes shapes an interaction in ways that make those outcomes "out of equilibrium" results.

20. It should be pointed out that this use of the term "defensive denial" diverges from its traditional meaning in the literature, where the term refers to justices who expect to lose the case on the merits voting against a case on cert.

21. Of course, a complete understanding of the cert process requires a much more elaborate model than has been offered here. Most immediately, I have not considered "opportunity costs" for choosing to decide a case, which must be important for the decision to deny or grant cert. As a result, within the current model, all cert denials are "defensive" denials by a nonconvergent Court trying to protect against evasion. This is naturally a stark oversimplification of a much more complex reality in which cert denials are likely to be motivated by a variety of considerations, as Perry's excellent account lays out (1991).

Court-State Interactions

National Judicial Power and the Dormant Commerce Clause

CLIFFORD J. CARRUBBA AND JAMES R. ROGERS

The institutional relationships of the Supreme Court extend beyond its inter-actions and dependence on Congress and the president to include the states that make up the American federal system. This essay turns its attention to these re-lationships and develops a game in which a court monitors states as they regu-late trade among themselves. Unlike those commentators who see Supreme Court oversight of interstate commerce as the product of an ascendant Court bending states to its will, this paper argues that the "dormant Commerce Clause" (DCC) originates as the strategic product of an institutionally weak Court. The paper lays out three lines of argument. First, it rejects the notion that observing a Court ruling against state governments and those governments complying with the ruling provides evidence of a strong Court. Secondly, the equilibria of the "weak Court" model in this essay directly implies the doctrinal contours of the dormant Commerce Clause, while the ascendancy hypothesis does not. Finally, this essay offers empirical support that the sincere preferences of a majority of justices in *Cooley v. Board of Warden* (53 U.S. 264 [1851]) sup-ported making interstate commerce the exclusive policy domain of Congress, a move that would have completely disbarred states from regulating interstate commerce. Nonetheless, the Court in *Cooley* embraced a conditional DCC doc-trine, a move that is inconsistent with the ascendancy hypothesis but is consis-tent with the strategic maneuverings of a weak Court. Our results suggest that the U.S. Supreme Court was not historically quite as powerful as it is often por-trayed, a conclusion that revises our understanding of the role of the Supreme Court in the development of the American political system.

The rise of the "dormant Commerce Clause" (DCC) is often portrayed as a doctrinal tour de force of a powerfully ascendant U.S. Supreme Court. Richard Bensel, for example, expresses a typical view when he writes: "By striking down state attempts to regulate interstate commerce, the federal courts simultaneously consolidated national judicial supremacy (over state sovereignty) and constructed a national marketplace" (2000, 325, n. 122). Similarly, Felix Frankfurter refers to the DCC as an "audacious doctrine" that requires that "state authority must be subject to such limitations as the Court finds it necessary to apply for the protection of the national community" (1937, 19). Echoing this, Martin Redish and Shane Nugent argue that the DCC is a "figment of the Supreme Court's imagination" in which the Court unilaterally usurped state authority by shifting "the political inertia against the states in the regulation of interstate commerce" (1987, 617). Similar sentiments can be found throughout DCC literature. In contrast, we argue that the dormant Commerce Clause is not quite the victory for the Court over state sovereignty that Bensel, Frankfurter, and others portray. Rather, we claim that it is a doctrine specifically designed in recognition of the *limits* of Court power.

To demonstrate our argument, we derive a game-theoretic model in which states interact with themselves and with a Court in regulating interstate commerce. While states comply with judicial rulings striking down state regulations of interstate commerce (when the Court chooses to rule against a state), nonetheless, the Court *avoids* ruling against states under certain conditions to avoid the embarrassment of handing down decisions states would ignore. We then demonstrate that the equilibria we identify in the game-theoretic model corresponds to the doctrinal contingencies of the dormant Commerce Clause. While the Court effectively prohibits some state burdens on interstate commerce, we also show that the point at which the Court's DCC doctrine begins to *permit* state burdens on interstate commerce is where the model predicts that states would no longer have incentives to enforce compliance to adverse judicial decisions among themselves. That is, the doctrine announced by the Court does not require state compliance to its dictates precisely where the model predicts that states would want to refuse to comply with Court decisions.

The rise of the dormant Commerce Clause therefore does not represent the ascendance of national judicial supremacy at the expense of state sovereignty. Rather, the dormant Commerce Clause as actually evolved is consistent with the strategic actions of a much weaker institution than that represented by the conventional story, and in significant part reflects the *inability* of the Court to assert national judicial supremacy over state sovereignty.

The Commerce Clause and State Interests in Free Trade

In this section we very briefly discuss the historical context that motivated the adoption of the Constitution's Commerce Clause. Doing so identifies the incentives state officials had (and have) both to embrace *some* limitation on their power to burden interstate commerce as well as incentives they have to oppose more extensive limitations. The models developed in the next section of the essay then formalize this story.

The Articles of Confederation asserted formal limits on state regulation of interstate commerce.[1] The national government, however, lacked effective authority under the Articles to prevent states from taxing and regulating interstate trade. This weakness was recognized early on as a major problem with the Articles of Confederation,[2] and by the late 1780s the problem was widely acknowledged as the most significant failing of the Articles. Indeed, the Annapolis convention of 1786—a meeting of officials from New York, New Jersey, Pennsylvania, Delaware, and Virginia—was specifically charged with drafting amendments to the Articles of Confederation to give the national government authority over "trade and commerce" and to create a "uniform system" among the states of "commercial intercourse and regulation" (Proceedings of the Commissioners 1786).

The Annapolis convention failed, however, not because of opposition to national supervision of interstate commerce, but because the commissioners concluded that the Articles of Confederation needed revisions more extensive than merely increasing national power over interstate commerce. National authority over interstate commerce, however, remained key in prompting calls for an entirely new constitution. Hamilton observed in 1788, for example, that "the want of a power to regulate commerce is by all parties" acknowledged as a "defect" of the Articles of Confederation (1788/1999, 111). Similarly, in his concurring opinion in *Gibbons v. Ogden* (9 Wheat 1 [1824]), Justice Johnson recalled that the absence of national authority over interstate commerce was "the immediate cause that led to the forming of a [constitutional] convention" in 1787 (9 Wheat 1, 224). While the constitutional text confers a positive power over interstate commerce to Congress, the primary aim of the Commerce Clause, James Madison explained, was as much to deprive states of the authority to regulate interstate commerce as it was to grant additional power to Congress.[3]

Of course, state officials of the time recognized that they would benefit in the aggregate from ceding control over interstate commerce to the national government. But that did not mean that they therefore lacked incentives to attempt unilaterally to burden commerce in their state's favor if they could get away with it. Among the states of that time, as among nations today, the politics of interstate trade are characterized by a version of the well-known prisoners' dilemma. On the one hand, everyone is better off if all barriers are eliminated relative to the situation in which all states are permitted to impose barriers. On the other hand, because the effect of lowering barriers to trade is to help exporting industries compete in foreign markets, each state would like their trading partners to eliminate their barriers to trade while unilaterally maintaining its own barriers. Thus, while each state would rather have a free-trade regime than not, each state also has an incentive unilaterally to defect from that regime and maintain its own barriers when it can. It is this tension—the incentive to cede power to the national government over interstate commerce and the continuing state-level incentives to defect from this free-trade regime—that, we argue below, generates the particular contours of the Court's dormant Commerce Clause doctrine.

It was universally acknowledged during the founding era that states needed to cede the right to regulate interstate commerce to national authorities in order to solve the collective action dilemma among the states. In the next section we formalize this story, motivate the role of a national court in regulating interstate commerce—and the incentives that states had to accede to *some* national judicial control of interstate commerce—and analyze the conditions under which the Court can (and cannot) enforce federal limits on the ability of states to burden interstate commerce.

Three Models

In this section, we consider three versions of a model in which states interact with each other in choosing whether to regulate interstate commerce. In the first version, we consider outcomes when states can induce compliance with a free-trade regime only through their individual actions. This corresponds to the situation of the states under the Articles of Confederation. The second version of the model adds a "weak" Court to the original game. The Court is "weak" in this version because it can only monitor state action; its only power over state action is the role its judgment serves as a device that communicates otherwise unknown information to the other states. This corresponds to the situation of the states under the 1787 Constitution, with a Court that holds only the power of "judgment." The third version of the model then considers the additional requirements necessary for the existence of the "strong" Court stipulated by the ascendancy hypothesis—a Court with the power to force states to submit to its will when they prefer not to.

A MODEL OF INTERSTATE TRADE WITHOUT A NATIONAL COURT

Assume there are three players: nature and two state governments. The governments are engaged in a repeated game of interstate commerce. Each period starts with nature drawing a cost of compliance for each state government. Nature draws a low cost, c_l, with probability p_l or a high cost, c_h, with probability $1 - p_l$. The actual cost that free trade imposes on intrastate interests is allowed to vary because it will presumably vary over time and in different economic markets.

There are two associated ways to think about these costs. First, in the short run, lowering trade barriers often generates economic and social costs. These costs arise from firms that cannot compete in the newly competitive environment closing down and thereby adversely affecting growth rates and unemployment. Thus, presuming legislators care about short-run economic outcomes in their state, the costs modeled can be considered actual economic and social costs of lowering barriers to trade. Second, these economic and social costs can be thought of as explicitly political costs. If the adversely affected sectors of the economy are politically organized, through business organizations, unions, and/or otherwise, these organized interests presumably would exert political pressure on elected officials. Maintaining free-trade policies thus imposes a political cost on the legislators in each state in the sense that they must forgo supplying protective legislation to intrastate interests that want protection and can affect the political prospects of the legislators.

However conceived, these costs are initially private information to the respective state's government. That is, the other states do not know with certainty how much interstate competition is threatening economic or political interests in other states—they only know with certainty how much it is threatening their own intrastate interests.

Once costs are drawn, the governments simultaneously decide whether to comply with the free-trade regime or to defect and unilaterally impose trade barriers against the other state. Each state receives some benefit, b, if the other state does not impose barriers against it in that period. Once payoffs are realized a discount factor, $\delta \in (0,1)$, is accrued and the next period begins. The discount factor makes future payoffs worth less than payoffs today.

SOLUTIONS TO THE INTERSTATE MODEL

When a game is infinitely repeated, it's a common result (called the "Folk theorem") that there is a large set of achievable equilibria. Anything from never cooperating to always cooperating can occur, depending on the strategies specified. But we believe that some of these equilibria are more likely than others.

If maintaining free trade is always mutually beneficial, $c_h < b$, the Pareto optimal solution (for discussion on the "Pareto optimal solution," see the book appendix) is never to allow defections. Under a whole range of t-period, renegotiation proof punishment strategies, this solution is achievable. For example, if one state imposes trade barriers, a t-period punishment phase is entered. In this punishment phase, the defecting state is expected to comply with the free-trade regime, while the other state punishes the defecting state by not complying. Assuming cooperation is sustainable, this regime ensures perfect compliance and, in expectation, all states are best off. Since there is nothing restricting cheap talk at the beginning of the game, there is no reason the states could not or would not coordinate on this solution. See appendix A to this essay for proof of the equilibrium.

Of course, this scenario is unrealistic. While the benefits of complying with a free-trade regime may exceed the costs most of the time, it is implausible that the benefits always will exceed the costs. Thus, for the rest of the analysis, we consider behavior when low costs are less than benefits, but high costs are greater than benefits, $c_l < b < c_h$.

This modification changes what governments would like to do, but not what they can do. Now governments only want to comply when costs are low. The expected utility of selective compliance, $[p_1(c_l)/1 - \delta]$, exceeds the expected utility of universal compliance, $[p_1(c_l) + (1 - p_1)(c_h)/1 - \delta]$, when $c_l < b < c_h$. Nonetheless, because the costs of compliance are private information, there is no way to tailor the punishment strategy optimally. The governments must punish or not punish independent of the actual costs of compliance. Thus, while the states would like to promote selective compliance, the options are to promote perfect compliance or nothing.

Without the ability to tailor their punishment strategies, the states did not cooperatively sustain free trade. This situation was certainly suboptimal compared to maintaining selective compliance. By definition, the payoff from selective compliance, $[p_1(c_l)/1 - \delta]$, was larger than the payoff from no compliance, 0. In fact, this situation quite possibly was the worst possible outcome for the states. As long as perfect compliance is net beneficial, $[p_1(c_1) + (1 - p_1)(c_h)/1 - \delta > 0]$, the states would have preferred even the unsustainable perfect compliance regime to no compliance. Thus, while the states might have preferred any level of trade regulations to none, the inability to self-enforce a selective compliance regime lead to a Pareto inferior outcome and quite possibly the worst possible outcome.

ADDING A WEAK COURT TO THE MODEL OF INTERSTATE TRADE

One way around the problem of not being able to tailor the punishment strategy to the actual cost of compliance is to create a monitoring mechanism. If the states can create an institution that is capable of evaluating the cost of compliance, they can achieve an equilibrium that Pareto dominates the outcome of the game without a monitoring mechanism.

To add the Court, we modify the model as follows. First, in addition to the two states, assume there are two additional types of actors: the Court and a pair of potential litigants (one per state). The Court is a national institution to which cases are brought, and the litigants are the individuals or groups adversely affected by a state government's decision to impose trade barriers. As before, each state draws a private cost of compliance and then decides whether to defect. But now, if a government chooses to impose a barrier to trade, a potential litigant can dispute the defecting state's action by filing suit in the national Court. Note, while potential litigants are free to bring a case, it is costly for them to do so. Let k_p be the cost to the plaintiff of litigating a case.

If a suit is filed, both sides argue the facts before the Court, and the defecting state's true cost of compliance becomes common knowledge. Once the true cost is known, the Court issues a ruling declaring whether the defecting state has unconstitutionally burdened interstate trade. If it has, then the Court issues a judgment indicating any compensation due from the state to the litigant for the unconstitutional burden.[4]

Finally—and significantly—any state found to have acted unconstitutionally is free to choose whether to comply with the ruling or not. Two costs are associated with this decision. For the government, there potentially is some fixed cost for not paying a judgment, k_j. If $k_j = 0$, it is costless to ignore the Court's ruling, and if $k_j > 0$, it is not costless. For the Court, there is some small fixed cost from having its decision ignored, k_c.[5] Once any judgments that are going to be paid have been paid, δ is accrued, and a new period begins.

Given this game, each actor's strategy sets and payoffs are as follows. State government strategy profiles consist of three elements: a probability of defecting on low costs, $p(D|c_l)$, a probability of defecting on high costs, $p(D|c_h)$, and a maximal size judgment they are willing to pay if caught defecting on cost i, pj_i ($PJ_i = \{pay, not\ pay\}$ for $i = l, h$). Payoffs are a function of the variable cost of compliance, c_l and c_h, the benefit of compliance, b, the cost of judgments paid, j_i, and the cost of not obeying rulings, k_j.

Litigant strategy profiles consist of only one element: a probability (a) with which to bring cases upon observing a defection. Payoffs are a function of the cost of bringing a case, k_p, and the benefit of judgments received, j_i.

Finally, Court strategy profiles consist of four elements: decisions over whether to rule against a government upon observing a defection on a low or a high cost, $r_i = \{constitutional, unconstitutional\}$ for $i = l, h$, and decisions over what size judgment to impose if the Court does rule against a government for a low or high cost defection, $j_i > c_i$ for $i = l, h$. Payoffs are a function of whether the governments comply with the law, whether the governments comply with Court decisions, and some small fixed cost that the Court pays if its decision is ignored (k_c). Unless stated otherwise, we assume the Court wants maximal compliance with the law. That is, the Court wants to maximize instances of compliance independent of the costs of compliance, where an instance is defined to be a government complying with the law ex ante or the government complying with an adverse ruling if caught having defected ex post. Anticipating the results somewhat, we assume these preferences, because we must demonstrate that even when a weak Court wants universal compliance, it can only facilitate selective compliance.

SOLUTIONS TO THE INTERSTATE MODEL WITH A COURT

As before, we know from the Folk theorem that there is a large set of achievable equilibria. Nonetheless, as before, we believe there is good reason to expect certain outcomes. To demonstrate why, we first define what we believe to be the most plausible punishment strategies, and then present the resulting on-equilibrium path behavior.

PUNISHMENT PATH BEHAVIOR. Governments ideally would like to enforce compliance when costs are low, but not when costs are high. Introducing a monitoring mechanism—the Court—allows them to do so. The punishment strategy that best takes advantage of the monitoring mechanism is defined as follows. If a state government is observed defecting on a low cost and that government does not obey an adverse ruling, that government must cooperate for t periods while the government it defected against does not cooperate. If at any point the government being punished does not cooperate, the punishment phase is restarted. No other behavior elicits punishment.[6]

The next two sections provide solutions to the model conditional upon the punishment strategy specified above. For our purposes, it is useful to derive two solutions, one when there is a relatively small fixed cost to ignoring the monitoring mechanism's ruling ($k_j < c_h$) and one where there is a relatively large fixed cost ($k_j > c_h$). When the cost of ignoring a ruling is small, the Court wields only the power of its judgment. When the cost of ignoring a ruling is large, the Court has some extrinsic enforcement mechanism it can rely on to enforce its rulings. We examine the behavior and the outcomes in both equilibria. Doing so permits us to compare the plausibility of both the ascendancy hypothesis and our hypothesis by testing their logical prerequisites and implications against the Court's actual behavior and doctrinal outcomes. The weak-court solution is considered first.

THE WEAK-COURT EQUILIBRIUM. The stage game is solved using subgame perfection. When to pay an adverse judgment, the equilibrium size of any judgments proposed, when to rule against a state government, the probability of a case being brought, and the probability of defecting over high and low costs are derived. Formal statement of this behavior is presented below and discussed subsequently through a series of propositions. Proof is provided in appendix B to this essay. We might underscore at this point that we draw on these observations in the next part of the essay and show that the equilibrium behavior identified in the observations reflects the behaviors respectively permitted or prohibited by the dormant Commerce Clause.

EQUILIBRIUM PATH BEHAVIOR WITH $k_j < c_h$

$$JP_i^* = \begin{cases} pay & \text{if } j_i \leq j_i^* \\ not\ pay & otherwise \end{cases}$$

$$j_i^* \leq \begin{cases} \dfrac{\delta - \delta^{T+1}}{1 - \delta}(p_1(1 - p[D|c_1])b + (1 - p_1)c_h) + k & \text{if } i = l \\ \varnothing & \text{if } i = h \end{cases}$$

$$r_i^* = \begin{cases} constitutional & \text{if } i = l \\ not\ constitutional & \text{if } i = h \end{cases}$$

$$a^* = \frac{c_l}{J_1^*}$$

$$p[D|c_i]^* = \begin{cases} 1 & \text{if } i = h \\[2em] \dfrac{k_j\left(\dfrac{1}{p_l} + 1\right)}{J_l^* - k_j} & \text{if } i = l \end{cases}$$

Observation 1: A government only pays a judgment when the cost of the judgment is less than the cost of ignoring a ruling plus any future punishment from not paying the judgment.

$JP_i^* = pay$ if and only if the size of the judgment is sufficiently small, $j_i \leq j_i^*$.

Observation 2: Since the Court only benefits when rulings are followed, the Court makes sure adverse judgments are sufficiently small.

For low-cost defections, judgments must be small enough that the cost of ignoring the Court's ruling plus the punishment imposed by the other government is greater than the cost of paying the judgment, $j_l^* \leq (\delta - \delta^{T-1}/1 - \delta)(p_l(1 - p[D|c_l])b + (1 - p_l)c_h) + k_j$. For high-cost defections, no adverse judgments are paid. The only cost of not paying a judgment on a high-cost defection is the cost of ignoring the ruling; this cost is less than paying a high cost, and paying the judgment is greater than paying the high cost ($k_j < c_h < j_h$).

Observation 3: As long as the Court experiences any cost from having a ruling ignored, the Court only rules against governments if it anticipates compliance with the judgment.

Since governments only pay adverse judgments on low-cost defections and the Court pays some small cost for having its rulings ignored, the Court only rules against governments on low costs.

Observation 4: Finally, governments are occasionally taken to court, are occasionally ruled against, and always obey the ruling.

Conditional on the above results, the governments and litigants find it optimal to randomize the remaining behavior. Litigants bring cases with a probability that makes governments indifferent over defecting on low costs, $a^* = (c_l/J_1^*)$, while governments always defect over high costs and defect over low costs with a probability that makes the litigants indifferent over bringing cases, $p[D|c_l]^* = [k_j(1/pl + 1)/J_l^* - k_j]$. Litigants make governments indifferent over defecting on low costs by making the probability of being caught on a low-cost defection times the cost of being caught on a low-cost defection equal to the cost of simply not defecting in the first place. Governments make litigants indifferent over bringing cases by making the cost of bringing a case equal to the probability of winning the case times the reward from winning the case.

In sum, when the cost of ignoring a ruling is sufficiently small, the Court can promote selective compliance, but no more. Governments will comply over low costs at least some of the time and obey an adverse Court ruling whenever caught not complying on low costs, but governments will never comply over high costs nor obey an adverse ruling if caught not complying over high costs.

This solution accounts for state support for the shift from the Articles of Confederation to the development of a "selective" or "contingent" dormant Commerce Clause doctrine under the 1787 Constitution. States could not sustain compliance with a free-trade regime among themselves under the Articles of Confederation. By creating a national monitoring mechanism (i.e., the Court) with no more than the power to hear cases and issue rulings, the governments would be able to promote selective compliance. Thus, even with weak institutional powers, the Court could provide the states with a Pareto improving outcome relative to its absence.

THE ASCENDANT (OR STRONG) COURT EQUILIBRIUM. This story changes when we allow the costs of ignoring the Court's ruling to be sufficiently large, $k_j > c_h$. In the previous solution, the behavior that emerges from the game depends solely on the preferences of the governments. This solution entirely depends on the preferences of the Court.

Once more, the stage game is solved using subgame perfection. And again, when to pay an adverse judgment, the equilibrium size of an judgments proposed, when to rule against a government, the probability of a case being brought, and the probability of defecting over high and low costs are derived. Proof is provided in appendix C to this essay.

EQUILIBRIUM BEHAVIOR WITH $k > c_h$

$$PJ_i^* = \begin{cases} pay & \text{if } j_i \leq j_i^* \\ notpay & \text{otherwise} \end{cases}$$

$$j_i^* \leq \begin{cases} \dfrac{\delta - \delta^{T+1}}{1 - \delta}\left(p_l(1 - p[D|c_l])b + (1 - p_l)c_h\right) + k & i = l \\ k & i = h \end{cases}$$

$$r_i^* = unconstitutional \qquad\qquad \begin{aligned} &\text{if } i = 1 \\ &\text{if } i = h \end{aligned}$$

$$a^* = 1$$
$$p[D|c_i]^* = 0 \qquad\qquad\qquad\qquad \text{if } i = l, h$$

Observation 5: A full-compliance regime arises if the Court wants a full-compliance regime.

Unlike the case where $k_j < c_h$ holds, we will no longer see defections from the legal regime. The logic still parallels the weak court solution. As before, a government only pays a judgment when the cost of the judgment is less than the cost of ignoring a ruling plus any future punishment from not paying the judgment. Thus, a judgment is paid if and only if the size of the judgment is sufficiently small, $j_i \leq j_i^*$.

Also as before, since the Court only benefits when judgments are paid, the Court will make sure adverse judgments are sufficiently small. For low-cost defections, the constraint does not change. Judgments against low-cost defections must be small enough that the cost of ignoring a Court ruling plus the punishment that will be imposed by the other government are greater than the cost of paying the judgment. Nonetheless, unlike before, judgments on high-cost defections now will be paid. Since the cost of ignoring a ruling is now larger than the cost of paying a high cost in the first place, judgments less than k_j can be imposed and governments will choose to pay them even though governments will not punish each other for not paying a judgment on a high-cost defection. Knowing judgments will be paid over both high and low costs, the Court is no longer indifferent over ruling against governments on high costs. Now the Court wants to and will rule against governments independent of the costs.

Next, since governments will always be ruled against, as long as the cost of bringing a case, k_p, is sufficiently small, litigants will always bring cases upon observing a defection. The litigant knows that it is assured of winning. Finally, knowing that they will always go to court and always lose, governments will never defect. Since judgments will always be awarded, and judgments are always at least as large as the cost of complying in the first place, it is a strictly dominant strategy for the governments to not defect in the first place.

In sum, if the Court wants universal compliance and the cost to ignoring the Court's ruling is sufficiently large, the Court can get universal compliance independent of government preferences. Of course, this solution assumes the Court wants universal compliance. If the Court only wanted selective compliance, that is what you would observe. In that case, the Court would simply rule against governments only when the Court observed a low-cost situation. Thus, while government preferences determine outcomes when the cost of ignoring a ruling is small, Court preferences determine outcomes when the cost to ignoring the Court's ruling is sufficiently large.[7]

The Doctrinal Strategy of the Dormant Commerce Clause

Above we considered the influence that an institutionally weak Court (which has only the power of judgment) and an institutionally strong Court (that can rely on an extrinsic force to ensure that its rulings are obeyed) could have on interstate trade relations. We demonstrated that both an institutionally weak Court and an institutionally strong Court could promote free trade among the states. So, which model more accurately characterizes the development of DCC doctrine? If the proponents of the ascendancy hypothesis are correct, we should observe behavior consistent with the strong Court model. To wit, the Court should rule against governments with impunity, governments should comply with those rulings, and therefore Court preferences alone should determine the shape of the doctrine. Conversely, if we are correct, we should observe behavior consistent with the weak Court model. The Court should only rule against governments when the Court anticipates governments will comply with the ruling and therefore government preferences should determine the shape of the doctrine.

We believe that the evidence weighs heavily in favor of the weak Court model. To demonstrate why, we develop three lines of argument. First, we reject the notion that merely observing the Court ruling against state governments and those governments complying with the rulings is evidence that a strong Court exists. We do this by demonstrating that the judicial outcomes predicted by our weak Court model are observationally equivalent to those predicted by the ascendancy hypothesis. Next, we demonstrate that the actual DCC doctrine is a partial-compliance regime specifically of the type our weak Court model predicts. States are not supposed to burden interstate trade in general, but exceptions are allowed when the cost of complying with federal law is demonstrably large. Of course, while this finding is consistent with our model, of itself it is not a refutation of the ascendant Court argument. If a majority of the Court was in favor of a partial compliance regime, that is what the ascendant

Court hypothesis predicts we should observe. Thus, the final step of our argument involves demonstrating that a majority of the Court in *Cooley* had sincere preferences for an exclusive DCC, the very position that the Court rejected in that case.

Taken together, the model and the evidence suggest that the DCC is the product of an institutionally weak Court rather than the product of an imperial Court. While a majority of the Court wanted to prohibit states from imposing *any* state burden on interstate commerce, they could not enforce their preferred doctrine and instead strategically adopted a doctrine that allows states conditionally to burden interstate trade.

THE OBSERVATIONAL EQUIVALENCE OF THE WEAK COURT MODEL AND THE ASCENDANCY HYPOTHESIS

The first point concerning the equivalence of the weak Court model and the ascendancy hypothesis is a simple one. It might be argued that observing state officials complying with Court DCC rulings, even when they do not like doing so, is prima facie evidence in support of the ascendant Court hypothesis.[8] As our model demonstrates, this conclusion, while intuitively appealing, is not true. While observing a Court ruling against a government and the government complying with the ruling is consistent with the ascendant court hypothesis (this is our Observation 5 above), it is also consistent with a Court that only has the power of judgment (this is our Observation 4 above). A weak *but strategic* Court only rules against a state government when it anticipates that the government is going to obey the ruling. Thus, one cannot conclude from the mere fact that when the Court announced a ruling, states were observed complying with it that, therefore, the Court was able to impose its will on the state governments whenever it chose to do so.[9]

THE STRATEGIC CONDITIONS OF THE DORMANT COMMERCE CLAUSE

Our second line of argument is that the equilibria of the weak Court model directly imply the actual contours of the DCC doctrine. To demonstrate this requires a brief foray into the doctrinal specifics of the dormant Commerce Clause. We first very briefly sketch the development of the dormant Commerce Clause up to the definitive rejection of an "exclusive" DCC doctrine *Cooley* and the Court's concomitant embrace of a conditional or partial DCC doctrine. We then identify the correspondence between the equilibria identified above and the doctrinal specifics of the dormant Commerce Clause. Specifically, we show that the Court's explicit consideration of the magnitude of state interest in determining the constitutionality of state laws under the DCC directly maps onto the respective "high cost/low cost" equilibria identified in the weak Court model above. When free trade in a market imposes high costs on a state (i.e., when states would realize a sizeable benefit from burdening interstate commerce), the model predicts that the Court will not strike down the law. And corresponding to that, we show that the DCC doctrine dictates that the Court gives state actions a constitutional pass in that situation. But when the costs to a state for sustaining free trade in a market are low, the model predicts that the Court will strike down the law and the state will comply. Corresponding to that, the DCC doctrine requires that the Court strike down state laws in that situation. Below, we more specifically identify the correspondence between the model's predicted behavior and the actual DCC doctrine for both the Court's "balancing test" and for its "almost per se unconstitutional" test.

THE DOCTRINAL RISE OF THE DORMANT COMMERCE CLAUSE. As is well known, the U.S. Constitution expressly grants authority over interstate commerce to Congress. The Constitution does not expressly grant to the Supreme Court a supervisory role over state regulations of interstate commerce when there is no congressional legislation to preempt those regulations. Yet early on, individual Supreme Court justices—notably Chief Justice John Marshall—entertained the possibility that state attempts to regulate interstate commerce were unconstitutional even when their laws did not conflict with specific congressional enactments. While ultimately resting the Court's decision in *Gibbons v. Ogden* on the preemptory effect of a congressional statute, the opinion in the case (written by Marshall) included in dictum that the Court "is not satisfied" that Ogden had persuasively "refuted" the notion that the commerce power was an "exclusive" grant of authority to Congress—and, hence, that states could never constitutionally regulate interstate commerce. Indeed, Justice William Johnson was so persuaded that he rejected the Court's statutory preemption rationale and concurred in judgment by arguing that the state law was unconstitutional because the federal commerce power "must be exclusive" even when unexercised by Congress.

While a number of justices continued to insist on the exclusive nature of congressional commerce authority,[10] the state of the law remained unsettled through the 1840s. No binding majority embraced the position that Congress's commerce power was exclusive. Beginning in *Pierce v. New Hampshire* of *The License Cases* (1847), however, Justice Levi Woodbury began floating an alternative position, arguing that Congress's authority was exclusive only when national uniformity was required in the regulation of interstate commerce, but that is was a nonexclusive, concurrent power when such uniformity was not required. By 1851 a majority of the Court had coalesced around Woodbury's intermediate position (although Woodbury was gone from the Court by that time), and announced that position in *Cooley v. Board of Wardens.* As Peter Hay and Ronald Rotunda observe:

> In its threshold inquiry the Court rejected the notion of an exclusive role for Congress . . . as an untenable doctrine. The Court also declined to adopt a state-directed posture validating all state regulation in the absence of specific Congressional prohibition. It has selected a middle ground, sometimes deciding that the area is appropriately regulated by the several states and at other times deciding that the area may not be regulated at all. (1982, 73)

The Court in *Cooley* did not specify the criteria by which it would distinguish a national as opposed to local subject. Nonetheless, the Court soon evolved the requirements that, in order to pass constitutional muster, a state law that discriminates against interstate commerce must be proven actually to advance a legitimate (i.e., nonprotectionistic) policy purpose and must be necessary to attain that purpose (*Minnesota v. Barber,* 136 U.S. 313 [1890]). More broadly, if a state law does not discriminate against interstate commerce but nonetheless burdens it, the Court will sustain the law only if the benefit of the law is shown to be greater than the cost the law imposes on interstate commerce.[11]

THE MAGNITUDE OF STATE INTEREST AND THE "BALANCING TEST." We consider the broadest doctrine first. That courts consider the costs and benefits of interstate commercial regulations to the states is expressly manifest in what has come to be called the *Pike* "balancing test." It should be underscored that while *Pike v. Bruce Church, Inc.* (397 U.S. 137 [1970]) was decided in 1970, the Court's opinion purports only to summarize and clarify its long-standing balancing test. Justice Potter Stewart wrote for the Court:

> Although the criteria for determining the validity of state statutes affecting interstate commerce have been variously stated, the general rule that emerges can be phrased as follows: Where the statute regulates even-handedly to effectuate a legitimate local public interest, and its effects on interstate

commerce are only incidental, it will be upheld unless the burden imposed on such commerce is clearly excessive in relation to the putative local benefits. If a legitimate local purpose is found, then the question becomes one of degree. And the extent of the burden that will be tolerated will of course depend on the nature of the local interest involved, and on whether it could be promoted as well with a lesser impact on interstate activities. Occasionally the Court has candidly undertaken a balancing approach in resolving these issues, but more frequently it has spoken in terms of "direct" and "indirect" effects and burdens. (*Pike,* 142, citations omitted)

Here the Court weighs the costs and benefits of the state legislation. The greater the benefit to the state relative to the costs imposed on other states (since those other states must assume the cost of the burdened commerce),[12] the more apt the Court is to sustain the burden the state's law places on interstate commerce. (In making the translation between the model and the case law, keep in mind that benefits foregone are the respective costs (high or low) of maintaining a free-trade policy in a given market.)

THE MAGNITUDE OF STATE INTEREST AND THE "ALMOST PER SE UNCONSTITUTIONAL" TEST. Of the class of state laws that burden interstate commerce, there is a subset of laws—those that discriminate against interstate commerce—to which the Court pays particularly close attention.[13] So, while the benefits to the law must still be greater than the costs, for this set of cases the Court applies a heightened form of scrutiny to the state's claims regarding the law. The reason is that these types of laws are much more likely to impose costs greater than local benefits relative to laws that merely burden interstate commerce but that do not discriminate against interstate commerce. Hence, discriminatory legislation lacks the internal check provided by intrastate political processes and makes it much more likely that the costs of discriminatory legislation to other states are greater than the local benefits (Hay and Rotunda 1982, 85; Rogers 1999b, 1101–4). Thus, the Court can more freely strike down discriminatory legislation, confident that the other states will back up its decision and that the discriminating state will not flout its decision.

There are three pertinent elements of the "almost per se unconstitutional" test. First, the discriminating state has the burden of proof. That is, for the discriminatory law to be sustained, the state must provide credible evidence that affirmatively establishes the need for the law. Secondly, the state must prove that the law advances a legitimate state interest. Finally, the state must establish that there is no nondiscriminatory alternative that would achieve the same legitimate purpose (*C & A Carbone, Inc. v. Clarkstown* 511 U.S. 383 [1994], 392).

The requirement that the state's law have a "legitimate" purpose—essentially meaning that state policies cannot pursue protectionistic purposes—exists simply to guarantee positive content to the dormant Commerce Clause doctrine. (If protectionism were a legitimate purpose, then the Court could strike down no state trade barrier.) That a state law that discriminates against interstate commerce must be shown as "necessary" to accomplish the state's purpose again only requires in these particular circumstances that states have no alternative means to achieve a given end than to burden the other states with the cost of its policy.

In summary, the doctrinal contours of the dormant Commerce Clause are directly suggested by the weak Court model. The court expressly compares the magnitude of state benefits to the costs imposed on the rest of the states in applying the balancing test. The Court also weighs the magnitude of state interest in applying the "almost per se unconstitutional" test. The distinction in the latter test is that it applies when state action actually discriminates against interstate commerce (rather than merely burdening it). Because any benefit that a state is likely to receive from directly discriminating against interstate commerce will come directly at the expense of other states, discriminating states bear the heavier burden of proving both the magnitude of their interest and the insufficiency of attaining that interest by other nondiscriminatory means.

The doctrinal intricacies, however, should not obscure the broad contours of the various tests and the direct correspondence between the elements of the various tests and the equilibria of the weak Court model discussed in part two of this essay. To wit, the higher the local benefit to protectionism, ceteris paribus, the more apt the Court is to sustain the state's law. But the higher the local benefit, the more apt the state is to flout an adverse judgment. The rule announced by the Court here is carefully calibrated so that it does not strike down state laws precisely when states would have a sizeable incentive to ignore the Court's ruling. So, too, the greater the cost imposed on other states, ceteris paribus, the greater the incentive the other states have to punish a state burdening interstate commerce, and the Court can credibly strike down the state burden knowing that the offending state will comply with its ruling.

The contours of the DCC doctrine here are calibrated such that the Court makes a decision adverse to a state's law only when a state has the incentive to comply and the other states have the incentive to act in a way to enforce the Court's decision. Thus, observationally, the Court's rulings are always obeyed. But this does not result from the intrinsic power of the Court, or from there somehow being a "norm of compliance" to doctrines that were announced a long time ago. Rather, the Court *appears* strong, because its doctrine is strategically calibrated to strike down state laws only when the other states would back up its decision. When that extrinsic enforcement power is absent, the Court's doctrine prevents the Court from a futile decision that announces the invalidity of a state's law but which would be ignored by the state.

We might underscore here that the doctrinal results discussed in this part of the essay are consistent with our model's predictions even if a majority of justices in *Cooley* preferred an exclusive dormant Commerce Clause doctrine. That is, given the strategic context in which the Court found itself vis-à-vis the states, even if a majority of justices preferred that states always be disbarred from regulating interstate commerce (i.e., even if they preferred an exclusive DCC), these justices would nonetheless act strategically and embrace the weaker, contingent DCC doctrine.

Of course, while the doctrinal specifics of the DCC are remarkably consistent with our model's predictions, we cannot conclude from this evidence that the ascendancy hypothesis is wrong. After all, if the sincere preferences of a majority of the Court supported a partial compliance regime, that is exactly what the ascendancy hypothesis would predict we should observe. In the next section we examine the available evidence over judges' sincere preferences at the time that they announced the conditional doctrine and reject this possibility.

Evidence of a Sincere Preference for Stronger DCC Doctrine by the *Cooley* Majority

We showed above that the equilibria to the weak Court model directly suggest the doctrinal contours of the dormant Commerce Clause. The ascendancy hypothesis has no such direct implication. Nonetheless, the ascendancy hypothesis is consistent with the promulgation of a conditional DCC if the substantive doctrinal preferences of a majority of a "strong Court" supported a conditional rather than an exclusive dormant Commerce Clause doctrine. In this section we show the evidence is just the opposite. The evidence, in fact, suggests that a majority of the justices on the Court in *Cooley* actually supported an exclusive DCC while announcing a conditional DCC in that case. The evidence is this: a majority of justices in *The Passenger Cases* (48 U.S. 144 [1849]) reportedly embraced the doctrine that the authority to regulate interstate commerce rests *exclusively* with the Congress, thereby disbarring states from adopting any such laws.[14] Nonetheless, two years later in *Cooley*, three of these justices defected from their earlier viewpoint and formed a majority around the position that states may conditionally regulate interstate commerce. Let us consider the evidence is somewhat greater detail.

In his concurring opinion in *The Passenger Cases* (there was no majority opinion), Justice James Wayne identified the majority opinion of the justices regarding the exclusivity of authority to regulate interstate commerce:

> [I]t will be well for me to say, that the four judges (McLean, Catron, McKinley, and Grier) and myself who concur in giving the judgment in these cases do not differ in the grounds upon which our judgment has been formed, except in one particular, in no way at variance with our united conclusion; and that is, that *a majority* of us do not think it necessary in these cases to reaffirm, with our brother McLean, what this Court has long since decided, that the constitutional power to regulate "commerce with foreign nations, and among the several States, and with the Indian tribes," *is exclusively vested in Congress, and that no part of it can be exercised by a State.* (410–11, parenthetical comment in original, emphasis added)

Indeed, Wayne's opinion expressly rejected the intermediate position that the Court would adopt two years later.[15] None of the justices listed by Wayne suggested that Wayne had done other than reported their sincerely held preference that states would not regulate interstate commerce. Nonetheless, when called upon to decide *Cooley* just two years later—a case that would pivot around the exclusivity of the interstate commerce power—three of these justices defected and instead embraced the conditional doctrine that has remained the law ever since. It should be underscored that all five justices remained on the Supreme Court and would have constituted a binding majority that could have officially announced a decision that the commerce power was exclusive to Congress.

Thus, a majority of the Court did not embrace this position when it would actually have mattered to the outcome of a case. When it was merely cheap talk, a majority of justices affirmed their sincerely held belief that the commerce power was exclusively vested in Congress and could not be exercised by the states. But when the viewpoint was no longer a matter of cheap talk, and would strike down a state, a majority of the Court—including those who had already been on record in favor of exclusivity—definitively rejected exclusivity and embraced a doctrine that permitted states conditionally to burden interstate commerce. So, the evidence is consistent with the results of our model and with the idea that the Supreme Court strategically adopted a "conditional" dormant Commerce Clause doctrine and is inconsistent with the ascendancy hypothesis.

Conclusion

The states had manifest incentives to reduce barriers to interstate trade. Doing so required the creation of a stronger national government and was one of the main reasons—perhaps *the* main reason—for replacing the Articles of Confederation with the 1787 Constitution. But in this stronger national government, the judiciary was "the least dangerous" branch, whose power lay only in its judgment. It did not, and does not, have the intrinsic authority to enforce its decisions.

Commentators have pointed to the dormant Commerce Clause doctrine as evidence that a powerfully ascendant Supreme Court brought the states to heel, bending them to its will. We disagree with this interpretation of the relationship between the DCC doctrine and judicial power. Our case against this interpretation of the DCC is sustained by three lines of argument. First, we develop a model that generates behavior that is observationally equivalent to the behavior relied on by those holding the ascendancy hypothesis. To wit, our model predicts that states always comply with the Court's rulings when it strikes down state trade barriers. Nonetheless, our Court remains weak and asserts its authority only so far as it is in the states' interests to do so. Even though justices may wish to go further and prevent states from ever burdening interstate commerce, they cannot do so without being embarrassed by noncomplying states. So, they strategically alter their decisions so as to avoid noncompliant behavior by the states. Nonetheless, it should be underscored that our model predicts *observed* compliance with the Court's rulings just as the ascendancy hypothesis does.

Secondly, our model accounts for the particular contours of the dormant Commerce Clause. Specifically, it predicts that the Court can credibly prevent states from burdening interstate commerce when they have little to gain from such burdens, but that the Court will permit states to burden interstate commerce when it is important to them to be able to do so. The model's predictions map onto the conditions under which the Court's DCC doctrine permits states to burden interstate commerce. Our model expressly accounts for the recognition of those conditions by the

Court, while the ascendancy hypothesis does not. At best, the ascendancy hypothesis must regard the conditional DCC as one of several alternatives available to the Court, depending on its underlying preferences. To wit, if the Court had truly evolved into an institution as powerful as suggested by the ascendancy hypothesis, then the Court could have gone all the way and forced the states to comply with a doctrine announcing that interstate regulation is "exclusively" the province of the Congress. That the Court did not do so, in this view, must be because the justices themselves did not believe in the idea that Congress had an exclusive grant of power over interstate commerce, and so they did not choose to assert their full power over the states in disbarring them ever from regulating interstate commerce. That development of the actual DCC doctrine, in this view, is at best no more than a chance alignment of sincere preferences on the part of the justices.

Finally, evidence from *The Passengers Cases,* which were decided just two years before *Cooley,* suggests that the sincere preferences of a majority of justices, in fact, *supported* the view that Congress had exclusive authority over interstate commerce. If this were true, and if the Court were as powerful as suggested by the ascendancy hypothesis, then the Court would have come to a different decision in *Cooley v. Board of Wardens* and would have announced an exclusive DCC doctrine in that case. But the Court announced no such doctrine in *Cooley.* Rather, three justices who had earlier been publicly identified with the "exclusive" DCC viewpoint instead defected and joined a majority that embraced a conditional approach to state burdens on interstate commerce.

Our theory is observationally equivalent to the ascendancy theory in predicting compliance by the states to the Court's DCC decisions. Our theory predicts the particular contours of the DCC doctrine, accounting for the contingencies under which states are permitted by the Court's doctrine to burden interstate commerce and when they are not. Finally, our theory explains why justices would embrace an exclusive DCC doctrine at one point in time (and in a case in which the doctrine did not affect the outcome), yet just two years later would change their allegiances and embrace a conditional doctrine.

The implication of our argument is that the U.S. Supreme Court was historically not quite as powerful as it is often portrayed, even vis-à-vis the states. This does not take anything away from the Court, or deny over two centuries of development in the relationship of the Court to other branches of government and to the states. Rather, the argument serves to underscore the continuing implications of Alexander Hamilton's observation regarding the power of a government institution that does not control the "purse" or "sword." Perhaps even today the lesson is that an institution whose sole power is that of judgment is "powerful" to the extent that its judgments are serviceable to the interests of other government actors, whether they be other branches of the national government or state governments.[16] In any event, our argument at least invites a revised understanding of the rise of the dormant Commerce Clause. It was likely not the product of an imperial judiciary foisting free trade upon recalcitrant states. Rather, the doctrine is more plausibly the product of an institutionally weak Court as it strategically accommodated the conditional interests of the states in free trade.

Appendix A

COOPERATION WITHOUT A COURT

The payoff from complying equals the cost of compliance, c_i, plus the continuation value of remaining on equilibrium path, CV_e^g. Since on-equilibrium path behavior entails perfect cooperation, $CV_e^g = (\delta/1 - \delta)$ $(p_l(-c_l) + (1 - p_l(-c_h)) + b)$. The payoff from defecting equals the continuation value of going on punishment path for t periods before returning to cooperation, $CV_p^g = (\delta - \delta^{t+1}/1 - \delta)(p_l(-c_l) + (1 - p_l)(-c_h)) + (\delta - \delta^{t+1}/1 - \delta) CV_e$. Thus, as long as $-c_h + (\delta/1 - \delta) (p_l(-c_l) + (1 - p_l(-c_h))$ $+ b \geq (\delta - \delta^{t+1}/1 - \delta)(p_l(- c_l) + (1 - p_l) (-c_h)) + (\delta^{t+1}/1 - \delta)(p_l(-c_l) + (1 - p_l(-c_h)) + b)$, perfect cooperation is sustainable. Simplifying yields $(\delta - \delta^{t+1}/1 - \delta) b \geq c_h$. For b and δ sufficiently large, or c_h sufficiently small, perfect cooperation is sustainable.

Appendix B

WEAK-COURT SOLUTION

Assume $k_j < c_h$. Working backward, the first step in the solution is to identify when governments pay adverse judgments. There are two possible scenarios, an adverse judgment on a low-cost defection and an adverse judgment on a high-cost defection. If the government defected on a low cost, the continuation value from paying the adverse judgment equals the cost of the judgment, j_l, plus the payoff from staying on equilibrium path, CV_e^g. Since on-equilibrium behavior here entails always defecting on high costs, probabilistically defecting on low costs, never paying adverse judgments on high costs, paying adverse judgments on low costs, and cases being brought against defecting governments with probability a, the payoff from staying on-equilibrium path is as follows: CV_e^g = $(\delta/1 - \delta)(p_l(p[D|c_l]a(-j_l) + (p[D|c_l](-c_l)))) + (\delta/1 - \delta)(1 - p[D|c_l])b$.

The continuation value from not paying the adverse judgment equals the cost of ignoring a Court ruling, k_j, plus the cost of being on punishment path for t periods before returning to equilibrium path. Since punishment path entails never defecting while being defected against for t periods, the punishment path payoff is $CV_p^g = (\delta - \delta^{t+1}/1 - \delta)(p_l(-c_l) + (1 - p_l)-c_{l_t})) + (\delta^{t+1}/1 - \delta)CV_e$. Paying an adverse judgment on a low-cost defection is a best reply when $-j_l + CV_e^g \geq -k_j + CV_p^g$. Solving for j_l, governments pay when $j_l^* \leq (\delta - \delta^{t+1}/1 - \delta)(p_l(1 - p[D|c_l]b + (1 - p_l)c_h)) + k_j$. Again, this holds for sufficiently large b, c_h, and δ.

If a government defects on a high cost, there is no punishment phase. Thus, the only incentive for a government to pay a high cost is if the cost of going against a ruling, k_j, is sufficiently large. Formally, the continuation value from paying an adverse judgment on a high-cost defection is $-j_h + CV_e^g$, and the continuation value from not paying is $-k_j + CV_e^g$. Solving for when $-j_h + CV_e^g \geq -k_j + CV_e^g$ yields $j_h^* \leq k_j$. Since $j_h > c_h$ must hold and we assumed $k < c_h$, this constraint is never met. So, governments never pay judgment on high-cost defections.

Anticipating what judgments the governments pay, it is a best reply for the court to rule against low-cost defections, issuing a judgment of size j_l^* upon observing a low-cost defection, and not rule against governments upon observing a high-cost defection (because of the positive cost, $k_c > 0$ of being ignored).

Given equilibrium behavior on the judgments, litigants bring cases with a probability that makes governments indifferent over defecting on low costs by making the expected cost of defecting on a low cost equal to the cost of complying, $-c_l = a(-j_l)$. Solving for a yields $a^* = (c_l/j_l^*)$. Because $j_l^* > c_l$ holds, we know $a^* \in (0,1)$.

Finally, the government defects on low costs with a probability that makes litigants indifferent over bringing cases. For a litigant to be indifferent over bringing a case, the expected payoff from bringing a case must equal the payoff from not bringing a case, zero. Thus, $p[c_l|D](j_l^* - k_p) + (1 - p[c_l|D])(-k_p) = 0$ must hold. Using the fact that by Bayes's rule $p(D|c_l) = [p(c_l|D)p_D/p_l]$, that governments always defect over high costs, $p(D|c_h)=1$, and that $p_D = p(D|c_l)p_l + p(D|c_h)(1 - p_l)$, we can solve these equations simultaneously to find $p(D|c_l)$. Doing so yields $p(D|c_l)^* =$

$[k_p(1/p_l) + 1]/(j_l^* - k_p)$. For j_l^* and p_l sufficiently large or k_p sufficiently small, $p(D|c_l)^* \in (0,1)$.

Appendix C

ASCENDENT COURT SOLUTION

Now assume $k_j > c_h$. In this case, start with the high-cost defection. Once again, the only incentive for a government to pay a high cost is if the cost of going against a ruling, k_j, is sufficiently large. And also like before, the continuation value from paying an adverse judgment on a high-cost defection is $-j_h + CV_e^g$, and the continuation value from not paying is $-k_j + CV_e^g$. Solving for when $-j_h + CV_e^g \geq -k_j + CV_e^g$ yields $j_h^* \leq k_j$. However, unlike appendix B, since k_j and j_h are both greater than c_h, and the court sets j_h, this constraint can always be met. Further, since the Court wants to maximize instances of compliance, it will set $j_h < k_j$. Given enforcement over high costs is achievable, for k_p sufficiently small all defections will be brought to Court, all governments will be ruled against, and all governments will pay the judgment.

Notes

1. Section IV of the Articles of Confederation provided that "the people of each State . . . shall enjoy therein all the privileges of trade and commerce, subject to the same duties, impositions, and restrictions as the inhabitants thereof respectively, provided that such restrictions shall not extend so far as to prevent the removal of property imported into any State, to any other State, of which the owner is an inhabitant."

2. Speaking of the old Congress under the Articles of Confederation, as early as 1782 Alexander Hamilton warned of the consequences of the oversight: "[V]esting Congress with the power of regulating trade ought to have been a principal object of the confederation for a variety of reasons. It is as necessary for the purposes of commerce as of revenue." Alexander Hamilton (1782/1987, 477). In 1785 James Madison drafted a set of resolutions regarding foreign trade for the Virginia House of Delegates. The second proposed resolution held: "Resolved, that the unrestrained exercise of the powers possessed by each State over its own commerce may be productive of discord among the parties to the Union; and that Congress ought to be vested with authority to regulate the same in certain cases." (James Madison 1785/1987, 482).

3. The Commerce Clause "grew out of the abuse of the power by the importing States in taxing the non-importing, and was intended as a negative and preventive provision against injustice among the States themselves, rather than as a power to be used for the positive purposes of the General Government, in which alone, however, the remedial power could be lodged." (James Madison 1829/1987, 521).

4. The "judgment" here is the return of the tax or penalty (see, e.g., *Cooley v. Board of Wardens,* 53 U.S. 299 [1951]) plus a possible contempt citation for disobeying the court's judgment. Further, losing the case means that the state politicians face the displeasure of the interest group that sought the protective law in the first place.

5. Note that this cost can be arbitrarily small. It just must be other than zero.

6. Note that this punishment strategy will not ensure perfect compliance on low costs. Rather, this strategy ensures maximal compliance over low costs, conditional on no compliance over high costs. Even with a monitoring mechanism, in this game, it is impossible to ensure perfect compliance over low costs without also requiring compliance over high costs. And if governments want to simply require perfect compliance, there is then no need to rely on a monitoring mechanism. Thus, we assume the punishment strategy is tailored to maximizing low-cost compliance while not leading to any high-cost compliance.

7. Technically, we do not observe governments being ruled against and complying in this game. Nonetheless, if there is any uncertainty over whether a government really complied with the law or not, we would observe governments being taken to court, ruled against, and obeying those rulings with a positive probability. A version of this model is solved in Carrubba (2002b). Proof can be provided upon request.

8. This is not to ignore the important issue of implementation and the ability of states to circumvent judicial rulings. Rather, we only argue our model predicts no more open flouting of judicial rulings than does the ascendancy theory, so the lack of such a phenomenon does not confirm the claims of the ascendancy theory as against our model.

9. This intuitive, but mistaken, claim has been made in other literatures as well. For example, Stone Sweet and Brunell (1998) argue that observing European Union (EU) member state governments complying with adverse European Court of Justice (ECJ) rulings is prima facie evidence that EU governments are constrained to obey ECJ rulings. See Carrubba (2002a, 2002b) for applications of the weak-Court model to the ECJ.

10. For example, Justice Joseph Story, in dissent in *New York v. Miln* (36 U.S. 102 [1837]), argued that "The power given to congress to regulate commerce with foreign nations, and among the states, has been deemed exclusive; from the nature and objects of the power, and the necessary implications growing out of its exercise. Full power to regulate a particular subject implies the whole power, and leaves no residuum; and a grant of the whole to one, is incompatible with a grant to another of a part" (158, 1837).

11. The different treatment of discriminatory and nondiscriminatory regulation is justified by appeal to a "political process" rationale. James Rogers (1999b) shows that the Court evolved doctrinal standards of how strictly to review state regulations of interstate commerce that were calibrated to the likelihood that an inefficient policy would be generated by the state's policy process. The doctrine the Court finally evolved essentially mimicked the Pareto criterion for efficiency.

12. The Court expressly weights costs and benefits. See, e.g., *Southern Pacific Co. v. Arizona* (325 U.S. 761 [1945]) and *Kassel v. Consolidated Freightways Corp* (450 U.S. 662 [1981]).

13. While all laws that discriminate against interstate commerce necessarily burden interstate commerce, the reverse is not true—state laws may burden interstate commerce without necessarily discriminating against interstate commerce.

14. Four of these justices did not believe that the dormant Commerce Clause was

implicated in the case, so that identification of that majority would not constitute binding precedent.

15. "Some of the judges of it have, in several cases, expressed opinions that the power to regulate commerce is not exclusively vested in Congress. But they are individual opinions, without judicial authority to overrule the contrary conclusion, as it was given by this Court in Gibbons v. Ogden" (411).

16. In a similar spirit, see also, for example, Rogers (2001b) argument that Congress tolerates judicial independence because of the informational contribution that judicial review makes to the policy process, a contribution that is often valuable to the policy interests of congressional majorities.

Strategic Games within the Judicial Hierarchy | **2**

A Court of Appeals in a Rational-Choice Model of Supreme Court Decision Making

THOMAS H. HAMMOND, CHRIS W. BONNEAU,
AND REGINALD S. SHEEHAN

The Supreme Court's place at the top of a judicial hierarchy is no guarantee that the lower courts will automatically follow its decisions. This means that compliance and implementation by lower courts is problematic, especially in light of the relative handful of cases heard by the Supreme Court compared to many thousands of cases passing through the lower courts, almost none of which will ever be reviewed by the Supreme Court. This paper develops a formal model of lower-court interactions with the Supreme Court. A key issue, it turns out, is whether the Supreme Court wants to comply with its own previous decisions. If the Court's composition has changed or if some of the justices' policy preferences have changed, some Court majority may prefer to modify the Court's previous policy if some appeals court decision provides the opportunity. So if an appeals court does not follow some previous Supreme Court policy, this appeals court is not necessarily being noncompliant; a majority on the new Supreme Court might actually prefer the appeals court's new policy to the old Supreme Court policy. For this reason, understanding the conditions under which the Court itself will maintain, or modify, its own previous decisions is critical to understanding the issue of appeals court compliance. The results from this model help clarify this critical issue.

Supreme Court justices—or at least the reigning majorities in cases—expect lower courts to cite, uphold, and implement their decisions. These expectations are clearly important. While the Supreme Court hears only a few dozen cases each year, the lower courts hear many thousands, and if the lower courts ignore Supreme Court decisions, those decisions will not become the law of the land in any practical sense. Hence, the question: How can the justices ensure that the lower courts will actually comply with the Supreme Court's decisions?

Early research concluded that there was a high degree of lower-court compliance with Supreme Court decisions (see, e.g., Baum 1978, Manwaring 1972, Songer and Sheehan 1990, Tarr 1977). However, this literature focused only on salient cases that were likely to receive Court scrutiny: anticipating higher-level review, lower-court judges may have been more likely to comply with Supreme Court decisions. But it may be less likely that the Supreme Court will review less salient lower-court decisions. Hence, the lower courts may have retained some freedom to pursue their own preferred policies, though how much freedom they actually had remained unclear.

Recognizing the potentially problematic nature of the Supreme Court's relationships with the lower courts, judicial scholars have increasingly resorted to the language of "principal-agent" theories. From this perspective (see, e.g., Songer, Segal, and Cameron 1994), the Supreme Court serves as the "principal," which has ultimate formal authority to make judicial decisions, and the lower courts serve as the "agents," which are supposed to make their own decisions in accordance with what the principal wants. However, as analysis of the economic theories of principal-agent relationships makes clear (see, e.g., Miller 1992), there are limits on the extent to which any principal is able to control its agents.

Several variables affect the extent of such control. One factor in many principal-agent relationships is *asymmetric information*. For example, if it is costly for the principal to determine what actions the agent has taken, the agent may be able to take actions that diverge from what the principal wants. However, asymmetric information is probably not a significant factor in relationships between the Supreme Court and the lower courts. For any one case, the members of the Court are normally able to discover, at a rather small cost, what actions the lower court has taken. This is because lower-court decisions and other information relevant to these cases must be publicly reported or otherwise made available to the Court. This makes it relatively easy for the justices, or at least their clerks, to find out what a lower court has actually done.

Another factor in many principal-agent relationships is that principals have *limited time and energy*. For example, while it may be easy for a Supreme Court justice or clerk to find out what happened in any one case, the fact that the lower courts decide thousands of cases every year places limits on what the justices can discover about the extent to which Supreme Court decisions are being implemented *in the aggregate*. In fact, by trying to understand what happened in any one lower-court case, the justices and their clerks are thereby reducing the time and energy they have available for examining the remaining cases. So, even if a lower court makes a decision at variance with some previous Supreme Court ruling, the chances may be relatively small that the Court will actually review and overturn that decision.

A third factor in some principal-agent relationships is that the principal is a *multimember body,* and the need for agreement among these members may constrain what actions they are collectively able to take in response to some action by the agent. For example, the Supreme Court has nine members and uses majority rule to adopt new legal policies. This means that any justice's desire to limit, modify, or overturn a lower-court decision must be able to gain the support of a Court majority. If no Court majority can be mobilized against the lower court decision, the decision will stand.

These problems facing the principal—asymmetric information, limited time and energy, and the difficulty for a multimember body to mobilize a collective response—can all limit the extent to which the principal is able to control the agent's actions. Indeed, for each of these "control problems" for the principal, there is likely to be an "evasion strategy" for the agent who wants to avoid being controlled. But while various kinds of lower-court strategies have been examined by the literature on compliance (see, e.g., Caminker 1994, Canon and Johnson 1999, Manwaring 1972, Songer and Sheehan 1990, Tarr 1977), this literature has not developed an explicit principal-agent theory of lower-court/Supreme Court interactions for use in developing a systematic understanding of the lower courts' evasion strategies. This lack of a systematic understanding of lower-court strategies means that it is not clear on what variables empirical research should focus when examining lower-court compliance with Supreme Court decisions.

Since there are at least three different kinds of control problems, this suggests that there could be at least three distinct theories of lower-court/Supreme Court interaction. This essay focuses on just the third kind of control problem: the need for the justices to construct a Court majority before they can respond to a lower-court decision. We focus on this last problem, because it most likely is the most intractable of the three. For example, we have already suggested that asymmetric information is probably not a significant factor in Supreme Court interactions with the lower courts. And for the justices' time-and-energy constraints, the justices could at least be imagined as being given the administrative resources to overcome more of these constraints and thereby supervise the lower courts more effectively. However, the nine-member Supreme Court cannot be as easily imagined as abandoning its reliance on majority rule as the basis for its decision making.

In this essay, then, we develop a formal model of lower-court inter-actions with the Supreme Court for use in determining the extent to which a lower court can make decisions that affect how, or even whether, a Supreme Court majority is able to respond.

In previous work—see Thomas Hammond, Chris Bonneau, and Reginald Sheehan (2005)—we developed a formal model of what decisions rational policy-maximizing justices should be expected to make in the Supreme Court's multistage decision-making process. This initial model includes the Supreme Court but no lower courts. The model shows that the final opinion adopted by the Court depends on a complex interaction between the policy preferences of the justices and the location of the status quo policy, that is, the Court's previously adopted policy, in relation to the justices' policy preferences. We extend this initial model by incor-porating a federal appeals court. For simplicity we assume just one appeals court judge, rather than a three-judge panel or the appeals court en banc, who makes the appeals court's decision. However, the general character of our results is not greatly affected if a multimember appeals court is con-sidered.

The construction of a formal model usually relies on some previously developed general understanding of the institution or process under in-vestigation. However, one of the most basic questions about the appeals courts has received remarkably little consideration. If an appeals court de-cision is appealed to the Supreme Court and the Court grants certiorari, does the *content* of the appeals court's decision influence the final decision the Supreme Court makes? In an effort to clarify some of the different kinds of interactions that appear to be possible between an appeals court and the Supreme Court, we develop three somewhat different versions of our model.

These three versions of our model fall into two different categories, de-pending on whether there is a clear and explicit Supreme Court precedent on the issue at hand in a case.

We develop the first two versions of our model for cases in which there is already an explicit Supreme Court policy. One version of our model re-flects what we call a "minimalist" perspective regarding appeals court influ-ence on the Supreme Court. From this perspective, an appeals court deci-sion merely provides an opportunity for Supreme Court justices to involve themselves in some case; in effect, what is assumed to matter to the justices is only that an appeals court made *some* decision—*any* decision—which was then appealed to the Supreme Court. This appeals court decision al-lows the justices to decide whether they want to give the case their full attention (by granting certiorari), and if the justices choose to hear the case, the minimalist perspective implies that they will completely disregard the content of the appeals court's decision when composing their own. After all, the Supreme Court is the principal, not the agent, so why should the justices feel constrained by what particular policy an appeals court endorsed in its decision? Thus, the justices' key concern is assumed to be whether they can craft a new policy that some Court majority prefers to the previous Court policy that is relevant to the case under consideration.

As it turns out, our initial model of Supreme Court decision making (with no lower court) can also be seen as representing the minimalist perspective on appeals court/Supreme Court interactions; because the content of the appeals court decision is, from this perspective, assumed to be irrelevant to the Court, the appeals court does not have to be explicitly incorporated in the first version of our model. All that is needed for the minimalist version of the model is an exogenous statement that an appeals court has made a decision on the case and that the Supreme Court will have an opportunity to review the case; decision making on the case can then proceed as in our initial model of Supreme Court decision making.

The second version of our model reflects more of a "maximalist" perspective on the appeals court's influence—or at least *potential* influence—on the Supreme Court's decision. Unlike the minimalist version, the maximalist version does require explicit incorporation of an appeals court. From the maximalist perspective, if an appeals court makes a decision that deviates from the Supreme Court's previous policy, what the appeals court is actually doing is implementing a new legal policy, though just in its own circuit, in place of the Supreme Court's previous policy. An appeal of the appeals court decision means that the Supreme Court is being forced to confront a new legal state of affairs involving the new policy the appeals court is implementing in its own circuit; since this new policy was *unilaterally* established by the appeals court, this is why we use the term "maximalist" to describe this version of our model. Some of the justices may approve of this new legal state of affairs—that is, they may approve of the new policy the appeals court is implementing in its own circuit—and want to have the Court enshrine this new legal state of affairs as explicit policy for the rest of the country. Other justices may disapprove of the new policy implemented by the appeals court in its circuit and want the Supreme Court's previous policy restored in that circuit. Of course, it may turn out (perhaps because of a deliberate appeals court strategy) that the Court is unable to muster a majority to overturn the appeals court decision. Thus, the justices' key concern here is whether they can craft a new policy that some Court majority prefers to the new legal state of affairs created by the appeals court's decision.

The maximalist version of our model shows that the outcome of the interaction between the appeals court judge and the Supreme Court depends not only on the policy preferences of the justices and the location of the previous Court policy (as in the minimalist version) but also on the preferences of the appeals court judge and the content of her decision. We show that under some preference configurations, the appeals court judge can, by endorsing her own most-preferred policy in her decision, thereby induce the Supreme Court to endorse her most-preferred policy as well; under other configurations, the best the appeals court judge can do is to endorse a policy that induces the Court to adopt the median justice's most-preferred policy; and under still other configurations, no matter what policy the appeals court judge endorses, the Court will adopt a policy at the ideal point of the justice writing the majority opinion. Despite the maximalist label for this version of our model, then, what policy the appeals court judge endorses in her decision actually has a rather variable impact on what policy the Supreme Court finally adopts.

These first two versions of our model presume that there is an explicit Supreme Court policy to which the appeals court is responding. However, for some kinds of issues, there may not be any clear and explicit Court policy. New issues of public law do occasionally arise (e.g., Internet law) that are not clearly governed by previous Court decisions or by any existing statute. For this kind of issue, then, an appeals court decision is clearly making new law. Thus, the question for the third version of our model is whether there exists some Supreme Court majority that can replace this appeals court decision with some policy of its own. The third version, like the second version, also generates a mixed picture of the influence the appeals court has on Supreme Court decisions. Under some conditions, the appeals court judge can ensure that her most-desired policy is affirmed by the Court, but under other conditions, the ideal point of either the median justice or the majority opinion writer will be chosen by the Court.

While our essay focuses primarily on appeals court *influence on* Supreme Court decision making, the three versions of our model clarify some important aspects of appeals court *compliance with* previous Supreme Court decisions. A key issue, it turns out, is whether the Supreme Court itself wants to comply with previous Court decisions. If the composition of the Court has changed, for example, or if some of the justices' policy preferences have changed, some Court majority may prefer to modify the Court's previous policy if some appeals court decision provides the opportunity. So if an appeals court does not comply with some previous Supreme Court policy, this appeals court should not necessarily be charged with noncompliance; a majority on the new Supreme Court might actually prefer the appeals court's new policy to the old Supreme Court policy. For this reason, understanding the conditions under which the Court itself will maintain, or modify, its own previous decisions is critical to understanding the issue of appeals court compliance. The results from our model help clarify this critical issue.

To develop these results, we structure the essay as follows. In the second part, we present the basic definitions and assumptions for all three versions of our model of appeals court interactions with the Supreme Court. The third part presents the results from the minimalist version of our model, the fourth part presents the results from the maximalist version, and the fifth part presents the results from the third version. The sixth part examines what happens when we modify a key assumption common to all versions of our model. The seventh part concludes the paper by discussing some issues involving empirical tests of the various versions of our model.

Definitions and Assumptions

All three versions of our model are based on the same fundamental set of assumptions and definitions. Referring to the appeals court judge and the Supreme Court justices simply as "actors," we begin with the following assumptions:

Assumption 1: Each actor has a most-preferred policy among the legal policies the Supreme Court might consider on a case.

Assumption 2: Each actor's sole objective is to have the Supreme Court adopt a policy as close as possible to his or her most-preferred policy on a case.

We also make an assumption about the issue space over which these actors have their preferences:

Assumption 3: Supreme Court policymaking on a case takes place in a one-dimensional issue space.[1]

Since each actor is assumed to have a policy he or she most desires (Assumption 1), this means that there is a point on the issue dimension (Assumption 3) that the actor prefers over any other point on the line. The following term is normally used in the spatial modeling literature here:

Definition 1: An actor's *ideal point* is his or her most-preferred point on the issue dimension in a case.

Thus, if an actor could unilaterally select the policy the Court adopts in some case, the actor would choose a policy at his or her ideal point. The ideal points of the justices on the issue dimension will be labeled J_1 for justice 1, J_2 for justice 2, and so forth. The ideal point of the median justice on the Court will be labeled J_{med}, and the ideal point of the chief justice will be labeled J_{CJ}.

Each actor is assumed to have a utility function generating utilities that *decrease monotonically* as policies diverge in either direction from the actor's ideal point. This relationship between the locations of the policies and how much each actor values the policies can be summarized as follows:

Assumption 4: Each actor has a utility function that is *single-peaked* on the issue dimension in a case.

That is, on the single issue dimension for a case, each actor considers policies that are farther and farther leftward from his or her ideal point, or farther and farther rightward, to be less and less desirable.

Among the policies on the issue dimension is the *status quo policy,* labeled SQ. For the minimalist version of our model, the status quo policy is simply some explicit Supreme Court policy, previously adopted, that the Court may or may not wish to modify, given the case currently under consideration.

For the maximalist version of our model, while the initial status quo policy is again some explicit and previously adopted Supreme Court policy, an appeals court may have issued a ruling on some case that creates a new legal policy in its own circuit. The legal state of affairs for the country will now exhibit a composite pattern: (a) there will be a new legal policy in the circuit of the appeals court that issued the new ruling, and (b) the previous Supreme Court policy will continue to hold in the rest of the country.[2] The key question here is how the Supreme Court will respond to this new legal state of affairs created by the appeals court. If the Supreme Court refuses an appeal of this appeals court ruling, this composite pattern will then persist as the legal state of affairs in the country.[3] If the Court reverses the appeals court ruling, the Court's previous policy will have been reestablished throughout the country. If the Court affirms the appeals court ruling, the appeals court ruling will have been established as explicit Court policy for the whole country. And if the Court modifies the appeals court ruling, this modification of the appeals court ruling will have been established as explicit Court policy for the whole country.

For the third version of our model, because there exists no previous Supreme Court policy, the initial status quo policy is actually established by the appeals court when it makes its decision. If this decision is appealed, each justice will then try to have the Court adopt an alternative policy that is as close as possible to his or her own ideal point.

Throughout our analysis, we will use the following terminology to refer to the set of policies a justice prefers to the status quo policy:

Definition 2: A justice's *preferred-to set of the status quo* is the set of policies the justice prefers to the status quo policy.

Similarly, we will want to refer to the set of policies a majority of justices prefer to the status quo:

Definition 3: The *win-set of the status quo* is the set of policies that is preferred to the status quo policy by a majority of justices on the Court.

For instance, given a five-member Court, if there is a set of points a majority, such as justices 1, 2, and 3, prefers to SQ, we will refer to this win-set as $W_{J1J2J3}(SQ)$. If there is a set of points less than a majority of justices prefer to SQ, we will use the same notation as for a win-set. Thus, justice 1's preferred-to set of SQ will be indicated by $W_{J1}(SQ)$, and if there is a set of points justices J_1 and J_2 both prefer to SQ, their joint preferred-to set is indicated by $W_{J1J2}(SQ)$.

In our graphical illustrations we depict a justice's preferred-to set by a horizontal, downward-facing bracket. In figure 1, for example, given an SQ on the issue dimension, we show the preferred-to set for each of the five justices, J_1 through J_5. One bracket shows the set of points that J_1 prefers to SQ, or $W_{J1}(SQ)$; a second bracket shows the set of points that J_2 prefers to SQ, or $W_{J2}(SQ)$; and so forth.

Note that the boundary of a justice's preferred-to set on the side away from SQ indicates the policy that, for the justice, produces an amount of utility equivalent to that produced by SQ. For example, justice J_3 in figure 1 is *indifferent* between SQ and a policy at the left-hand boundary of $W_{J3}(SQ)$. Thus, a preferred-to set of SQ contains only those policies the actor *prefers to* SQ. Since the actor is indifferent between SQ and the policy at the other end of the preferred-to set, this policy at the other end is *not* included in the preferred-to set.

Note also in figure 1 that in the region where these brackets overlap

FIGURE 1 Preferred-to sets and win-sets for five justices

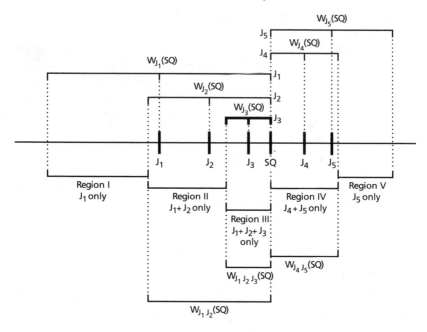

(one above the other), the number of brackets that overlap tells us how many justices prefer the set of points in the overlapping region to SQ. For example, what we have labeled Region I indicates the set of points that only J_1 prefers to SQ. Region II indicates the set of points that only J_1 and J_2 prefer to SQ. Region III indicates the set of points that only J_1, J_2, and J_3 prefer to SQ. Region IV indicates the set of points that only J_4 and J_5 prefer to SQ. And Region V indicates the set of points that only J_5 prefers to SQ. This simple diagrammatic device—how many of these bracket-lines overlap each other for any given portion of the line?—will be useful in showing how many justices prefer some policy to SQ.

We must occasionally refer to policies that are farther from the status quo policy than some win-set or preferred-to set. We will use the word "outside" to refer to these particular policies:

Definition 4: The policies and justices that lie "outside" a win-set or a preferred-to set are those policies or justices with both of the following features:
(a) they are on same side of SQ as the win-set or preferred-to set; and,
(b) they are farther from SQ than the win-set or preferred-to set.

Thus, in figure 1, it is the policies to the left of $W_{J3}(SQ)$ that will be said to lie "outside" $W_{J3}(SQ)$.

We will also use a related term, "minority-side":

Definition 5: A "minority-side" policy or justice lies on the side of SQ that contains only a minority of the justices' ideal points.

Thus, in figure 1, justices J_4 and J_5 are the minority-side justices, and the minority-side policies are those that lie to the right of SQ.

When there are no policies a justice prefers to SQ, this means that his or her preferred-to set is empty. A justice has an empty preferred-to set of SQ only when his or her ideal point is identical to SQ. Similarly, when a majority of justices have no points they all prefer to SQ, this means that their win-set of SQ is empty; this will happen when SQ lies at or between the ideal points of two or more of these justices.

The total number of justices will be denoted by J, and a bare majority of the J justices will be denoted by *maj*. We assume that there is an odd number of justices (as with the Supreme Court), and when there is an odd number of justices, *maj* can be computed from a simple formula: *maj* = $(J + 1)/2$. While for reasons of diagrammatic clarity our illustrations all involve just five Supreme Court members (i.e., J = 5, so *maj* = 3), our model holds for a Court of any size, including nine members.

We will be constructing what the formal modeling literature generally calls a "perfect information" model. For such a model, the following assumption holds:

Assumption 5: Each actor knows the ideal point of every other actor, and all actors know and understand what the decision-making procedures are.

Our rationale for assuming that the justices know each others' ideal points stems from the justices' close working relationships; on the current Court, for example, several of these relationships extend back many years. It may thus be possible for the justices to make relatively accurate predictions of the locations of each others' ideal points on any one case; this would allow each justice to make relatively accurate predictions of the consequences of any particular choice he or she might make at each stage of the decision-making process. Moreover, because many justices serve on the Court for many years, it should also be possible for appeals court judges to determine, with a substantial degree of accuracy, what the views of the Supreme Court justices are likely to be on many legal issues of mutual interest. In fact, of all our national decision-making institutions, it may be for the Supreme Court and the appeals courts that these perfect-information conditions, often assumed in formal modeling, are most closely approximated.

We assume that the appeals court judge and the Supreme Court justices are rational. The standard definition of "rationality" is that a rational justice attempts to gain Supreme Court adoption of a policy as close as possible to his or her own ideal point. Since the Court's decision-making process has multiple stages, we can make the following assumption:

Assumption 6: Each actor will make those choices at each stage of the decision-making process that help ensure that a policy as close as possible to the actor's ideal point will be approved by a majority of the Supreme Court justices on the final vote.

This is precisely what Lee Epstein and Jack Knight (1998) argue that a "strategically rational" justice would do. Hence, our general view (in agreement with Epstein and Knight) is that if an actor is "rational," this implies that the actor will be "strategically rational" as well.

On occasion, strategic rationality may force the justice to make decisions at the earlier stages that go against what the justice would do if he or she were the sole decision maker for the Court. For example, consider an appeals court ruling that is more "conservative" than current Court policy. A "liberal" justice would thus want to overturn this conservative ruling and restore the status quo ante. However, if this liberal justice expects that the Court as a whole would actually uphold the conservative appeals court ruling, thereby enshrining it as official policy for the entire country (and not just for the circuit of the appeals court that made the ruling), he would rationally vote *not* to grant certiorari on the case; this is what has been called "defensive denial" in the literature. Rational behavior will thus sometimes require the justice to reject options he would otherwise support if he were the sole judicial decision maker, or require that he endorse options he would otherwise prefer to reject.

While our initial model of Supreme Court decision making (Hammond, Bonneau, and Sheehan 2005) involves all five stages of the Court's five-stage decision-making process (involving first certiorari, then the original vote on the merits, then opinion assignment, then coalition formation, and then the final vote on the merits), for the purposes of this essay we simplify development and presentation of our initial model of Supreme Court decision making in three ways. First, we focus primarily on what policy would be adopted at the final stage, and since coalition formation and the final vote are so closely intertwined, we analyze them together. Second, we assume that the chief justice will always be the opinion assignor; according to standard Court procedures, he can become the opinion assignor simply by voting with the majority on the original vote on each case, and he would have an incentive to do this because he can best advance his own policy goals by controlling the opinion assignment.[4] This is a simplifying assumption and does not affect our results in any substantial fashion. Third, we assume that there is another justice with an ideal point that is the same as that of the chief justice; this allows the chief justice to avoid self-assignment and still get an opinion that is identical to what he would write himself. Despite these simplifications, the resulting model still allows us to develop a sound understanding of the strategic relationships between the appeals court and the Supreme Court.

In the next three sections we use this library of concepts, assumptions, and notational and diagrammatic tools to model the appeals court judge's interactions with the Supreme Court.

Version 1: The Minimalist Model of Appeals Court/Supreme Court Interactions

In the minimalist perspective on the role of the appeals court, the Supreme Court justices view the appeals court decision merely as an opportunity to get involved in a case, should enough justices desire. In fact, as we have already noted, our initial model of Supreme Court decision making, with no appeals court, can also serve as the minimalist version of our model of appeals court/Supreme Court interactions.

We begin with a series of propositions characterizing the relationship between the location of SQ and the location of J_{med}, the ideal point of the median justice. This relationship has a critical impact on what majority opinion will be written and on what the final vote will be on this opinion. We standardize our illustrations of these propositions by presuming that J_{med} is always located to the left of SQ.

We begin by noting that if SQ is located at J_{med}, SQ cannot be replaced by any other policy. The reason is that upsetting SQ requires at least *maj* votes from justices who would agree to replace SQ with some other policy. But if SQ is at J_{med}, there will be at most *maj* − 1 justices to the left of SQ who want to replace SQ with some policy to its left, and at most *maj* − 1 justices to the right of SQ who want to replace SQ with some policy to its right. We can summarize this argument as follows:

FIGURE 2 If SQ is at the median justice's ideal point, SQ cannot be upset

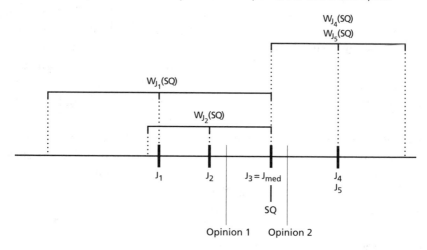

Proposition 1: If SQ is at J_{med}, there exists no policy that a majority of justices prefer to SQ.

To illustrate, consider figure 2, in which SQ is located at the ideal point of justice J_3, the median justice (so $J_3 = J_{med}$). Assume that Opinion 1 has been proposed. While it lies inside the preferred-to sets of two justices, J_1 and J_2, three votes are needed for it to replace SQ. Similarly, if Opinion 2 has been proposed, three votes are needed for it to replace SQ, but it lies inside the preferred-to sets of only two justices, J_4 and J_5. In neither case, then, can SQ be upset.

In contrast, if SQ is not located at J_{med}, SQ can be upset:

Proposition 2: If SQ is not at J_{med}, there exists a set of policies— $W_{Jmed}(SQ)$—that a majority of justices prefer to SQ.

When SQ is not at J_{med}, the existence of this set of policies—$W_{Jmed}(SQ)$— always gives a majority an opportunity to replace SQ with some other policy. However, $W_{Jmed}(SQ)$ also acts as a constraint on what proposals could gain majority support over SQ; in particular, the right-hand and left-hand boundaries of $W_{Jmed}(SQ)$ are the boundaries of the set of feasible replacement policies.

These arguments about J_{med} and $W_{Jmed}(SQ)$ have a further implication:

Proposition 3: If the median justice, at J_{med}, prefers some proposal to SQ, this means that there will also be a majority of justices (i.e., there will be at least *maj* − 1 other justices) who prefer this proposal to SQ; if the median justice, at J_{med}, prefers SQ to some proposal, this means that there will also be a majority of justices (i.e., there will be at least *maj* − 1 other justices) who prefer SQ to this proposal.

Hence, we can assert the following:

Proposition 4: Support of the median justice is both *necessary* and *sufficient* for SQ to be replaced by some other policy within $W_{Jmed}(SQ)$.

In addition, the following is also implied:

Proposition 5: The preferred-to set of SQ of a justice will be contained by the preferred-to set of SQ of each justice whose ideal point lies outside the first justice's ideal point.

And this next proposition immediately follows:

Proposition 6: $W_{Jmed}(SQ)$ will be contained by the preferred-to set of SQ of each justice whose ideal point lies outside J_{med}.

To illustrate propositions 2 through 6, consider figure 3, in which SQ is not located at J_{med}. First consider Opinion 1 at the point labeled "*" at the left end of the $W_{Jmed}(SQ)$ bracket. Because Opinion 1 lies inside $W_{Jmed}(SQ)$, and because $W_{Jmed}(SQ)$ lies inside $W_{J1}(SQ)$ and $W_{J2}(SQ)$, this means that Opinion 1 could gain the support of a Court majority— J_1, J_2, and J_3—to replace SQ. Opinion 2 at J_{med} could also gain the three

FIGURE 3 Only opinions inside $W_{Jmed}(SQ)$ can upset SQ

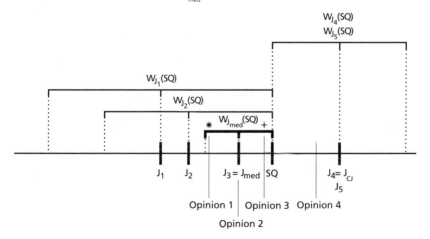

votes necessary to replace SQ, as could Opinion 3 at the point labeled "+" at the right end of the $W_{Jmed}(SQ)$ bracket. In contrast, consider Opinion 4, which lies on the minority side. Since it lies inside the preferred-to sets of only two justices—J_4 and J_5—it could not gain the necessary three votes to upset SQ. In this case, then, SQ could be upset by Opinions 1, 2, and 3—or any other policy in $W_{Jmed}(SQ)$—but not by Opinion 4.

The analysis has focused thus far on the sets of policies that various justices prefer to the status quo, but nothing has indicated precisely what final policy would be adopted in place of SQ. It turns out that how these dissatisfied justices respond to the majority opinion can have a significant impact on what final policy is selected by the Court. For all three versions of our model, then, we will make the following critical assumption:

Assumption 7: Each justice who is not the majority opinion writer will respond *passively* to the majority opinion writer's draft opinion; in particular, if the draft opinion is better than SQ for a justice, he or she will simply join the opinion, and if the draft opinion is worse than SQ for a justice, he or she will simply write or join a dissent.

This assumption means that the justices who are not the majority opinion writer will not actively try to gain support for some alternative to the draft majority opinion. That is, they will treat their own decision-making agenda as containing just two options: SQ and the majority opinion writer's draft opinion. In effect, the justices are voluntarily ceding control of the Court's decision-making agenda to the majority opinion writer. Hence, we will refer to a model based on Assumption 7 as an "agenda-control" model of decision making on the Court.[5]

Given Assumption 7, the following can be easily deduced:

Proposition 7: The majority opinion writer's opinion will be the point inside $W_{Jmed}(SQ)$ that is closest to his or her own ideal point.

Now recall two of our simplifying assumptions for all three versions of our model, that the chief justice always votes with the majority on the original vote and so becomes the opinion assignor, and that there is another justice whose ideal point is identical to that of the chief justice, and so could be assigned by the majority opinion by the chief justice. These two assumptions, when combined with Proposition 7, allow us to complete this first version of our model.

Note, in particular, that what policy the majority opinion writer will adopt inside $W_{Jmed}(SQ)$ depends on where his or her ideal point is located: he or she can have an ideal point that lies on the majority side of

FIGURE 4 An opinion writer with an ideal point inside $W_{J_{med}}(SQ)$ can write the opinion at his or her ideal point

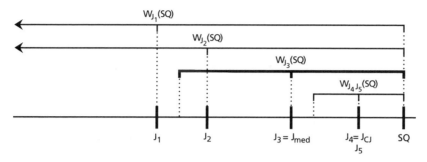

SQ or on the minority side of SQ. If the opinion writer has a majority-side ideal point, we can easily summarize his or her best strategy:

Proposition 8:
   (a) If the opinion writer's ideal point lies inside $W_{Jmed}(SQ)$, the opinion writer will draft an opinion at his or her own ideal point;
   (b) If the opinion writer's ideal point lies outside $W_{Jmed}(SQ)$, the opinion writer will draft an opinion just inside the outside boundary of $W_{Jmed}(SQ)$.

For example, consider the Court in figure 4. Assume as shown that justice J_4 is the chief justice and that justice J_5 has an ideal point at the same location as J_4. The chief justice here will vote on the majority side on the original vote, gain control of the opinion assignment, and then assign the opinion to justice J_5. Since justice J_5's ideal point lies inside $W_{Jmed}(SQ)$ here (i.e., inside $W_{J3}(SQ)$), Proposition 8a applies, so justice J_5 can write an opinion at his or her own ideal point of J_5; in fact, an opinion at J_5 would gain the support of all five justices, because it lies inside all five of their preferred-to sets.

Next, consider figure 5, in which the chief justice at J_1 and his compatriot at J_2 have ideal points that lie outside $W_{Jmed}(SQ)$. In this case, Proposition 8b applies, and the best justice J_2 can do is to write an opinion at the point labeled "*," which is just inside the outside boundary of $W_{Jmed}(SQ)$. An opinion at * would gain the support of justices J_1 (the chief justice), J_2 (the opinion writer), and J_3 (the median justice), though not the support of justices J_4 and J_5, each of whom prefers SQ to the policy at *.

In contrast, if the chief justice and his compatriot have minority-side ideal points, the chief justice would have to vote with the majority on the

FIGURE 5 An opinion writer with an ideal point outside $W_{J_{med}}(SQ)$ will have to write the opinion at * inside $W_{J_{med}}(SQ)$

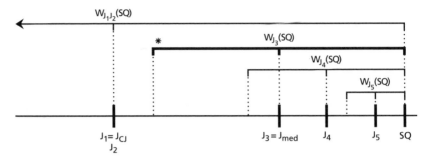

original vote in order to control opinion assignment, and his compatriot would have to do the same to be eligible to write the majority opinion. Assuming that a minority-side chief justice and his compatriot have thus voted with the majority, what opinion would be written? The answer is as follows:

Proposition 9: If the opinion writer's ideal point lies at SQ or to the minority side of SQ, the opinion writer will draft an opinion just inside the SQ-boundary of $W_{Jmed}(SQ)$.

For example, assume in figure 3 that justice J_4 is the chief justice and that his like-minded compatriot on the minority side is justice J_5. Note that a minority-side chief justice such as justice J_4 has a strong incentive to vote with the majority so as to control opinion assignment. If he does not vote with the majority, someone on the majority side will control the assignment, and the result here will be one of two different opinions: if the median justice, J_3, writes the opinion, she will write an opinion at her own ideal point of J_3, and if either justice J_1 or J_2 writes the opinion, the opinion will be written at * at the left-hand boundary of $W_{J3}(SQ)$. In either case, these opinions at * and J_3 are both worse than SQ for the minority-side chief justice at J_4.

To avoid such a loss, the chief justice could become the majority opinion assignor by voting on the majority side on the original vote, and for justice J_5 to become the majority opinion writer, he would have to vote on the majority side on the original vote as well. Having gained control of the opinion assignment, the chief justice would then assign the opinion to justice J_5. However, justice J_5 could not write an opinion at his own ideal point or at any other minority-side point; any such opinion would lie outside $W_{Jmed}(SQ)$ and so could not gain majority support. Instead, he would have to write a majority-side opinion, and the majority-side opinion that is closest to his own minority-side ideal point would be an opinion located at "+," which lies on the majority side but very close to SQ. Since this opinion at + lies inside $W_{Jmed}(SQ)$, it would gain support from a majority of the justices (i.e., from justices J_1, J_2, and J_3). While this opinion at + would be slightly worse than SQ for both the chief justice and justice J_5, it is nonetheless better for both of them than the opinions at * or J_3 that would otherwise result.

   This completes development of our minimalist (version 1) model of appeals court/Supreme Court interactions. The most basic result is simply that the majority opinion writer will have to draft an opinion that lies inside the preferred-to set of the median justice.

Version 2: The Maximalist Model of Appeals Court/Supreme Court Interactions

   In both the minimalist and the maximalist versions of our model, the initial status quo policy is simply some explicit and previously adopted Supreme Court policy. In contrast to the minimalist version, however, the maximalist version distinguishes between an explicit policy the Court has previously adopted (this is the initial status quo policy) and the legal policies that are actually being implemented in the country at any one time; we refer to the latter as "the legal state of affairs." This legal state of affairs can differ from explicit Supreme Court policy, because the appeals court has the authority to adopt and unilaterally implement a new policy in its own circuit and then maintain this new policy over time, at least until its new policy is appealed to the Supreme Court and the Court issues its own ruling on the case. The potential impact of the appeals court's ruling, which creates the new legal state of affairs, stems from the fact that some Court majority may actually prefer this new legal state of affairs, or some modification of it, to the Court's own explicit and previously adopted policy.[6] The maximalist version of our model is based on the premise that whatever Court majority is able to coalesce in support of what particular policy will be influenced by what particular legal state of affairs has been created by the appeals court's ruling; in effect, then, the Supreme Court's decision-making process will pivot around this new legal state of affairs.

   Hence, the key question becomes: Is there some policy the appeals court judge could adopt (thereby creating a new legal state of affairs) so that the Supreme Court would respond by endorsing the policy the appeals court judge most prefers? As we will demonstrate, the location of the new legal state of affairs created by the appeals court ruling can have a significant effect on what policy the Supreme Court would subsequently adopt.

In our analysis, "SQ_1" will refer to the Court's previously adopted policy, and "SQ_2" will refer to the new legal state of affairs created by the appeals court ruling. What policy, if any, the Court chooses to replace SQ_1 depends on an interaction among *five* variables: the location of the chief justice's ideal point, J_{CJ}; the location of the median justice's ideal point, J_{med}; the location of SQ_1; the location of the appeals court judge's ideal point; and the location of the appeals court judge's ruling. We will determine what policy, SQ_2, the appeals court judge would adopt (i.e., what new legal state of affairs she will create) by determining, for each possible SQ_2, what policy the Supreme Court would adopt in response; the appeals court judge would then adopt that SQ_2 that leads the Supreme Court to adopt the policy closest to the appeals court judge's ideal point.

Our analysis begins by noting that there are six possible configurations for J_{CJ}, J_{med}, and $W_{Jmed}(SQ_1)$, as shown in figure 6. For each of these six basic configurations, we can determine what policy the majority opinion writer on the Supreme Court would adopt, to be labeled "$*_1$," assuming version 1 of our model (the minimalist version). Then we will determine for each of these six configurations what policies the Court's majority opinion writer would adopt, to be labeled "$*_2$," assuming version 2 of our model (the maximalist version) and given the various possible locations of the appeals court judge's ideal point. We can then compare the relative locations of $*_1$ and $*_2$ to determine what differences there are in the outcomes from the minimalist and maximalist versions of our model.

In figure 6, we first identify the six possible configurations for J_{CJ}, J_{med}, and $W_{Jmed}(SQ_1)$ and determine what the minimalist outcome, $*_1$, would be. In diagram (a), J_{CJ} is located outside $W_{Jmed}(SQ_1)$; by Proposition 8b, the majority opinion writer would write an opinion at $*_1$, which is just inside the left-hand boundary of $W_{Jmed}(SQ_1)$. In location (b), J_{CJ} is located inside $W_{Jmed}(SQ_1)$ but to the left of J_{med}; by Proposition 8a, the opinion writer would write an opinion, $*_1$, at his own ideal point of J_1, which is the same as the chief justice's ideal point of J_{CJ}. In diagram (c), J_{CJ} is located precisely at J_{med} inside $W_{Jmed}(SQ_1)$; again by Proposition 8a, the opinion writer would write an opinion, $*_1$, at J_{med}, which is the same as J_{CJ} and J_1. In location (d), J_{CJ} is located inside $W_{Jmed}(SQ_1)$ but to the right of J_{med}; again by Proposition 8a, the opinion writer would write an opinion, $*_1$, at J_{CJ}. In diagram (e), J_{CJ} is located precisely at SQ_1; by Proposition 9, the

FIGURE 6 The six possible configurations for the chief justice, the median justice, and $W_{J_{med}}(SQ)$

(a)

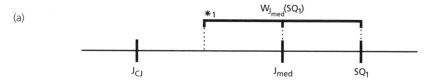

(b)

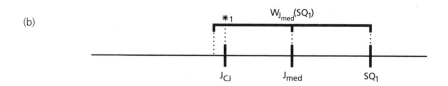

(c)

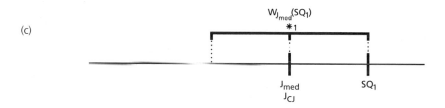

(d)

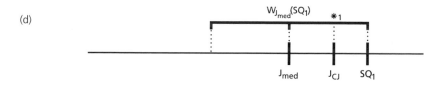

(e)

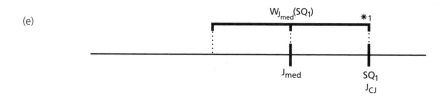

(f)

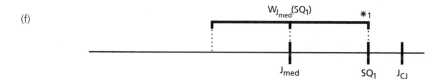

opinion writer would write an opinion at $*_1$, just inside the right-hand boundary of $W_{Jmed}(SQ)$. And in location (f), J_{CJ} is located on the minority side of SQ_1; again by Proposition 9, the opinion writer would write an opinion at $*_1$, just inside the right-hand boundary of $W_{Jmed}(SQ)$.

These six results—the six locations of $*_1$—show what the outcome would be for each of the six configurations, given version 1 of our model (in which the justices ignore the content of the appeals court decision).

Now consider what the outcomes would be from version 2 of our model. For each of the six diagrams in figure 6, note that an appeals court could, in principle, adopt some SQ_2, which could be located in a large number of different places. In our next six sets of figures, we determine how the location of the Court's final opinion would change in response to the various locations of SQ_2 that are possible.

In figure 7, we consider what happens with the configuration in figure 6(a), in which J_{CJ} is located outside $W_{Jmed}(SQ_1)$. In version 1 of our model, the opinion writer at J_1 would write an opinion at $*_1$, which is just inside the left-hand boundary of $W_{Jmed}(SQ_1)$. Now consider what would happen if the appeals court judge issues her own ruling, SQ_2, and the Supreme Court justices respond according to version 2 of our model, by trying to produce a Court policy that is majority-preferred to the new legal state of affairs, SQ_2, which was created by the appeals court.

Diagram (a) in figure 7 shows that if the appeals court judge creates a new legal state of affairs at SQ_{2a}, the left-hand boundary of $W_{Jmed}(SQ_{2a})$ would lie farther leftward than the left-hand boundary of $W_{Jmed}(SQ_1)$. The result is that the Supreme Court opinion written by majority opinion writer J_1 would move leftward from $*_1$ to $*_2$ so that it is now located at J_{CJ}, the chief justice's ideal point (and thus at J_1 as well). In diagram (b), if the appeals court judge creates a new legal state of affairs at SQ_{2b}, the left-hand boundary of $W_{Jmed}(SQ_{2b})$ will be at J_{CJ}, so the majority opinion writer's opinion, $*_2$, would have to lie *inside* $W_{Jmed}(SQ_{2b})$, so the resulting opinion would not move quite as far leftward from $*_1$ as in diagram (a). In diagram (c), the appeals court judge creates a new legal state of affairs at SQ_{2c}, which is an even shorter distance rightward from SQ_1, which means that the left-hand boundary of $W_{Jmed}(SQ_{2c})$ also moves leftward even less; as a result, the opinion writer must write an opinion further rightward, at $*_2$ as indicated. In diagram (d), the new legal state of affairs, SQ_{2d}, is located precisely at SQ_1; the opinion writer's resulting policy of $*_2$ is located at the same place as $*_1$. In diagram (e), SQ_1 is replaced by an SQ_{2e}, which lies to its left; as a result, the opinion writer would have to write an opinion at $*_2$, which now lies to the right of $*_1$. And in diagram (f), SQ_1 is replaced by an SQ_{2f} which is located right at J_{med}. What results is an opinion, $*_2$, which must also be located at J_{med} (because $W_{Jmed}(SQ_{2f})$ is empty).

Now consider the pattern in the final opinions, $*_2$, which are produced. For the first six diagrams in figure 7, note that $W_{Jmed}(SQ_{2 \ldots})$ is contracting inward toward J_{med} and has contracted to emptiness by diagram (f), when SQ_2 reaches J_{med}. The result is that the majority opinion writer's opinion, $*_2$, is moving farther and farther from J_{CJ} and closer and closer to J_{med}. But once SQ_2 begins to move leftward away from J_{med}, $W_{Jmed}(SQ_2)$ begins to expand leftward again; this enables the opinion writer to write a new opinion, $*_2$, which is closer and closer to J_{CJ}; see diagrams (g), (h), and (i). In fact, when SQ_2 reaches J_{CJ} (diagram j) and beyond (diagram k), the opinion writer can again write an opinion at J_{CJ}, which is his own ideal point as well.

We can condense this complex pattern of changes into one single diagram, which we call a *phase diagram;* see figure 8. This diagram shows where the final policy, $*_2$, is located as SQ_2 moves continuously from the extreme right to the extreme left; see the dashed "maximalist outcomes" line. The horizontal axis of the diagram shows the locations of J_{CJ} (and thus of the opinion writer, J_1), J_{med}, SQ_1, and $*_1$ (the outcome from the minimalist version of our model). The vertical axis of the diagram likewise shows the locations of J_{CJ}, J_1, J_{med}, SQ_1, and $*_1$. To interpret this diagram, imagine an SQ_2 that starts out at the extreme right and moves leftward to the extreme left: for each possible location of SQ_2 on the horizontal axis, the dashed "maximalist outcomes" line in the graph shows the location of the final policy, $*_2$, that would result on the vertical axis.

We can now address the key question: given the outcomes that would result from each possible appeals court opinion (i.e., the various SQ_2s in figure 8), what opinion would the appeals court judge choose to write? From figure 8, we see that an appeals court judge with an ideal point that lies anywhere to the right of J_{med} (see the horizontal axis in figure 8) has an incentive to make a decision at J_{med}. The reason is that an appeals court decision (i.e., an SQ_2) anywhere to the right of J_{med} (on the horizontal axis) would result in a final Supreme Court opinion some distance from J_{med} and thus closer to J_{CJ} (on the vertical axis); the best that this appeals court judge could achieve would be a final Court opinion at J_{med} (on the vertical axis), and this could be produced only by an appeals court decision at

FIGURE 7 Outcomes for diagram (a) in figure 6

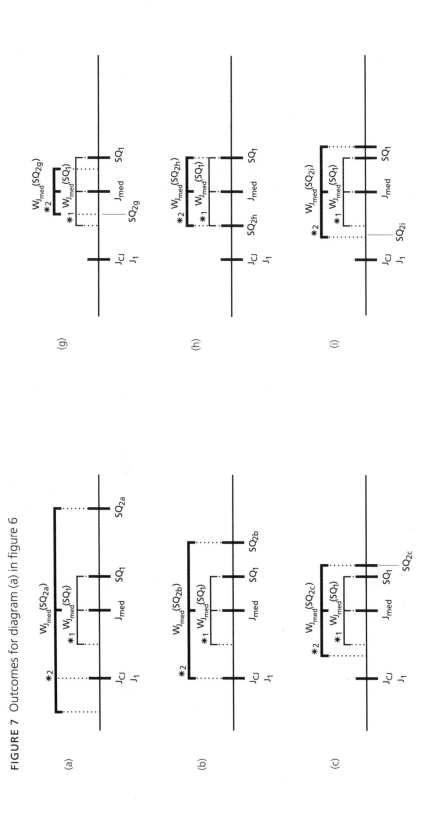

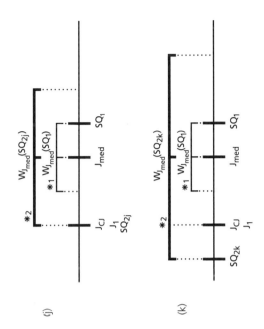

(d)

(e)

(f)

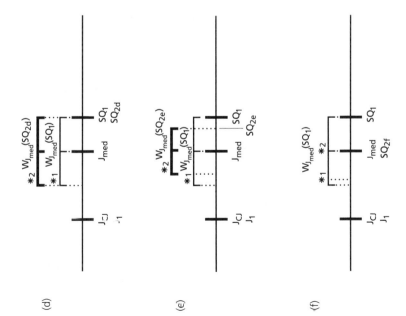

(j)

(k)

FIGURE 8 Phase diagram for diagram (a) in figure 6

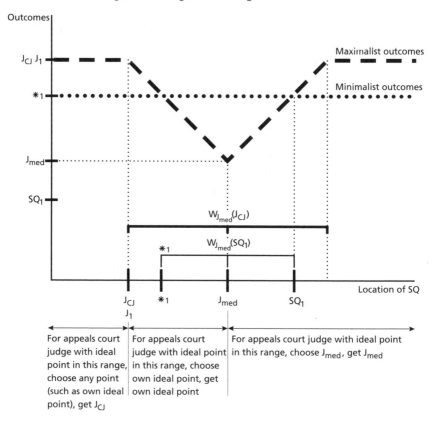

J_{med} (on the horizontal axis). We summarize this strategy at the bottom of figure 8 with the label, "For appeals court judge with ideal point in this range, choose J_{med}, get J_{med}."

However, an appeals court judge with an ideal point that lies at or between J_{CJ} and J_{med} would have an incentive to issue an appeals court decision at her own ideal point. The reason is that such a decision (on the horizontal axis) would produce a Supreme Court decision at the appeals court judge's own ideal point (on the vertical axis). We summarize this strategy at the bottom of figure 8 with the label, "For appeals court judge with ideal point in this range, choose own ideal point, get own ideal point."

Finally, given an appeals court judge whose ideal point lies at or to the left of J_{CJ} (on the horizontal axis), a final Supreme Court opinion at J_{CJ} (on the vertical axis) would be produced, no matter what decision the appeals court judge makes. Thus, for example, the appeals court judge could make an appeals court decision at his or her own ideal point (on the horizontal axis), and the result would be a Supreme Court opinion at J_{CJ} (on the vertical axis). We summarize this strategy at the bottom of figure 8 with the label, "For appeals court judge with ideal point in this range, choose any point (such as own ideal point), get J_{CJ}."

The next five figures—figures 9, 10, 11, 12, and 13—repeat this mode of analysis for the five remaining possible configurations of J_{CJ}, J_{med}, and SQ_1 shown in figure 6; for reasons of space we do not present the underlying sequence of cases for each figure as we did in figure 7.

For all but figure 10, the three strategies for the appeals court judge are the same as for figures 8 and 9: "Choose J_{med}," "Choose own ideal point," and "Choose any point." However, which particular strategy is best for the

FIGURE 9 Phase diagram for diagram (b) in figure 6

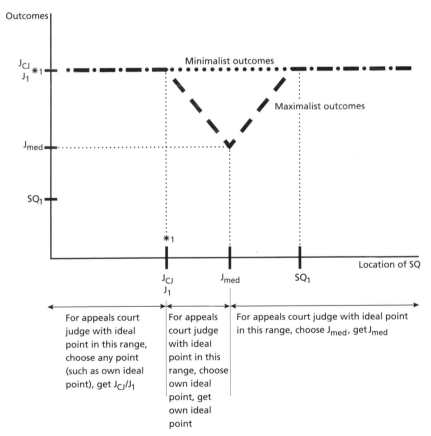

FIGURE 10 Phase diagram for diagram (c) in figure 6

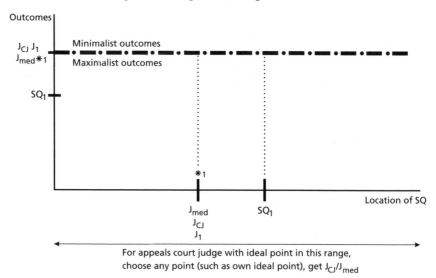

appeals court judge with any particular ideal point will change from figure to figure (that is, from configuration to configuration), as will the particular portion of the issue dimension in which it is optimal to choose each of these strategies. For figure 10, the final Supreme Court outcome will always be at J_{med} no matter what decision the appeals court judge makes.

In sum, the maximalist version of our model suggests that the relationship between an appeals court judge and the Supreme Court can exhibit very different characteristics. In particular, the appeals court judge's ability to move Supreme Court decision making in the direction he or she desires depends on the locations of the initial status quo policy, the chief justice's ideal point, the median justice's ideal point, the appeals court judge's ideal point, and the appeals court judge's legal ruling. With some configurations, the appeals court judge has maximal influence: she can issue a ruling at her own ideal point and the result will be a Supreme Court opinion at her own ideal point. With other configurations, the best the appeals court judge can do is to make a decision at the median justice's ideal point and get a Supreme Court opinion at that median justice's ideal point. And with still other configurations, whatever decisions the appeals court judge makes will have no impact at all on the Supreme Court's final opinion: the result will be an opinion at the opinion writer's ideal point.

We conclude that there is no single way of characterizing the relationship between the Supreme Court and an appeals court: the extent of the

FIGURE 11 Phase diagram for diagram (d) in figure 6

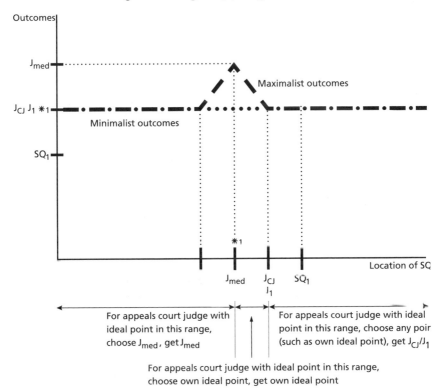

appeals court judge's influence (if any) depends on the configuration in a case.

Version 3: When There Is No Supreme Court Policy

The first two versions of our model of appeals court/Supreme Court interactions are premised on an assumption that the Supreme Court has previously established a clear and explicit policy; the key question in each case is whether the Court will replace its previous policy with a new policy. In contrast, the third version of our model is premised on the assumption that the Supreme Court has *not* previously established any clear and explicit policy. Hence, what serves as the "status quo policy" for the Court is simply whatever decision the appeals court makes on the case. The key question here is then: In the absence of any prior Supreme Court policy, what policy should an appeals court judge adopt so as to get a final Supreme Court policy as close as possible to her ideal point?

FIGURE 12 Phase diagram for diagram (e) in figure 6

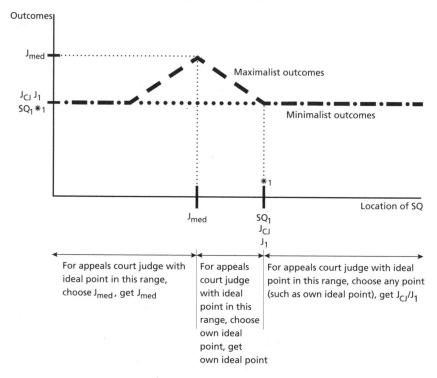

Not surprisingly, given the results thus far, the best strategy for the appeals court judge depends on the relative locations of the ideal points of the chief justice, J_{CJ}, the median justice, J_{med}, and the appeals court judge, to be labeled A. There are just four basic configurations that need to be examined:

- J_{CJ} and A are on opposite sides of J_{med};
- A lies between J_{CJ} and J_{med};
- J_{CJ} lies between A and J_{med}; and
- J_{CJ} and J_{med} have the same ideal point.

All other configurations are simply mirror images (left-to-right/right-to-left) of these four basic orderings.

First, consider the configuration in which J_{CJ} and A are on opposite sides of the median justice, who is justice J_3 here. For an example, see the diagrams in figure 14, in which the actors' ideal points are in the following left-to-right order: first J_{CJ} and J_2 (who have the same ideal point), then J_3 (the median justice), then J_4, then J_5, and then A; notice that J_{CJ}

and A are on opposite sides of J_{med}. We begin by examining a series of possible choices by the appeals court judge to see what choice produces the best final outcome for her. In diagram (a), the appeals court judge chooses a policy, labeled SQ_1, at her own ideal point of A, so the median justice's preferred-to set is $W_{Jmed}(SQ_1)$. This means that the chief justice (always voting with the majority) is the opinion assignor, and assigns the opinion to J_2; since J_2's ideal point falls inside $W_{Jmed}(SQ_1)$, he can write an opinion at J_2 and this opinion, indicated by $*_1$, will gain majority support (from J_{CJ}, J_2, and J_3) against SQ_1. Hence the outcome in diagram 1 from an opinion at SQ_1 will be a policy at $*_1$.

In diagrams (b), (c), and (d) the appeals court judge's policy choices, at SQ_2, SQ_3, and SQ_4 respectively, will still allow the opinion writer, J_2, to write an opinion at his own ideal point; these opinions are labeled $*_2$, $*_3$, and $*_4$ respectively. But in diagram (e), in which the judge has chosen a policy at SQ_5, $W_{Jmed}(SQ_5)$ does not allow J_2 to select a policy at his own ideal point; the best he can do here is to select a policy at the left-hand end of $W_{Jmed}(SQ_5)$, which is the policy at $*_5$ as shown. In diagram (f), the judge has chosen a policy, SQ_6, which is located at J_{med}, and the resulting outcome, $*_6$, is at J_{med}. In diagram (g), the judge has chosen a policy, SQ_7, which is located to the left of J_{med}; the opinion writer, J_2, would thus choose

FIGURE 13 Phase diagram for diagram (f) in figure 6

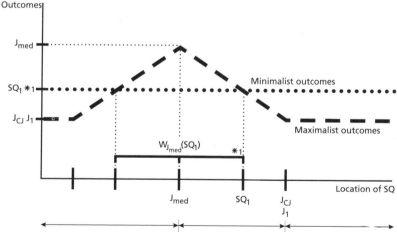

FIGURE 14 Outcomes when the chief justice and the appeals court judge are on opposite sides of the median justice

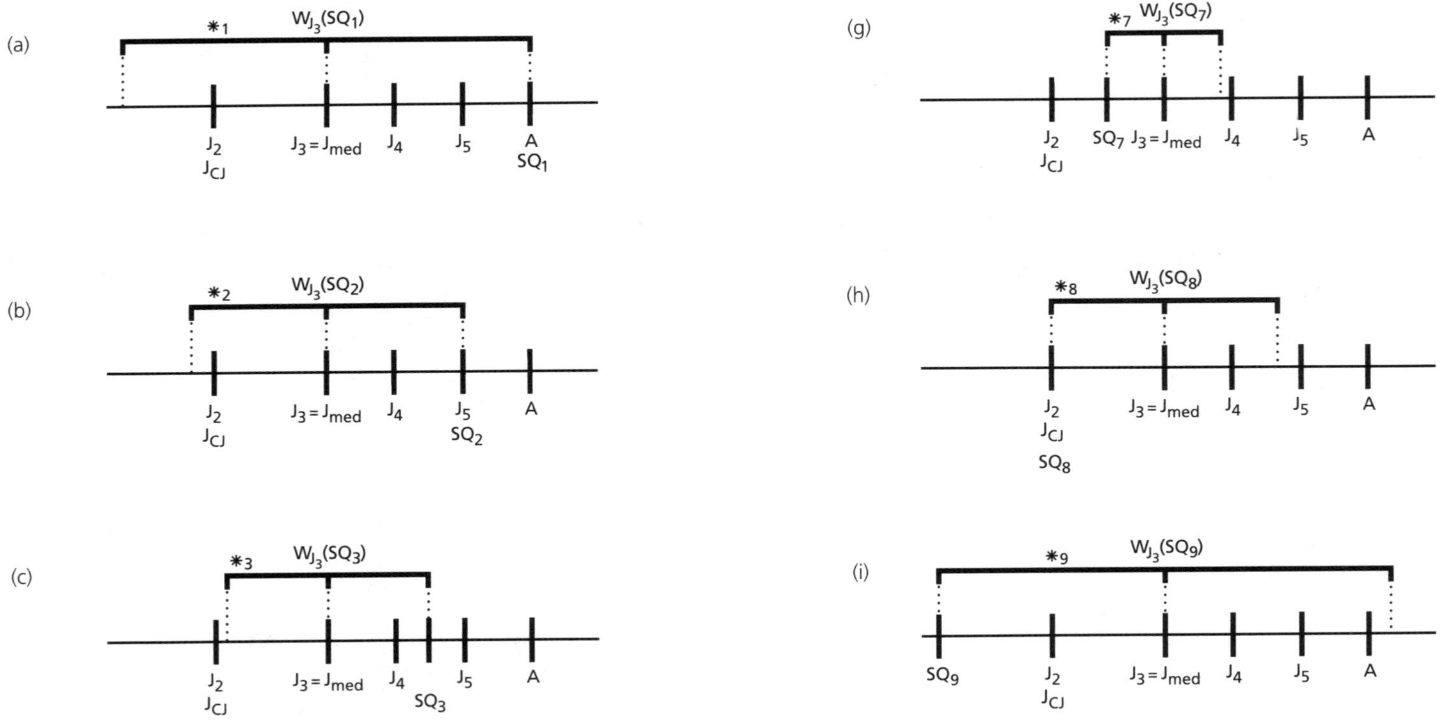

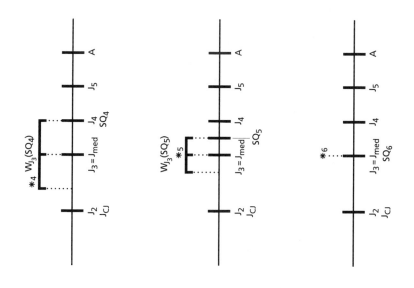

(d)

(e)

(f)

a policy, $^*_7$, at the left-hand end of the resulting win-set, $W_{Jmed}(SQ_7)$. In diagram (h), the judge has chosen a policy at SQ_8, which is far enough to the left so that J_2 is now located inside $W_{Jmed}(SQ_8)$ and so can choose a policy at his own ideal point; the result is the policy at $^*_8$. Finally, in diagram (i), the judge has chosen a policy at SQ_9, which is also far enough left so that J_2 is located inside $W_{Jmed}(SQ_9)$ and so can choose a policy at his own ideal point; the result is the policy at $^*_9$.

Note in each case that the opinion writer, justice J_2, writes his opinion inside $W_{Jmed}(SQ_{...})$, which means that this opinion will be able to gain the support of a Court majority against the appeals court's policy. Hence, a Court majority will always grant certiorari to this case, because these justices expect that the outcome will always be better for them than the policy previously selected by the appeals court judge.

The results from diagrams (a) through (i) in figure 14 are summarized in the phase diagram in figure 15. The horizontal axis shows the location of the appeals court judge's policy choice in relation to the actors' ideal points. The vertical axis shows the location of the outcome in relation to

FIGURE 15 Phase diagram for the diagrams in figure 14

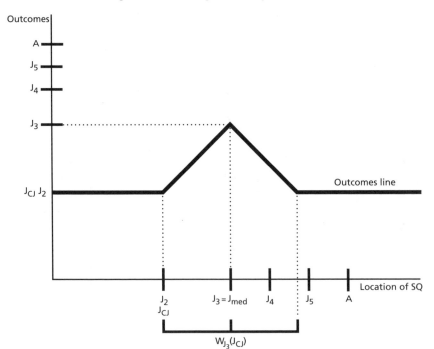

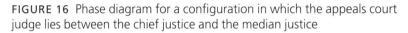

FIGURE 16 Phase diagram for a configuration in which the appeals court judge lies between the chief justice and the median justice

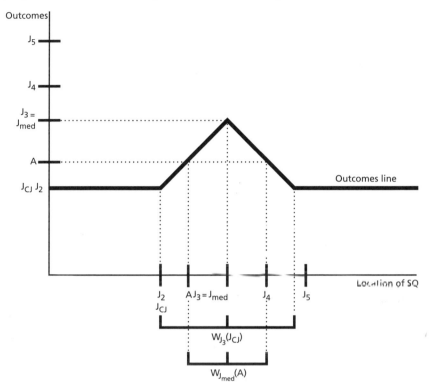

the actors' ideal points. The solid "outcomes line" shows what policy the Supreme Court would adopt for each decision that the appeals court judge could make. Inspecting the diagram in figure 15, we see on the vertical axis that with A at the top, the policy closest to A is at the top of the "hill," and the appeals court policy that produces this result is a policy at J_{med}. Hence, we have the following:

Proposition 10: If A is at or to one side of J_{med}, and J_{CJ} and his compatriot, J_2, are on the other side of J_{med}, then the appeals court judge's best strategy is a policy at J_{med} so that the Supreme Court's final policy choice would be at J_{med}.

Next, consider a configuration in which the appeals court judge's ideal point lies between J_{CJ} and J_{med}. The phase diagram is shown in figure 16. Interestingly, there are two equally good but quite different "best" strategies for the appeals court judge here. The reason is that the line traced hor-

izontally rightward from A on the vertical axis intersects the solid outcomes line in *two* places: one results from a policy at A on the horizontal
axis, and the other results from a policy at the right-hand boundary of
$W_{Jmed}(A)$. Hence we have:

Proposition 11: If A is at J_{CJ}, or lies between J_{CJ} and J_{med}, then the appeals
court judge has two best strategies—one at each boundary of
$W_{Jmed}(A)$—so that the Supreme Court's final policy choice would
be at A.

However, since one of these two best strategies for the appeals court judge
is to pick a policy at A, her own ideal point, it seems most plausible to
think that she will always select the policy at A rather than a policy some
distance away at the other end of $W_{Jmed}(A)$, even though they both produce an outcome at A.

Next, consider the configuration in which J_{CJ} lies between A and J_{med}.
The summary results are shown in the phase diagram in figure 17. Here
there is a wide range of best strategies for the appeals court judge, though
in none of them does she get her ideal point as an outcome. As we can see
in the diagram, a line traced horizontally from A on the vertical axis does
not intersect the outcomes line anywhere, but it is parallel to the closest
parts of the outcomes line in two regions—to the left and to the right of
$W_{Jmed}(CJ)$. To summarize, then, we have:

Proposition 12: If J_{CJ} lies between A and J_{med}, then the appeals court
judge's best strategy is to choose any policy to the left (and including)
the left-hand boundary of $W_{Jmed}(J_{CJ})$ or any policy to the right (and
including) the right-hand boundary of $W_{Jmed}(J_{CJ})$, so that the Supreme Court's final policy choice would be at J_{CJ}.

However, since the left-hand range (the set of policies to the left, and
including, the left-hand boundary of $W_{Jmed}(J_{CJ})$) includes the appeals
court judge's own ideal point of A, it seems most plausible to think that she
will simply select this policy at A rather than any of the many other policies that would yield the same outcome—J_{CJ}—as would the choice of A.

Finally, we note that if J_{CJ} is located at J_{med}, the particular choice by the
appeals court judge is irrelevant:

Proposition 13: If J_{CJ} is at J_{med}, the outcome will be at J_{med} (and thus at J_{CJ})
no matter what policy the appeals court judge selects.

The reason, of course, stems from the fact that no matter what policy,
$SQ_{...}$, the appeals court judge selects, there will be a nonempty

FIGURE 17 Phase diagram for a configuration in which the chief justice lies between the appeals court judge and the median justice

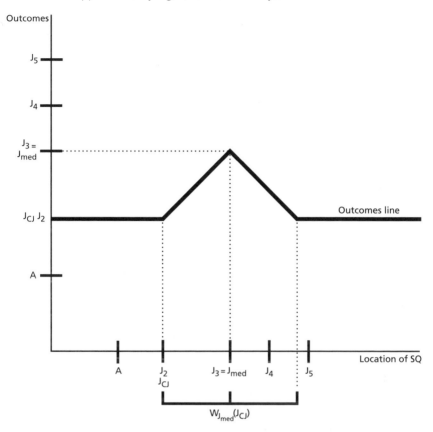

$W_{Jmed}(SQ \dots)$, and if the opinion writer (who has an ideal point at J_{CJ}, and thus at J_{med} as well) writes an opinion at J_{med}, this opinion would necessarily fall inside $W_{Jmed}(SQ \dots)$ and so would automatically attract majority support. Given this simple logic, no diagram need be presented.

These four propositions summarize the appeals court judge's best strategies when there is no prior Supreme Court policy.

An Alternative Assumption: Active Rather than Passive Justices?

We must now raise a question about an assumption common to all versions of our model. Recall Assumption 7, that the justices respond *passively* to the opinion drafted by the majority opinion writer: as long as the opinion is better than SQ for a justice, that justice will support the

FIGURE 18 Minimalist and maximalist outcomes when the justices are active policy-maximizers

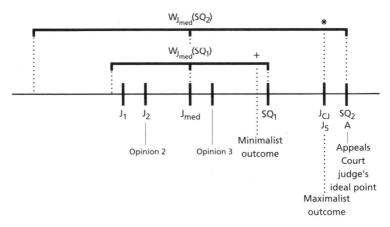

opinion over SQ. This "agenda-control" assumption is a plausible way of modeling the widely held view of judicial politics scholars that the policy preferences of the majority opinion writer can greatly affect the final opinion that the Supreme Court adopts on a case. However, the assumption has some implications that raise questions about its validity. The key question is this: Why would rational policy-maximizing justices allow the opinion writer to set their decision-making agenda on a case?

To address this question, we present two illustrations that suggest the assumption of passive justices may be incompatible with an even more fundamental assumption we make—that the Supreme Court justices are rational policy-maximizers.

First, consider figure 18, in which the initial status quo policy is at SQ_1 and the chief justice and his opinion-writing compatriot, who is justice J_5 here, have minority-side ideal points as indicated. (This configuration is a key aspect of figure 13, which in turn is derived from diagram (f) in figure 6.) Recall that SQ_1 represents the location of the Court's current policy, explicitly established by some Court opinion at a previous date. Now apply the minimalist version of our model to this configuration. Since the chief justice and justice J_5 seek control of the decision, they would both vote with the majority on the original vote, the chief justice would gain control of opinion assignment and would assign the opinion to justice J_5, and justice J_5 would then write the final opinion at the policy labeled +, which lies just inside the right-hand boundary of $W_{Jmed}(SQ_1)$. Thus, the policy at + is the minimalist outcome here.

Next, apply the maximalist version of our model to this same configuration. Assume that the appeals court judge has an ideal point at A, as indicated, near the right-hand end of the issue dimension. Assume also that the appeals court judge then selects a new policy for her circuit that results in a legal state of affairs at SQ_2, which is located at her own ideal point of A. The set of points the median justice, at J_{med}, prefers to this new legal state of affairs is $W_{Jmed}(SQ_2)$, and note that $W_{Jmed}(SQ_2)$ extends so far to the right that it includes J_{CJ} and J_5. The chief justice and justice J_5 could thus express support for their own ideal points on the original vote, the chief justice would thereby gain control of opinion assignment, he would assign the majority opinion to justice J_5, and justice J_5 would then write the Supreme Court's opinion, indicated by *, at his own ideal point of J_5 (which is, of course, identical to the chief justice's ideal point of J_{CJ}). Since the opinion at * is preferred by a majority of justices to the legal state of affairs at SQ_2 (in fact, * is *unanimously* preferred to SQ_2), the opinion at * will be the maximalist outcome. In other words, the appeals court judge's opinion, which initially created a legal state of affairs at SQ_2, causes a substantial change in Supreme Court policy, from the initial policy at SQ_1 to the final policy at *. The appeals court judge has thereby managed to move Supreme Court policy rightward and much closer to her own ideal point.[7]

However, recall our initial assumption that the previous Supreme Court opinion had established a policy at SQ_1. But even though the appeals court judge creates a new legal state of affairs at SQ_2, this point at SQ_2 is not enshrined in any kind of explicit Supreme Court opinion or policy. Instead, the Court's *official* policy remains at SQ_1 (after all, the Court has not yet responded to the appeals court decision), and it is critical to notice that justices J_1, J_2, and J_{med} all prefer SQ_1 (and even the policy at +) to every policy lying to the right of SQ_1, *including the policy at *.* Hence, there would seem to be little reason to think that justices J_1, J_2, and J_{med} would support an opinion at * (as proposed by justice J_5, the majority opinion writer) simply because * is better for each of them than SQ_2; after all, both * and SQ_2 are worse for these justices than SQ_1, the current status quo policy.

Three possible inferences can be drawn from the existence of this problem. One possible inference is simply that the maximalist version of our model needs just a minor modification. Note that this problem can arise only in the configurations diagrammed in figures 6(f) and 13, and we could eliminate the problem simply by specifying that the opinion writer must always draft an opinion that falls inside $W_{Jmed}(SQ_1)$.

However, this proposed solution is not entirely satisfactory. In figure 18, for example, this solution means that justices J_1, J_2, and J_{med} will simply ignore the opinion writer's effort to impose the *-vs.-SQ_2 agenda by considering only the policies inside $W_{Jmed}(SQ_1)$; that is, these three justices will consider only those responses to SQ_2 they find better than the Supreme Court's current policy at SQ_1. For these three justices, only an opinion inside $W_{Jmed}(SQ_1)$ would induce them to abandon the policy at SQ_1 and agree to something else; the majority opinion writer's proposed policy at * would simply be ignored by all three justices, because it is worse for them than SQ_1. From this perspective, then, the best the chief justice and justice J_5 could do is produce a draft opinion at +. But this opinion at + is just what is predicted by the minimalist interpretation of the role of the appeals court. In sum, the appeals court judge may be able to unilaterally change the legal state of affairs in her circuit, but she cannot unilaterally change the Supreme Court's own policy—only the justices themselves can do this. So if the justices can simply ignore the legal state of affairs created by the appeals court judge's opinion, the second possible inference can be identified: perhaps the maximalist version of our model rests on questionable assumptions regarding the Supreme Court's response to the appeals court decision, and so the maximalist version may have to be rejected in favor of the minimalist model.

But even this second inference may underemphasize the significance of the problem. A third possible inference, which is even more fundamental, would lead us to reject the minimalist model as well. This challenge involves the assumption that the majority opinion writer can exercise agenda control over the Supreme Court's decision-making process. From this perspective, the key question is this: Why would the other justices grant the majority opinion writer *any* degree of agenda control at all?

To illustrate, consider figure 18 again. If justices J_1, J_2, and J_{med} are refusing to abandon SQ_1 for *, even when led to this choice by justice J_5 (the opinion writer who, by Assumption 7, controls the Court's agenda), why would these same three justices then acquiesce to a policy at +? After all, these three justices all prefer other policies within $W_{Jmed}(SQ_1)$, such as a policy at J_{med}, to the policy at +; so why would policy-maximizing justices accept a policy at +, when they could get an even better policy such as J_{med}? In other words, the passive behavior presumed by the agenda-control assumption may be *irrational* for the policy-maximizing justices who are not writing the majority opinion.

In Hammond, Bonneau, and Sheehan (2005), we examine this issue in detail and propose an alternative model we refer to as the "open-bidding" model. From the perspective of the open-bidding model, a justice in figure 18 who dislikes the draft majority opinion at + (i.e., the draft opinion is not at his or her ideal point) would be assumed to *actively* draft and promote an alternative to +, the majority opinion writer's proposal. Of course, the only way a dissatisfied justice, such as justice J_2, can attract a majority to a counteropinion is to write it in such a way that the median justice (and therefore at least *maj* − 1 other justices as well) prefers it to justice J_5's opinion; for example, note that Opinion 2 is closer to J_{med} than is the opinion at +, so the median justice at J_{med} (and justices J_1 and J_2 as well) would support Opinion 2 over the draft opinion at +. Of course, this counteropinion from justice J_2 would stimulate a response by the majority opinion writer, justice J_5, but the only way that justice J_5 can attract a majority back to his own side is to revise the draft majority opinion so that it is even closer to J_{med} than Opinion 2; thus, justice J_5 might produce Opinion 3 (and we note that a majority of justices—J_{med}, J_{CJ}, and J_5—all prefer Opinion 3 to Opinion 2).

The only way justice J_2 could respond is with an opinion even closer to J_{med} than Opinion 3. The ultimate result of this back-and-forth process, which is always aimed at attracting the support of the median justice (and thus the support of a Court majority), is a final opinion located directly at J_{med}: the reason is that whichever side can gain the support of the median justice can become the majority, and the only way the support of the median justice can be *guaranteed* is to write an opinion at her ideal point of J_{med}.

Hence, the open-bidding version of our model, or something like it that generates outcomes at J_{med}, may characterize Supreme Court decision making more accurately than any model built on agenda-control assumptions. But if this is true, it means that the widespread belief that it matters who writes the majority opinion might have to be abandoned; the final opinion will end up at J_{med} no matter who the official opinion writer is. In figure 18, for example, justices J_2 and J_5 both draft opinions, but their competition for the support of the median justice drives the final outcome to J_{med}.[8]

This open-bidding argument can be applied to all three versions of our model of appeals court interactions with the Supreme Court. In version 1, in which the justices ignore the content of the appeals court decision, competing Court majorities will drive the opinion to J_{med}. In version 2, in which the appeals court is changing the legal state of affairs for the Court, competing Court majorities will again drive the final opinion to J_{med}, no matter what legal state of affairs was created by the appeals court judge.

And in version 3, in which the Supreme Court has no previous policy and the initial status quo is created by the appeals court judge, competing Court majorities will again drive the final opinion to J_{med}, no matter what opinion was initially written by the appeals court judge. Thus we have:

Proposition 14: If the justices do not grant agenda-control authority to the majority opinion writer (i.e., Assumption 7 does not hold), then the outcome will be at J_{med} for every configuration of preferences in all three versions of our model of appeals court interactions with the Supreme Court.

If the open-bidding logic more accurately characterizes how rational policy-maximizing justices would behave on the Supreme Court (compared to the agenda-control logic), who writes the majority opinion for the Supreme Court is irrelevant, as is the content of the appeals court opinion. Instead, outcomes in all kinds of cases would hinge simply on what the median justice most wants.

This fundamental debate about the nature of Supreme Court decision making is one that cannot be settled here; further theorizing and a substantial amount of empirical testing will be required. Until this debate is resolved, it may be impossible to draw a definitive conclusion about which version (if any) of our model of appeals court interactions with the Supreme Court is most valid. However, empirical investigation may help illuminate some of the choices to be made. We conclude the essay in the next section by discussing some of these empirical issues.

Conclusion: Empirically Evaluating the Models

If the various versions of our model of appeals court interactions with the Supreme Court were tested empirically, how should these tests be conducted? We have four observations to make.

Our first observation involves the diagrams in figures 8 through 13, which show the outcomes expected from the maximalist (version 2) interpretation of the role of the appeals court (given the six basic configurations of the locations of the chief justice's ideal point, the median justice's ideal point, and the initial status quo policy). As noted earlier, each diagram shows the solid "maximalist outcomes" line, but the same diagrams also indicate the "minimalist outcomes" with a dotted line; these are the outcomes that would be expected from the minimalist (version 1) interpretation of the role of the appeals court.

For example, in figure 8, the opinion writer is justice J_1 and in version 1 would write an opinion just inside the left-hand boundary of $W_{Jmed}(SQ_1)$, no matter what the appeals court judge does. In figures 9 through 12, this opinion writer would be able to write an opinion at his own ideal point of J_1, no matter what the appeals court judge does. And in figure 13, the opinion writer would write an opinion just inside the right-hand boundary of $W_{Jmed}(SQ_1)$, no matter what the appeals court judge does.

Note that with some configurations—see in particular figures 8 and 13—the minimalist and maximalist outcomes differ almost completely. Only at two points in these two diagrams—the two places where the "minimalist outcome" line crosses the "maximalist outcome" line—are the minimalist outcomes and the maximalist outcomes the same.

However, with other configurations—see figures 9, 11, and 12—the minimalist and maximalist outcomes differ only in the region of $W_{Jmed}(J_{CJ})$, the set of policies the median justice considers to be better than the chief justice's ideal point. For all other policies, the minimalist outcomes and the maximalist outcomes are the same.

And with the remaining configuration—see figure 10—the minimalist and maximalist outcomes are completely identical everywhere.

For purposes of empirical testing, then, it would appear that configurations such as figure 10 should be avoided. One could not discriminate between the minimalist and maximalist interpretations. And it appears that the configurations in figures 9, 11, and 12 are less than ideal. Only for some locations of the individuals' ideal points and the status quo policy could one discriminate between the two interpretations. It thus appears that the configurations in figures 8 and 13 would be best suited to empirical testing, because the two interpretations predict different outcomes almost everywhere.

Our second observation is that the entire class of models we have been developing, both here and elsewhere (see Hammond, Bonneau, and Sheehan 2005), require empirical measures of several critical variables. Depending on which version of our model is being tested, these variables are:

(a) the ideal point of each of the Supreme Court justices on the case under consideration;
(b) the location of any initial status quo policy previously selected by the Supreme Court and that holds for the case under consideration (this is not relevant for version 3);

(c) the ideal point of the appeals court judge on the case under consideration; and,

(d) the location of the policy choice made by the appeals court judge on the case under consideration.

All these variables, it should be emphasized, require placement of a point *on a common left-right metric.*

Measurement of all these variables on this common metric would be no small task. However, this kind of measurement problem has been successfully addressed in the congressional literature (e.g., Poole and Rosenthal 1997). Moreover, the database of Supreme Court votes needed for estimating the justices' ideal points is available, as is a database that could be used for estimating the ideal points of appeals court judges (see, e.g., Giles, Hettinger, and Peppers 2001). Nonetheless, while estimating the ideal points of the judges and justices would seem to be a manageable (though difficult) exercise, estimating the locations of the policy choices of the judges and justices (i.e., their opinions) on the same left-right scale as their ideal points would likely be far more difficult; it might require a process by which their opinions are read and coded and their locations on the common left-right metric quantitatively estimated.

Our third observation is that the three different versions of our model of appeals court interactions with the Supreme Court have been constructed in something approximating an empirical vacuum. As noted in our introduction, even the most recent and comprehensive discussions of the federal appeals courts (see, e.g., Songer, Sheehan, and Haire 2000) give no clear indication of whether the *content* of the appeals court decisions should be expected to have any kind of impact on the justices' decisions. For this reason, we think that it would be desirable for a qualitative assessment to be made of the role, if any, that appeals court decisions play in Supreme Court decision making. For example, an assessment of the various versions of our model might be based on interviews with those intimately familiar with the justices' decision-making practices regarding appeals court decisions (such as former clerks and even retired justices). Even if the interviews suggest that the versions of our model presented here are unsatisfactory, some of the issues raised by our modeling might prove useful in structuring some of the interview questions.

Our last observation involves our derivations, for versions 2 and 3 of our model, of what would be the best strategy for the appeals court judge. Just as it would be useful to gain a qualitative sense of how Supreme Court justices have responded to appeals court decisions, it would be useful to conduct a qualitative assessment of whether the strategies we derive seem to be actually used, in any sense at all, by appeals court judges. Interviews with those intimately familiar with these judges' decision-making practices (such as their former clerks and perhaps even retired judges themselves) might produce some insights as to whether any version of our model adequately characterizes how the appeals court judges actually behave on cases they expect might be appealed to the Supreme Court.

Whatever the outcome of these investigations, we noted in our introduction that some research had been conducted on lower-court compliance with Supreme Court decisions. But we also noted that none of this research had been guided by any kind of explicit, formally developed principal-agent model of appeals court interactions with the Supreme Court. While none of the versions of our model here may turn out to be *the* definitive model of these interactions, we do think that our general kind of approach will prove to be a useful, perhaps even essential, aspect of future investigations.

Notes

1. For empirical evidence that Supreme Court decision making in recent decades has been largely characterized by a single underlying issue dimension, see Grofman and Brazill (2002), Brazill and Grofman (2002), and Martin and Quinn (2002).

2. However, if the legal case involves a federal administrative agency, the Circuit Court of Appeals for the District of Columbia will have original jurisdiction, and so the "circuit" for which the appeals court's new policy was unilaterally established is, in effect, the entire country. Hence, the legal state of affairs here will *not* have a composite nature.

3. For several years this is what characterized judicial policy regarding university admissions involving affirmative action: one policy largely outlawing affirmative action in university admissions was established in the Fifth Circuit's 1996 decision in *Hopwood v. Texas* 78 F.3d 932 (1996), but other policies with varying degrees of support for affirmative action continued to hold in other circuits. It was not until the University of Michigan decisions by the Supreme Court in 2003 (*Grutter v. Bollinger* 539 U.S. 982 [2003] and *Gratz v. Bollinger* 539 U.S. 244 [2003]) that these conflicts among the circuits were resolved.

4. At the end of the next section we clarify the costs to a minority-side chief justice if he fails to control opinion assignment.

5. An assumption that the majority opinion writer exercises control over the Supreme Court's decision-making agenda is implied, we think, by the judicial politics literature, which emphasizes the importance of which justice becomes the majority opinion writer. The implications of an alternative assumption are discussed in part VI.

6. One possible reason for why some Court majority may want to diverge from the Court's own previously adopted policy is that there is preference change or turnover among justices on the Court. In fact, given the agenda-control assumption (Assumption

7), just changing who writes the opinion could result in a change in policy even if there is no preference change or turnover among the justices on the Court.

7. Since this final outcome at * is worse for justices J_1, J_2, and J_{med}, they would presumably vote against certiorari. But the chief justice and justice J_5 comprise *maj* − 1 of this five-member Court, so the "rule of four" standard for certiorari would be met, and decision making would proceed, as described, with the opinion at + as the final outcome under the original assumptions of the model.

8. In fact, the median judge could even construct a sequence of these competing coalitions herself and, by playing one off against the other, drive the final result to J_{med}, her own ideal point; she would not even need to rely on the initiative of any other justices. In other words, if there is any one justice on the Court who is in a position to control the Court's decision-making agenda, it is the median justice, not the majority opinion writer.

Appeals Mechanisms, Litigant Selection, and the Structure of Judicial Hierarchies

CHARLES M. CAMERON AND LEWIS A. KORNHAUSER

The previous essay elaborated on the theme of compliance in a judicial hierarchy. This essay pulls back to ask broader questions about judicial hierarchies that inquire into the logic of hierarchies as ways of minimizing and correcting errors. Three models are developed. The first approaches the question from a "macro" perspective of the adjudicatory system. It identifies conditions on the relative rates at which wrongly decided cases are appealed and the rates at which errors are corrected and introduced by an appellate process to determine when the addition of another appellate tier would be desirable. The essay then provides two *team* models of appeal that provide microfoundations for an analysis of hierarchy. The first of these team models shows the power of litigant selection of cases to appeal in the determination of the structure of the hierarchy when courts simply correct errors. With perfect selection by litigants, the optimal hierarchy in an error-correcting judiciary has exactly three tiers. The second of these team models shows that litigants will appeal only hard cases and that the rate of appeal will be a function of the quality of the court.

Judicial systems are typically organized as hierarchies, with rights of appeal from level to level. Why is this? Because appeals mechanisms are ubiquitous in court systems, this question is fundamental for our understanding of the structure and operation of judicial organizations.

We begin this essay with a structural analysis of appellate processes. The analysis characterizes the appellate process in terms of systemic features rather than individual behavior. In particular, we identify five key variables that allow a characterization of the performance of appeals processes. We then turn to consider specific ways of organizing appeals and focus in particular on appeals initiated by the litigants themselves, a method we call "litigant selection." Analysts of judicial systems, we believe, need to build models of appeals processes where the conduct of the actors is endogenous; these models typically will be game theoretic. Given a game-theoretic model of judicial and litigant conduct, we can use the structural apparatus in the first part of the essay to characterize the performance of the system. In this way, we explore how institutional design structures individual conduct, which in turn determines systematic performance. We next illustrate this style of analysis by presenting a simple game theoretic model of appeals and relate this model to the structural systemic analysis presented earlier.

How does this essay relate to others that study appeals processes? Broadly speaking, the theoretical study of judicial appeals remains in its infancy. Steven Shavell (1995) outlined the first and only structural analysis of appeals and hierarchy. In his analysis, Shavell assumes that error rates at both the trial and appellate levels are functions of litigant and state resources invested in the case. The conditions he places on these error rates invoke, but are not derived from, individually rational behavior. He argues that the costs of hierarchy are justified if litigants select the "right" cases—that is, the wrongly decided ones—to appeal. He assumes a system of fees and penalties will assure this outcome.[1] Andrew Daughety and Jennifer Reinganum (2000), in contrast, use a game-theoretic model to examine the informational properties of litigant selection of appeals. In this interesting model, the defendant and the appellate court both receive signals about the legal preferences of a superior court; the appellate court can make deductions about the defendant's private information from the appeal. A handful of theoretical papers examine other judicial appeals mechanisms.[2]

The Structure of an Appellate Process

Figure 1 displays a simple appellate system. In the figure, cases enter the system and are probabilistically sorted by a trial judge, either correctly or incorrectly (this is the bottom box in the figure). These cases—correctly or incorrectly adjudicated—may be appealed, at the indicated rates (the arrows from the lower box to the shaded circle). In turn, appealed cases may be correctly or incorrectly sorted at the appellate stage (as indicated by the various arrows and corresponding probabilities). This yields a sorting of cases after the appeals process, shown in the upper box in the figure.

SOME DEFINITIONS

We can characterize an appeals process from level t to level $t + 1$ by five parameters: (1) p^t, the error rate at t (with $1 - p^t$ as the nonerror rate at t); (2) q_R^t, the probability that a case rightly decided at level t will be appealed

FIGURE 1   Structural parameters in an appeals system

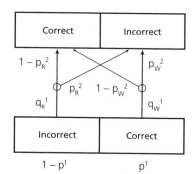

to level $t + 1$; (3) q_W^t, the probability that a case wrongly decided at level t will be appealed to level $t + 1$; (4) $1 - p_R^{t+1}$, the probability that, on appeal, a correctly decided case will be upheld at $t + 1$; and, (5) $1 - p_W^{t+1}$, the probability that, on appeal, a wrongly decided case will be reversed at $t + 1$. We will refer to these probabilities by name in the following ways. We shall call p_R^{t+1} the *conditional error introduction rate at t + 1* because it reflects the conditional probability that the appellate court will introduce an error. And we call $(1 - p_W^{t+1})$ *the conditional error correction rate at t + 1.*[3]

In addition, we call q_W^t / q_R^t the *selection ratio at t;* it is the ratio of the probability a wrongly decided case is appealed to the probability a correctly decided case is appealed. An appeals process is *selective, selection-neutral,* or *anti-selective* as this ratio is greater than, equal to, or less than 1 respectively.

We call $(1 - p_W^{t+1} / 1 - p^t)$ the *error correction ratio at t + 1;* it is the ratio of the conditional error correction rate at $t + 1$ to the nonerror rate at t. An appeals process is *error correcting, error-correction neutral,* or *anti-error correcting* as this ratio is greater than, equal to, or less than 1 respectively.

We call (p_R^{t+1} / p^t) the *error introduction ratio at t + 1;* it is the ratio of the conditional error introduction rate at $t + 1$ to the error rate at t. An appeals process is *error introducing, error introduction neutral,* or *anti-error introducing* as this ratio is greater than, equal to, or less than 1 respectively.[4]

A FUNDAMENTAL THEOREM

In appendix A to this essay, we use these definitions to prove a theorem about the desirability of an add-on appeals process. Our metric for evaluating a judicial hierarchy is the total number of errors remaining after the operation of the hierarchy.

Theorem 1: An add-on hierarchy is superior to the underlying court structure if and only if (1) the add-on hierarchy is sufficiently selective at T, or (2) the add-on hierarchy is sufficiently error correcting at $T + 1$, or (3) the addition of the $T + 1$ level sufficiently improves the performance in the underlying court structure.

Two simple corollaries follow immediately from the theorem (again, proofs are in appendix A).

Corollary 1.1: An add-on hierarchy that is error-introduction neutral and error-correction neutral is superior to the underlying court structure if and only if the added appeals process is sufficiently selective.

Corollary 1.2: Consider an add-on appeals process that is selection neutral. If the new tier does not reduce errors in the tiers below, the add-on hierarchy is superior to the underlying court structure if and only if the error-correction ratio exceeds the error-introduction ratio for the add-on appeals process.

The corollaries indicate the following. If the new tier improves performance below, selectivity in the new tier is not necessary to guarantee the superiority of the new hierarchy. Otherwise, it is a necessary condition, at least when the appeals process is error-introduction and error-correction neutral. However, selectivity in the new tier is not sufficient to guarantee the superiority of the new hierarchy, even if performance below degrades. Rather, when performance below degrades, the additional appeals process must be *sufficiently* selective to overcome the degradation in the quality of adjudication at the lower tiers.

Corollaries 1.1 and 1.2 make clear that the desirability of hierarchy does not require, as Shavell (1995, 394) assumes, that the error-introduction ratio be less than the error-correction ratio. Examination of the critical equation (H1), in appendix A, shows that an add-on hierarchy may be superior to the underlying hierarchy even when the error-introduction rate exceeds the error correction rate. This can occur, for example, if the appeals rate from T to $T + 1$ is sufficiently low for cases correctly decided at T.[5] Of course, this appeals rate might not be sufficiently low when economically rational litigants face a high error-introduction rate. It can also occur if the addition of the new tier sufficiently improves performance in the tiers below, for example, by improving litigant selection. But why should a new tier affect behavior below? We return to this rather subtle point later.

Motives, Information, and Mechanisms

The preceding structural analysis of judicial hierarchy, which identified five key variables in an appeals process, treated these variables parametrically. In actual appellate systems, the key probabilities are endogenous. Selectivity and other rates reflect the choices of litigants and judges operating within a specific institutional setting, a setting that structures the actors' incentives and brings to bear specific technologies of information revelation (e.g., the rules of evidence and judicial inference). Thus, working models of judicial hierarchies need to show how different institutional structures and procedural rules lead to different conduct by the actors and thus different performance of the system, in terms of the five key variables. Working models of this kind will typically be game theoretic.

This section acts as a bridge to game theoretic models of appeals mechanisms, by discussing two of the more problematic elements in models of appeals: assumptions about the motives of judges and assumptions about information.

THE SOURCES OF JUDICIAL ERROR

The ability of different mechanisms to detect and correct errors depends on the underlying cause of errors.[6] Two different approaches—the "principal-agent" (or just "agency") approach and the "team" approach—make very different assumptions about the sources of judicial errors and consequently lead to different models of appeals mechanisms.

Principal-agent models of adjudication focus on conflicting interests among judges to explain the existence of hierarchy. Each judge has a preference relation among policies (or, more simply, over case outcomes) and seeks to implement her preferences through her decisions. Hence, "errors" reflect deliberate malfeasance or rebellion by judges. From this perspective, the real source of error in judicial systems is a dearth of reliable judges.

Because the agency approach views judges as political actors, each striving to promote her policy interests, the design of the system will focus on controlling those conflicts rather than efforts to achieve correct answers. Hence, the agency approach to hierarchy directs attention to appeals mechanisms incorporating strategic auditing by superiors, structured competition among lower-court judges to induce compliance (tournaments), "whistle-blowing" by dissenters on collegial courts, and litigant decisions to appeal, the latter a device to reveal litigants' knowledge of malfeasant actions. It is worth noting that some features of the U.S. judicial hierarchy seem difficult to reconcile with an agency approach. An example is the specialization of trial courts in fact-finding. The underlying assumptions of the agency approach would seem to suggest a system in which appellate courts have the authority to redetermine the facts of a case. Otherwise, a trial judge can partly achieve her desired outcomes through her assessment of the facts.

The team approach presents a very different view of adjudication. In this approach, members of the judiciary are treated as if they are a member of team, in the sense of Ray Radner: they all share a common goal and an identical utility function (Marshak and Radner 1972). The most obvious goal is deciding cases "correctly." This aspiration makes sense in a context in which all judges *agree* on what constitutes correct answers, since they share the same utility function. One might imagine other goals as well, for example, minimize the number of cases brought before the judiciary, or maximize certainty in the law. But "maximize the number of correctly decided cases" seems particularly sensible in the team context.

In the team approach, the principal source of judicial error is hidden information. If judges knew *all* relevant information about the cases, there would be no errors. However, some knowledge is very costly to acquire or verify, so error is inevitable in a world with resource constraints (and, possibly, bounded rationality and variable degrees of judicial skill). In terms of appeals the team approach stresses litigant selection of appeals, as a device to reveal information hidden to judges but known by litigants.

Which approach—agency or team—is the "right" or "best" way to model adjudication? The answer, of course, depends on the modeler's interests. If the modeler is interested in value conflicts and their consequences, then the agency approach is obviously more appropriate. But there is more to the story of adjudication than value conflict—in fact, from a purely positive perspective, most litigation most of the time involves little conflict over fundamental values. To the extent that the modeler is interested in the political economy of "normal" cases rather than extraordinary ones, the team approach is very appealing. Finally, the team approach offers an attractive avenue for creating real (as opposed to straw man) versions of what political scientists like to call "the legal model." Having both agency (political) and team (legal) models of the same phenomenon may be extremely useful for structuring empirical work and, ultimately, understanding why judicial systems are organized the way they are and operate the way they do.

INFORMATION STRUCTURES IN APPELLATE PROCESSES

In game-theoretic models of appeals, what information structures are worth considering? The answer depends on one's view of litigation. Two stand out: the "implementation" view of adjudication and the "law-creation" view.

In the "implementation" account of adjudication, an initial trial is about determining facts asymmetrically known by the litigants.[7] Then, given the relevant and admissible facts that emerge, the trial court applies a definite legal rule to determine judgment (Kornhauser 1992). Within this framework, appeals involve correcting lower courts' errors in implementing legal rules. Within a team model, these errors might occur because relevant information isn't revealed at trial, information that might emerge at appeal, thus allowing error correction, or, errors might occur because the trial judge simply makes a mistake in applying law to facts, a mistake that might be corrected through more careful review at the appellate stage. Within the U.S. system of appeals, in which the fact-finding role of trial courts is privileged and little if any additional factual material emerges on appeal, only the second possibility would seem to deserve serious consideration.

In contrast, in the "law-creation" account of adjudication, the key issue is really the absence of a definitive legal rule—there is a "gap" in the law. Of course, an initial trial may *still* be about determining facts. However, the thorny problem for the trial judge, even after the facts emerge, is to make a judgment in the absence of a definitive rule: she must "guess" the "best" rule and apply it. (Note that in a team model, every judge in the same position with the same information would proceed similarly, and the "best" rule—once discovered—will be compelling for all.) Within this account, appeals allow additional or more-intense deliberation about the "best" rule, correcting faulty inferences about the best rule.

This view of litigation directs attention to a handful of information structures, among the multitude of possible ones. In particular, within the team framework:

1. Implementation of Existing Rules

    A. Losing litigant has unrevealed private information about the trial judge's fact-law match (litigant knows the judge made a mistake), so that the act of appeal may signal judicial error. The appellate judge (1) may or (2) may not receive additional information about the correct fact-law match during the appeal hearing itself.

B. The losing litigant does not have private information about the trial judge's fact-law match (litigant has no special knowledge of judicial error). In this case, the act of appeal is simply a lottery rather than a signal. As before, additional information about the fact-law match (1) can or (2) cannot be revealed to the appellate judge during the appeal hearing itself.

2. Creation of New Rules

A. Losing litigant has unrevealed private information about the "best rule" for filling the gap, so that the act of appeal is a signal about this information. Then, additional information about the best rule (1) can or (2) cannot be revealed to the appellate judge during the hearing itself.

B. Losing litigant does not have unrevealed private information about the "best rule" for filling the gap, so that the act of appeal is the act of appeal is simply a lottery rather than a signal. Then, additional information about the best rule (1) can or (2) cannot be revealed to the appellate judge during the hearing itself.

As an example, the model in Daughety and Reinganum 2000 analyzes the information structure in 2.A.(1). In their model, the losing litigant receives a noisy signal about the likely rule ultimately to be chosen by the highest court (the "best rule"), but so does the judge during the appeals process. The task for the appellate judge is to best use both signals efficiently.

In our view, an important research task for analysts of judicial systems is to explore each of these information structures and show how different institutional designs lead to different conduct by the actors and different performance by the system, especially in terms of the five variables identified earlier.

Litigant Selection and Appeals

We now formulate a game in which selection, error-correction, and error-introduction ratios are determined endogenously. We focus on the team context, to create a legal model of hierarchy. And, we consider legal implementation, focusing on information structure 1.A (1). We provide a particularly simple model, not as a final word on the subject, but to illustrate some of the relevant ideas.

PRELIMINARIES

There are two classes of litigants—plaintiffs and defendants—and, depending on the game, one, two, or three tiers of judges. Defendants have a type $\beta \in \{l, \bar{l}\}$, (liable and not liable, respectively). Nature selects Defendant's type as l with common knowledge probability p_0. Plaintiff and defendant each have two actions open to them in the event the judicial system has more than one tier. Suppose the system has T tiers. If a judgment at tier $t < T$ is adverse to its interest, losing litigant j at level t may either appeal ($s_j^t = 1$) or not appeal ($s_j^t = 0$). (A judgment at tier T cannot be appealed.) Let σ_j^t denote the probability of an appeal by losing litigant j at tier t. A judge i at tier t reaches a judgment $v_i^t \in \{l, \bar{l}\}$ (defendant held liable or not liable, respectively). Let p_i^t denote the probability that judge i at tier t reaches judgment $v_i^t = l$. And, let v_F denote the final judgment prevailing in the judicial system; that is, v_F is the decision of the judge at the highest tier in the system to hear the case.

In this team model, all judges wish to maximize the expected number of rightly decided cases in the system. In addition, lower court judges wish to avoid reversal; they suffer a loss ε if a case is reversed. The utility of judge i at level t is then given by:

$$u_i^t = \begin{cases} 1 - J_i \varepsilon \text{ if } v_F = \beta \\ 0 - J_i \varepsilon \text{ if } v_F \neq \beta \end{cases}$$

where J_i is an indicator variable taking the value 1 if i's judgment is ultimately reversed and 0 otherwise.

The defendant pays damages d in the event that $v_F = 1$ (that is, she is held liable in the end); otherwise she pays 0. In addition, a litigant incurs a cost c each time she appeals.

The defendant's utility is then given by

$$u_D = \begin{cases} -d - I_D c \text{ if } v_F = l \\ 0 - I_D c \text{ if } v_F = \bar{l} \end{cases}$$

where I_D equals one plus the number of appeals the Defendant makes.[8]

The plaintiff suffers a loss λ; but this occurs regardless of the play of the game and so can be normalized to zero. Should the plaintiff prevail in litigation he will receive damages d from the defendant in the event that $v_F = l$; otherwise he receives 0. The plaintiff's utility is then given by

$$u_p = \begin{cases} d - I_p c \text{ if } v_F = l \\ 0 - I_p c \text{ if } v_F = \bar{l} \end{cases}$$

where I_p equals the number of appeals the plaintiff makes.

The information structure is the following. Initially, the defendant's type β is private information; hence, it may be rational for the defendant and plaintiff to engage in litigation (however, we do not actually model the pretrial settlement process). At the end of the trial, the defendant's type is revealed to *both* litigants. This assumption reflects the operation of discovery and the litigants' special knowledge of their circumstances. However, the defendant's type is revealed to judge i at tier t only with probability π_i^t (c^t/n^t), that is, with a probability that is a function of the judge's caseload.[9] More specifically, as a result of the trial and the judge's deliberation concerning matters of fact and law, the judge at tier t receives a "hard signal" $x^t \in \{0,\beta\}$, where 0 denotes a noninformative hard signal.[10] We assume that if a defendant's type is ever revealed by a "hard signal"—verifiable and legally admissible evidence combined with judicial reasoning that team members see as determinative—then all subsequent judges also know the defendant's type. We assume $\pi^{t\prime} < 0$. Let μ_i^t be the belief of judge i at tier t that defendant is liable ($\beta = l$).

FLAT ORGANIZATION

As a benchmark, we first consider a flat organization. The "equilibrium" is straightforward, because, in effect, there is only one player, the judges at the first tier, each of whom acts unilaterally. If the judge learns the defendant's type from the hard signal, it rules accordingly. Otherwise, it relies on its prior beliefs. A strategy $\rho_i^1(x^1, p_0)$ for judge i is a probability of ruling "l", given the hard signal and the initial probability the defendant is liable.

Proposition 1: In a one-tier hierarchy, the following characterizes judge i's strategy:

$$\rho_i^1(x^1, p_0) = \begin{cases} 1 \text{ if } \mu_i^1 > \dfrac{1}{2} \\ \alpha \in [0,1] \text{ if } \mu_i^1 = \dfrac{1}{2} \\ 0 \text{ if } \mu_i^1 < \dfrac{1}{2} \end{cases}$$

Proof: The expected value of $v^1 = l$ is $\mu_i^1(1) + (1 - \mu_i^1)(0)$, while the expected value of $v^1 = \bar{l}$ is $\mu_i^1(0) + (1 - \mu_i^1)(1)$. The former will be greater than the latter as $\mu_i^1 > < = (1/2)$. Note that if the hard signal reveals the defendant's type, then $\mu_i^1(x^1, p_0) = 1$ or $\mu_i^1(x^1, p_0) = 0$ as $x_1 = l$ or $x_1 = \bar{l}$, respectively. Absent an informative hard signal, $\mu_i^1(x^1, p_0) = p_0$.

In expectation, the proportion of correctly decided cases is $\Pi(c^1/n^1) = \pi^1(c^1/n^1) + (1 - \pi^1(c^1/n^1))\max\{p_0, 1 - p_0\}$. This proportion is higher as π^1 increases, so that informative hard signals are more likely. It also increases as p_0 tends toward 0 or 1, so that relying on prior beliefs tends to sort the litigants properly.

TWO-TIER HIERARCHY

We now consider a two-tier hierarchy. In this game, a losing litigant may appeal to a higher court, which is obliged to hear the appeal. This is a signaling game, since the appeal may reflect the hidden information of the appellant. There are three types of equilibria to consider: a separating equilibrium; a hybrid, or partial pooling equilibrium; and a pooling equilibrium.

SEPARATING EQUILIBRIUM. In this equilibrium, the litigants separate in appeals: if the defendant's type was not revealed at trial, the losing litigant does not appeal in correctly decided cases ($v^1 = \beta$), thus ending the game; but the losing litigant does appeal (so $s_j^1 = 1$) in incorrectly decided ones ($v^1 \neq \beta$). Given this behavior by the litigants, the appellate court always reverses the trial court (in the absence of a hard signal that the losing litigant has improperly appealed—an out-of-equilibrium event). But a hard signal upon appeal must be rather likely, for it is this possibility that drives the correctly losing litigants to separate from incorrectly losing ones.

Conceptually, an equilibrium of this game requires the specification of strategies for seven players: the trial judge, the appellate judge, a losing defendant of type l, a losing defendant of type $\bar{l}$, a losing plaintiff who knows the defendant's type is l, and a losing plaintiff who knows the defendant's type is $\bar{l}$. However, in the separating equilibrium, we may describe the strategy of all losing litigants identically, conditioning only on whether the trial judgment was correct or incorrect, given the defendant's type. Consequently, as the following proposition shows, the separating equilibrium is quite simple.

Proposition 2a: In a two-tier hierarchy, if $\pi^2(c^2/n^2) \geq 1 - (c/d)$, then the following is an equilibrium: judge i at tier 1 adopts the strategy

$$\rho_i^1(x^1, p_0) = \begin{cases} 1 \text{ if } \mu_i^1 > \dfrac{1}{2} \\ \alpha \in [0,1] \text{ if } \mu_i^1 = \dfrac{1}{2} \\ 0 \text{ if } \mu_i^1 < \dfrac{1}{2} \end{cases}$$

A losing litigant j at tier 1 adopts the strategy

$$\sigma_j^1(v^1, x^1, \beta) = \begin{cases} 1 \text{ if } v^1 \neq \beta \\ 0 \text{ if } v^1 = \beta \end{cases}$$

and an appellate judge i at tier 2 adopts the strategy

$$\rho_i^2(s_j^1, x^2, x^1, p_0) = \begin{cases} 1 \text{ if } \mu_i^2(s_j^2, x^2, x^1, p_0) \geq 1/2 \\ 0 \text{ otherwise} \end{cases}$$

and $\mu_i^2(s_j^2, x^2, x^1, p_0)$ is determined by Bayes's Rule whenever possible. If a hard signal ever reveals β, the appellate judge believes the hard signal regardless of an appeal.

Proof: See appendix B.

A striking feature of this equilibrium is that every case is adjudicated correctly: the expected number of errors is zero! But, the caseload for the appellate judge is just its share of the cases incorrectly decided at the first level, which on average is $(1 - \pi^1(c^1/n^1))\min\{p_0, 1 - p_0\}C^1$. If the trial judges are overburdened, their accuracy (π^1) will be low. Then, if prior beliefs are not very useful in sorting litigants correctly at trial, the appellate caseload may be large. And in turn, if the appellate caseload is heavy, the critical condition on appeals accuracy ($\pi^2 \geq 1 - c/d$) may fail and the separating equilibrium will not be possible.

SEMISEPARATING (PARTIAL POOLING) EQUILIBRIUM. Suppose the probability of a hard signal on appeal isn't high enough to ensure separation of types. Then the following is an equilibrium: the trial judge acts as above; absent a hard signal at trial, a losing litigant definitely appeals an incorrect judgment and may appeal a correct one. Thus, no appeal is a sign of guilt by the losing litigant (but a payoff irrelevant one because this ends the game). An appeal, however, has an ambiguous meaning. Absent a hard signal on appeal, the appellate court reverses some judgments but affirms others. This equilibrium involves rather delicate mixing.

Proposition 2b: If $\pi^2 < 1 - (c/d)$, the following is an equilibrium: The trial judge plays the strategy

$$\rho_i^1(x^1, p_0) = \begin{cases} 1 \text{ if } x^1 = l, \text{ or if } x^1 = 0 \text{ and } p_0 > \dfrac{1}{2} \\[2mm] \alpha \in [0,1] \text{ if } x^1 = 0 \text{ and } p_0 = \dfrac{1}{2} \\[2mm] 0 \text{ if } x^1 = \bar{l}, \text{ or if } x^1 = 0 \text{ and } p_0 < \dfrac{1}{2} \end{cases}$$

An incorrectly losing plaintiff plays the strategy

$$\sigma_P^1(v^1 = \bar{l}, x^1, \beta = l, \rho_i^1(\cdot)) = \begin{cases} 1 \text{ if } x^1 = \beta = l, \text{ or if } x^1 = 0, \beta = l \\[1mm] \text{and } \rho_i^2(v^1 = \bar{l}, x^1 = x^2 = 0) \geq \dfrac{c - d\pi^2}{d(1 - \pi^2)} \\[3mm] 0 \text{ if } x^1 = 0, \beta = l \\[1mm] \text{and } \rho_i^2(v^1 = \bar{l}, x^1 = x^2 = 0) < \dfrac{c - d\pi^2}{d(1 - \pi^2)} \end{cases}$$

A correctly losing plaintiff plays the strategy

$$\sigma_P^1(v^1 = \bar{l}, x^1, \beta = \bar{l}, \rho_i^1(\cdot)) = \begin{cases} 1 \text{ if } x^1 = 0, \beta = \bar{l} \\[1mm] \text{and } \rho_i^2(v^1 = \bar{l} = x^2 = 0) > \dfrac{c}{d(1 - \pi^2)} \\[3mm] \dfrac{p_0}{1 - p_0} \text{ if } x^1 = 0, \beta = \bar{l}, \\[2mm] \text{and } \rho_i^2(v^1 = \bar{l}, x_1 = x_2 = 0) = \dfrac{c}{d(1 - \pi^2)} \\[3mm] 0 \text{ if } x^1 = \beta = \bar{l}, \text{ or if } x^1 = 0, \beta = \bar{l} \\[1mm] \text{and } \rho_i^2(v^1 = \bar{l}, x^1 = x^2 = 0) < \dfrac{c}{d(1 - \pi^2)} \end{cases}$$

An incorrectly losing defendant plays the strategy

$$\sigma_{D=i}^1(v^1 = l, x^1, \rho_i^1(\cdot)) = \begin{cases} 1 \text{ if } x^1 = \bar{l}, \text{ or if } x^1 = 0 \\[1mm] \text{and } \rho_i^2(v^1 = l, x^1 = x^2 = 0) \leq \dfrac{d - c}{d(1 - \pi^2)} \\[3mm] 0 \text{ if } x^1 = 0 \\[1mm] \text{and } \rho_i^2(v^1 = l, x^1 = x^2 = 0) > \dfrac{d - c}{d(1 - \pi^2)} \end{cases}$$

A correctly losing defendant plays the strategy

$$\sigma^1_{d=l}(v^1 = l, x^1, \rho^1_i(\cdot)) = \begin{cases} 1 \text{ if } x^1 = 0 \\ \text{and } \rho^2_i(v^1 = l, x^1 = x^2 = 0) < 1 - \dfrac{c}{d(1-\pi^2)} \\[2mm] \dfrac{1-p_0}{p_0} \text{ if } x^1 = 0 \\ \text{and } \rho^2_i(v^1 = l, x^1 = x^2 = 0) = 1 - \dfrac{c}{d(1-\pi^2)} \\[2mm] 0 \text{ if } x^1 = l \text{ or if } x^1 = 0 \\ \text{and } \rho^2_i(v^1 = l, x^1 = x^2 = 0) > 1 - \dfrac{c}{d(1-\pi^2)} \end{cases}$$

Finally, the appellate judge plays the strategy

$$\rho^2_i(v^1 = \bar{l}) = \begin{cases} 1 \text{ if } \mu^2_i = 1, \text{ or if } x^1 = x^2 = 0 \\ \text{and } \sigma^1_P(x^1 = 0, \beta = \bar{l}) > \dfrac{p_0}{1-p_0} \\[2mm] \dfrac{c}{d(1-\pi^2)} \text{ if } x^1 = x^2 = 0 \\ \text{and } \sigma^1_P(x^1 = 0, \beta = \bar{l}) = \dfrac{p_0}{1-p_0} \\[2mm] 0 \text{ if } \mu^2_i = 0, \text{ or if } x^1 = x^2 = 0 \\ \text{and } \sigma^1_P(x^1 = 0, \beta = \bar{l}) < \dfrac{p_0}{1-p_0} \end{cases}$$

$$\rho^2_i(v^1 = l) = \begin{cases} 1 \text{ if } \mu^2_i = 1, \text{ or if } x^1 = x^2 = 0 \\ \text{and } \sigma^1_D(x^1 = 0, \beta = l) > \dfrac{1-p_0}{p_0} \\[2mm] 1 - \dfrac{c}{d(1-\pi^2)} \text{ if } x^1 = x^2 = 0 \\ \text{and } \sigma^1_D(x^1 = 0, \beta = l) = \dfrac{1-p_0}{p_0} \\[2mm] 0 \text{ if } \mu^2_i = 0, \text{ or if } x^1 = x^2 = 0 \\[2mm] \text{and } \sigma^1_D(x^1 = 0, \beta = l) < \dfrac{1-p_0}{p_0} \end{cases}$$

Beliefs are determined by Bayes's Rule whenever possible. If a hard signal ever reveals β, the appellate judge believes the hard signal regardless of an appeal.

Proof: See appendix B.

These strategies may look forbiddingly complex, but the play of the game is actually quite simple. If a hard signal occurs at trial, the trial judge rules accordingly, and there is no appeal. If no hard signal emerges at trial, what happens depends on the initial probability that the defendant is liable.

If $p_0 > .5$ and the trial judge's signal is uninformative, the trial judge holds the defendant liable. An incorrectly losing defendant appeals with certainty. A correctly losing Defendant appeals with probability $(1 - p_0/p_0)$ (which lies between 0 and 1). Given an appeal by a defendant but no hard signal on appeal, the appellate judge sustains with probability $1 - (c/d(1 - \pi^2))$ and reverses with the reciprocal probability. An incorrectly losing plaintiff appeals with certainty; and the appellate court reverses. (When the trial signal is uninformative, there are no correctly losing plaintiffs given the strategy of the trial judge.)

If $p_0 < .5$, absent a hard signal at trial, the trial judge holds the Defendant not liable. An incorrectly losing plaintiff appeals with certainty. A correctly losing plaintiff appeals with probability $(p_0/1 - p_0)$ (which lies between 0 and 1). Given an appeal by a plaintiff but no hard signal on appeal, the appellate judge again sustains with probability $1 - (c/d(1 - \pi^2))$ and reverses with the reciprocal probability. An incorrectly losing defendant appeals with certainty and the appellate judge reverses. (When the trial signal is uninformative, there are no correctly losing defendants given the strategy of the trial judge.)

POOLING EQUILIBRIUM. There are two possible pooling equilibria: an "everyone appeals" equilibrium, and a "no-one appeals" equilibrium.

A moment's reflection shows that the former cannot be an equilibrium. Because litigants pool, the appellate judge's beliefs must be the same as those of the trial judge in cases lacking a hard signal at either level. Consequently, in those cases, the appellate judge will uphold the trial judge's verdict. But this means that an appeal by a losing litigant in a correctly decided case can never be profitable (since either a hard signal is received, resulting in an affirmance, or one is not received, again resulting in affirmance).

A "no-appeals" equilibrium can hold if the probability of a hard signal is rather low. But this equilibrium is vulnerable to forward induction-style refinements. In this equilibrium, no litigants appeal. But if one did, the appellate judge (absent a hard signal) must affirm the lower court—in the equilibrium, an appeal (an out-of-equilibrium event) is taken as a signal of guilt. (Otherwise, losing litigants will appeal, breaking the equilibrium). Given this interpretation of an appeal, no one appeals. Although this is an equilibrium, an obvious issue is, is it reasonable for the appellate judge to believe that an appeal signals guilt rather than innocence? Note that for correctly losing litigants, a no-appeal equilibrium dominates no appeal (since if there is a hard signal, his guilt emerges, and if not, the judge believes he is guilty and affirms anyway). By construction, no appeal must also be more appealing than appeal for an incorrectly losing litigant. But it must be the case that, for any response by the appellate judge to an appeal, appeal is more attractive for an incorrectly losing litigant than for a correctly losing litigant (because of the possibility of a hard signal, which would vindicate the incorrectly losing litigant). Hence, if the appellate judge sees an appeal, she should put no weight on an appeal from an incorrectly losing litigant.[11] But given this reasoning, an appeal could only come from an incorrectly losing litigant, which should compel the judge to reverse, even absent a hard signal. Hence, this equilibrium appears implausible.

The reasoning establishes:

Proposition 2c: No universally divine pooling equilibrium exists in the two-tier game.

Discussion

The two-tier separating equilibrium performs well, but it is fragile. It can exist only if judicial accuracy in the upper tier is quite high. But if judicial accuracy in the lower tier is poor, then the upper tier's caseload can be very high, and its accuracy correspondingly low. In that case, the partial pooling equilibrium—which is far less desirable—looks more probable. The equilibrium in the following section seems to point to a easy structural "fix" for the two-tier system's vulnerability.

We now consider a three-tier hierarchy and focus on a truly remarkable separating equilibrium. In this equilibrium, litigants separate at the first level of appeals, so that only incorrectly decided cases appeal. In the intermediate court, all appealed initial judgments are reversed (in equilibrium). Then, losing litigants make no appeals to the "Supreme Court." Hence, all cases are resolved correctly! Unlike the separating equilibrium in the two-layer hierarchy, separation does not depend on high levels of accuracy at the second level. Rather, the key in constructing the equilibrium is a high level of accuracy at the *highest* level—even though this court hears no cases. If a correctly losing litigant makes a "bogus" appeal to the intermediate court and the case is reversed (absent a hard signal), then the litigant who initially (correctly) won has an incentive to appeal to the Supreme Court, which is very likely to receive a hard signal and decide the case correctly. Conversely, in a case that is initially incorrectly decided but corrected upon appeal, the correctly losing litigant will have no incentive to appeal to the high court, if the accuracy level at that level is sufficiently high. This high level of accuracy is quite reasonable, given the Supreme Court's low caseload (actually, zero in equilibrium).

Proposition 3: If $\pi^3 > 1 - (c/d)$, the following is an equilibrium in the three-tier hierarchy game:

$$\rho_i^A(p_0, x^1, v^1, s^1, x^2, v^2, s^2, x^3) = \begin{cases} 1 \text{ if } \mu_i^3(\cdot) \geq \dfrac{1}{2} \\ 0 \text{ otherwise} \end{cases}$$

$$\sigma_j^2(p_0, x^1, v^1, s^1, x^2, v^2) = \begin{cases} 1 \text{ if } v^2 \neq \beta \\ 0 \text{ otherwise} \end{cases}$$

$$\rho_i^2(p_0, x^1, v^1, s^1, x^2) = \begin{cases} 1 \text{ if } \mu_i^2(\cdot) \geq \dfrac{1}{2} \\ 0 \text{ otherwise} \end{cases}$$

$$\sigma_j^1(p_0, x^1, v^1) = \begin{cases} 1 \text{ if } v^2 \neq \beta \\ 0 \text{ otherwise} \end{cases}$$

$$\rho_i^1(p_0, x^1) = \begin{cases} 1 \text{ if } \mu_i^1(\cdot) \geq \dfrac{1}{2} \\ 0 \text{ otherwise} \end{cases}$$

Beliefs are determined wherever possible by Bayes's Rule. If a hard signal ever reveals the defendant's type, the beliefs of subsequently acting judges are fixed accordingly. Following an appeal of the intermediate court's judgment, in the absence of any hard signals the high court believes an error occurred at the intermediate court.

Proof: See appendix B.

Conceptually, the conditional error introduction rate at the Supreme Court is small enough so that it dissuades bogus appeals. This, in turn, allows the conditional error correction rate at the penultimate stage to be very high (even absent much judicial accuracy), thereby encouraging "legitimate" appeals.

The following Corollary is striking:

Corollary 3: There is never a need to have more than three tiers in a judicial hierarchy, regardless of the caseload.

Proof: The error rate in the equilibrium detailed in Proposition 3 is zero. Adding additional layers cannot improve upon this performance. And, the equilibrium is robust to the caseload.

This remarkable result obviously reflects the strong assumptions in the model. It is important to identify the critical assumption, which is: *after trial, both litigants know whether the defendant is truly liable.* The hierarchy then exploits their hidden but mutual knowledge, implicitly encouraging them to police the outcome via appeals.

It is also tempting to interpret Propositions 2 and 3 in the following way. If the caseload in a judicial system is sufficiently small, a two-tier hierarchy is "good enough" to exploit the power of litigant selection. But if the caseload becomes too burdensome, a three-tier hierarchy—and no more than three tiers—is needed to gain the full benefit of litigant selection. In fact, the historical development of state judicial systems in the United States follows this stylized script (see Kagan et al. 1978). And broadly speaking, so does the history of the federal judiciary (Frankfurter and Landis 1928). Of course, functionalist "just-so" stories can never adequately account for actual historical developments. But the models may suggest some fruitful directions for historical research on judicial hierarchies.

One implication of Proposition 3, however, appears quite counterfactual. Proposition 3 seems to imply that few judges are needed at the trial level (since judicial accuracy there is immaterial), and few judges are needed at tier two (because accuracy there is also, in equilibrium, immaterial). But, on the assumption that a larger panel implies a more accurate judgment on the law, several judges are probably needed at the highest level—even though these judges hear no cases.

Reflection suggests, however, that many judges are surely required, at least at the trial level. Recall the key assumption in the model: both litigants learn all private information during trial, even if the judges do not. For trials to proceed in a sufficiently informative way to assure mutual revelation, surely considerable judicial resources are required.[12] (In addition, of course, trial courts make judgments of law, an activity not addressed by the model in this essay). Thus, tier one may require many judges. A relatively sparse layer of intermediate appellate judges is then necessary to process the large number of appeals from an inaccurate trial court; each intermediate appellate judge need not have great accuracy. Accuracy at the top, however, is essential, so we should expect a reasonably sized panel of judges prepared to act en banc on any given appeal. The current structure of trial courts in the United States arguably fits that description. There are many trial judges, but they do not sit in panels; they serve only to guide fact-finding. Supreme courts in the United States generally have large panels of five to nine judges. There are many intermediate appellate courts that usually sit in panels of three.

The Structural Consequences of Litigant Selection

Our simple models of litigant selection illustrate the complexity of the structural relations within a judicial hierarchy. Here we briefly illustrate the use of the theorems in the first part of the essay—the structural analysis—by applying them to the game theoretic models in the second part of the essay. We focus on the move from a flat organization to a two-tiered hierarchy, first in the separating equilibrium and then in the partial pooling equilibrium. Application of the theorems to the move to a three-tiered hierarchy is similar, and is omitted for brevity. Within our framework, of course, theorem three shows that adding a fourth or higher tier cannot improve the performance of the hierarchy.

ADDING A SECOND TIER: SEPARATING EQUILIBRIUM

Our propositions 2a to 2c indicate the possible consequences of moving from a flat organization of a judicial system to a two-tiered hierarchical organization. Consider first the separating equilibrium described in proposition 2a. When the second tier is sufficiently accurate, the two-tiered hierarchy correctly decides every case. This occurs because the appeals process is highly—indeed, infinitely—selective as $q_R^{1|2}$, the probability that a case rightly decided at level 1 will be appealed to level 2, is simply 0, while $q_W^{1|2}$, the probability that a wrongly decided case at level 1 will be appealed to level 2, equals 1. The second tier thus introduces no errors and, as every wrongly decided case is appealed, it corrects all errors from below.

This analysis is consistent with an application of our theorem 1 from section 2 concerning add-on hierarchies. Perhaps the simplest way to see this is to use (H3). In the case of a two-tier hierarchy, the two-tier hierarchy will be superior to the flat organization, if

$$\frac{1-p_W^{2|2}}{1-p^{1|2}} > \frac{q_R^{1|2}}{q_W^{1|2}}\frac{p_R^{2|2}}{p^{1|2}} - \frac{\Delta^2}{q_W^{1|2}C_W^{1|2}(1-p^{1|2})} \qquad \text{(H3.a)}$$

In the separating equilibrium, $q_R^{1|2} = 0$, $q_W^{1|2} = 1$, and $1 - p_W^{2|2} = 1$, so (with a little algebra) H3.a reduces to $C_W^{1|2} > -\Delta^2$. However, using the earlier definitions, $\Delta^2 = C_W^{1|1} - C_W^{1|2}$. Substituting and rearranging reduces H3.a to: $C_W^{1|1} > 0$. This inequality is met in any reallocation hierarchy that simply reallocates some of the trial judges in the flat organization to an appellate tier. Thus, though the addition of an appellate tier degrades the quality of justice at the trial level, it may improve the performance of the system as a whole.[13]

ADDING A SECOND TIER: PARTIAL POOLING EQUILIBRIUM

We now consider the partial pooling equilibrium, which arises when the appellate tier is not sufficiently accurate to enforce the separating equilibrium. We begin with a "direct" comparison of the two organizational forms, by calculating the expected errors in the two-tier hierarchy with a partial pooling equilibrium. In the appendix, we prove

Proposition 2d: In the semiseparating equilibrium of the two-tier game, the expected proportion of correctly decided cases of the court system is $1 - (1 - \pi^{1|2})(1 - \pi^{2|2})(1 - p_0)$, if $p_0 > .5$, and $1 - (1 - \pi^{1|2})(1 - \pi^{2|2})p_0$ if $p_0 \leq .5$.

Proposition 2d states that, in the semiseparating equilibrium, if a hard signal is likely at either the trial or appellate level, correct adjudication will be likely as well. Similarly, if the defendant is probably liable ($p_0 \approx 1$) or probably not liable ($p_0 \approx 0$), correct adjudication is probable. But if a hard signal is unlikely both at trial and on appeal and the Defendant is approximately equally likely to be liable as not liable, the probability of correct adjudication approaches one-half—a coin toss. This is far from the perfect adjudication of the separating equilibrium.

The following corollary follows immediately from proposition 2d and the observation that in the flat organization the total number of errors is $(1 - \pi^1(c^{1|1}/n^{1|1}))\min\{p_0, 1 - p_0\}$.

Corollary: A two-tiered hierarchy under the partial pooling equilibrium is an improvement over a flat organization if and only if $(1 - \pi^{1|1}) > (1 - \pi^{1|2})(1 - \pi^{2|2})$.

This corollary states that in the partial pooling case, the two-tiered hierarchy *reduces error if it reduces the probability that the judicial system receives no hard signal.* We have already noted in our discussion of the separating equilibrium that creating a second tier by reallocating judges from a trial bench to an appellate bench will degrade the quality of the trial courts; that is, $(1 - \pi^{1|1}) > (1 - \pi^{1|2})$. The accuracy of the appellate process must thus be sufficiently high to overcome this deficit.

Theorem 1 yields the same conclusion, in a somewhat less direct manner. Perhaps the simplest approach is to use (H0). In this case, (H0) indicates that the two-tier hierarchy will be superior to the flat organization, if

$$C_W^{1|1} > C_W^{1|2}(1 - q_W^{1|2}) + C_W^{2|2}$$

(recalling that $A^{1|T} = 0$). Using the definitions for caseloads of wrong cases, this becomes

$$p^{1|1}C^{1|1} > C_W^{1|2}(1 - q_W^{1|2}) + C_R^{1|2}q_R^{1|2}p_R^{2|2} + C_W^{1|2}q_W^{1|2}p_W^{2|2} \tag{H0.a}$$

To evaluate this expression, we need to specify the values of the key systemic variables that characterize the appellate tier in the partial pooling equilibrium. We employ the "aggregate" approach discussed in note 12, focusing on the case of $p_0 > \frac{1}{2}$.[14] First, $p^{1|1}$, the error rate at level 1 in the flat organization, equals $(1 - \pi^{1|1})(1 - p_0)$. Second, $q_R^{1|2}$, the probability that a case rightly decided at level 1 will be appealed to level 2, is $(1 - \pi^{1|2})$ $(1 - p_0)/\pi^{1|2} + (1 - \pi^{1|2})p_0$.[15] Third, $q_w^{1|2} = (1 - \pi^{1|2})(1 - p_0)\backslash(1 - \pi^{1|2})(1 - p_0) = 1$, that is, the probability that a wrongly decided case at level 1 will be appealed to level 2 is equal to 1. Fourth, $1 - P_R^{2|2}$, the probability that, on appeal, a case correctly decided at level 1 will be upheld, is $\pi^{2|2} + (1 - \pi^{2|2})(1 - (c/d(1 - \pi^{2|2}))$. Fifth, $1 - p_W^{2|2}$, the probability that, on appeal, a wrongly decided case will be reversed, equals $\pi^{2|2} + (1 - \pi^{2|2})(c/(d(1 - \pi^{2|2}))$. Finally, note that $C_W^{1|2} = (1 - \pi^{1|2})(1 - p_0)C^{1|2}$ and $C_R^{1|2} = (\pi^{1|2} + (1 - \pi^{1|2})p_0)C^{1|2}$.

Employing $p^{1|1}$ and $q_W^{1|2}$, (H0.a) reduces to

$$(1 - \pi^{1|1})(1 - p_0)C^{1|1} > C_R^{1|2}q_R^{1|2}p_R^{2|2} + C_W^{1|2}q_W^{1|2}p_W^{2|2}$$

Substitution of the additional key values and some algebra yields

$$(1 - \pi^{1|1})(1 - p_0)C^{1|1} > (1 - p_0)(1 - \pi^{1|2})(1 - \pi^{2|2})C^{1|2},$$

so that if the initial caseload in the two organizational forms is the same, the conclusion in the corollary is immediate. Of course, the number of disputes brought to a court system will often depend on the quality of justice provided by the system.

Conclusion

In this essay, we first conducted a structural analysis of appeals procedures, the first complete analysis of this kind that we know. We then discussed possible information structures that might arise in judicial hierarchies. Finally, we examined one of these in a rather stylized, game-theoretic setting. The purpose of the game-theoretic analysis was less to propose models of courts that one could take to data, than to conduct a series of thought experiments aimed at sharpening our theoretical intuitions about the logic and incentives in appeals system. The game-theoretic models point to the value of litigant selection, particularly in the situation of judicial implementation. The intuition is simple but illuminating: *litigant selection places the burden of appeals on informationally advantaged actors.* The separating equilibrium in the three-tier hierarchy suggests the remarkable power of this mechanism, even in the face of relatively weak technologies of judging. We suspect litigant selection will be less potent in situations of law creation, because the litigants are not likely to be informationally advantaged relative to judges.[16] Presumably, the absence of information asymmetries precludes a striking structural result, like the three-tier result in the implementation models (Corollary 3). Nonetheless, if the initial trial provides the litigants with good information about the prospects of reversal (that is, the probability a higher court will find a better rule), litigants will still screen out the least promising cases for law creation. In short, the logic of litigant selection seems compelling in systems of appeals.

Appendix A: Comparing a T-tier hierarchy and a T+1 tier Hierarchy

We employ the following notation:

$C \equiv C^1$, the total number of cases to be decided in the system

$n \equiv$ total number of judges in the system

$T \equiv$ the total number of tiers (indexed by t)

$n^t \equiv$ the total number of judges at tier t

$C^t \equiv$ the total number of cases at tier t

$q_w^t \equiv$ the proportion of wrongly decided cases at level t that are appealed to level $t + 1$

$q_R^t \equiv$ the proportion of rightly decided cases at level t that are appealed to level $t + 1$

$p^t \equiv$ the error rate at t with $(1 - p^t)$ the nonerror rate at t.

$p_R^t \equiv$ probability that a rightly decided case at level $t - 1$ will be wrongly decided at t, conditional on its being appealed to level t.

$p_w^t \equiv$ probability that a wrongly decided case at level $t - 1$ will be wrongly decided at t, conditional on its being appealed to level t.

We now prove a theorem about the desirability of an *add-on appeals process* (which yields an *add-on hierarchy*). In an add-on hierarchy, we append an appeals process to an existing court structure. Theorem 1 identifies conditions under which an add-on hierarchy is superior to the underlying court structure standing alone.

First, define the *caseload of correctly decided cases* and the *caseload of incorrectly decided cases* at tier t in a T-level hierarchy. At tier 1, these are: $C_R^{1|T} = (1 - p^{1|T}) C^{1|T}$ and $C_W^{1|T} = p^{1|T} C^{1|T}$ (note the superscript indicating the "height" of the hierarchy). At the higher levels, $t > 1$, they are: $C_R^{t|T} = C_R^{t-1|T} q_R^{t-1|T} (1 - p_R^{t|T}) + C_W^{t-1|T} q_W^{t-1|T} (1 - p_W^{t|T}$ and $C_W^{t|T} = C_R^{t-1|T} q_R^{t-1|T} p_R^{t|T} + C_W^{t-1|T} q_W^{t-1|T} p_W^{t|T}$, respectively.

Our metric for evaluating a judicial hierarchy is the total number of errors remaining after the operation of the hierarchy. The total number of errors in a T-tier hierarchy is simply the unappealed errors at each of the lower levels, plus the errors at tier T. Define the sum of unappealed errors in the levels lower than t' in a T-tier hierarchy as $A^{t|T} = \Sigma_{t=1}^{t'-1} C_W^{t|T} (1 - q_W^{t|T})$. (We define $A^{1|T} \equiv 0$. The total number of errors in a T-tier hierarchy is then $E^{T|T} = A^{T|T} + C_W^{T|T}$. Finally, define $\Delta^{T+1} \equiv A^{T|T} - A^{T|T+1} + C_W^{T|T} - C_W^{T|T+1}$. Note that this is the *errors reduced in tiers 1 to T by adding tier T + 1.* (If the addition of the $T + 1$ tier increases errors in tiers 1 to T, then Δ^{T+1} is negative.) We can now state Theorem 1:

Theorem 1: An add-on hierarchy is superior to the underlying court structure if and only if (1) the add-on hierarchy is sufficiently selective at T, or (2) the add-on hierarchy is sufficiently error correcting at $T + 1$, or (3) the addition of the $T + 1$ level sufficiently improves the performance in the underlying court structure.

Proof: Moving from the T-level hierarchy to the $T + 1$ hierarchy reduces errors, if

$$A^{T|T} + C_W^{T|T} > A^{T|T+1} + C_W^{T|T+1}(1 - q_W^{T|T+1}) + C_W^{T+1|T+1} \tag{H0}$$

$$\Leftrightarrow A^{T|T} - A^{T|T+1} + C_W^{T|T} - C_W^{T|T+1} > C_R^{T|T+1} q_R^{T|T+1} p_R^{T+1|T+1}$$
$$- C_W^{T|T+1} q_W^{T|T+1}(1 - p_W^{T+1|T+1})$$

$$\Leftrightarrow \Delta^{T+1} + C_W^{T|T+1} q_W^{T|T+1}(1 - p_W^{T+1|T+1}) > C_R^{T|T+1} q_R^{T|T+1} p_R^{T+1|T+1} \tag{H1}$$

that is, the errors reduced in tiers 1 to T by the addition of tier $T + 1$, plus the errors corrected directly by tier $T + 1$, are greater than the errors introduced directly by tier $T + 1$.

Rearranging (H1) yields

$$\frac{q_W^{T|T+1}}{q_R^{T|T+1}} > \frac{p_R^{T+1|T+1}}{C_W^{T|T+1}} \frac{C_R^{T|T+1}}{1 - p_W^{T+1|T+1}} - \frac{\Delta^{t+1}}{q_R^{T|T+1} C_W^{T|T+1}(1 - p_W^{T+1|T+1})}.$$

Multiplying the first term on the right-hand side of this expression by $(C^{T|T+1}/C^{T|T+1})$ yields

$$\frac{q_W^{T|T+1}}{q_R^{T|T+1}} > p_R^{T+1|T+1} \frac{C^{T|T+1}}{C_W^{T|T+1}} \frac{C_R^{T|T+1}}{C^{T|T+1}} \frac{1}{1 - p_W^{T+1|T+1}} - \frac{\Delta^{T+1}}{C_W^{T|T+1}(1 - p_W^{T+1|T+1})}$$

Noting that $(C^{T|T+1}/C_W^{T|T+1}) = (1/p^{T|T+1})$ and $(C_R^{T|T+1}/C^{T|T+1}) = 1 - p^{T|T+1}$, we then have

$$\frac{q_W^{T|T+1}}{q_R^{T|T+1}} > \frac{p_R^{T+1|T+1}}{p^{T|T+1}} \frac{1 - p^{T|T+1}}{1 - p_W^{T+1|T+1}} - \frac{\Delta^{T+1}}{q_R^{T|T+1} C_W^{T|T+1}(1 - p_W^{T+1|T+1})}. \qquad \text{(H2)}$$

(H2) establishes the first part of the theorem because it states that (H1) holds if and only if the selection ratio at level T is greater than the error introduction ratio at $T + 1$ times the inverse error correction ratio at $T + 1$, minus a weighted version of the errors reduced in tiers 1 to T by adding tier $T + 1$.

To establish part (2) we simply rewrite (H2) as

$$\frac{1 - p_W^{T+1|T+1}}{1 - p^{T|T+1}} > \frac{q_R^{T|T+1}}{q_W^{T|T+1}} \frac{p_R^{T+1|T+1}}{p^{T|T+1}} - \frac{\Delta^{T+1}}{q_W^{T|T+1} C_W^{T|T+1}(1 - p^{T|T+1})}. \qquad \text{(H3)}$$

(H3) states that the add-on hierarchy is superior if the error-correction ratio at $T + 1$ is greater than the inverse selection ratio at T times the error-introduction ratio at $T + 1$, minus a weighted version of the errors reduced in tiers 1 to T by adding tier $T + 1$.

Part (3) of the theorem follows immediately from (H1), by rewriting it as

$$\Delta^{T+1} > C_R^{T|T+1} q_R^{T|T+1} p_R^{T+1|T+1} - C_W^{T|T+1} q_W^{T|T+1}(1 - p_W^{T+1|T+1}). \qquad \text{(H4)}$$

This completes the proof.

We now consider the corollaries to the theorem.

Corollary 1.1: An add-on hierarchy that is error-introduction neutral and error correction neutral is superior to the underlying court structure, if and only if the added appeals process is sufficiently selective.

Proof: We rewrite (H2) on the assumption that the appeals process is error-introduction and error-correction neutral. The reallocation hierarchy will be superior to a flat organization, if and only if

$$\frac{q_W^{T|T+1}}{q_R^{T|T+1}} > 1 - \frac{\Delta^{T+1}}{q_R^{T|T+1} C_W^{T|T+1}(1 - p_W^{T+1|T+1})} \qquad \text{(H2.1)}$$

If $\Delta^T+1 \leq 0$, so that addition of the $T+1$ tier either degrades performance in the lower tiers or leaves them unaffected, a necessary condition for (H2.1) to hold is that $q_w^T/q_R^T > 1$: the appeals process from T to $T+1$ must be selective. But if $\Delta^{T+1} > 0$, so that addition of the $T+1$ tier improves performance below, (H2.1) can hold even if the appeals process from T to $T+1$ is antiselective.

Corollary 1.2: Consider an add-on appeals process that is selection neutral. If $\Delta^{T+1} \leq 0$, the add-on hierarchy is superior to the underlying court structure if and only if the error correction ratio exceeds the error introduction ratio for the add-on appeals process.

Proof: We rewrite (H3) on the assumption that the add-on appeals process is selection neutral:

$$\frac{1 - p_W^{T+1|T+1}}{1 - p^{T|T+1}} > \frac{p_R^{T+1|T+1}}{p^{T|T+1}} - \frac{\Delta^{T+1}}{q_W^{T|T+1} C_W^{T|T+1}(1 - p^{T|T+1})} \qquad \text{(H3.1)}$$

The LHS of (H3.1) is the error-correction ratio. The first term in the RHS of (H3.1) is the error-introduction ratio. Under the maintained assumptions, the RHS of (H3.1) is greater than the error-introduction ratio. Hence, if (H3.1) is to hold, it is necessary that the error-correction ratio exceed the error-introduction ratio.

Up to this point, we have not drawn a sharp distinction between adding a new tier using additional judicial resources, and adding a new tier by reallocating a fixed number of judges. But suppose judicial performance degrades when per-judge caseload increases (that is, resources-per-case decreases). Now consider some court structure with T tiers and n judges. Should an institutional designer reallocate judges to create tier $T+1$? Doing so adds a new layer of appeals, which might seem to be a good thing, if, say, the error-correction rate exceeds the error-introduction rate at $T+1$. But it will also increase per-judge caseloads below, and thus degrade judicial performance in the lower levels.

Theorem 1 indicates that the direction and magnitude of Δ^{T+1} and the relationship among the selection, error-correction, and error-introduction ratios at T and $T+1$ will be critical in evaluating a reallocation hierarchy.

Suppose judicial performance is very sensitive to caseload, so removing judges from lower tiers decreases substantially the conditional error correction rate and increases substantially the conditional error-introduction rates and the error rates. Then Δ^{T+1} may be negative in sign and large in magnitude. Given this, the performance of the new tier will have to be very good indeed to offset the degradation in judicial performance below. Conversely, if judicial performance is relatively insensitive to per-judge caseloads, so Δ^{T+1} is negative but modest in size, the new tier need not perform so well. Finally, if the addition of the new tier dramatically improves litigant selection of cases in the lower tiers, so Δ^{T+1} is positive in sign despite the degradation in judicial performance, the new hierarchy can be superior even if the new tier itself performs rather poorly. This somewhat counterintuitive result underscores the need to examine behavioral models of hierarchy, moving beyond a purely the structural analysis.

Appendix B: Proof of Propositions

PROOF OF PROPOSITION 2A

We proceed to show, by backward induction, that each player's strategy is in equilibrium, given the strategies of other players.

APPELLATE JUDGE   There are four possibilities to consider: (1) an incorrectly losing litigant appeals from a judgment based on an uninformative signal at trial, but the appellate judge receives an informative signal; (2) a (correctly or incorrectly) losing litigant appeals from judgment based on an uninformative signal to the trial judge, *and* the appellate judge also receives an uninformative signal; (3) an incorrectly losing litigant appeals from a judgment based on an informative signal at trial; and (4) a correctly losing litigant appeals, and either the trial judge or the appellate judge receives an informative signal. (Recall that an informative signal to a court reveals the defendant's type with complete accuracy and becomes common knowledge to the judiciary.)

In case (1), the hard signal on appeal fixes the appellate judge's beliefs at 0 or 1, and the judgment follows from the logic of Proposition 1. In case (2), the litigants' strategy and Bayes's Rule fix the appellate judge's beliefs at either 0 or 1 (the former when the appellant is the defendant, the latter when the appellant is the plaintiff). Given these beliefs, the judgment again follows immediately. Case (3) is an out-of-equilibrium event, so Bayes's Rule has no bite. But the beliefs indicated in the proposition fix the appellant judge's beliefs according to the hard signal, and again the indicated judgment follows. Now consider case (4), which occurs only off the equilibrium path, as the trial judgment is improperly appealed. Again, Bayes's Rule has no bite, but the specified beliefs require the appellate judge to believe the informative signal. The appellate judge thus upholds the judgment of the trial court.

LOSING LITIGANT   There are two cases. (1) The trial court received an informative signal, and (2) the trial court received an uninformative signal.

1. Suppose no informative signal at trial ($x^1 = 0$). We consider the optimal responses of an incorrectly and correctly losing litigant in turn.

A. An incorrectly losing litigant will definitely appeal, because doing so will result in either (1) an informative hard signal on appeal ($x^2 = \beta$) leading to reversal, or (2) a believed signal of innocence in the absence of a hard signal ($x^2 = 0$), from Bayes's Rule, again leading to reversal.

B. Given $x^1 = 0$, a correctly losing litigant will not appeal if the expected value from appeal is less than the sure value from not appealing, that is, for a correctly losing plaintiff $(1 - \pi^2)d + \pi^2 0 - c \leq 0 \Rightarrow \pi^2 \geq 1 - (c/d)$ and for a correctly losing defendant $(1 - \pi^2)0 + \pi^2(-d) - c \leq -d \Rightarrow \pi^2 \geq 1 - (c/d)$. This is the condition indicated in the Proposition.

2. Suppose an informative signal at trial ($x^1 = \beta$). Again we consider the optimal responses of a correctly losing and incorrectly losing litigant in turn.

A. A correctly losing litigant will not appeal, given the specified off-the-equilibrium path beliefs (the appellate judge believes the hard signal and thus will rule the same way as the trial judge, gaining the correctly losing litigant nothing but costing him an additional c).

B. An incorrectly losing litigant will definitely appeal, because the appellate judge's (off the equilibrium path) belief is that the hard signal was correct, and so he reverses.

TRIAL JUDGE   Given separation by the litigants and the appellate judge's strategy, the trial judge knows that a correct outcome will occur regardless of his judgment. But, the epsilon loss from reversal means the trial judge is not indifferent between his actions—he wants to judge correctly. Accordingly, he follows the utility-maximizing strategy indicated in Proposition 1.

PROOF OF PROPOSITION 2B

We proceed, as in the proof of proposition 2a, by backward induction and show that each player's strategy is in equilibrium given the strategies of other players.

APPELLATE JUDGE   If a hard signal ever reveals the defendant's type, the appellate judge rules accordingly. Suppose there is no hard signal at trial or on appeal.

If the plaintiff is the losing party at trial, then the expected value to the appellate judge of reversing is $p_0\sigma_p^1(v^1 = \bar{l}, x^1 = 0, \beta = 1, \rho_i^2(v^1 = \bar{l}, x^1 = x^2 = 0))(1) + (1 - p_0)\sigma_p^1(v^1 = \bar{l}, x^1 = 0, \beta = \bar{l}, \rho_i^2(v^1 = \bar{l}, x^1 = x^2 = 0))(0)$, which is equal to p_0, when $\sigma_p^1(\cdot) = 1$, which it will be if $\rho_i^2(v^1 = \bar{l}, x^1 = x^2 = 0) \geq (c - d\pi^2/d(1 - \pi^2))$ (from above).

The judge's expected value of sustaining a judgment for a defendant on appeal is $p_0\sigma_p^1(v^1 = \bar{l}, x^1 = 0, \beta = \bar{l}, \rho_i^2(v^1 = \bar{l}, x^1 = x^2 = 0))(0) + (1 - p_0)\sigma_p^1(\cdot)(1)$. The expected values of the two are equal when $\sigma_p^1(v^1 = \bar{l}, x^1 = 0, \beta = \bar{l}, \rho_i^2(\cdot)) = (p_0/1 - p_0)$. Clearly, if $\sigma_p^1(\cdot) > (p_0/1 - p_0)$, the appellate judge will hold the defendant liable with certainty, and hold the defendant not liable with certainty if the strict inequality is reversed.

LOSING LITIGANT   Recall that there are three types of losing litigants, losing plaintiffs, losing defendants of type l and losing defendants of type $\bar{l}$. We treat them simultaneously. If the defendant's type is revealed at trial ($x^1 = \beta$), then $v^1 = \beta$. In this case, the (correctly) losing litigant will not appeal, given the specified off-the-equilibrium path beliefs of the appellate judge (the appellate judge believes the hard signal and thus rules the same way as the trial judge, gaining the correctly losing litigant nothing but costing him an additional c).

If the defendant's type is not revealed at trial ($x_1 = 0$), an incorrectly losing plaintiff will appeal if the expected value of the appellate lottery is greater than submitting to the incorrect trial verdict, that is, appeal if $\pi^2 d + (1 - \pi^2)(d\rho_i^2(v^1 = \bar{l}, x^1 = x^2 = 0) + (1 - \rho_i^2(\cdot))0) - c > 0 \Leftrightarrow \rho_i^2(v^1 = \bar{l}, x^1 = x^2 = 0) > (c - \pi^2 d/(1 - \pi^2)d)$ and not if the inequality goes the other way. (It will be shown momentarily that the former inequality holds.) Similarly, an incorrectly losing defendant should appeal if $\pi^2 0 + (1 - \pi^2)(-d\rho_i^2(v^1 = l, x^1 = x^2 = 0) + (1 - \rho_i^2(\cdot))0) - c > -d \Leftrightarrow \rho_i^2(v^1 = l, x^1 = x^2 = 0) < (d - c/(1 - \pi^2)d)$, and not if the inequality goes the other way. (It will be shown momentarily that the former inequality holds.)

If the defendant's type is not revealed at trial ($x^1 = 0$), a correctly losing plaintiff may appeal. Recall, however, that, given the strategy of the trial judge, the value of p_0 determines whether there are correctly losing plaintiffs or correctly losing defendants. Thus, there are correctly losing defendants if and only if $p_0 \geq \frac{1}{2}$ while there are correctly losing plaintiffs if and only if $p_0 \leq \frac{1}{2}$.

A correctly losing plaintiff will appeal, if $\pi^2 0 + (1 - \pi^2)(d\rho_i^2(v^1 = \bar{l}, x^1 = x^2 = 0) + (1 - \rho_i^2(\cdot))0) - c \geq 0 \Leftrightarrow \rho_i^2(v^1 = \bar{l}, x^1 = x^2 = 0) > (c/(1 - \pi^2)d)$, and not if the inequality goes the other way. If this relation holds with equality (and the trial signal is uninformative), a correctly losing plaintiff will be indifferent between appealing and not appealing, and so can mix. Similarly, if the defendant's type is not revealed at trial, a correctly losing defendant will appeal, if $-d\pi^2 + (1 - \pi^2)(-d\rho_i^2(v^1 = l, x^1 = x^2 = 0) +)1 - \rho_i^2(\cdot))0) - c > -d \Leftrightarrow \rho_i^2(v^1 = l, x^1 = x^2 = 0) \leq 1 - (c/(1 - \pi^2)d)$, and not if the inequality goes the other way. Again, if this relation holds with equality, a correctly losing defendant will be indifferent between appealing and not appealing and so can mix (absent a hard signal at trial). A similar exercise for an appealing defendant leads to the strategy indicated by $\rho_i^2(v^1 = l)$.

It only remains to show that $\rho_i^2(v^1 = \bar{l}, x^1 = x^2 = 0) = (c/d(1 - \pi^2))$ compels an incorrectly losing plaintiff to appeal, while $\rho_i^2(v^1 = l, x^1 = x^2 = 0) = 1 - (c/d(1 - \pi^2))$ compels an incorrectly losing defendant to appeal. To establish the first part, note that $(c/d(1 - \pi^2)) > (c \quad d\pi^2/d(1 - \pi^2)) \; \forall \pi^2 > 0$; the result then follows from plaintiff's appeal strategy, above. To establish the second part, note that $1 - (c/d(1 - \pi^2)) = (d(1 - \pi^2) - c/d(1 - \pi^2)) < (d - c/d(1 - \pi^2)) \; \forall \pi^2 > 0$. The result then follows from defendant's appeal strategy, above.

TRIAL JUDGE   The trial judges behaves in the by-now familiar fashion, using hard signals if available and otherwise efficiently using prior beliefs.

PROOF OF PROPOSITION 2D

Using the above strategies, if $p_0 > .5$, the probability of a correct outcome is $\pi^1 + (1 - \pi^1)\{\pi^2 + 1 - \pi^2)[(1 - p_0)(1)(c/d(1 - \pi^2)) + p_0[(1 - p_0/p_0)(1 - (c/d(1 - \pi^2))) + (2p_0 - 1/p_0)]]\}$ which simplifies to the expression in the Proposition. Similarly, if $p_0 \leq .5$ the probability of a correct outcome is $\pi^1 + (1 - \pi^1)\{\pi^2 + (1 - \pi^2)[(1 - p_0)\{((p_0/1 - p_0))(1 - (c/d(1 - \pi^2))) + (1 - 2p_0/1 - p_0)\} + p_0(1)(c/d(1 - \pi^2))]\}$ which again simplifies as indicated.

PROOF OF PROPOSITION 3

The proof proceeds via backward induction.

HIGH COURT (TIER 3) JUDGE   Appeals to the high court are out-of-equilibrium events, so Bayes's Rule has no bite. However, we require the high court judge's beliefs to be fixed in the natural way if any $x^t \neq 0$, ($t = 1, 2, 3$). In that case, the indicated judgments follow from Proposition 1. Absent a hard signal, the most-favorable belief to appeals (and difficult for the equilibrium) is that an appeal of the intermediate court's judgment signals $v^2 \neq \beta$. We assume this belief. But again, given this belief, the indicated judgment follows immediately.

LOSING DEFENDANT AT LEVEL 2   If x^1 or $x^2 = \beta$, the defendant surely appeals adverse $v^2 = l \neq \beta$ because in this case, following appeal, $\mu_i^3 = 0$ (from the specified out-of-equilibrium beliefs) and the defendant prevails. Conversely, if x^1 or $x^2 = \beta$ and $v^2 = l = \beta$, Defendant definitely does not appeal, because in this case, $\mu_i^3 = 1$ (from the specified out-of-equilibrium beliefs) and the defendant loses at additional cost of c. If $x^1 = x^2 = 0$, incorrectly losing defendant surely appeals, because either $x^3 = \beta$ and thus $\mu_i^3 = 0$ and high court reverses, or $x^3 = 0$ and thus $\mu_i^3 = 0$ (from the specified out-of-equilibrium beliefs) and high court again reverses. If $x^1 = x^2 = 0$, the correctly losing defendant appeals if and only if the expected value of appealing is greater than or equal to the expected value of not appealing, to wit, $(1 - \pi^3)0 + \pi^3(-d) - c \geq -d \Rightarrow \pi^3 \leq 1 - (c/d)$. But this contradicts the condition on high court accuracy assumed in the equilibrium.

LOSING PLAINTIFF AT LEVEL 2   The argument for the plaintiff is analogous and omitted for the sake of brevity.

INTERMEDIATE APPELLATE (TIER 2) JUDGE   There are three cases. Case (1) $x^1 = \beta$. An appeal following a hard signal at trial is an out-of-equilibrium action so Bayes's Rule has no bite. We specify that the appellate judge believes the hard signal (so that $\mu_i^2 = 0$ or 1, as $x^2 = \bar{l}$ or l, respectively), and the indicated judgments follow immediately from Proposition 1.

Case (2) $x^1 = 0$, $x^2 = \beta$. In this case, $\mu_i^2 = 0$ or 1, as $x^2 = \bar{l}$ or l, respectively, and the indicated judgment follows from Proposition 1.

Case (3) $x^1 = 0$, $x^2 = 0$. Given the appellate strategies of the litigants and Bayes's Rule, $\mu_i^2 = 0$ if the losing defendant appeals, and $\mu_i^2 = 1$ if the losing plaintiff appeals. Again, the indicated judgment follows from Proposition 1.

LITIGANT LOSING AT TRIAL   There are two cases. Case (1) Incorrectly losing litigant. An appeal definitely is reversed by the court at tier 2, with or without a hard signal. Following the reversal, at tier 2, the correctly losing litigant does not appeal so that the correct judgment stands. Hence, an incorrectly losing litigant at trial definitely appeals.

Case (2) Correctly losing litigant. If there is a hard signal at trial, an appeal gains nothing and costs c, so is not undertaken. Suppose no hard signal at trial. If a hard signal emerges at appeal, the appellant loses again, and further appeal is hopeless. If a hard signal does not emerge at appeal at tier 2, the appellant definitely wins at tier 2. But (from above) the (now incorrectly) losing litigant, after appeal, will definitely appeal to the high court. Hence a correctly losing defendant should appeal (absent a hard signal at trial) if and only if $\pi_i^2(-d) + (1 - \pi_i^2)(\pi_i^3(-d) + (1 - \pi_i^3)0) - c \geq -d \Rightarrow \pi_i^3 < 1 - (c/d(1 - \pi_i^2))$. But this contradicts the condition assumed in the equilibrium (i.e., even if $\pi_i^2 = 0$). The condition for a correctly losing plaintiff is identical and a derivation is omitted for the sake of brevity.

Notes

Cameron gratefully acknowledges support from NSF Grant 0079952 and the Center for the Study of Democratic Politics, Woodrow Wilson School of Public and International Affairs, Princeton University. Kornhauser acknowledges support from the Max E. Greenberg and Filomen D'Agostino Research Fund of NYU School of Law.

1. Schwartz 1995 criticizes Shavell 1995 on this point, suggesting that perfect separation of "legitimate" from "illegitimate" appeals (or initial cases) may not be compatible with individually rational behavior.

2. Cameron, Segal, and Songer 2000 consider strategic auditing, as does Spitzer and Talley 1998. Cameron 1993 sketches a model of judicial tournaments (see also Kornhauser 1995). Judicial tournaments are then explored in more detail in McNollgast 1995. Shavell 1995, footnote 2, provides citations to the literatures on appeals by employers and in administrative agencies.

3. Note that Shavell 1995 does not fully characterize an appeals process because the paper does not define q_R^t and q_W^t.

4. Appendix A to this essay provides the proof for a theorem about the desirability of an *add-on appeal process*.

5. Shavell's model compares the "optimal" flat organization to the "optimal" two-tiered hierarchy.

6. Parts of this section draw heavily on Kornhauser 1995.

7. As is well known, an initial informational asymmetry across the litigants is essential; otherwise, they will settle (if possible).

8. We assume the defendant pays the court costs for the trial.

9. We assume that cases are divided equally over judges and that the judges divide their time equally over cases. It is straightforward to show that error-minimizing judges should allocate their time equally over objectively indistinguishable cases.

10. Obviously, this is a rather special judicial technology. In Cameron and Kornhauser 2003, we consider a technology in which trials and appeals are always somewhat informative but never perfectly so.

11. This is refinement D1 in Cho and Kreps 1987, and is equivalent to Banks and Sobel's universal divinity.

12. Phrased differently, as the resources devoted to "fact-finding" at the trial level increase, the probability that there is mutual revelation of type to the parties approaches 1.

13. We note a rather subtle issue in defining the key structural variables of section 2. They may be calculated in several different ways. They might defined in terms of the behavior required by the equilibrium strategy or in terms of actual equilibrium behavior. These variables might also be defined at each information set—when the trial court re-

ceived a hard signal and when it did not. Or, the variables might be defined simply in aggregate terms. As the variables may have different values at different information sets, we choose to define a "aggregate" variable specified in terms of actual equilibrium behavior. The definition permits us to invoke Theorem 1 and its corollaries. For example, consider $1 - p_R^{2|2}$, the probability that, on appeal, a case correctly decided at level 1 will be upheld. This event has a probability 0, because, in equilibrium, no correctly decided cases are appealed. On an actual, aggregate-behavior definition, this variable is thus undefined. Using a definition based on the equilibrium strategy at different information sets, the value of $1 - p_R^{2|2} = 1$, if there was a hard signal. If there was no hard signal, then the probability $1 - p_R^{2|2}$ equals $\pi^{2|2}((C^{2|2}/n^{2|2}))$, the probability that the appellate court receives a hard signal that reveals the appellant's type. By contrast $1 - p_W^{2|2}$, the probability that, on appeal, a wrongly decided case will be reversed, does occur in equilibrium, and it equals 1 under both an aggregate behavioral definition and on a definition that relies on equilibrium strategies at each information set.

14. The case of $p_0 < \frac{1}{2}$ is virtually identical in reasoning and is omitted for the sake of brevity.

15. This is the rightly decided appealed cases, over all rightly decided cases.

16. But, see Daughety and Reinganum 2000 for a contrary view.

Informative Precedent and Intrajudicial Communication

ETHAN BUENO DE MESQUITA AND MATTHEW STEPHENSON

Precedent is another feature of the institutional environment of the Supreme Court. The justices both interact with precedents set by previous Courts and rely on precedents to gain the compliance of the lower courts. By deferring to precedent, policy-oriented appellate judges can improve the accuracy with which they communicate legal rules to trial judges. An information model of this process yields new implications and hypotheses regarding conditions under which judges maintain or break with precedent, the constraining effect that precedent has on judicial decision making, the voting behavior of Supreme Court justices, the relationship between a precedent's age and its authority, the effect of legal complexity on the level of deference to precedent, the relative stability of rules and standards, and long-term patterns of legal evolution. Perhaps most important, this essay demonstrates that "legalist" features of judicial decision making are consistent with an assumption of policy-oriented judges.

Political scientists have long recognized the importance of courts as political actors. However, while an extensive literature examines the judiciary's strategic interaction with the other branches of government (e.g., Ferejohn and Weingast 1992, Gely and Spiller 1992), less attention has been paid to the effects of the institutional structure of the courts themselves on patterns of judicial decision making. Yet models of the judiciary's unique institutional dynamics are essential to understanding the courts, just as analyses of congressional committees (e.g., Gilligan and Krehbiel 1990, Shepsle and Weingast 1987) or the bureaucracy (e.g., Moe 1982) are essential to understanding the legislative and executive branches. In this essay, we develop a formal model that demonstrates how the problem of communication between different levels of a hierarchical court system, such as the one in the United States, can, under some conditions, create incentives for judges to defer to precedents established in prior cases, and how this constraining effect influences the policy decisions made by the courts.

This approach sheds light on the perplexing and controversial debate over the relative importance of legal versus policy concerns in judicial decisions. Scholars subscribing to policy-oriented models argue that judges are concerned with the external effects of their rulings on allocations of risk, wealth, power, or opportunity.[1] Judges may be motivated by policy concerns because of partisan loyalties, a sincere desire to effect particular changes in the world, or pursuit of promotion or reelection. Whatever the reason, the policy-oriented judge cares about actual judicial "outputs" more than any particular method of arriving at those outputs. Others, however, argue that judges are concerned with "legalism," that is, with correctly following the rules and norms of proper judicial reasoning. A legalist judge maximizes utility by adhering faithfully to these internal rules, regardless of the external result. The purely policy-oriented judge and the purely legalist judge are, of course, ideal types, and few scholars, if any, believe that judges are motivated solely by concern with external effects or by fidelity to internal norms. Nonetheless, these two sets of factors are often presented as competing explanations for judicial behavior, and their relative importance is the subject of heated debate (e.g., Knight and Epstein 1996; Segal and Spaeth 1996a, 1996b; Songer and Lindquist 1996).

We demonstrate that "legalist" principles are, at least in some cases, compatible with—and in fact explained by—judges' concerns with the external policy effects of their rulings. Focusing on one central principle of judicial decision making in Anglo-American legal systems—stare decisis, or deference to precedent—we show that purely policy-oriented judges will often defer to legal precedent, even when doing so requires them to issue decisions that deviate from the rulings they otherwise would prefer. Appellate judges can use prior cases to increase the accuracy of their communication with trial judges. Often, a judge may modify the substantive ruling in order to purchase this increased accuracy in communication. Thus, in the model we present, it is not the case that policy-oriented judges ignore precedent, nor is it the case that judges care about precedent instead of, or in addition to, caring about policy. Rather, judges care about precedent *because* they care about policy.

In addition to demonstrating this basic idea, our model has the advantage of being able to account systematically for both adherence to and departure from precedent. Specifically, our comparative static analysis shows how variation in four parameters—the distance between the existing legal rule and the deciding judge's ideal, the age of the existing precedent, the difficulty of intelligibly integrating existing precedent with new rulings, and the precision or imprecision of communication between judges—affects the relative likelihoods that a judge will adhere to or break with existing legal precedent. Our model also has implications for how much judges are able to change the substantive law without ever openly breaking from established precedent. Further, our informational model of stare decisis sheds light on other important empirical puzzles in the study of judicial decision making. We reconcile the seemingly contradictory observations that arguments from precedent play a major role in U.S. Supreme Court deliberation and adjudication, and yet justices consistently vote their preferences rather than following established precedents. Our approach also offers an explanation for why long lines of cases might evoke both deference and skepticism. Finally, our model yields several novel hypotheses, including predictions regarding the types of legal issues in which long lines of precedent will emerge, the relative stability of clear rules versus flexible standards, and patterns of long-term legal evolution.

Competing Theories of Judicial Decision Making

We focus on the principle of stare decisis,[2] which dictates that judges ought to apply rules and principles laid down in prior cases, because it is, or at least is claimed to be, one of the most important principles of judicial decision making in the Anglo-American common law system (e.g., Schauer 1987). Judges are not, under ordinary circumstances, supposed to overturn "settled law" (Nelson 2001).[3] Our focus on stare decisis also results from its salience for the more general question of the nature of judicial preferences. Judicial deference to established precedent is a focus of the debate between the policy-oriented and legalist models of judicial decision making, because these models seem to offer such different predictions for how important precedent will be in practice. A legalist judge is expected to place great weight on the stare decisis principle and consequently is expected to defer to prior decisions even when that judge would have decided the precedent-setting case differently.[4]

By contrast, it is not clear why a policy-oriented judge would ever defer to constraints imposed by prior decisions. It may be that judges often agree with the principles laid down in old cases and follow them for that reason, but if this is the case, then stare decisis is merely a description of—rather than a reason for—patterns of judicial decision making. To the extent that a legal precedent exerts a causal influence on at least some judicial decisions, it must be the case that in these decisions, judges would prefer to issue a different ruling if the precedent did not exist. Thus, a policy-oriented judge would be expected to attach little importance to established precedent when making decisions.

Scholars have offered a number of reasons why even a policy-oriented judge might want to respect established legal precedent. One argument—the one most familiar to lawyers—is that stability in the law is in itself a valued policy goal, and judges would therefore be willing to defer to an established legal rule, because the act of deference itself advances their policy preference for stability. But this explanation has a difficult time accounting for adherence to precedent in areas of law where stability and the need for long-term planning are less salient. Perhaps more important, stability in the law is a collective good; for a given judge to sacrifice other policy goals for the sake of stability, that judge must believe that other judges will also value stability sufficiently highly that they will not overturn precedent. But, if a judge believes that other judges do place a high value on stability, that judge may be tempted to break with precedent and establish a new legal rule, because it will be respected by future courts with little overall loss in legal stability. Additionally, the value of legal stability is considerably reduced to a judge if the stable legal rule is objectionable (Kornhauser 1989). While the need for stability may be enough when the judge is indifferent between legal rules, it is a less plausible basis for deference to precedent when the judge has strong substantive preferences between rules.

Another suggestion as to why policy-oriented judges might respect the principle of stare decisis is that judges want their own precedents followed, and therefore follow precedents set by others (Landes and Posner 1976, Rasmusen 1994). Because judges prefer a world in which all precedents, including their own, are respected to a world in which no precedents are respected, they will attempt to enforce universal respect for precedent by punishing judges who "defect."[5] While there may be some of this tit-for-tat in the real world, this explanation has several problems as a general account of the practice of stare decisis. First, it relies on the empirically dubious assumption that judges look to other judges' respect for legal precedent when determining whether to follow precedent set by those judges. Second, it has trouble accounting for why the precedents of retired judges are ever followed without reference to even more complicated, and empirically problematic, punishment mechanisms. Third, in the absence of such mechanisms, this explanation also does not explain well why some judges break with some precedents but follow others. In a simple model where judges expect general retaliation for any break with existing precedent, if they break once they have no reason not to break always.

A third possibility is that policy-oriented judges do not care about precedent per se, but recognize the need to preserve their institutional power and legitimacy. Because this legitimacy derives in part from a public belief that judges apply a specialized set of legal skills, including the ability to interpret and apply established legal precedents, as well as a belief that judges are politically neutral interpreters of law, policy-oriented judges will want to perpetuate the belief that they make decisions according to precedent (Cox 1976, Maltz 1980). This may, in turn, lead them to modify their decisions sometimes to show more respect for precedent to enhance their institutional power. However, the collective action objection applies to this explanation as well; the overall effect of any particular decision on institutional legitimacy is likely to be small, while the policy ramifications of the case itself often are large. Moreover, the effect of a decision on public perception of the court's legitimacy may have more to do with the content of the decision than whether it involved overturning a precedent (e.g., Hyde 1983, Nelson 2001).

Finally, several studies point out that deference to precedent may be valuable even to policy-oriented judges because of the informational function that judicial precedents serve (e.g., Shapiro 1972, Rehnquist 1986). The informational perspective is composed of two types of explanations for deference to precedent. First, reasoning from precedents may improve communication between appeals courts, allowing for judicial specialization and error correction (e.g., Kornhauser 1989, Macey 1989). A more pessimistic version of the same basic argument is that the practice of stare decisis is essentially an "information cascade" in which rational agents ignore their own information and imitate the behavior of preceding decision makers, often leading to uncorrected inefficient results (Talley 1999).

We suggest a second informational function the doctrine of stare decisis might serve. This function involves communication between high courts and lower courts. The basic idea is that the development of lines of cases can communicate a legal principle better than any individual case could. An initial case may invoke a general phrase or principle, such as "due process," "reasonable," "compelling interest," and the like; future cases develop and give meaning to these inherently vague phrases. Hence, a lower court can learn more about the appellate court's view of the proper interpretation of, say, a due process balancing test by examining a line of ten cases in which the same test was applied than by reading the first (or the last) ruling the appeals court issued. Similarly, an initial case might declare a bright-line rule that, though clear, is both over- and underinclusive.[6] Further cases can carve out exceptions and make qualifications so that the line of cases applying the rule offers lower courts a much more nuanced test than that announced by the original decision.

Our model explores this second type of informational use of legal precedent, a use that we believe has been neglected in the scholarly discussion of judicial decision making and that has not been formally developed or rigorously analyzed. In so doing, we provide an account of judicial decision making that explains why policy-oriented judges are expected to be influenced by precedent, while also capturing cases where judges break from precedent.

THE MODEL

Consider a simple judicial system consisting of an appellate judge and a trial judge. The appellate judge hears a limited number of cases, and, through the decisions in these cases, the appellate judge can announce how the law ought to be interpreted. The trial judge decides the vast majority of cases. We make the simplifying assumption that when making decisions, the trial judge attempts to apply established law, without reference to the trial judge's own personal policy preferences. There are several possible substantive defenses of this assumption that could ultimately be modeled explicitly. These include considerations such as promotion being dependent on strict adherence to the law established by appellate decisions, a desire not to be overturned on appeal, or other factors. For the purposes of this model, it suffices to assume that some mechanism exists that leads the trial judge to behave as a faithful agent of the appellate judge. While we assume a nonstrategic trial judge, we do address the conditions under which a strategic trial judge might behave in this way later in the analysis section of the essay.

The trial judge's understanding of appellate rulings is imperfect, and the trial judge often does not decide cases exactly as the appellate judge would have. The appellate judge cannot correct all these "mistakes" by altering or reversing the trial court's decision on appeal. This may be because the appellate court's jurisdiction is discretionary and many appeals are not heard (e.g., U.S. Supreme Court review of circuit court decisions), or because many cases are not appealed at all despite the existence of an automatic right to an appeal (e.g., federal circuit court review of district court decisions). Thus, the appellate court judge, in order to successfully influence the application of the law to the majority of cases, needs to communicate a preferred interpretation of the law to the trial court as accurately as possible, subject to time and resource constraints.

The appellate judge has preferences over the legal rule defined on a unidimensional continuum.[7] Denote the appellate judge's ideal point, $j \in \mathbb{R}$. The policy continuum might represent, for example, the level of care exercised by a defendant in a civil action, with j representing the minimum amount of care the appellate judge believes a defendant must exercise to avoid liability. That is, the appellate judge in this example believes that all defendants who exercise a level of care less than j ought to be liable, and all defendants who exercise a level of care above j ought to escape liability. As such, j is the appellate judge's ideal legal rule. The trial judge has no preference over the policy dimension per se; rather, the trial judge tries to implement whatever the appellate judge has declared to be the proper legal rule.

When deciding a case, the appellate judge issues a ruling with two components. First, the appellate judge announces a substantive holding on the proper application of the legal rule to the case at hand. This substantive holding corresponds to a point in the policy space, denoted by $r \in \mathbb{R}$. Second, the appellate judge declares whether this substantive holding is consistent with existing precedent or whether the appellate judge is breaking with precedent. "Precedent" here means the line of appellate cases on the relevant legal issue that have been decided prior to the present case and that have never been overruled by a subsequent appellate case. Prior decisions are not assumed to all have been made by the current appellate judge. Rather, one can think of the game beginning with an existing line of precedent that may have been established before the current appellate judge took office. If the appellate judge issues a holding and declares that it is consistent with precedent, then the case is added to the relevant line of cases, and the trial judge will interpret the appellate judge's substantive holding in the context of the other substantive holdings in the line in order to ascertain the legal rule the appellate judge wishes to enact. If, however, the appellate judge declares a break with precedent, then a new line of cases is established, and the trial judge will treat the most recent appellate decision as the exclusive statement of the legal rule.[8] The number of cases in the line of precedent, including the decision being made in the current round, is denoted by t. Thus a line of precedent is a series of substantive rulings $(r_1, r_2, \ldots, r_{t-1})$, where r_{t-1} is the most recent ruling and the current appellate judge issues ruling r_t.

The declaration that the appellate judge is maintaining or breaking from precedent is communicated perfectly to the trial judge. However, the communication of the substantive holding of each ruling is inherently noisy. Thus the trial judge, when attempting to understand an appellate ruling, observes t signals, each drawn from a normal distribution with variance σ^2. The means of these distributions are the r's associated with the substantive holdings of the different cases in the line of precedent. The trial court judge averages these signals to estimate the legal rule.[9] Thus, the trial judge's estimate of the legal rule is a sum of a series of normally distributed random variables. Such a sum is itself a normally distributed random variable.[10] Consequently, the trial court's estimate can be treated *as if* it were a single signal, denoted by x, drawn from a normal distribution with mean $\mu_t = (\Sigma_{i=1}^{t} r_t / t)$ and variance (σ^2/t) (DeGroot 1970).

It is important to stress that the trial judge does not actually believe that all of the observed signals are drawn from a single distribution. If the trial judge did believe this, signals far from the estimated mean would make the trial judge less confident in this estimate. However, the trial judge recognizes that the various observed signals are drawn from different distributions with different means, reflecting earlier decisions, potentially made by different appellate judges. Given that the trial judge aggregates these signals, each additional signal, no matter how far it is from the mean, decreases the variance of the trial judge's estimate of the legal rule to be implemented. This variance is the variance of the trial judge's estimate, not the trial judge's estimate of the variance of a single underlying distribution.

If the appellate judge breaks with precedent, there is only one decision in the line of cases, so $t = 1$ and the trial judge receives a signal drawn from a normal distribution with mean $r_{t=1}$, the most recent appellate holding, and variance σ^2. The mean of the distribution of the signal in the period prior to the current appellate judge's decision is denoted μ_{t-1}, and, we refer to this value as "existing precedent." Because x (the value of the draw from the distribution of the trial court's estimate) is the only information the trial judge has, it is the trial judge's best guess as to what the appellate judge wants. Consequently, the trial judge will treat x as the controlling legal rule when deciding cases.

The appellate judge's utility has two components. First, the appellate judge would like the decisions of the trial court judges to be as close as possible to the appellate judge's own ideal point. That is, the appellate judge wishes to minimize $|x - j|$. The reason for this is that any cases that fall in this interval are cases the trial judge will get "wrong" from the appellate judge's point of view. Again, consider a case in which the policy dimension represents the level of care taken by a tort defendant. If the defendant exercised a level of care less than the minimum of x and j, the trial court will correctly find the defendant liable. Similarly, if the defendant exercised a level of care above the maximum of x and j, the trial court will correctly find the defendant not liable. However, when the defendant exercised a level of care in the interval between x and j, the trial court will rule incorrectly. In this event, if $x > j$, the trial court will mistakenly find liability, while if $x < j$, the trial court will mistakenly find no liability. The larger the size of the interval $|x - j|$, the larger the number of cases that will be decided incorrectly. We assume that the appellate judge's utility function is quadratic—that is, the appellate judge wants to minimize the expected value of the square of the distance between x and j, which is equal to $((\mu_t - j)^2 + (\sigma^2 / t))$.

Second, if the appellate judge does not announce a break with precedent, it is costly to offer a ruling, r_t, that is substantively different from the existing precedent, μ_{t-1}. We are agnostic as to the relative importance of these two factors in the appellate judge's utility calculation; we weight the importance of the latter by the parameter $\alpha \geq 0$ on which we perform comparative static analysis.[11] Thus, the utility cost associated with changing the law while claiming to adhere to precedent is $\alpha(\mu_{t-1} - r_t)^2$. If the appellate judge breaks with precedent, this cost does not apply.

This cost arises because writing an opinion that intelligibly integrates existing precedent with a change in the substance of the legal rule becomes increasingly difficult as the distance between precedent and the substantive holding grows. Thus, there are real costs in intellectual effort and research associated with such a decision. If these costs are not invested, that is if the appellate judge were to declare that a decision was consistent with precedent without explaining how the substance of the ruling and prior rulings could be intelligibly integrated, then the trial judge would be unable to make decisions with reference to the full line of cases. This aspect of the model captures the intuition that trial judges would have difficulty simply averaging signals that are quite distant from one another. Trial judges are only able to aggregate such signals if the appellate judge has invested substantially in explaining how to do so. This effort is costly to the appellate judge and becomes more costly the greater the distance between the appellate holding and existing precedent, reflecting the increasing difficulty of the trial judge's task. In our model, the intuition that it would be difficult for the trial judge to aggregate a sharply divergent holding into existing precedent is captured by the costliness to the appellate judge of making such a holding.

One might object to the assumption that judges bear a cost when maintaining precedent but do not bear a cost when breaking with precedent. However, the assumption is benign with respect to the conclusions of our model. Our analytic results are unchanged by the addition of a fixed cost for breaking with precedent. Such a cost would change the actual point at which appellate judges break, but would not affect the comparative statics. There is a second, more conceptual justification for making this assumption. Any cost from breaking with precedent, beyond the loss of information already modeled, would arise from legalist values. We omit legalist values from the judicial utility function in order to see whether the norm of stare decisis is consistent even with purely policy-oriented judges and, indeed, whether what appear to be legalist values may emerge as a result of policy motivations.

The expected utility to the appellate judge is therefore:

$$EU = -\left((\mu_t - j)^2 + \frac{\sigma^2}{t} \right) - \tilde{\alpha}(\mu_{t-1} - r_t)^2,$$

where $\tilde{\alpha} = \alpha$, if the appellate judge maintains precedent, and $\tilde{\alpha} = 0$, if the appellate judge departs from precedent.

Analysis

THE APPELLATE JUDGE'S DECISION

The appellate judge has two choices to make. The appellate judge must select a substantive holding (r_t) and must also decide whether to declare a break with precedent. These two decisions are interrelated. To determine whether or not to break with precedent, the appellate judge must first know the expected outcomes, which are a function of the different substantive rulings the appellate judge would issue, depending on whether precedent is maintained or not. Thus, we work backward, first determining the appellate judge's optimal substantive holding contingent on whether the judge has broken with or maintained precedent.

If the appellate judge breaks with precedent, the second term of the judge's expected utility function is zero, because $\tilde{\alpha} = 0$. Further, because the appellate judge has broken with existing precedent, t reverts to 1. Therefore, the line of cases considered by the trial judge contains only the appellate judge's most recent decision, that is, $\mu_{t=1} = r_{t=1}$. It is obvious that the appellate judge's expected utility in this case is maximized when $r_t = \mu_t = j$. Thus, if an appellate judge breaks with precedent, the substantive holding will be the judge's ideal legal rule, and the judge's expected utility in this case, *EU(break)*, is $-\sigma^2$.

If the appellate judge does not break with precedent, the decision is more complicated. The appellate judge would like to issue a ruling that moves precedent toward the judge's own ideal point, but is constrained by the cost of deviating too much from the line of precedent of which this decision becomes a part. The appellate judge thus chooses r_t by solving the following maximization problem:

$$\max_{r_t}\left\{-\left[(\mu_t - j)^2 + \frac{\sigma^2}{t}\right] - \alpha(\mu_{t-1} - r_t)^2\right\}. \tag{1}$$

Note that μ_t, the mean of the distribution of the trial judge's estimate of the legal rule, is a function of r_t. In particular, $\mu_t = [(t-1)\mu_{t-1} + r_t]/t$. Thus, we can rewrite the maximization problem as:

$$\max_{r_t}\left\{-\left[\left(\frac{(t-1)\mu_{t-1} + r_t}{t} - j\right)^2 + \frac{\sigma^2}{t}\right] - \alpha(\mu_{t-1} - r_t)^2\right\}. \tag{2}$$

Solving for the first order condition yields:

$$r_t^* = \mu_{t-1} + \frac{t(j - \mu_{t-1})}{1 + \alpha t^2}.$$

Knowing the optimal substantive holding, r_t^*, allows us to calculate the mean of the new distribution from which the trial court judge will draw an estimate of the proper legal rule. This new mean, μ_t^*, is given by:

$$\mu_t^* = \frac{(t-1)\mu_{t-1} + r_t}{t} = \frac{j + \alpha t^2 \mu_{t-1}}{1 + \alpha t^2}. \tag{3}$$

Now, to find the appellate judge's expected utility from issuing a decision consistent with precedent, *EU(maintain)*, we substitute r_t^* and μ_t^* into the expected utility function. This yields:

$$EU(maintain) = -\left[\left(\frac{j + \alpha t^2 \mu_{t-1}}{1 + \alpha t^2} - j\right)^2 + \frac{\sigma^2}{t}\right]$$
$$- \alpha\left[\mu_{t-1} - \left(\mu_{t-1} + \frac{t(j - \mu_{t-1})}{1 + \alpha t^2}\right)\right]^2,$$

which simplifies to:

$$EU(maintain) = -\frac{\alpha t^2}{1 + \alpha t^2}(j - \mu_{t-1})^2 - \frac{\sigma^2}{t}. \tag{4}$$

In our model, the central benefit to appellate judges of maintaining precedent is informational. The more cases the trial judges have to refer to, the more accurately they will understand the legal rule for which that line of cases stands. Thus, the appellate judge wishes to maintain precedent because it makes communication with trial courts less noisy. However, the use of precedent comes at a price. In particular, appellate judges bear a cost for deviating substantively too far from the line of precedent they claim to uphold. This constrains judges who are maintaining precedent from implementing a legal rule that matches their personal ideal, as can be seen in the model. When precedent is maintained, $\mu_t^* = (j + \alpha t^2 \mu_{t-1})/(1 + \alpha t^2)$ $\neq j$ (unless $\alpha = 0$ or $\mu_{t-1} = j$). The rule applied by the trial court when precedent is maintained is biased away from the current appellate judge's ideal point (j) in the direction of the old precedent (μ_{t-1}). Further, it is interesting to note that the appellate judge, when maintaining precedent, chooses the holding $r_t^* = \mu_{t-1} + [t(j - \mu_{t-1})/(1 + \alpha t^2)]$, which is not equal to existing precedent (μ_{t-1}) or the appellate judge's ideal point (j), unless, by chance, $j = \mu_{t-1}$ or $t = 1 + \alpha t^2$. This ruling is always in the direction of the appellate judge's ideal point, but may be more or less extreme, relative to existing precedent. If $t > 1 + \alpha t^2$, the appellate judge will issue a ruling further from existing precedent than the appellate judge's ideal point. Otherwise, the appellate judge will issue a ruling between the ideal point and existing precedent.

While the appellate judge can make sure, by announcing a break with precedent, that the mean of the trial court's signal is equal to the appellate judge's ideal point, the variance of this signal (that is, the noisiness of communication) will be higher. Again, this can be seen clearly in the model, because $\sigma^2 > (\sigma^2/t)$ as long as $t > 1$. The appellate judge thus faces a trade-off between the accuracy with which the legal rule is communicated to the trial courts and the proximity of that rule to the appellate judge's ideal. The appellate judge determines whether or not to break with precedent by comparing the expected utilities associated with each choice, breaking with precedent if and only if:

$$EU(break) - EU(maintain) = \sigma^2 \frac{1-t}{t} + \frac{\alpha t^2}{1 + \alpha t^2}(j - \mu_{t-1})^2 > 0$$

$$\Leftrightarrow \frac{\alpha t^3}{(t-1)(1 + \alpha t^2)}(j - \mu_{t-1})^2 - \sigma^2 > 0. \quad (5)$$

The trial judge in this model is not a strategic actor. Rather, the trial judge simply follows the instructions of the appellate judge, aggregating all existing holdings in the line if precedent has been maintained, but considering only the appellate judge's most recent ruling if precedent has been broken. Because the focus of our model is the appellate judge's decision, taking the trial judge's aggregation rule as given, we do not formally analyze the ramifications of strategic behavior by the trial judge. Nonetheless, because we justified this simplifying assumption in part by claiming that trial judges want to please their superiors on the appellate bench or avoid being overturned on appeal, one might wonder if the trial judge would be better off attempting to deduce and implement the current appellate judge's ideal point, rather than following existing precedent. This turns out, however, not to be the case.

The trial judge could, of course, form an unbiased approximation of the appellate judge's ideal point by inverting the maximization problem that the appellate judge solved in equation (2), conditioning on the trial judge's estimate of preexisting precedent, μ_{t-1}.[12] That is, the trial judge could observe the signals associated with the first $t-1$ rulings in the line of precedent and use this information to estimate the precedent the current appellate judge faced. Then, conditioning on this preexisting precedent, the trial judge could invert the appellate judge's maximization problem to estimate what value of j would have caused the current appellate judge to issue the ruling the trial judge observed. This estimate is unbiased, because the expected value of the trial judge's observation of any holding, r_i, in the line of precedent is r_i.

Notice, though, that the information regarding preexisting precedent can be used only to help the trial judge figure out what the current appellate judge's maximization problem was. Having done this, the only information the trial judge has regarding the appellate judge's ideal point is the signal that the trial judge observes, which is drawn from a normal distribution with mean equal to the current appellate judge's ruling, r_t^*. The variance of this distribution is σ^2, not (σ^2/t). Consequently, following this inversion procedure cannot lead the trial judge to a better estimate of the appellate judge's ideal point than would be achieved if the appellate judge had simply broken with precedent and issued a ruling exactly at the appellate judge's ideal point. Indeed, because the trial judge approximates preexisting precedent with error, the estimate of j deduced from the inversion procedure is less precise than the estimate the trial judge would have formed if the appellate judge had broken with precedent.

The appellate judge only maintains precedent when the ruling of a trial judge who follows that precedent (that is, averages all the signals) will, in expectation, be closer to the appellate judge's ideal point than it would have been had the appellate judge broken with precedent. Since the trial judge's estimate of the appellate judge's ideal point formed by the inversion procedure is even worse than that produced by a break with precedent, the trial judge is more likely to please the appellate judge (and less likely to be overturned) by following precedent than by trying to deduce the appellate judge's ideal point. If this were not the case, the appellate judge would have broken with precedent. Thus, the trial judge would be better off acting as a faithful agent of the appellate judge, deciding cases according to precedent when instructed to do so.[13]

Results

COMPARATIVE STATICS

Comparative static analysis on the parameters of this model yields a number of results regarding how these parameters affect the relative desirability of maintaining or breaking with existing precedent.

It is clear from equation (5) that the desirability of breaking with precedent decreases as σ^2, the noisiness of each individual signal, increases. The intuition is that as communication between appellate and trial courts becomes less precise, the extra information provided by situating a decision in a line of precedent becomes more valuable to the appellate judge. Equation (5) also implies that increasing $|j - \mu_{t-1}|$, the distance between the appellate judge's ideal point and existing precedent, increases the attractiveness of breaking with precedent. Because a large distance between existing precedent and the appellate judge's ideal point constrains how much the appellate judge can move the expected trial court decision, the appellate judge is less willing to trade off control over the substantive rule for increased accuracy of transmission.

Equation (5) additionally shows that breaking with precedent becomes more attractive as α, the marginal cost of making a substantively divergent decision within an existing line of precedent, increases. The reason for this is that, when α is close to 0, the appellate judge can move μ_t very close to j, even while maintaining precedent. Thus, the informational benefit of situating the current decision in a long line of cases comes at very little cost in terms of substance. However, as α grows, the appellate judge's ability to move the legal rule close to j becomes more constrained, making adherence to existing precedent less attractive. One can see this by examining equation (3). Assuming that precedent is maintained, the distance that the legal rule will be moved is given by $|\mu_t^* - \mu_{t-1}|$ $= |(j - \mu_{t-1})/(1 + \alpha t^2)|$, which is clearly decreasing in α.

Deriving the comparative statics on t, the number of cases in the line of precedent, is more complicated. Because t is a discrete variable, to calculate the change in the attractiveness of breaking with precedent as the age of the precedent increases, we take the first differences of equation (5) with respect to t:

$$[EU_{t+1}(break) - EU_{t+1}(maintain)] - [EU_t(break) - EU_t(maintain)] \equiv$$

$$FD(t) = -(j - \mu_{t-1})^2\, \alpha \frac{\alpha t^4 + 2\alpha t^3 + \alpha t^2 - 2t^3 + 2t + 1}{(1 + \alpha t^2 + 2\alpha t + \alpha)(1 + \alpha t^2)t(t-1)} \qquad (6)$$

A little algebra demonstrates that this first-difference can be positive or negative, depending on α and t. In particular:

$$FD(t) < 0 \text{ if } \frac{2t^3 - 2t - 1}{t^4 + 2t^3 + t^2} \equiv \bar{\alpha}(t) < \alpha \qquad (7)$$

$$FD(t) > 0 \text{ if } \frac{2t^3 - 2t - 1}{t^4 + 2t^3 + t^2} \equiv \bar{\alpha}(t) > \alpha.$$

Increasing t decreases the desirability of breaking with precedent when $\alpha > \bar{\alpha}(t)$; otherwise increasing t increases the desirability of breaking with precedent. It is important to note that this threshold, $\bar{\alpha}(t) = (2t^3 - 2t - 1)/(t^4 + 2t^3 + t^2)$, is itself a decreasing function of t. There are two cases to consider in understanding this result. The first is when $\alpha > \bar{\alpha}(2)$ (the lowest possible values of $\bar{\alpha}(t)$ when the appellate judge chooses to maintain existing precedent). In this case, for all values of t, the attractiveness of breaking with precedent is decreasing as t increases. That is, for a sufficiently large α, older precedents are always less vulnerable than younger precedents. This case is illustrated in figure 1. If, however, $\alpha < \bar{\alpha}(2)$, then increases in t increase the attractiveness of breaking with precedent for a certain number of periods. Specifically, increases in t will increase the likelihood of breaking as long as α is below the threshold value of $\bar{\alpha}(t)$. But, as t increases, this threshold value decreases, meaning that α will eventually be greater than the threshold. At that point, the effect of increasing t switches so that increases in t decrease the desirability of breaking with precedent. This case is illustrated in figure 2.

FIGURE 1 EU(break) – EU(maintain) with $\alpha > \bar{\alpha}(2)$

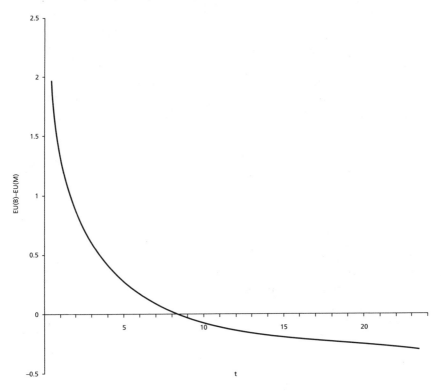

To understand the intuition behind these comparative statics, recall that an increase in t has two effects on the desirability to the appellate judge of maintaining the line of precedent. On the one hand, an increase in t increases the constraint on how much the judge can move the substantive legal rule, making older precedents less attractive. On the other hand, an increase in t improves the accuracy with which the legal rule is communicated to the trial court, making older precedents more attractive. When α is sufficiently high, the information effect always overwhelms the constraining effect. The reason for this is that when α is high, the appellate judge's ability to move the legal rule is already so constrained that the marginal effect of an increase in t on this constraint is negligible. However, when α and t are sufficiently low, the constraining effect of an increase in t is more important to the judge than the effect on information, thereby making an increase in t increase the attractiveness of breaking with precedent. As t increases further, the information effect of marginal increases in t will eventually overwhelm the constraining effects; no

FIGURE 2 EU(break) − EU(maintain) with $\alpha < \bar{\alpha}(2)$

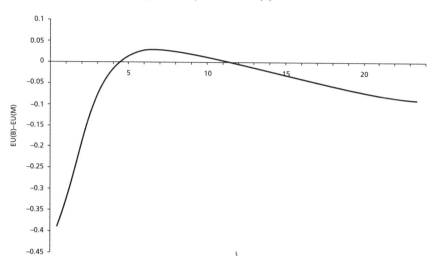

matter how low α is, when t is sufficiently high, the appellate judge is already so constrained that the marginal constraining effect of an increase in t is again negligible.[14]

LIMITS OF LEGAL CHANGE

An interesting question in the context of our model is, how far on the substance dimension can a legal rule move without a judge ever claiming to have broken from precedent? Is this distance bounded or unbounded? That is, how far would precedent move, if, over an infinite series of turns, each appellate judge's ideal point was such that that judge was exactly indifferent between moving existing precedent and breaking with it, leading these judges to move μ_t as far from μ_{t-1} as is possible—always in the same direction—without declaring a break from existing precedent? Returning to the tort liability example discussed earlier, imagine that over time appellate judges want a progressively stricter standard of care. We want to know whether it is possible for the standard of care to become infinitely more strict than the original standard announced by the first judge to consider the question, without any judge ever openly breaking with established precedent.

Of course, the idea that there are multiple appellate judges deciding cases in sequence implies a dynamic model, beyond the scope of this project. Nonetheless, our model does provide a framework that allows us to gain some theoretical leverage on this problem. If an appellate judge does not know what the ideal points of future judges will be, it is reasonable for the current judge to assume that the probability of a future judge having preferences any given distance to the left of existing precedent is the same as the probability of that judge having preferences the same distance to the right. Under such a symmetry assumption, the expected ideal point of a future judge lies at existing precedent. Consequently, the appellate judge's best guess of future precedent is current precedent, and so the decision problem in the dynamic model reduces to the one-shot problem analyzed above.[15]

Therefore, we can find the maximum distance the legal rule can move under these conditions (i.e., $\max|\mu_\infty - \mu_1|$) by solving the following constrained infinite sum:

$$\sum_{t=2}^{\infty}\{\mu_t^* - \mu_{t-1}\} = \sum_{t=2}^{\infty}\left\{\frac{j + \alpha t^2\,\mu_{t-1}}{1 + \alpha t^2} - \mu_{t-1}\right\}$$

$$= \sum_{t=2}^{\infty}\left\{\frac{j - \mu_{t-1}}{1 + \alpha t^2}\right\},$$

$$s.t.\ \frac{(j - \mu_{t-1})^2\,\alpha t^3}{(1 + \alpha t^2)(t - 1)} - \sigma^2 = 0. \tag{8}$$

By making the constraint an equality, we impose the condition that in each round, the preferences of the appellate judge are such that the legal rule moves as far as is possible without the appellate judge preferring to break with precedent. Solving the constraint for $(j - \mu_{t-1})$ and substituting, we find that the sum is equal to:

$$\frac{\sigma}{\sqrt{\alpha}}\sum_{t=2}^{\infty}\frac{1}{t}\frac{\sqrt{t-1}}{\sqrt{t}\sqrt{1 + \alpha t^2}}. \tag{9}$$

Notice that if $\alpha \neq 0$ this can be bounded above as follows:

$$\frac{\sigma}{\sqrt{\alpha}}\sum_{t=2}^{\infty}\frac{1}{t}\frac{\sqrt{t-1}}{\sqrt{t}\sqrt{1 + \alpha t^2}}$$

$$< \frac{\sigma}{\sqrt{\alpha}}\sum_{t=2}^{\infty}\frac{1}{t}\frac{1}{\sqrt{\alpha t^2}} = \frac{\sigma}{\alpha}\sum_{t=2}^{\infty}\frac{1}{t^2} = \left(\frac{\pi^2}{6} - 1\right)\frac{\sigma}{\alpha}. \tag{10}$$

Thus, the distance that can be moved in one direction without a break from precedent is finite, even over an infinite number of turns. Specifically, the legal rule cannot move a distance greater than $((\pi^2/6) - 1)(\sigma/\alpha)$ from the decision in the first case in the line of precedent without at least one judge deciding to break. We can find comparative statics on the actual point of convergence by referring directly to equation (9). Notice that if α is very small, so that judges are relatively unconstrained by the precedential line in which they are writing, this distance is quite large, whereas as α gets large, the distance shrinks. Similarly, as σ becomes large, the distance that can be moved gets larger, because judges are willing to write opinions in line with precedent even when the substantive holdings of those decisions are very far away from the substantive position of the existing precedent.

Discussion

RESOLUTION OF SOME EMPIRICAL PUZZLES

Our model provides a new perspective on when, why, and how judicial decisions are constrained by existing precedents. This perspective helps account for empirical observations of judicial behavior that are otherwise difficult to reconcile. To take a striking example, consider the role of deference to precedent in Supreme Court decision making. On the one hand, a rigorous analysis of voting patterns on the Court finds that justices who vote against a "landmark" case—that is, a case that establishes an important precedent—tend not to switch their voting pattern in subsequent cases, even though the "landmark" case decision ought to constitute a legal precedent (Segal and Spaeth 1996a). This seems to be strong evidence that judges, at least at the Supreme Court level, do not feel constrained by legal precedents as such. On the other hand, if it is really the case that the justices do not attach much importance to precedent, then it is hard to explain why they devote so much time and intellectual energy to it in their deliberations, and why they place so much emphasis on it in most of their decisions. Analysis of the U.S. Supreme Court decision-making process, after all, reveals that arguments from precedent vastly outnumber all other kinds of arguments in attorneys' written briefs, the Court's written opinions, and the justices' arguments in conference discussions (Knight and Epstein 1996, Phelps and Gates 1991). If it were really the case that judges cared about case outcomes rather than precedent, then all the emphasis on arguments from precedent would seem a waste of resources. But if precedent is really influencing justices' decisions, then the persistent patterns of continuous dissent from landmark decisions is difficult to explain.

Our model accounts straightforwardly for this seeming contradiction. Justices care about precedent precisely because they care about policy; if they can sufficiently improve their communication of the proper legal rule by integrating their decision with an existing line of cases, they will do so, even if it means somewhat modifying the legal rule they announce and expending some energy on writing a compelling and coherent opinion that integrates seemingly divergent rulings. Thus, though our model does not formalize the process of formulating a judicial opinion, it is entirely consistent with the observation that judges put a lot of time and attention into trying to integrate their preferred outcome into an established line of cases.

However, in our model, if an appellate judge decides that the additional accuracy is not worth the sacrifice in terms of substantive policy, then the judge will vote to break with precedent. If a given judge dissents in a landmark case, therefore, that judge will usually continue to dissent in subsequent cases. After all, in our model, judges do not care about precedent per se, so there is no reason for a judge to vote to uphold a legal rule that is far from that judge's ideal simply because that rule had been established in a prior case. An appellate judge will only vote to adhere to precedent if in doing so the legal rule can be moved sufficiently closer to the judge's ideal point that the gain in terms of accuracy is worth the cost in terms of substance.

A second apparent empirical anomaly that our model illuminates is the seemingly schizophrenic attitude of judges toward long-established precedents. On the one hand, many would quote approvingly Justice Oliver Wendell Holmes's quip that "it is revolting to have no better reason for a rule of law than that it was laid down in the time of Henry IV. It is still more revolting if the grounds upon which it was laid down have vanished long since, and the rule simply persists from blind imitation of the past" (1897). On the other hand, it is often thought that a legal rule with a long history is worthy of particular deference. Thus, lawyers and judges sometimes argue, implicitly or explicitly, against tampering with long-established legal rules even while disagreeing with their substantive content. Again, our model suggests a simple reconciliation of these apparently contradictory notions. Recall from the comparative statics that increasing t has two effects. It constrains the judge's ability to affect the substance of the legal rule, leading to the frustration embodied in Holmes's remark. However, an old precedent—that is, a long line of cases—though difficult to move, has a great deal of informational value. The consequence is that old precedents become entrenched so that even when judges disagree with the substantive rules, they are reluctant to overrule them.

NEW HYPOTHESES

In addition to offering new insights into these important empirical puzzles, our model also suggests a number of new hypotheses regarding patterns of judicial decision making. First, recall the comparative statics on the parameter σ, which measures the inherent difficulty in communication between appellate and trial judges. The model demonstrated that, as σ increases, the attractiveness of breaking with precedent decreases. Substantively, this implies that areas of law that are highly complex and not amenable to simple legal regulation are more likely to develop long lines of cases, with both high levels of deference to precedent and evolution and change of legal rules within the precedent. However, when the legal issue is simple, making communication of the legal rule less difficult, judges have little use for precedent. They will either follow the old rule exactly or change it completely.

Next, our model offers a new perspective on the long-standing debate about the relative merits of rules and standards (e.g., Kaplow 1992, Schlag 1985, Sullivan 1992). Typically, standards contain general principles— for example, "due process" or "negligence"—whereas rules use more specific and precise language. Strict liability tort regimes and statutes of limitations are examples of such legal rules. In terms of our model, rule-like holdings might correspond to relatively higher values of α, whereas standards might correspond to lower values of α (recall that α measures the costs to judges of effecting substantive legal changes while claiming consistency with an existing line of precedent). This is because it is easier for judges to adapt the broader, more general language of standards, while claiming fidelity to the original principle, than it is for judges to alter an unambiguous legal rule. As shown above, as α increases, the distance a judge will move the substance of existing precedent while maintaining that precedent decreases, but, as a result, the desirability of breaking with precedent increases. Thus, our model calls into question the conventional view that rules are more stable and predictable than standards. We find a trade-off between two types of stability. Rules will be associated with periods of little substantive change punctuated, more frequently, by sudden breaks. Standards, conversely, will be characterized by more constant, but gradual, substantive change but will be overturned outright less often. While we do not have a normative position regarding this trade-off, our model demonstrates that the question of whether rules or standards foster greater stability and predictability is more complex than is commonly appreciated.

Finally, our model suggests patterns that should emerge in the long-term evolution and development of law in an Anglo-American common law system. Recall that when α is sufficiently low, legal rules are less vulnerable to being overruled when they are very young and when they are very old. A judge can easily adapt the substance of a young precedent to reflect personal policy preferences, making a break with precedent unnecessary. And, while a very old precedent strongly constrains judge's ability to influence the substance of the law, it provides tremendous informational value. Middle-aged precedents are more vulnerable to being overruled. Thus, when α is sufficiently low, we might expect the following pattern of legal development. When courts initially confront a new legal issue, the law will likely be characterized by a number of false starts. The legal rule specified by the first judge to confront the issue will be refined by a number of subsequent judges, but as the rule solidifies, it becomes more vulnerable to being overruled. This occurs because, as the rule develops, it may begin to exert a significant constraint on the decisions of judges before it can provide sufficient informational benefits to compensate for this constraining effect. Thus, we expect several rules to be proposed, refined, and ultimately rejected. However, once a legal rule survives the precarious intermediate stage of its development, it will become increasingly entrenched, overturned only if it is confronted by a judge with substantially divergent preferences.

Conclusion

We have developed an informational model of judicial decision making in which deference to precedent is useful to outcome-oriented appellate judges, because it improves the accuracy with which they can communicate legal rules to trial judges. Although we believe that our model makes a significant contribution to understanding judicial decision making, it is important to highlight that much work remains to be done in developing informational theories of judicial behavior. For example, while we have discussed a series of judicial decisions made over time, we have only modeled judges as one-shot decision makers. A formal treatment of repeated decision making might offer important insights, especially regarding the potentially moderating effect of the belief that one has multiple opportunities to effect changes in a substantive legal rule. Further, several possibilities exist for game-theoretic extensions of our simple decision-theoretic model. A particularly interesting avenue to explore would be a game with multiple appellate judges with diverse policy preferences. Another possibility is to model trial court judges as strategic actors with policy preferences of their own.

Nonetheless, our model yields interesting implications and hypotheses regarding conditions under which judges will maintain or break with precedent, the constraining effect that precedent has on judicial decision making, the voting behavior of Supreme Court justices, the relationship between a precedent's age and its authority, the effect of legal complexity on the level of deference to precedent, the relative stability of rules and standards, and long-term patterns of legal evolution. Perhaps most important, we have demonstrated that "legalist" features of judicial decision making are consistent with an assumption of policy-oriented judges. Thus, the informational approach to the study of judicial behavior can generate new insights and help to reconcile long-standing debates in the literature.

Notes

This article originally appeared in *American Political Science Review* 96(4) (2002): 755–66, and is reprinted with the permission of Cambridge University Press. We are indebted to Scott Ashworth, Bruce Bueno de Mesquita, Charles Cohen, Eric Dickson, Gilles Serra, Ken Shepsle, Judge Stephen Williams, several anonymous referees, and the participants in the Harvard Rational Choice Lunch Group, the Harvard Political Economy Research Workshop, the Texas A&M Conference on Institutional Games and the U.S. Supreme Court, and the William H. Riker Conference on Constitutions, Voting, and Democracy at Washington University for valuable comments. Stephenson gratefully acknowledges support from the John M. Olin Center for Law, Economics, and Business. Bueno de Mesquita gratefully acknowledges support from the Center for Basic Research in the Social Sciences.

1. Both the "attitudinal model" (Segal and Spaeth 1993) and the "strategic model" (Knight and Epstein 1998) of judicial behavior are "policy oriented," in that both models assume judges are primarily concerned with substantive outcomes.

2. *Stare decisis et non quieta movere*—"stand by the thing decided and do not disturb the calm."

3. One aspect of this principle is the idea that lower courts are supposed to follow the precedents set by higher courts (vertical stare decisis). This is not much different from the principle in many hierarchical organizations that subordinate units are supposed to follow the directions and guidelines laid down by their superiors. A more interesting aspect of the stare decisis principle—and one more unique to judicial decision making—is the principle that courts are supposed to follow their own prior decisions (horizontal stare decisis).

4. This might not always be the case, because there might be some other "legal" principle, e.g., the proper interpretation of a statute, that could trump the principle of deference to decided cases even for a legalist judge. Nonetheless, as a general rule, it is safe to

assume that legalist judges in a common law system would attach substantial weight to precedent.

5. If there is not specific, targeted retaliation against particular judges for failing to follow precedent, the general judicial interest in precedent-following alone is insufficient, because respect for precedents is a collective good and individual judges' dominant strategy would be to free ride (Macey 1989).

6. A bright-line rule is a rule that minimizes ambiguity by setting well-defined and simple categories of prohibited and permissible behavior.

7. We will refer to the judge's preferences over this continuum as policy preferences; however, we use policy broadly, to reflect public-policy preferences, normative judgments regarding fairness or justice, or a weighted combination of various factors.

8. The discrete binary choice between maintaining and breaking with precedent is a simplifying assumption. Clearly, in the real world, multiple lines of precedent may be in play in any given decision and the judge may decide to maintain parts of existing precedent. Framing the issue in the manner that we do captures in starkest form the same essential decision problem that would arise in more complex adjudicative choices.

9. The trial judge could, in theory, aggregate these signals in some other way (for example, by taking a weighted average), and this would, in turn, change the optimal decision of the appellate judge. We focus attention on a simple average for the following reasons. First, including the possibility of a weighted average would not alter the appellate judge's basic decision problem—the trade-off between greater precision (if the appellate judge's holding is aggregated with those of other judges) and the opportunity to announce the judge's most preferred legal rule (if the trial judge looks only at the appellate judge's ruling). The unweighted average is thus the simplest among a class of similar aggregation rules, any of which might be reasonable, depending on other background institutional assumptions. Second, calculating the optimal weighted average is itself a complex problem that depends on the appellate judge deriving the optimal weights as a function of the appellate judge's preferences and existing precedent. Third, not only is this calculation complex for the appellate judge, but the proper weights, once calculated, would have to be communicated to the trial judge. This communication, like the communication of the substantive holding, would be inherently noisy. Thus, the calculation and transmission of appropriate weights—essentially, a more refined and sophisticated principle of stare decisis—introduces another level of complexity, which, though interesting, is beyond the scope of this essay and is therefore left to future research.

10. In particular, if $X_i, \ldots, X_n$ are independent random variables and $X_i \sim N(\mu_i, \sigma_i^2)$, $i = 1, \ldots, n$ and $a_1, \ldots, a_n$ are constants such that $a_i \neq 0$ for at least one i, then the random variable $a_1 X_1 + \ldots + a_n X_n$ is normally distributed with mean $a_1 \mu_1 + \ldots + a_n \mu_n$ and variance $a_1^2 \sigma_1^2 + \ldots + a_n^2 \sigma_n^2$. (DeGroot 1970, 38). In our case, because the trial judge is taking an average, $a_i = (1/t)$, $\mu_i = r_i$, and $\sigma_i^2 = \sigma^2$ for $i = 1, \ldots, t$. Consequently the average of the signals is itself a random variable with mean $\mu_t = (\Sigma_{i=1}^{t} r_i)/t$ and variance (σ^2/t).

11. If $\alpha > 1$, this implies that the cost of writing the decision is weighted more heavily than how close the trial court's decision is to the appellate court's ideal point. If $0 \leq \alpha < 1$, the closeness of the trial court decision to the appellate judge's ideal point is weighted more heavily. If $\alpha = 0$, adherence to precedent is costless no matter how much the legal rule is changed substantively; in this special case, the appellate judge would always claim

to adhere to precedent, because doing so imposes no constraints whatsoever on the distance the appellate judge can move the legal rule.

12. This is only possible if the trial judge knows α and σ^2. If not, the trial judge is unable even to entertain the possibility of trying to deduce the appellate judge's ideal point from the observed signals.

13. This is not to say that an aggregation rule other than averaging might not lead to superior outcomes in some circumstances. As discussed earlier, the optimal aggregation rule is a function of a host of complex institutional factors beyond the scope of this model. Nonetheless, the basic logic—that the appellate judge's choice to maintain precedent implies that the trial judge will do better by following precedent than by attempting to deduce the appellate judge's ideal point—holds under any aggregation rule.

14. Note also that as t goes to infinity, the appellate judge is completely constrained by the old precedent. In this case, the value of α does not matter, and the payoff of an appellate judge who maintains precedent converges to $-(j - \mu_{t-1})^2$.

15. Of course, this is also the case if each appellate judge is myopic, caring only about the payoff in the current round.

Decision Making by an Agent with Multiple Principals

Environmental Policy in the U.S. Courts of Appeals

STEFANIE A. LINDQUIST AND SUSAN B. HAIRE

Institutional games for both higher and lower courts become especially complex in the realm of environmental policymaking. Environmental policymaking has long been depicted as the result of interaction between a wide variety of policy actors, including the courts, Congress, and the presidency. This essay shifts attention to the U.S. Courts of Appeals to examine judicial decision making in pollution control cases from 1984 to 1996 in order to assess the extent to which judges respond to the complex, multiple institutional forces in their decision-making environment. From a principal-agent perspective, circuit judges are hypothesized to respond to the policy preferences of multiple principals. The empirical results support this premise, suggesting that circuit court judges' decisions are influenced by Supreme Court preferences in this policy area and, to a lesser degree, to shifts in the environmental policy preferences of Congress. Although judges' decisions were not directly influenced by presidential policy preferences, they did reflect the substantial influence of an executive branch agency, the Environmental Protection Administration, particularly when the agency advocated an anti-environmental position.

Judges on the United States Courts of Appeals face a complex set of job requirements and constraints. In terms of their job requirements, circuit court judges must dispose of a mandatory docket comprised of cases arising in multiple issue areas, many of which are highly technical. Often, these caseloads are extremely heavy; in some circuits, judges decide hundreds of cases each year, drafting full opinions in many of them. Moreover, circuit judges decide cases in randomly assigned panels and generally do not distribute their workload on the basis of individual judges' substantive expertise. Thus, they must familiarize themselves with case law and statutory provisions in a wide array of often highly complicated doctrinal areas.

In addition to these workload burdens, circuit judges are also subject to other influences stemming from the institutional environment in which they work. Although federal judges are appointed for life and enjoy considerable independence, they render decisions within a complex institutional environment that generates important decision-making norms. For example, federal judges face pressure from the executive branch, particularly when the courts review decisions by administrative agencies seeking to implement the president's policy agenda. Indeed, as generalists, federal judges (in connection with statutory mandates) have developed a policy of deference to the judgments of administrative agents, which likely accounts in part for the high rates of success agencies enjoy in court. Similarly, canons of statutory construction frequently lead judges to defer to legislative preferences. To enhance its control over courts' interpretation and implementation of federal statutes, Congress may incorporate carefully worded judicial review provisions or override judicial decisions through statutory amendments. Lower federal court judges must also defer to the policy pronouncements of their principals at the Supreme Court; research shows that circuit judges often vote in a manner that is consistent with changing Supreme Court preferences (Johnson 1979, Songer and Sheehan 1990). And, in some policy areas, lower federal court judges, particularly those in the appeals courts, are faced with claims advanced by interest groups involved in the litigation process as parties or amicus curiae.

These factors are particularly pronounced in cases involving administrative regulation of the environment. Environmental protection constitutes a highly politicized policy area that has attracted considerable attention from political elites as well as from the public at large. The enactment, interpretation, and implementation of environmental statutes have involved the participation of Congress, the executive branch, and the federal judiciary, as well as attracted the active involvement of multiple interest groups on both sides of the issue. As a result, cases involving the interpretation and implementation of environmental law offer a promising context in which to study the manner in which judges on the courts of appeals respond to these competing interests. As William Eskridge and Philip Frickey (1994, 32) have observed, "Law is not simply a prediction that preexists the sequential, hierarchical, and purposive interaction of institutions. It is, instead, a product of that interaction—an equilibrium, that is, a balance of competing institutional pressures." This statement is particularly apt in the context of environmental law.

In this essay, therefore, we examine judicial decision making in pollution control cases decided by the U. S. Courts of Appeals from 1984 to 1996. In doing so, we are able to assess the extent to which circuit judges respond to multiple institutional forces in their decision-making environment, including the influence of Congress, the president, and the Supreme Court. After considering existing theoretical perspectives, we argue that these three policy players, in particular, represent multiple principals to the appeals courts as agents. In our empirical model, we test this theoretical framework to assess whether circuit judges make decisions that are consistent with the preferences of multiple principals, all of whom are interested in influencing the impact of environmental policies, at times in ways that lead to competition and conflict. In what follows, we begin with a discussion of environmental policymaking during the relevant period, with a particular emphasis on cooperation and competition between the courts, Congress, and the presidency over environmental policy outcomes.

Environmental Policymaking in the 1980s and 1990s

The "environmental decade" of the 1970s marked the first wave of legislation addressing pollution control. During that historic period (actually beginning in 1969), Congress enacted numerous laws aimed at environmental degradation, including the National Environmental Policy Act of 1969 (NEPA), the Clean Air Act Amendments of 1970, the Federal Water Pollution Control Act (Clean Water Act) Amendments of 1972, and the Resource Conservation and Recovery Act of 1976 (RCRA).[1] The decade ended with the passage of the Comprehensive Environmental Response, Compensation, and Liability Act (CERCLA) of 1980, which contains the Superfund provisions allowing for the allocation of responsibility among polluters. These statutes were the result of intense public focus on environmental issues during the period. And while the Democratically controlled Congress frequently played a more dominant role in the process of formulating environmental statutes, the presidential administrations of Richard Nixon, Gerald Ford, and Jimmy Carter all cooperated on environmental issues. The courts also proved to be hospitable for the airing of environmental grievances (Blumm 2001). In general, the 1970s marked a period in which the three branches of government were unified in addressing American citizens' environmental concerns.

With the election of Ronald Reagan in 1980, however, the political dynamics on environmental issues changed significantly. Reagan was elected on a platform of deregulation, small government, and pro-business initiatives. The Reagan administration, with the assistance of the new Republican Senate in 1981, was able to appoint ideologically conservative agency heads to EPA and the Departments of Agriculture, Interior, and Energy and advocated sharp budget cuts to programs devoted to environmental protection. Yet, even in the face of a Republican Senate and the pro-business Reagan administration, Congress was still able to pass legislation in the 1980s strengthening RCRA. In addition, Congress passed the Superfund Amendments and Reauthorization Act of 1986. In 1987 a Democratically controlled Congress passed the Clean Water Act Amendments of 1987.[2] Thus, in the 1980s, Congress remained at the forefront of environmental policy, clearly setting the agenda at the national level. Furthermore, Reagan's pro-business policies vitalized environmental organizations, which sought to counteract Reagan's message. This enthusiasm for environmental concerns continued throughout the presidency of George H. W. Bush, who, chastened by the backlash against the Reagan administration's anti-environmental policies, made a greater effort to accommodate environmentalists.

During this period too, Reagan and George H. W. Bush were able to staff the courts with like-minded conservatives, and the Supreme Court's shift toward the right was manifested in cases such as *Chevron v. National Resource Defense Council* (104 S.Ct. 2778 [1984]), insulating the Reagan administration's actions from scrutiny by more liberal judges. The conservative Rehnquist Court also rendered decisions undermining environmentalists' standing to sue to enforce environmental protection laws (McSpadden 1997), a trend that continued into the next decade.

By the early 1990s, other pressing issues, including the economy, overshadowed the environment on the national agenda. The election of Bill Clinton and Al Gore in 1992 was greeted with hope by many environmentalists, but Clinton failed to capitalize on his shared partisan affiliation with Congress to enact much environmental legislation in the early years of his presidency (Vig 1997). After the 1994 congressional elections and Republican ascendancy there, the Clinton administration adopted a more aggressive position toward protecting the environment, but Clinton's efforts were largely defensive in nature. At the same time, the judiciary, now dominated by Reagan and Bush appointees, became less receptive to environmental claims in general (McSpadden 1997).

Within this shifting policy context, the federal circuit courts have shouldered a considerable amount of the workload associated with implementation of federal environmental statutes. The lower courts constitute the forum for most regulatory policy issues that are litigated in the federal system. A substantial proportion of cases filed in the federal system are appealed to the circuit courts, while some are filed directly in the courts of appeals following the final decision of the relevant agency (usually EPA). Moreover, when judges on the courts of appeals decide an environmental case, they are often faced with a complex task. Environmental statutes and regulations set forth legal standards that often depend on highly technical and scientific information. In some circumstances, statutes may be ambiguously worded, thus leaving agencies and the courts to clarify parties' legal obligations. Furthermore, in many situations that arise in connection with pollution control, the courts, rather than the EPA or the Corps of Engineers, constitute the key institution that must implement environmental policy created by the elected branches.

For example, some environmental statutes include citizen suit provisions that allow private persons and organizations to sue in federal court to enforce statutory mandates. Other statutes provide for individuals or corporations to settle the costs of pollution cleanup among themselves through litigation in federal court, as provided by Superfund provisions. The efficacy of "private attorneys general" either to enforce environmental protection statutes or to allocate elimination costs clearly depends on the courts' receptivity to these private lawsuits, rather than on the activities of administrative agencies. Indeed, one congressional purpose underlying citizen suit provisions is to allow an "end run" around recalcitrant agencies that refuse to enforce environmental laws as Congress sees fit (Smith 1998). The circuit courts are at the center of this implementation process, because they render the final judgment on most environmental appeals and thus often bear the responsibility to determine legal policy in the area of pollution control.

Circuit Court Judges as Environmental Policymakers: A Principal-Agent Framework

As implementers of federal environmental policy, circuit court judges find themselves in a decision-making context in which the policy parameters are defined by several institutional actors, including the Supreme Court, Congress, and the president. We draw on principal-agent theory to assess the interactions between circuit judges, as agents, and these three principals. In environmental policy, principal-agent theory highlights the issues that arise when each principal relies on circuit judges as agents to implement statutory and administrative guidelines. In many circumstances, given goal conflict and information asymmetry between principal and agent (Brehm and Gates 1999), the principals cannot perfectly control the agent's actions.

In its most basic formulation, principal-agent theory suggests that circuit judges as agents should and often will respond to the preferences of political actors that exercise supervisory control over the circuit courts. Within the federal judicial hierarchy, the most obvious supervisory role is assumed by the Supreme Court. The High Court is expected to correct circuit court decisions that are inconsistent with the justices' preferences. Indeed, as agents, lower federal court judges appear to respond to the preferences of the Supreme Court in many circumstances. Empirical studies of search-and-seizure cases support the expectation that circuit court judges make decisions that are largely consistent with Supreme Court justices' preferences (Cameron, Segal, and Songer 2000; Songer, Segal, and Cameron 1994). While simple superior-subordinate dyads are appropriate models for policy areas like criminal procedure where the courts dominate the policy domain, they may be unrealistic when studying environmental policy where other political principals attempt to control judicial policymaking. Thus, before outlining our specific expectations concerning the influence of each principal on judicial decision making in the circuit courts, we provide a brief discussion of the special issues created by the existence of multiple principals in this decision-making context.

Although a multiple principals-agents perspective has not been fully developed in studies of lower court decision making (but see Brent 1999), scholars have employed these frameworks to account for interactions between Congress, the president, the Supreme Court, and administrative agencies. In particular, positive political theorists provide insight into the dynamic created by multiple principals, which permit bureaucratic agents to shift the policy status quo away from the position preferred by the enacting legislative coalition (McCubbins, Noll, and Weingast 1987, 1989). One model by Matthew McCubbins, Roger Noll, and Barry Weingast (1989) demonstrates that bureaucratic policy "drift" will not be corrected as long as the policy position taken by the agent is within the Pareto optimal set defined by the preferences of the president, House, and Senate. Because each principal may veto legislation, any policy position promulgated by the agency that falls within the Pareto optimal set will have the support of at least one of these players. If two principals attempt to correct the bureaucratic shift in policy, the agent would turn to the (third) most proximate principal who could veto the correction advanced by the other principals.

The McCubbins, Noll, and Weingast model may guide the development of a multiple-principal perspective to understand the institutional environment faced by circuit judges when rendering environmental decisions. In cases raising statutory legal claims, circuit judges may be viewed as agents to the political branches as well as agents to the Supreme Court. Indeed, Congress often explicitly relies on courts to implement regulatory policy by enabling courts to police compliance with legislative mandates through litigation brought by private attorneys general. Nonetheless, circuit judges are motivated by their own policy concerns. As a result, when interpreting environmental statutes, a circuit judge may prefer to shift policy outcomes away from the enacting coalition's ideal point toward her own preference point. And she may do so without repercussion in the form of statutory override as long as her judicial decision falls within the Pareto optimal set defined by the policy preferences of her principals.

Yet, given that circuit court judges are part of a decentralized judicial hierarchy and render decisions with limited geographic impact—in contrast to the more centralized policymaking by administrative agencies—circuit court decisions are less likely to generate a response by the political branches. And clearly, courts cannot be viewed as subject to political control exercised by the elected branches in any conventional sense. Federal courts cannot simply be equated with administrative agencies, because the latter do not enjoy the independence protections provided in Article III of the U.S. Constitution.

Congress and the president do enjoy some, more limited means to influence the federal courts, however. The political branches control the judicial appointment process, may construct judicial review provisions to constrain judges' discretion in interpreting statutes, can enhance the role of favored groups in litigation, and can alter federal court jurisdiction (Jackson 1998, Resnik 1998, Shipan 1997). Conversely, the Supreme Court exercises far more direct control over circuit court outputs, enhancing the likelihood that circuit judges will conform to the Court's preferences on environmental policy. Although the Court's docket is small, the threat of reversal is real. Moreover, participation by interest groups in the certiorari process ensures that "fire alarms" are sounded whenever a circuit deviates from the High Court's preferences (cf. McCubbins and Schwartz 1984). Thus, we expect that the principals' influence over circuit courts will vary depending on the likelihood of corrective action on the part of the individual principal. In their study of seven agencies, Dan Wood and Richard Waterman (1991) found that the agencies responded to the exercise of direct political control, particularly in the form of executive appointments. Similarly, circuit judges, as agents, might be expected to weigh more heavily the preferences of those principals who exercise direct supervisory control over their activities.

Circuit court judges' responsiveness to their principals' preferences is also likely to stem from considerations unrelated to strategic responses to other institutional actors. In particular, circuit judges face internal constraints associated with workload demands and with appellate court decision-making norms. In recent decades, circuit courts have faced an exponential increase in caseload (Krafka, Cecil, and Lombard 1995) and have adapted to the burgeoning caseload by altering traditional processes of appellate litigation (Baker 1994). Overworked judges may be sensitive to case outcomes that are likely to increase future litigation. By rendering decisions that conform to congressional preferences, for example, circuit judges may attempt to ensure the clarity and consistency of precedent, thus reducing further litigation over statutory meaning or effect. Similarly, circuit judges may wish to avoid remand or reconsideration of their decisions, which may follow from an en banc challenge or reversal by the Supreme Court. Judges faced with significant workload demands may also rely on cues from principals as an efficient decision-making device. Decision-making norms may further serve to promote efficient case disposition. Certain norms, including those associated with canons of statutory construction, deference to administrative agencies, and hierarchical stare decisis, explicitly define the appropriate boundaries of the court's relations to other institutional participants in the regulatory process, such as Congress and the Supreme Court. Workload constraints and decision-making norms may therefore prompt circuit judge-agents to act sincerely in the interests of their principals.

Thus far, our principal-agent perspective suggests that, whether acting sincerely or strategically, circuit judges are expected to make judicial policy that is consistent with the preferences of the Supreme Court, Congress, and the president. By recognizing the existence of multiple principals and evaluating their influence on circuit judge-agents, research may capture the broader institutional context (e.g., Moe 1985). Recognition of multiple principals for circuit judges, however, shifts the theoretical focus because of the possibility that principals will not agree on goals. Considerable disagreement over goals in the environmental policy arena existed during the 1980s and 1990s. Where divergent goals exist, it is unclear which principal's goals the agent will choose to follow. We expect the Supreme Court's effect to be magnified because of its supervisory role over the appeals courts in the federal judicial hierarchy. Another possibility is that the agent will choose "the most cognitively salient" goal held by any particular principal (Mitnick 1980, 15).

Extending this logic to our analysis of lower-court environmental policy, one might expect, for example, that judges will respond to clear information concerning the preferences of principals and possibly weigh more heavily the preferences of the principal who dominates the policy agenda. In the hypotheses below, we provide more detail on specific expectations suggested by this framework.

Hypotheses

Our framework highlights the influence of those principals who possess lawmaking authority: Congress, the presidency, and the Supreme Court. However, we also develop and test expectations regarding the influence of other actors, namely the EPA and interest groups, who are interested in environmental policy, but who do not possess lawmaking authority or tools of supervisory control over circuit court judges.

MULTIPLE PRINCIPALS: CONGRESS, THE PRESIDENT, AND THE SUPREME COURT

In the case of multiple principals, the principal with the most "cognitively salient" goals may be the most influential in the policymaking environment. This seems uniquely applicable to Congress when particular statutory issues are raised in court. Judges would be expected to be sensitive to the policy position of Congress in areas where the legislative branch has dominated the policy agenda. When legislative activity is high, judges simply have more information about congressional preferences. In environmental policy, Congress leads the agenda (Flemming, Wood, and Bohte 1999). Over the last three decades, the policy positions taken by Congress on pollution-control issues have varied. Interestingly, congressional policy efforts in this area are often at odds with the ideological content of other actors' policy initiatives. For example, with public support in the mid-1980s, Congress passed several laws that strengthened pollution-control standards, in spite of the position taken by President Reagan.

Circuit judges may be responsive to legislative preferences for a variety of other reasons as well. First, Congress may draft judicial review provisions to ensure case results more proximate to legislative intent. In their discussion of bureaucratic drift, McCubbins, Noll and Weingast (1989) observe that Congress appreciates the difficulties associated with altering or overriding bureaucratic interpretations of regulatory statutes that fail to conform to legislative intent. Because ex post legislative changes or oversight are unlikely to restore the original coalition's agreement and preferred policy outcome, the governing coalition in Congress must rely on ex ante controls over agency action to ensure compliance with legislative preferences. Since Congress also relies on the courts as agents, it may create statutory controls to ensure that judicial interpretations conform to the enacting coalition's policy preferences. As Charles Shipan (1997) noted in his study of telecommunications statutes, Congress devises judicial review provisions so as to influence court decisions reviewing agency action. In addition, by granting standing to certain affected constituencies through its enactments, Congress can use the courts as additional watchdogs to identify agency noncompliance (Smith 1998).

Second, decision-making norms in statutory cases frequently draw on agency theory and induce judges to take into account the preferences of Congress. For example, principles of statutory construction involving legislative intent hold that judges' interpretations should further the purposes of the enacting coalition. Yet, preserving the original coalition's intent may also require fidelity or attention to current legislative preferences.[3] In this regard, John Ferejohn has observed:

> [I]nsofar as courts in particular have allegiance to statutes—that is, to the duly encoded preferences of the enacting Congress—they should be careful to devise interpretive methods that protect statutes from contemporary political responses, and in particular do not provoke congressional responses that are very far from the statutory desires of the enacting coalition Such courts would engage in what might be called "strategic jurisprudence," in that they would have to take account of the preferences of the sitting Congress in interpreting statutes. Only by doing so would such courts be able to act as "sophisticated honest agents" of the enacting Congress. (Rodriguez 1994, quoting Ferejohn, 1992)

Finally, concern over legislative initiatives to override federal court decisions may lead strategic judges to take into account the preferences of the sitting Congress. Very little research has explored this question at the courts of appeals. Richard Revesz (2001), for example, was unable to detect evidence of congressional influence over circuit court decisions in his study of the D.C. Circuit's review of the health and safety decisions of twenty federal agencies. These findings are limited to one specific court, however. Because the proposition is worthy of further empirical evaluation, we offer a counterhypothesis:

H_1: As support for pro-environmental policies by the sitting Congress increases, the likelihood of a circuit judge voting in favor of the pro-environmental position will increase.

Consideration for the legislature frequently stands at the forefront of the debate over whether judicial policy is responsive to democratic political influences. Yet the president may actively pursue his own legislative initiatives, and through the veto power, he may formally shape the content of environmental statutes. The executive branch is also a primary player in the formulation of regulatory policy, with pollution-control issues included in the presidential domestic policy agenda since the Nixon administration. In the 1980s, the Reagan administration drew fire from environmental activists for introducing regulatory reform that reduced the burdens associated with environmental controls (Kovacic 1991). The policy stance of George H. W. Bush's administration was more hospitable to environmental interests, with the appointment of officials who were more supportive of governmental regulation in the area of pollution control. And although Clinton did not pursue environmental issues as aggressively as some environmentalists would have preferred, his administration was probably the most receptive to concerns over pollution control.

For reasons similar to those concerning Congress, we expect that judges will broadly gauge current presidential preferences when deciding a regulatory policy issue. To begin with, federal judges may seek to further the policy goals of the executive branch because of the president's lawmaking authority. Indeed, any "correction" by the legislative branch requires the president's approval.[4] Judges also may consider executive branch preferences because of their more self-interested concern over the enforcement and implementation of judicial interpretations of regulatory statutes.[5] Officials in the executive branch are responsible for ensuring compliance with judicial standards in regulatory policy. Therefore, judges may anticipate varying levels of cooperation according to their perceptions of presidential support for a policy stance.

Still, we anticipate the effect of presidential policy preferences to be less pronounced than that of legislative preferences for several reasons. Some scholars predict that judges will be less responsive to changes in presidential preferences because administration officials lack the tools necessary to reverse court rulings on statutory questions (Gely and Spiller 1990). Moreover, we noted above that norms induce judges to ascertain the preferences of Congress. Canons of statutory construction do not encourage a similar sensitivity to presidential policy preferences. Not surprisingly, one empirical analysis of decision making in environmental cases before the lower courts found that judges' decisions often were contrary to the policy leanings of the current administration (Wenner and Dutter 1988). McCubbins, Noll, and Weingast also note that, in the environmental context, legislators recognize the ex post influence presidents may wield over administrative agencies, because presidents appoint high-ranking agency personnel. Thus, they suggest that "an enduring theme in Congress will be to build in protections against undue influence by the President" (1989, 435). If Congress is successful in its efforts to insulate regulatory decisions from undue presidential influence, the effects may be seen in judicial interpretations of legislative enactments as well. With these caveats in mind, we offer our second hypothesis:

H_2: As support for pro-environmental policies by the sitting president increases, the likelihood of a circuit judge voting in favor of the pro-environmental position will increase.

In addition to Congress and the president, the courts of appeals are also agents to their principal at the Supreme Court. Judicial decision making in the U.S. Courts of Appeals is expected to be influenced by the Court for a number of reasons. First, the potential for review and reversal by the High Court may lead lower-court judges to align themselves to the preferences of the Supreme Court. The Supreme Court, as principal, appears to grant certiorari to strengthen control over its agents (Cameron, Segal, and Songer 2000). The High Court also may choose outcomes that will reduce the costs of supervising the lower courts (Cohen and Spitzer 1996). Therefore, the Supreme Court's supervisory authority is believed to be more effective when upper-court precedent provides specific, unambiguous directives to lower-court judges.

Empirical research has demonstrated that the Supreme Court does exercise considerable control over its agents at the circuit court, as the evidence indicates that the circuits respond to the Court's preferences. For example, Donald Songer, Jeffery Segal, and Charles Cameron (1994) evaluated the degree to which the Court is able to control circuit court decision making in search-and-seizure cases from 1961 to 1990, of which only 2 percent were actually reversed by the Supreme Court. Although the monitoring activity of the Supreme Court was therefore extremely limited, Songer, Segal, and Cameron found that circuit judges were generally faithful to the Supreme Court's changing policy preferences, even after controlling for case facts. Other studies have reached similar results in other issue areas (Johnson 1979, Gruhl 1980, Songer 1987, Songer and Sheehan 1990). Fear of reversal alone may not account for the degree to which lower courts respond to the Supreme Court, however. Similar to our arguments concerning the effect of Congress, we propose here that circuit judges, as agents, are more likely to respond to Supreme Court directives when supported by decision-making norms. In this context, norms associated with hierarchical stare decisis may contribute to circuit court responsiveness to upper-court directives. In the context of environmental policy, we would expect circuit judges to be most likely to respond when there is recent High Court precedent that offers specific standards concerning the statute being raised in the appeal. For these reasons, we offer our third hypothesis:

H_3: As Supreme Court precedent for the pro-environmental position in- creases, the likelihood of a circuit judge voting in favor of the pro- environmental position will increase.

OTHER CONTEXTUAL INFLUENCES ON JUDICIAL POLICYMAKING

The first three hypotheses set forth above constitute our main focus: the manner in which the circuit courts respond to Congress, the presi- dency, and the Supreme Court when making regulatory decisions. But the context of judicial decision making is still more complex. Other actors and institutions also compete for influence in the judicial policymaking process.

Whereas general positions on policy issues are established by presi- dents,[6] the position of the administration in a particular case is often rep- resented by the agency-litigant. In environmental matters, EPA has played a leading role in establishing national pollution-control standards. During the 1980s and 1990s, courts examined the agency's interpretation of statutory obligations, such as whether EPA should consider cost- benefit trade-offs when establishing abatement standards and whether it was appropriate to use economic incentives to achieve such standards (Kovacic 1991, O'Leary 1993). Judicial review of enforcement efforts also included considering whether the EPA (or state environmental enforce- ment agency) should be more lenient toward polluters attempting to meet standards (e.g., extensions on timetables).

The same efficiency concerns described above also likely motivate judges on the appeals courts to rely on information provided by agencies and defer to the judgment of administration officials. With respect to administrative agencies, standards of judicial review embodied in the Administrative Procedures Act and reinforced by Supreme Court precedent such as *Vermont Yankee* and *Chevron* mandate that judges acknowledge some level of deference to administrative agencies, rather than exercising de novo review in all circumstances. These deferential standards reflect the recognition that generalist courts are not as qualified as administrative agencies to render judgments on technical issues and that efficiency will be promoted by allowing agencies some discretion in pursuing their statutory obligations. Scholarship on the lower federal appeals courts clearly establishes that federal agencies, including the EPA, are more likely to prevail (Songer and Sheehan 1992). These findings are interpreted as evidence that stronger parties are more often able to prevail in litigation. A federal agency's strength may stem from considerable resources and expertise.

Armed with legal talent in their own agency, the Department of Justice, and the U.S. Attorneys' offices, the EPA clearly does not lack legal resources. As a repeat player, the EPA also may be more persuasive than its opponents as a result of the substantive and process expertise it possesses. In this respect, "generalist" appeals court judges with a high workload can find themselves yielding to the substantive expertise of an agency in cases that are technical in nature. As one scholar found, there is a "prudent unwillingness to engage in policy making functions for which the courts are . . . ill-suited. This is particularly true for the technically complex fact-finding and analysis decisions that dominate EPA's agenda"[7] (Kovacic 1991, 694).

Recurring appearances in a single policy area also contribute to an agency's substantive legal expertise, because litigators have more opportunities to fine-tune their knowledge of circuit law. In the EPA, this familiarity may have a cumulative effect as a result of appeals in multiple circuits; government litigators can draw on their experiences from litigation in one circuit when framing issues and arguments for a similar case in another. In addition, as a recurring litigant in the same circuit, EPA attorneys will become more familiar with circuit practices and individual judges' preferences. Drawing on this familiarity, the EPA can tailor arguments that will be more appealing to a particular circuit or panel. In light of the foregoing discussion, therefore, we offer the following hypotheses concerning the influence of the EPA in litigation before the courts of appeals:

H_4: When the EPA supports the pro-environmental position in a case, the likelihood of the circuit judge voting for that position increases.

H_5: When the EPA supports the anti-environmental position in a case, the likelihood of the circuit judge voting for the pro-environmental position decreases.

Any thorough analysis of regulatory decisions in the courts of appeals cannot ignore the influence of interest groups in the process. Pluralist theories of democratic politics view organized interests as vital to the functioning of the political system (Lowi 1979). Within the institutional context examined here, interest groups play an important informational role in environmental policymaking. In addition to providing expertise to inform judges in the decision-making process, organized interests alert judges to the preferences of multiple, competing principals, thereby reducing any informational asymmetries that may exist (Banks and Weingast 1992, Hettinger and Zorn 1999).

In environmental policy, groups tend to stake out opposing ends of the policy spectrum. At one end, industrial groups allege that environmental regulations undermine economic stability through excessive costs and difficult compliance requirements (O'Leary 1993). Groups supporting this argument include trade associations, such as the National Coal Association, or corporate public interest organizations, such as the Mountain States Legal Foundation. These business and property interests have increasingly appeared in the appeals courts since the 1980s to challenge administrative regulations before they could take effect (Wenner 1990). Organizations that represent environmental interests in the courts include the Sierra Club, Environmental Defense Fund, and the Natural Resources Defense Council. These groups have challenged agency regulations for not sufficiently meeting legislative directives. In addition, environmental groups have sponsored citizen suits in which individuals seek judicial enforcement of pollution-control standards (Wenner 1990).

If part of the coalition of interests involved in the content of legislation, these groups can provide lower-court judges with information on the preferences and likely actions of the legislative and executive branch. Moreover, these groups have become repeat players in the courts as they have increasingly litigated claims over time (Wenner 1990). Their experience and resources permit them to engage in forum shopping to find the most receptive lower court (O'Leary 1993). Whether interest groups successfully forum shop in the lower courts is subject to debate. One analysis of federal district court decisions found that interest groups fared no better than other types of litigants (Epstein and Rowland 1991). Conversely, another analysis suggests that the informational role of interest groups may tip the balance as individual litigant success in state supreme courts was more likely when supported by amicus (Kuersten, Songer, and Kaheny 1998). In light of these considerations, we suggest that:

H_6: As the number of interest groups filing for (against) the pro-environmental position increases, the likelihood of the circuit judge voting in favor of the pro-environmental position will increase (decrease).

COMPLETING THE MODEL: JUDICIAL POLICY PREFERENCES AND
CASE CHARACTERISTICS

Our framework thus far suggests judicial decision making in the lower courts will be shaped by multiple principals and other actors in the policy process. We have also assumed that circuit judges' decisions will be shaped, in part, by the judges' policy preferences, although we have not staked out a position that such ideological considerations will play a paramount role in environmental cases. Nevertheless, we expect that judicial policy preferences will affect case outcomes to some degree. Moreover, we recognize that all cases are not directly comparable, even in this relatively narrow field of environmental law. Thus, we must identify case characteristics that will enable us to control for these unique influences.

The inevitable exercise of judicial discretion in statutory interpretation would suggest that judges have the potential to act on their own policy preferences. Models of decision making in the U.S. Courts of Appeals have long suggested a relationship between the policy preferences of judges and their voting behavior (Goldman 1975; Songer and Davis 1990; Songer and Haire 1992; Songer, Segal, and Cameron 1994). Research on lower-court decision making indicates differences in judicial attitudes are well captured by variables that correspond to selection processes[8] (Carp and Rowland 1983, Goldman 1997, Songer and Haire 1992). Generally, the findings of these studies suggest that in recent years judges appointed by Republican presidents are more conservative than those appointed by Democratic presidents. In the context of environmental law decisions of the U.S. Courts of Appeals, William Kovacic (1991) found Reagan judges much more likely to support burden-reducing measures when compared to Carter judges. Overall, one would expect recruitment processes to lead to the selection of those who share the views of their appointing president.[9] Therefore, our measure of judicial attitudes is represented by the policy preferences of the president at the time of the judge's appointment.

H_7: As the liberalism of the appointing president increases, the likelihood of the circuit judge voting in favor of the pro-environmental position will increase.

Many cases raise "easy" issues with clearly applicable legal standards. In these cases, there is little doubt about the outcome, regardless of the preferences of other relevant actors. In easy statutory cases, canons of construction provide judges with a framework for analysis; judges are admonished that "if language is plain and unambiguous it must be given effect" (Llewellyn 1950, 401, 403). Not surprisingly, it is common for opinion authors to begin their analysis with the statutory text. Yet the analysis does not always end with the text of the statute where ambiguous language or meaning exists. In such circumstances, judges often look to "legislative intent" and "statutory purpose" to guide their interpretation. In the case of ambiguous legal standards, judges thus clearly enjoy broader discretion in the interpretive process.

In pollution-control cases, judges apply and interpret a wide range of environmental statutes. The titles of pollution-control statutes emphasize their purpose: prevention and cleanup of polluted areas. Nevertheless, these statutes vary to the extent that they include precise or broad statutory mandates. For example, some scholars have found that the broad mandate of NEPA has undermined its effectiveness as a policy instrument (Wenner and Dutter 1988). Judges and scholars alike have criticized CERCLA (the Superfund) for its lack of clarity. In contrast, statutes that deal with a specific regulatory area, such as those establishing standards for clean air and water, are more likely to be successful as a result of their narrow focus and more specific technical standards (Wenner and Dutter 1988). Where Congress has been particularly clear and has set forth precise technical standards, it reduces judicial discretion to diverge from Congress's intent to protect the environment. For these reasons, we offer the following hypotheses concerning the nature of the regulatory statutes involved in pollution-control cases:

H_8: When a case raises a claim based on narrowly defined regulatory statutes, the likelihood of the circuit judge voting in favor of the pro-environmental position will increase.

Research Design

VARIABLE MEASUREMENT

To test these hypotheses, we examine judicial voting in pollution-control cases decided by the U.S. Courts of Appeals from 1984–1996.[10] Since our analysis focuses on statutory claims, we excluded those cases that did not raise a statutory issue. Judges' votes were coded as "1" if they supported the pro-environment position. For example, a judge supported the pro-environment position if she voted in favor of more stringent air quality standards or against claims of industrial polluters and insurance companies that they were not financially liable for cleanup of a site. If the judge opposed the "pro-environment" position, their vote was coded "0."

We collected data from a variety of sources to test our hypotheses. Our framework requires that we develop measures that represent known policy positions of each principal and other policy actors. These measures are detailed below with descriptive statistics reported in the appendix to this essay.

CONGRESSIONAL ENVIRONMENTAL POLICY PREFERENCES. To measure Congress's preferences concerning environmental policy, we used the League of Conservation Voting (LCV) scores. As outlined above, our theoretical expectations do not suggest that circuit judges will respond to the preferences of individual legislators, or, for that matter, individual chambers. Instead, we expect that circuit judges will respond to shifts in the overall position of Congress as indicated by legislative activity in this policy area. From 1989 to 1996, for the year of the judicial decision, this variable was calculated by averaging the scores for the membership in each house before calculating the mean for the two chambers. Before 1989, LCV calculated the scorecard by Congress. Since our perspective suggests that judges' assessments of legislative preferences are derived from current legislative activity, we chose not to lag this variable.

ENVIRONMENTAL POLICY PREFERENCES OF THE SITTING PRESIDENT. To assess the policy position of the current administration, we used a measure that takes the LCV scorecard calculated for Congress and identifies those instances when the president took a position on the legislation.[11] The result is a measure of the proportion of times the president took a pro-environment position on roll calls selected for the LCV scorecard. The failure to take a position did not affect a president's score.

SUPREME COURT. Our theoretical framework suggests that the influence of the Supreme Court in regulatory policy will depend on the strength and clarity of signals sent to the lower court through precedent. Therefore, our measure incorporates both the directionality and intensity of pollution-control policy emanating from the High Court for each statutory area.[12] To develop this measure, we began by identifying all cases in the U.S. Supreme Court Database that dealt with pollution control. Each case was then classified according to the statute involved. A measure of Supreme Court influence for that statute was calculated by multiplying the number of decisions in that term by the directionality of the decisions in the particular statutory area.[13] Once a measure of Supreme Court preference was identified for a statute in a term, we linked that measure to courts of appeals' decisions where the primary issue focused on that same statute.

ENVIRONMENTAL PROTECTION AGENCY. To test our hypotheses that judges defer to the position of this agency, we coded two dummy variables that identified whether the EPA was a direct party, and whether the agency-litigant was representing the pro- or anti-environmental position. In cases where both of these variables are coded "0," the EPA was not a direct party in the appeal.

INTEREST GROUPS. To test whether judges are more likely to vote in favor of a group's policy position when that group participates as amicus, we coded dummy variables that identified whether one or more amicus briefs were filed by an industry (antienvironment) or environmental group, and whether the brief was unopposed by another group. In cases where these variables are coded "0," no amicus briefs were filed or briefs were filed in the same case by opposing groups.

JUDICIAL POLICY PREFERENCES. To measure the general policy predisposition of each judge (as selected for by the appointing president), we used the NOMINATE score of the president at the time of appointment. Lower values on this score represent more liberal policy positions. Therefore, we expect the variable to be negatively related to pro-environmental voting.

TYPE OF STATUTE. To test whether narrowly defined pollution control statutes contribute to pro-environmental voting, we coded a dummy variable that indicated whether the claim was brought under a clearly defined regulatory statute, including the Clean Air Act, Clean Water Act, pesticide acts, Safe Drinking Water Act, and the RCRA. In those instances where the case raised claims under multiple pollution-control statutes, the statute coded for this variable was determined by the amount of space allotted to the statutory legal analysis in the opinion. Those cases coded as "0" included those that focused on the National Environmental Policy Act (NEPA), CERCLA, Administrative Procedures Act, and other statutes with miscellaneous pollution control provisions such as the Federal Tort Claims Act and maritime laws.

STATISTICAL METHOD

A logistic regression model was used to assess the effects of these independent variables on judges' votes. In the first table, we report the coefficient, the robust standard error,[14] and the probability associated with the one-tailed t-test. To assess model performance, the log-likelihood is reported along with the pseudo R^2. In the second table, we provide additional information to assess the relative impact of each independent variable on the probability of a pro-environment vote. In the last portion of our analysis, we use a statistical simulation procedure to explore the interactive relationships between agents' preferences and the positions of their principals and other actors in environmental policy.

Results

Although judicial voting tends to be skewed toward a pro-environmental outcome, a number of hypothesized factors affected the likelihood of a vote in that direction to a statistically significant degree. Judges' voting behavior corresponded with their policy preferences as selected for by the appointing president. Most important, given our theoretical focus, the results presented in table 1 also suggest that two principals—Congress and the Supreme Court—significantly affect judicial voting. Notably, precedential signals from the High Court were effective in shaping subsequent decision making on the U.S. Courts of Appeals in pollution-control cases. Judges on these courts also supported positions consistent with the environmental policy preferences of the sitting Congress. In contrast, the policy stance taken by the current president does not appear to be related to judicial voting behavior. Instead, a more direct influence from the executive branch was realized through the Environmental Protection Agency. Whether it supports the pro- or anti-environment position, this agency finds overwhelming judicial support. In contrast, interest groups with a

TABLE 1 Logit model of circuit judges' votes in environmental cases

VARIABLE	COEFFICIENT	STANDARD ERROR	p-VALUE
Principals in the policymaking process			
Presidential environmentalism	−0.004	0.005	0.17
Supreme Court environmentalism	0.72	0.29	<0.01
Congressional environmentalism	0.15	0.06	0.01
Other institutional influences			
EPA direct party—pro-environmental	1.24	0.42	<0.01
EPA direct party—anti-environmental	−1.55	0.57	<0.01
Environmental group amicus advantage	0.17	0.84	0.42
Industry group amicus advantage	−0.70	0.66	0.15
Judicial policy preferences			
Appointing president's NOMINATE score	−0.90	0.26	<0.01
Case type			
Federal regulatory statute	1.04	0.38	<0.01
Constant	−7.21		
Pseudo R-squared	0.22		
Percent predicted correctly	71.51		
Log-likelihood	−262.81		

N=509. Robust standard errors calculated using the Huber-White procedure with clustering on panels. P-values are based on one-tailed tests.

stake in the policy process found little support for their claims.[15] Similar to the findings of prior research, this analysis also indicates the need to control for case content. Cases brought under narrowly defined regulatory statutes were more likely to be associated with pro-environmental voting.

Although these results provide some insight into the factors that influence judicial decision making, we performed additional calculations to assess more thoroughly the relative contributions of each independent variable. Following an approach developed by Gary King, Michael Tomz, and Jason Wittenberg (2000), we use a technique of statistical simulation to generate substantive information on the influence of these variables, including an assessment of the uncertainty surrounding the estimates.

The information in table 2 provides a straightforward way of assessing the impact of each independent variable on the predicted probability of a vote in support of environmental values, ceteris paribus.[16] The figures indicate the average impact of a change in each independent variable on the probability of a pro-environmental vote, while holding all other variables, including those that were not statistically significant, at either their

TABLE 2 Effect of explanatory variables on probability of pro-environmental vote

VARIABLE	TYPE CHANGE	AVG. CHANGE	95% CONFIDENCE INTERVAL	
			LOWER	UPPER
Principals in the policymaking process				
Presidential environmentalism	Min → Max	−0.09	−0.28	0.10
Supreme Court environmentalism	Min → Max	0.53	0.12	0.82
Congressional environmentalism	Min → Max	0.36	0.07	0.63
Other institutional influences				
EPA direct party—pro-environmental	0 → 1	0.19	0.06	0.33
EPA direct party—anti-environmental	0 → 1	−0.36	−0.58	−0.1
Environmental group amicus advantage	0 → 1	0.01	−0.53	0.27
Industry group amicus advantage	0 → 1	−0.16	−0.45	0.12
Case type				
Federal regulatory statute	0 → 1	0.25	0.07	0.41
Judicial policy preferences				
Appointing president's NOMINATE score	Min → Max	−0.18	−0.29	−0.07

NOTE: Tables shows the average impact of a change in each independent variable holding all other variables in the equation constant at either their mean (for interval variables) or mode (for dummy variables). Entries are based on 5,000 simulated sets of coefficients drawn from their sampling distribution.

mean (for interval variables) or mode (for dummy variables). The type of change for each variable represents the difference between the observed minimum and maximum for interval or ordinal measures and the presence or absence of dichotomous variables.

The average change in the probability of a pro-environmental vote fell by 18 percent when comparing voting by judges selected during the most conservative administrations (generally, Reagan and Bush appointees) against those selected by the most liberal presidents (generally, Johnson, Carter, and Clinton appointees). These additional calculations also suggest the sometimes-dramatic effect of Supreme Court precedent within the judicial hierarchy. On average, the probability of a pro-environmental vote increased by 53 percent when circuit judges rendered decisions following pro-environmental Supreme Court precedent, as opposed to anti-environmental precedents in the relevant statutory area. Influences from the other branches of government were pronounced as well. When moving from a legislative session where members of Congress offered the lowest level of support for environmental values to one that offered the high-

FIGURE 1 Probability of pro-environmental vote by policy preferences

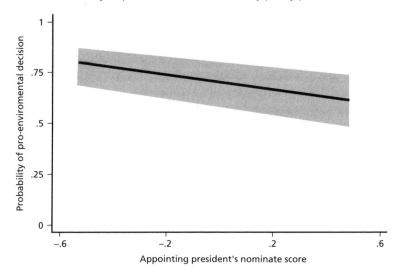

NOTE: Judicial policy preferences measured by NOMINATE score of appointing president. Tinted areas indicate 95 percent confidence intervals around mean probability.

est level of support, the average change in the predicted probability of a pro-environment vote rose by 36 percent. When the EPA is a litigant supporting the pro-environment position, the average change in the predicted probability of a pro-environmental vote was an increase of 19 percent; however, more dramatic effects were noted when the EPA supports the opposing side, as the estimated average change in the probability of a pro-environmental vote dropped by 36 percent.

The underlying premises of our theoretical framework posit that the effects of these factors are complex and interactive. For example, we suggested that goal conflict between circuit judges and principals would vary and that circuit judges would weight goals of particular principals differently, depending on the decision-making context. To explore these ideas and examine further the uncertainty surrounding the parameter estimates, we estimated the probability of a pro-environment vote at different levels of our independent variables, while holding other variables at values that represent their central tendency. In figure 1, we begin by examining more closely the influence of judicial policy preferences on the predicted probability of a vote in support of the pro-environment position.[17]

The figure suggests that most judges' votes during this time period

FIGURE 2 Probability of pro-environmental vote by Supreme Court's environmental decisions and judicial policy preferences

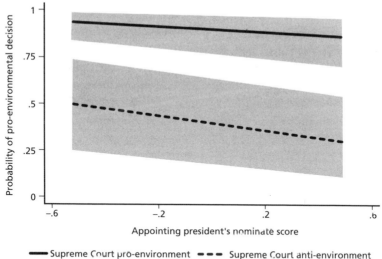

NOTE: Judicial policy preferences measured by NOMINATE score of appointing president. Tinted areas indicate 95 percent confidence intervals around mean probability when Supreme Court had issued two decisions in the prior year interpreting the statute at issue in a pro-environmental fashion and when the Court had issued two decisions in the prior year interpreting the statute at issue in an anti-environmental fashion.

supported the pro-environment position. The probability falls, but not dramatically, as the policy views of the appointing president become more conservative. Uncertainty associated with the predicted probability was greatest for judges appointed by conservative presidents.[18] To examine this relationship under varying institutional contexts, we present additional plots in the remaining figures below.

Our theoretical framework suggests that lower-court judges may vote on the basis of their policy preferences but that circuit judges will also respond to directives issued by the Supreme Court. Overall, figure 2 indicates that the ideological content and intensity of Supreme Court precedent affect the probability of pro-environmental voting in the lower courts. Even judges appointed by the most conservative presidents were overwhelmingly more likely to support the pro-environment position when High Court decisions clearly pointed in that direction. Similarly, judges appointed by liberal presidents demonstrated very different voting tendencies that corresponded to variation in the position of the High Court. More uncertainty clearly surrounded the predicted probability of

FIGURE 3 Probability of pro-environmental vote by congressional environmental position and judicial policy preferences

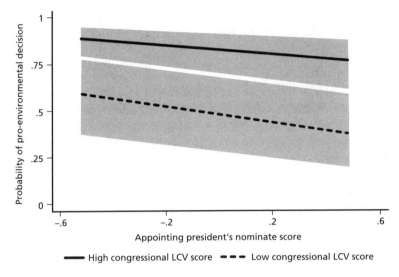

NOTE: Judicial policy preferences measured by NOMINATE score of appointing president. Tinted areas indicate 95 percent confidence intervals around mean probability in two situations: when the average congressional LCV score is at its highest and when the average LCV score is at its lowest.

judicial voting when Supreme Court signals were characterized as "anti-environmental."

Although judicial ideology influences the probability of pro-environmental voting, figure 3 demonstrates the important influence of congressional policy positions on judicial voting. When the LCV score for Congress was at its lowest during the time period, the probability of pro-environmental voting was substantially lower than that estimated for the period marked by "high" environmental scores for Congress. Again, greater uncertainty surrounded the predicted probability of judicial voting when legislative support for environmental values was at its lowest.

Discussion

Environmental policymaking has long been depicted as the result of interaction between a wide variety of policy actors, including the courts, Congress, and the presidency. This empirical analysis provided an opportunity to assess systematically the relative influence of particular actors on judicial behavior in pollution-control cases decided in the lower courts. Using a principal-agent perspective, we hypothesized that circuit judges would respond to the policy preferences of multiple principals. Our results offer some support for this premise. As we expected, circuit judges responded dramatically to signals from the Supreme Court in this policy area and, to a lesser degree, to shifts in the environmental policy preferences of Congress. Of the three principals identified in our framework, we did not find support for a hypothesized relationship between presidential policy preferences and circuit judges' decision making. Given the relatively weak position of the president as principal to circuit judges, it should not be surprising that we did not find empirical support for such an effect. With regard to legislation, the president formally possesses only a limited power to veto bills. Moreover, in environmental policy, studies have documented that Congress, not the president, generally sets the policy agenda. However, we should note that the influence of the EPA on judicial decision making in the appeals courts was dramatic, particularly when the agency advocated an anti-environmental position.

This analysis lends further support to the view that the Supreme Court, as principal, influences subordinates in the federal court system. Still, we believe a few points should be emphasized. After estimating several models of judicial voting, we found the effectiveness of signals from the Supreme Court depended on distinguishing between statutory areas. In several models of judicial voting, we used other measures of Supreme Court policy positions[19] and found that broad measures of Supreme Court influence were not related to judicial voting in the U.S. Courts of Appeals. Recent existing research on Supreme Court-circuit court interactions has focused on a policy area where judicial activity is ongoing and ideologically charged (Cameron, Segal, and Songer 2000; Songer, Segal, and Cameron 1994). In that context, broad measures of Supreme Court ideology may be used to gauge the effect of the principal on their lower-court agents. However, in pollution-control case law, High Court activity is sporadic, making review less likely. In addition, Supreme Court decision making in this policy area may not always be characterized by the same liberal-conservative ideological cleavages. Therefore, lower-court judges in this issue area are responsive, but only after the Supreme Court issues clear directives in the form of precedent. We argued earlier that the effects of the Supreme Court, as principal, will be heightened when decision-making norms support adherence to upper-court precedent that also provides unambiguous cues for lower courts to follow. These findings tend to support that view. Further support for this interpretation was suggested by additional models we estimated; in those models, we found the effect of Supreme Court precedent to be diminished after two years of the decision date.

The statistical simulation also uncovered more information surrounding the interaction of principals' goals with agent preferences. Judicial policy preferences affected the probability of pro-environmental voting, but this relationship varied with the influence of Supreme Court precedent and congressional preferences. When these principals pushed toward pro-environmental voting, conservative judges were more likely to vote contrary to their attitudes. In contrast, when these same principals leaned toward anti-environmental positions, greater uncertainty surrounded the predicted probability of judicial voting and contributed to the likelihood that judges would fall back on their policy preferences. Although we can only speculate on this point, these findings do suggest that congruence between judicial decision making, judicial policy preferences, and the positions taken by the Supreme Court and Congress may depend on the policy context as well as the degree to which multiple principals and agents share goals.

Our findings regarding congressional influence may also be interpreted as supporting a more strategic account of circuit judges' voting behavior. Revesz's (2001) failure to find evidence of congressional influence over D.C. Circuit judges' review of administrative agencies' decisions led him to conclude that circuit judges probably voted their sincere preferences in such cases without considering legislative reactions. Revesz presented two alternative interpretations of his results: (1) that judges do not act strategically but rather vote their sincere preferences in agency cases, or (2) that judges do vote strategically but view the possibility of legislative override as so small as to be inconsequential. The latter interpretation is supported in part by the empirical evidence; in a recent study of congressional responses to federal circuit court decisions, the authors found that, for the period 1990 to 1998, Congress proposed legislation to override only 106 such decisions, not all of which was eventually enacted (Lindquist and Yalof 2001). Thus, the likelihood of override in any particular case—given the thousands of cases rendered by the circuit courts each year that interpret federal statutes—is infinitesimal. Moreover, the strategic account suggests that judges will have sufficient information to calculate the probability of congressional response, which must not be so low that it is essentially meaningless within the context of any particular case. In the courts of appeals, judges face time pressures and workload constraints that reduce the likelihood that they can effectively engage in such a calculation process envisioned.

While our findings in environmental cases do not parallel those reported by Revesz, we hesitate to conclude unequivocally that our model supports a strategic account of circuit court decision making, although we do not rule it out. As Baum (1997, 20) has pointed out, "Scholars who infer goals and motives from behavior should be sensitive to complexities and open to alternative interpretations." Our results are potentially consistent with both a sincere and strategic view of principal-agent interactions. Judges may sincerely choose to consider congressional preferences in accordance with norms of statutory interpretation, thus creating the relationship between congressional preferences and judicial voting behavior found in our statistical model. Conversely, judges may also be acting strategically as they anticipate an adverse congressional response in the form of legislative override, even though in the case of circuit court decisions, the likelihood of such an override is close to zero. And it is possible that judges act strategically not so as to embody their policy preferences into law over the long run, but rather to avoid other forms of conflicts or ramifications related to workload. Judges may seek to satisfy legislative preferences because it serves to avoid legislative or litigant responses that may increase appellate litigation. Indeed, where judges interpret statutory guidelines in a manner that is inconsistent with Congress's policy preferences, litigants may experience increased incentives to challenge the particular interpretation further.

We note also that the limited impact of attitudinal factors in comparison to the more pronounced impact of congressional and Supreme Court preferences suggests that circuit judges do act as "sincere" agents to a large degree. Yet as noted above, the influence of judicial attitudes was not uniform. In fact, when influential principals' positions strayed away from the pro-environmental position of the enacting coalition, judicial voting behavior became more consistent with their attitudes. In such situations, judges (particularly conservative judges) may feel themselves less constrained by the initial pro-environmental policy domain that is often embodied in pollution control statutes.

Appendix

The table below contains descriptive statistics of the variables used in the analysis.

TABLE 3 Descriptive statistics

VARIABLE	MEAN	STD. DEVIATION	MINIMUM	MAXIMUM
Pro-environmental decision	0.62	.49	0	1
Presidential environmentalism	37.65	40.28	0	100
Supreme Court environmentalism	−0.88	0.644	−2	2
Congressional environmentalism	49.83	3.11	43	55
EPA direct party—pro-environmental	0.39	0.49	0	1
EPA direct party—anti-environmental	0.13	0.34	0	1
Environmental group amicus advantage	0.12	0.33	0	1
Industry group amicus advantage	0.06	0.24	0	1
Federal regulatory statute	0.61	0.49	0	1
Appointing president's NOMINATE score	0.10	0.42	−0.52	0.48

N=509 judicial votes.

Notes

We are indebted to Rick Dunn and Kevin Pybas for their invaluable research assistance. The order of the authors' names is random; equal contributions were made by each.

1. This discussion is drawn in substantial part from Kraft and Vig (1997).

2. Of course, not all environmental initiatives were successful during the Reagan administration. Congress was less successful in enacting legislation to address acid rain, to amend the Clean Air Act, and to modify laws dealing with pesticides.

3. Furthermore, in the case of environmental legislation, Congress was generally active throughout the relevant period, reevaluating and amending relevant statutes. As a consequence, current legislative preferences would often be relevant to judges' deliberations.

4. Presidents also exercise lawmaking authority through the use of executive orders.

5. We address below legal norms that support deference to the position of the agency.

6. We also note that the preferences of an agency head, and the actions of administrative agencies, are not always consistent with presidential policy preferences.

7. Judges on the D.C. Circuit, however, have debated the role and ability of judges to scrutinize these science-policy issues. For example, Judge David Bazelon argued that courts should focus their inquiry on procedures rather than substantive, scientific issues (*International Harvester Co. v. Ruckelshaus*, 478 F.2d 615 [1973]). In contrast, Judge Harold Leventhal advocated an approach where judges take a "hard look" at the substantive decision of an agency (*Greater Boston Television Corp. v. FCC*, 444 F.2d 841 [1970]).

8. Although Songer, Segal, and Cameron (1994, 2000) also suggest that prosecutorial experience, region, and religion (whether or not the judge was Catholic) are indicators of ideology, they do not offer a theory-based explanation for their inclusion of these variables. Whereas prosecutorial experience would likely affect one's perception of search-and-seizure questions, it is less clear how being from the South and Catholic affect judicial voting in other areas. Studies of political behavior generally suggest north-south distinctions are no longer helpful to delineating differences in policy preferences. Our own analysis of the U.S. Courts of Appeals database did not find these indicators to be related to judicial voting (1984–96) after controls were introduced for the individual circuits.

9. Prior research also suggests that the attitudes of lower federal court judges, particularly those at the trial level, may be shaped by influences at the local level (Wenner and Dutter 1988). We estimated alternative models with measures of localism, including indicators of state ideology and policy liberalism (Berry et al. 1998; Erikson, Wright, and McIver 1993) and an indicator measuring state-level membership in environmental groups. None of these variables was found to affect judicial voting. We dropped them from the final model, because we did not want to exclude votes by judges from the D.C. Circuit.

10. The universe of cases with published decisions was identified through LEXIS. We stratified the list by year and then coded every third case so that we ended up with a sample that made up approximately 30 percent of the universe. After deleting mixed votes, votes of judges who could not be identified, and cases where judges did not apply or interpret a statute, we were left with 509 votes.

11. We thank Rick Dunn for his efforts in developing this measure. After identifying the bills used by LCV to calculate the score, the annual report of Presidential Position Votes by Congressional Quarterly was used to identify the position of the president.

12. A measure of intensity also will minimize problems associated with case selection in the U.S. Courts of Appeals. As noted earlier, High Court precedent should have a direct, immediate effect on all levels of the judicial branch. As district court judges and administrative agencies alter their decision making to comply with Supreme Court precedent, the influence on the appeals courts will be expected to diminish.

13. This list was generated by searching the U.S. Supreme Court Database (with case citation as the unit of analysis) for all cases that dealt with an environmental policy issue. Then, each case was examined further to exclude those that did not address with pollution control (for example, land-use questions dealing with protected wildlife). For statutes where the High Court did not decide a single case during the time period, we used a composite measure derived from all pollution-control cases for that term. We anticipate a lagged effect of one year. For example, a Supreme Court decision from the 1983 term would be expected to influence decisions of appeals court judges in the year following (1984). A total of eighteen Supreme Court cases were identified during the time frame (1983–95). The ideological content of Supreme Court precedent governing a particular statute was coded according to the definitions provided by Spaeth (1997). Conservative precedent was coded −1 and liberal precedent was coded +1. If more than one decision was decided during that term and the ideological content was mixed, this variable was coded 0.

14. Because our individual-level observations are not truly independent, we report robust standard errors (White 1980) with observations clustered by panel. This estimator of variance allows us to relax the assumption of independence across observations.

15. We tested a model that included other measures of group influence, such as whether they were direct parties in litigation. The results of these alternative models all indicated that the presence of groups did not affect judicial voting in the appeals courts to a statistically significant degree.

16. Following the procedure set forth in King, Tomz, and Wittenberg (1999) and using the CLARIFY software package they discuss in this work, we randomly drew 5,000 sets of coefficients from their sampling distribution. After setting all variables at their central values, we estimated first differences (King 1989) for each explanatory variable in the model. The values of each explanatory variable used to calculated the first differences were 0 and 1 for dummy variables and the minimum and maximum values observed for interval variables. Average impact is the change in the probability of a pro-environmental vote (averaged over the 5,000 simulations) given the increase in the independent variable (holding constant all other variables at their central values).

17. Following King, Tomz, and Wittenberg (1999), we repeated the expected value algorithm 5,000 times to approximate a 95 percent confidence interval around the probability of a pro-environmental vote. The results are presented in figures 1 through 3.

18. The vertical bars, representing 95 percent confidence intervals, are longest when the appointing president's NOMINATE score places the judge at the conservative end of the ideological spectrum.

19. We used two measures of economic liberalism that were derived from Supreme Court decisions during the time period. One measure was broadly defined to include economic and labor cases, while another measure was narrowly defined to include regulatory cases only. Since our analysis focused on pollution control, we could not use the Segal and Cover scores that are appropriate for analyses of civil rights/liberties cases (Epstein and Mershon 1996).

Studying Courts Formally

LAWRENCE BAUM

Formal theory has a long history in the study of judicial behavior.[1] But its use was sporadic until the 1990s, when it emerged with surprising speed as a major approach to the analysis of judges' choices.

This development has brought enormous benefits to the field. Scholarship on judicial behavior had largely lost contact with broad theoretical issues. As a result, it had lost direction as well. A hallmark of the formal approach is its emphasis on explicit theoretical premises and systematic tracing of their behavioral implications. With that emphasis, formal research has helped to refocus scholars' attention on fundamental questions about the bases for judicial behavior. In conjunction with other developments, growth in the use of formal theory has made the study of judging more lively and more productive than it had been for a long time.

Contributions of this Volume

The essays in this volume highlight several patterns in formal analysis of courts. To begin with, the contributors are an eclectic group. While political scientists predominate, also included are legal scholars and people with training in both disciplines. Some are best characterized as students of courts with an interest in formal theory, others as formal theorists with an interest in courts, while still others are difficult to assign to one category or the other.

This melding of judicial scholars and formal theorists is a very good thing. Formal theory emerged as an important analytic approach to the study of courts largely through the work of scholars who were formal theorists first of all. Some of these scholars were unfamiliar (or unimpressed) with the existing research on judicial behavior. Perhaps inevitably, their arrival aroused negative reactions from judicial scholars who were suspicious of formal theory and of those who advocated its use.

Tensions between the two groups have not dissipated altogether, and there is continuing disagreement about the value of formal theory for an understanding of judicial behavior. But the tensions have declined considerably, and those who differ in their assessment of formal approaches increasingly show a healthy respect for the other side. More important, formal theorists have grown more knowledgeable about the courts, and judicial scholars have developed more expertise in formal theory. As a result, the work of both groups has strengthened, and increasingly people in each group benefit from the contributions of the other.

Many of the contributors to this volume are at early stages in their academic careers. That is no accident. A major reason for the accelerating progress of research on the courts is the high-quality work done by new scholars. More than ever, those scholars who emerge from graduate school (or from law school) knowing a lot about the courts also know a lot about other things, including theory and methodology. Only a portion of those scholars take a formal approach to study of the courts; whatever their approach, they are doing a great deal to advance our understanding of judicial behavior.

There is a substantial body of research on decision making within multimember courts that is explicitly formal or that has formal elements (e.g., Boucher and Segal 1995; Brenner 1979; Caldeira, Wright, and Zorn 1999; Hammond, Bonneau, and Sheehan 2005; Kornhauser 1992; Maltzman, Spriggs, and Wahlbeck 2000; Rohde 1972b). However, in recent years, scholars who take a formal approach have given particular attention to relationships between courts or, more often, between courts and the other branches of government. That emphasis is reflected in this volume. Some of the essays are efforts to explain the behavior of a single participant in relationships between policymakers, usually the Supreme Court, while others are concerned with the behavior of multiple participants. In each of the essays, whatever its focus, there is a sensitivity to the governmental context in which judges choose among alternatives; the central theme is interdependence.

This theme of interdependence contrasts with the image of the independent judge that has characterized a good deal of research, especially on the Supreme Court (Segal and Spaeth 2002). At this point, there is only a small body of systematic empirical studies on the extent to which judges' choices actually are constrained by other decision makers (e.g., Bergara, Richman, and Spiller 2003; Sala and Spriggs 2004; Segal 1997; Songer, Segal, and Cameron 1994; Spiller and Gely 1992).[2] Moreover, the findings of these studies are subject to multiple interpretations. It may turn out that the image of independence carries a considerable element of truth. But there is no doubt about the value of exploring the ways that courts might take other bodies of government into account and of testing for the forms and degree of constraint.

One attribute of the essays in this volume is their diversity. Some develop their theoretical positions mathematically, while others offer verbal formulations. Some papers test propositions empirically, others develop hypotheses for later tests, and a few work inductively from interesting empirical regularities to theoretical arguments.

As some examples will suggest, the essays range widely in their substantive interests. Georg Vanberg examines the relationship between courts and prospective implementers of their decisions.[3] Ethan Bueno de Mesquita and Matthew Stephenson explore the value of precedent to appellate judges. Stefanie Lindquist and Susan Haire analyze an array of influences on court of appeals decisions in environmental law in terms of an agent with multiple principals. The essays by Maxwell Stearns and by Cliff Carrubba and James Rogers analyze aspects of the commerce clause of Article I of the U.S. Constitution from different perspectives. Christopher Zorn examines litigation decisions by the solicitor general on behalf of the federal government.

What most characterizes the essays as a whole is their sophistication and creativity. Scholars who do formal work on the courts have moved well beyond relatively simple depictions of judicial behavior, and the contributors to this volume provide a series of insightful and nonobvious ways of thinking about courts. A few examples will serve to underline this trait:

1. Scholars almost always think of policy-oriented judges as people who want to enact their own preferred policies into law. In James Rogers's formulation, things are not so simple. Judges recognize that their own conceptions of good policy may be wrong, and legislators may have an advantage because they aggregate information across a large number of people. Thus, a Supreme Court justice who seeks good policy might happily adopt a doctrine of deference to congressional judgments even when the justice's preferences differ from those of Congress. In advancing this idea, Rogers points to a new way of thinking about good policy as a judicial goal.[4]

2. It seems obvious that Congress and the executive branch constrain the Supreme Court to a greater degree in interpretation of statutes than in constitutional interpretation. After all, it is far easier for Congress to overturn a statutory decision. Largely for this reason, formal analyses of

the interplay between Congress and the Court have dealt primarily with statutory law (see Segal 1997). But Andrew Martin provides reasons to predict just the opposite. In turn, his argument suggests that we need to rethink our assumptions about the relationship between Court and Congress in both statutory and constitutional law.

3. Understandably, formal analyses of relationships between higher and lower courts emphasize the conflict of interest between the two. In these analyses, judges at each level have policy preferences they would like to advance. To the extent that the preferences of higher-court and lower-court judges differ, each may act strategically to advance their own preferences. Charles Cameron and Lewis Kornhauser offer a conception of the judges at the two levels as a team (Radner 1972) with the shared goal of "deciding cases 'correctly'" (see also Kornhauser 1995). As they point out, one benefit of this conception is that it provides a perspective for exploration of the role of law in decision making.

4. Thomas Hammond, Reginald Sheehan, and Chris Bonneau examine how the decisions of the federal courts of appeals might impinge on the choices of Supreme Court justices. They draw out the implications of "minimalist" and "maximalist" conceptions of the impact that courts of appeals exert on the Supreme Court. In doing so, they call attention to the ways that lower-court decisions can structure the choices of reviewing courts. Their distinction also offers a way to consider the alternatives from which justices choose in cases.

The essays in this volume nicely illustrate the vitality of formal research on the courts. Perhaps their greatest contribution is the hypotheses they lay out for testing and the lines of prospective research they chart. They provide a substantial set of agendas for the future, agendas that judicial scholars can use whether or not they take a formal approach in their own work.

Some Directions for the Future

The scholarship in this volume, diverse as it is, also highlights widely shared assumptions and perspectives among scholars who do formal research on courts. The value of work that incorporates these assumptions and perspectives has been amply demonstrated. At the same time, it is useful to step back and consider implications of the dominant approaches to formal models of the courts. In turn, that consideration points to new directions that formal research might take.

BUILDING MODELS

With some important exceptions, formal work on judicial behavior has begun with two linked assumptions: judges pursue good policy, and they do so strategically.[5] Both assumptions have very reasonable bases, but there is also room for disagreement about their validity.

Formal theorists' emphasis on good policy as judges' central (often only) goal is shared by the preponderance of political science scholarship on judicial behavior. Since the early days of systematic research on judicial behavior, scholars have found this to be a useful simplifying assumption (e.g., Rohde and Spaeth 1976, Schubert 1965). Further, research on judicial behavior has focused heavily on the U.S. Supreme Court, for which the assumption has considerable basis in reality. Institutional characteristics of the Court such as the life term reduce the relevance of justices' self-interest to their decisions. The Court's selection of primarily "hard" cases reduces the relevance to decisions of justices' interest in making good law, however strong or weak that interest may be. By default, good policy emerges as central, and most close observers of the Court—whether or not they are scholars—recognize its centrality.

Yet, even for the Supreme Court, other goals may play a significant part in the decision process. For one thing, justices can be presumed to care about interpreting the law well, in light of their training, their career experience, and the context in which they make choices. Of course, making good law does not serve their self-interest, but the same is true of making good policy. Thus, there is no prima facie reason to assume that either law or policy takes primacy in the justices' hierarchies of goals.

Nor do institutional characteristics of the Supreme Court rule out behavior based on self-interested goals. The occasional justice may act to advance an interest in an elective position or promotion to chief justice. The most obvious result is that such a justice might avoid unpopular positions, but career ambitions might have more subtle effects as well. All justices can be presumed to prefer lighter workloads to heavier ones, and this motivation is the most reasonable explanation of the substantial decline in the number of cases that the Court hears since the outset of the Rehnquist Court in 1986 (Hellman 1997, O'Brien 1997). Since the Court's decisions may influence its workload, this goal can play a role in decision making on the merits.

Once we move to other courts, the relevance of considerations other than policy becomes obvious. For one thing, career goals are potentially quite powerful. Members of lower federal courts may seek promotion. In nearly every state, judges must secure reelection or reappointment to retain their positions. For some of these judges, career ambitions may do more than modify courses of action based on judges' policy preferences; they might play the dominant role that they do for many officials in the other branches of government.

If workload considerations are relevant even in courts that enjoy discretionary jurisdiction, they have considerably greater impact in the preponderance of courts whose jurisdiction is primarily mandatory. Faced with more cases than they can decide fully in the time available (or the time they wish to allocate to their work), judges encourage settlement between the parties, adopt mechanisms to reach summary decisions, or both. Little has been done so far to analyze this reality in the context of judges' policy goals. How do judges achieve the maximum impact on policy while rationing the number of full decisions they reach? It would be a useful step to build into models of the federal courts of appeals the screening process through which a high proportion of appeals are disposed of with limited consideration by judges (see Baker 1994). Certainly, the impact of time pressures should be taken into account, as it is in the essay by Lindquist and Haire in this volume.

Then there is the law. One implication of the theory of motivated reasoning (Kunda 1990) for courts is that the degree of legal ambiguity to cases is critical. If Supreme Court justices give little weight to legal considerations in their decisions, it is because the law is only a limited constraint in cases that are close on legal grounds. There are few other courts in which the average level of legal ambiguity is nearly as high. In intermediate appellate courts without discretionary jurisdiction, that level is considerably lower, because so many cases seem to have obvious outcomes. Not only are legal considerations likely to exert greater impact on decisions in such courts than in the Supreme Court, but these considerations can be expected to weigh more heavily in judges' conscious calculations.

Given all this complexity, it is not surprising that formal theorists have followed other students of judicial behavior in focusing on the Supreme Court and, to a lesser degree, the other courts that are most similar to the Court. But complexity is not absent even at the Supreme Court level. Models that posit only policy goals as a basis for judicial choices will continue to provide insights on judicial choices, but there is a need for models that incorporate other goals. The most obvious possibility, though not the only useful one, is models of judges who balance legal and policy goals. While scholars are familiar with the much-discussed distinction between legally "easy" and "hard" cases, they have not done a great deal with this distinction in their analyses of decision making. The effort by Lindquist and Haire to capture the effects of this distinction is one example of what can be done.

The "hardness" of cases is one dimension along which the relative importance of various judicial goals may vary. Hierarchies of goals are likely to differ by court and even by individual judge as well as by case. Modeling this heterogeneity presents challenges, but it can also lead to new insights about judicial behavior. The Bueno de Mesquita and Stephenson essay in this volume depicts policy-oriented appellate courts and law-oriented trial courts. Whether or not one accepts that dichotomy, it may be possible to gain insight about judicial hierarchy by thinking about a supreme court that is more policy-oriented than the courts below it.[6]

If policy is preeminent in formal theories as a judicial goal, strategy as a means to advance judges' goals is embedded even more deeply in those theories. Scholars who take a formal approach almost universally depict judges who pursue their goals strategically. In other words, policy-oriented judges take the positions that will best advance what they regard as good policy, even if doing so requires that they depart from their most preferred positions. The sincere judge makes only occasional appearances in this body of work (Ferejohn and Weingast 1992, Spiller and Spitzer 1995).

In the study of judges, as in other arenas, formal theorists typically take strategic behavior for granted. It is thought that a judge who seeks to make good policy necessarily acts in ways that best advance this goal; to act otherwise would be naive and self-defeating. Thus, Supreme Court justices act to avoid overrides of their decisions by Congress, members of courts of appeals act to avoid reversal by the Supreme Court, and judges on all multimember courts act to bring their court as close as possible to their own preferred position.

That some strategic behavior of this sort occurs is absolutely clear. Indeed, compromise and persuasion are inherent to collective decision making by appellate courts (Kornhauser and Sager 1993, 52–53). But it is not obvious that judges always act strategically on behalf of their policy goals. Where self-interest is directly and significantly implicated by people's choices, as it is in the economic arena, then the person who does not act strategically is naive or at least in error. Judicial policy is a different matter altogether. What judges gain from behaving strategically is expressive rather than instrumental: the pleasure of playing a game and the satisfaction that is derived from achieving something desirable. These are potentially powerful motivations. But judges also may gain something expressive from acting on their preferences sincerely: the pleasure of doing what they see as the right thing. As described by legal scholar and federal judge Richard Posner (1995, 123), "for judges as for ordinary citizens voting has a consumption value that is independent of its instrumental, power-exercising value." This too can be a powerful motivation.

Certainly, judges lose something by behaving sincerely: they sacrifice opportunities to advance what they regard as good policy. But they also avoid the need to compromise, to subordinate their preferences to those held by other people. Sincere behavior offers another advantage: it is considerably easier for judges simply to act on their conceptions of good policy than to go through the complex calculus that is sometimes required to engage in effective strategy. Intracourt strategy may also require considerable time and energy for interpersonal persuasion.

It is very difficult to guess what the mix of sincere and strategic behavior looks like. My own guess is that most judges engage in a mix of the two and that the mixes vary considerably among judges.[7] From what we know about past and current Supreme Court justices, some seemed to obtain satisfaction primarily from helping to achieve good policy in the Court and in government as a whole, while others most enjoyed the opportunity to state their own positions. William O. Douglas and William Brennan had similar preferences on most judicial issues, but it appears that they acted on those preferences in quite different ways.[8]

The accuracy of my guess is quite uncertain. But if it seems reasonable to relax the assumption that judges are all strategic all the time, then models should begin to take this complication into account. What consequences follow if one of the calculations judges make is the relative benefits of sincere and strategic behavior in particular situations? We might posit, for instance, that strategic behavior is more common when it requires limited rather than substantial departures from judges' most preferred positions. Further, we might expect more strategic behavior from judges in situations in which there is no direct alternative of sincere behavior (e.g., opinion assignment, case selection) than in those that offer substantial opportunities for sincere self-expression (e.g., dissenting opinions). In situations in which judges lack the opportunity to express their views directly, they should be more likely to act strategically.

Of course, the possibility of nonstrategic behavior also has implications for judicial interdependence. The sensitivity to other policymakers that characterizes formal theories of judicial behavior rests on an assumption that judges act in order to influence ultimate policy outcomes. To the extent that judges act instead to cast votes and write opinions that constitute good policy as they see it, their incentives to take into account other courts and the other branches of government may be limited. Thus, to take one example, the frequency with which Congress overrides federal court decisions (Eskridge 1991a) might reflect judicial indifference to the possibility of overrides more than judicial miscalculation.

Indifference toward the political environment is realistic to the extent that its consequences are limited. For a well-established supreme court, occasional legislative overrides carry low costs. For a supreme court that is newer and less institutionalized, direct conflicts with the other branches may exact much greater costs. Even judges who are inclined to behave sincerely have incentives to avoid elimination or marginalization of their court. Thus, the standard depiction of John Marshall's strategic behavior toward the other branches of the federal government (e.g., Graber 1998, McCloskey and Levinson 2005, chapters 2 and 3) rings true, and we would expect judges on new or newly active supreme courts in other nations to display similar sensitivity to their environments.

Treating strategic behavior as a variable rather than a constant presents a substantial analytic challenge, because it requires a departure from the usual assumptions and approaches of formal theory. To a lesser degree, the same is true of variation in goal orientations among judges, courts, and cases. At the same time, this is the kind of challenge that formal theory is well equipped to address. One of the benefits that formal models can provide is a better understanding of the consequences of differing goals and means for patterns of judicial behavior.

TESTING MODELS

In this early stage of concerted formal work on courts, scholars have given greater emphasis to developing models than to testing them. But empirical tests of propositions from formal models have become more common, as reflected in several of the essays in this volume.

Effective tests of these propositions often are difficult for all the reasons that apply to hypothesis testing in general. These difficulties aside, there is a fundamental problem of observational equivalence, the similarity between the behavior that would follow from the assumptions of a model and the behavior that would occur for other reasons. Quite frequently, different judicial goals or means can be expected to produce similar actions.

One example is familiar to students of judicial behavior. To what extent do Supreme Court justices take the possibility of congressional overrides into account when they interpret statutes? In all likelihood, strategic voting of this type probably does not require justices to depart frequently and substantially from their most-preferred policy positions. For the most part, then, sincere and strategic behavior will look about the same. Differentiating between the two requires fairly precise measurement of justices' preferences and of the conditions under which strategic judges would depart from their preferences to reduce the chances of an override. Scholars have made progress in this measurement task (e.g., Segal 1997, Sala and Spriggs 2004; see Martin and Quinn 2002), but we are still some distance from the desired precision.

A somewhat different example is the role of precedent in Supreme Court decision making. Students of the Court disagree strongly about the extent to which justices depart from their most-preferred policies to adhere to Court precedents. To the extent that justices do give weight to precedent, what motivates them to do so? The most obvious answer is that they care about precedent for its own sake, because they believe that stability in the law is desirable. But some scholars have argued that an orientation toward precedent is instead a means to advance justices' policy goals. In this volume Bueno de Mesquita and Stephenson present an insightful analysis to show how adherence to precedent may increase the effectiveness with which an appellate court communicates its position to lower courts. Lee Epstein and Jack Knight (1998, 163–77) argue that justices pay attention to precedent because their public legitimacy depends on the perception that they do so. Thus, adherence to precedent is consistent with quite different theories of judicial behavior.

In these ambiguous situations, the assumptions with which an empirical analysis begins have considerable impact on the interpretation of its findings. When formal models posit that judges are strategic and policy oriented, evidence consistent with those assumptions is treated as verifying them. In effect, in situations of observational equivalence, ties are broken in favor of the model. Further, evidence of behavior in the direction predicted by a model often is treated as establishing that all behavior is consistent with the model's assumptions.[9]

Of course, these rules of interpretation are common in research of all types. But they are especially prevalent in the testing of formal models, because so many of the scholars who do research in this area are strongly convinced that the basic assumptions underlying their models are accurate.[10] This viewpoint is also reflected in generalizations about judicial ends and means from illustrative evidence (e.g., Cohen and Spitzer 1994, Gely and Spiller 1990).

These rules of interpretation have been useful in thinking about the possible consequences of policy-oriented strategy for judicial behavior. To a degree, scholars have been extending the early inquiries of Walter Murphy (1964), using more formal analysis to probe what behavior might look like under an assumption of strategic action to advance policy goals. In the process, they have achieved a good deal. It is important, for instance, to understand why decision making that follows legal norms might actually reflect judges' efforts to achieve good policy rather than an interest in good law for its own sake. Nor have we exhausted such inquiries.

We also need, however, to work toward more rigorous tests of the assumptions that underlie formal models. One step is to move from searching for evidence that some judicial behavior is strategic and policy oriented to ascertaining the extent of such behavior. In assigning opinions, to what degree do chief justices act to advance their policy goals and to what extent do other goals underlie their choices? If it is true that Supreme Court justices modify their positions in cases to reduce the likelihood of a congressional override, how far are they willing to compromise in this effort?

Finding meaningful answers to these questions will not be easy, because even small imperfections in model specification and variable measurement can make considerable difference for the results. I have already noted the most vexing problem, measuring judges' policy preferences. One important task for students of judicial behavior is to develop tests of hypotheses that are not so dependent on precise measurement.

The essays in this volume reflect the progress scholars already have made in developing and undertaking good tests of hypotheses about judicial ends and means. We need to continue progress in testing the assumptions that underlie competing conceptions of judicial behavior (see Hettinger, Lindquist, and Martinek 2004). Here too, formal theory is well suited to make a major contribution.

Concluding Thoughts

As my comments suggest, some daunting challenges confront formal theorists of judicial behavior. But judged by a realistic standard, progress so far has been impressive. Research that takes a formal approach has offered new ways of thinking about judicial behavior, developed important propositions about patterns of behavior, and contributed empirical tests of some of those propositions. Perhaps most important, this body of work has helped to stimulate advances by students of judicial behavior whose own approaches are not formal. If our understanding of judges is considerably better now than it was fifteen years ago, the work of formal theorists has contributed to that advance in important ways.

The essays in this volume underline that contribution. They also demonstrate how far formal work on the courts has progressed. The sophistication and creativity of these essays is impressive. They advance our thinking about an array of issues in the study of courts, and they point the way for further advances in theory and theory testing.

I referred earlier to the growing integration of formal and nonformal work on judicial behavior. The book reflects that integration process. It should help to foster continued integration by raising issues and hypotheses for scholars of all theoretical and methodological persuasions to consider. As a consumer of research on courts and judges, I look forward to the field's continuing progress in grappling with the difficult issues that concern scholars in the field.

Notes

1. Some examples of early work with substantial elements of formal theory are Schubert (1959, ch. 4; 1962), Rohde (1972a, 1972b), Baum (1977), and Brams and Muzzio (1977).

2. Also relevant is the body of empirical research on lower-court responses to Supreme Court decisions (Canon and Johnson 1999, ch. 2).

3. Vanberg frames his analysis in broad terms, applicable to constitutional courts in the United States and elsewhere. Vanberg (2001) tests a model of legislative-judicial interaction in the German Constitutional Court. This extension of scope beyond courts in the United States is useful in any instance and especially valuable for analysis of issues that are specific to high courts.

4. Rogers (2001b) offers a similar informational perspective on Congress.

5. Because terminology varies a good deal, I should clarify what I mean by strategic behavior (see Baum 1997, 90–92). Judges behave strategically when they take actions intended to advance their goals in collective decisions of their own court or decisions of other bodies. In the context of voting on case outcomes and doctrines, strategic judges may (but not always must) take positions that differ from the ones they most prefer, in order to achieve the best results. Sincere judges simply vote in accord with their preferences.

6. As the essay by Cameron and Kornhauser suggests, it is also possible to gain insights from models that depict law rather than policy as the primary basis for judicial action. In courts without discretionary jurisdiction, it would be useful to follow the implications of positing workload as the primary consideration for judges.

7. On variation in sincere and strategic behavior in Congress, see Martin (2001).

8. On Douglas, see Simon (1980) and Urofsky (1990); on Brennan, see Eisler (1993) and Clark (1995).

9. There are exceptions to this interpretive rule, exemplified by Andrew Martin's nuanced interpretation of his findings in his essay in this volume.

10. Certainly there are circumstances in which an interpretation based on a formal model is to be preferred to alternative interpretations. One occurs when the model provides a unified framework for a set of findings that otherwise would require a variety of explanations. Another is when a model's predictions are contrary to conventional wisdom and are well supported by empirical findings.

For scholars whose primary goal is successful prediction, this discussion of choices between alternative models is largely beside the point; so long as a model predicts behavior well, the validity of its motivational assumptions is irrelevant. But if we are interested in understanding why judges or other actors make particular choices, then distinguishing between models with different assumptions is an important task.

A Primer on Game Theory

JAMES R. ROGERS

This "primer" sketches several important concepts in game theory. Its goal is not to provide a comprehensive introduction to the subject; there are a number of good books dedicated to that purpose.[1] Rather, the goal is to supply readers unfamiliar with game theory with a few tools to help them understand the basic structure of the arguments in the more-theoretical essays in this volume. I'll discuss five topics. First, I provide a basic apologia for formal game theory. Secondly, the central idea in game theory, the idea of a "Nash equilibrium," is defined and explained. Next, we'll focus on several important concepts in game theory: how actions that are never taken (actions off the equilibrium path) nonetheless can have a dramatic affect on observable outcomes; how repeating a game can change equilibrium outcomes relative to playing a game just once; and, finally, how the play of a game can signal information about a player or about aspects of the world at large.

Game Theory and the Virtue of Abstraction

The central idea in game theory is that the players recognize that they are interacting with other players. As in recreational games, the actions you take are often affected by your assessment of how the other player (or players) will respond. The other player is simultaneously thinking about your play in the same way, knowing full well that your play will depend on your assessment of what I will play and, in turn, what I will play depends on my assessment of how you will respond, and so forth. This awareness, and the different actions it implies, is what is meant by players being "strategic."

It is important, however, to understand how game theory extends beyond recreational games. First, recreational games are often competitive in that one player or team wins, while the other player or team loses. But these sorts of win-lose games are only a special class of the set of games understood as strategic interaction between two or more individuals. Games in politics, economics, and other dimensions of life can have different outcomes—outcomes in which what one player gains does not necessarily come at the expense of another player. Games in real life exist in which more than one player can gain (or "win") at the same time or, indeed, in which all the players lose at the same time. So, while it's often useful to gain an understanding of game theory by thinking of the interaction that players have in recreational games, we need to be careful that we don't limit our idea of game theory to the special class of games where some players "win" at the expense of other players "losing."

Secondly, while game theory is not inherently formal and mathematical,[2] scholarly applications of game theory tend toward mathematical abstraction. People sometimes complain that this abstraction makes game-theoretic models "unrealistic" and that, therefore, game theory is not very useful for studying the real world. Further, even simple game-theoretic models can prove daunting to the reader unfamiliar with the type of reasoning they represent. So what's the value added of the exercise if models are both unrealistic and off-putting?

First, the unrealism of game-theoretic models—or of any model, for that matter—is not a vice, it is a *virtue*. As with any abstraction (whether prosaic, mathematical, graphical, or some combination), the value of the abstraction hinges on the model's usefulness. The very unrealism of a model, if properly constructed, is what makes it useful. For an every-day example, consider the instrumental abstraction of a city street map. It is obvious that street maps are highly abstracted representations of the real topography of a city. Maps utterly distort what is *really* there and leave out numerous details about what a particular area looks like. But it is precisely *because* the map distorts reality—because it abstracts away from a host of details of what is really there—that it becomes useful. A map that attempts to portray the full details of a particular area would be too cluttered to be useful or too large to be stored in a glove compartment. So it is with the game-theoretic models. They seek to abstract away from a host of details that are not relevant to the phenomenon under study. It is the very abstraction that permits us analytically to "hold everything else equal" and to focus on the most salient aspects of the phenomenon.

Of course, everything is not always equal, and omitted details can matter. Just as with street maps, there can be better models and worse models for particular purposes. Maps that abstract away from too much detail won't be useful in finding a particular street or address. Models that abstract away from too much pertinent detail aren't useful for understanding the phenomenon being studied. The trick, then—which is as much a matter of aesthetic taste as it is intellectual judgment—is to develop models that provide just enough detail to be useful for their intended purpose without being so complex as to confuse rather than illuminate.

Further, maps, just like other models, can be initially off-putting abstractions from reality for those unfamiliar with them. Many maps use specialized symbols and representations that require some time and effort to learn. Of course, simply because maps can be simplifying abstractions from reality doesn't mean that we always use them. Sometimes it's easier to write directions to your house in words; sometimes it's easier to draw a map. The basis of your choice is instrumental—what best accomplishes the goal of directing someone to your house successfully. So it is with models. There is nothing inherently wrong with a model that is written entirely in words. Sometimes, however, it's more convenient for a given purpose to use symbols and equations. Again, the choice is instrumental.

To be sure, as with the stylization of maps, sometimes the abstractions may be initially off-putting to a person untrained in what the symbols mean. But as with the increasing usefulness of abstract maps relative to written directions when routes become complicated, attempts to understand more-complex phenomena can benefit from the convenience and parsimony of more-mathematically abstract models relative to more-prosaic models. And, of course, reasonable people can have different personal preferences for written directions relative to mapped-out directions. Reasonable people can also disagree over whether a particular map is detailed enough to serve its purpose (or whether the map contains superfluous and distracting details). So, too, scholars have different preferences over using more prosaic models relative to more mathematical models. Scholars can further disagree whether a specific model, whether prosaic or mathematical, is, on the one hand, sufficiently detailed to help us understand the phenomenon under investigation or, on the other hand, so detailed that the phenomenon is obscured rather than illuminated. To the extent that mathematizing concepts in a model help us effectively to express, manipulate, or reason from those concepts, it's a useful enterprise. To the extent that mathematization doesn't achieve a useful purpose, then there's no reason to mathematize an otherwise perfectly understandable prosaic model.

We next consider several specific concepts in game theory. First, we define the notion of "equilibrium"—specifically, "Nash equilibrium." Then we examine a few basic ideas in game theory that are employed by some of the essays in this volume.

Nash Equilibrium

A central concept in most (but not all) game theory today is the idea of a "Nash equilibrium," named after Nobel laureate John Nash. The concept is so widely used that the "Nash" is often dropped and it is simply referred to as "equilibrium." The analytical advance in game theory (at least relative to decision theory) is that it can accommodate phenomena in which outcomes depend on the interaction of choices of more than one person. But when that's true, it means that I need to know something about your choice in order to make my choice, and you need to know something about my choice in order to make your choice. A Nash equilibrium defines the case in which no player in a game wishes to change strategies, given the strategies that the other players are playing.

We begin with a simple example of a game in "normal form." One benefit of formal modeling is that it requires that analysts precisely specify who is acting, what actions they can take, and how they value the outcomes in the game. (Analysts often find the exercise in and of itself helps them to think more clearly about the phenomena that they want to study.) Consider the simple normal form game in table 1. This is a version of the best known game—the prisoners' dilemma.[3]

Before we solve the game, we need to understand its setup. There are two players, A and B. Each has a choice of two strategies, U (up) or D (down) for player A, and L (left) or R (right) for player B. Each player then

TABLE 1 The prisoners' dilemma

		PLAYER B	
		L	R
PLAYER A	U	(5,5)	(0,8)
	D	(8,0)	(1,1)

receives a payoff from each combination of strategies the two players choose. For example, if player A plays U and player B plays R, then player A receives a payoff of 0 and player B receives a payoff of 8.

For simple normal-form games, it's easiest to express them in the form of a table such as table 1. But as games become more complex—more players, more strategies, and more outcomes—they become increasingly difficult to express in the form of a table. Instead, they need be expressed even more abstractly (but more compactly than in a table) as a set of players, N, a strategy set for each player, S_i, $i \in N$, and a utility, or payoff, function for each player, U_i, $i \in N$.

To understand how the more-abstract way of expressing a game works, it is sometimes useful to take the simple tabular form of a game and translate it into the more-abstract form described just above. Stating the game in table 1 in normal form requires that we identify the set of players, N = {A, B}, the set of strategies available to each player, S_A = {U, D}, S_B = {L, R}, and the payoff or utility function, U_i, for each player, $i \in N$, which are defined as below. (The ordered pairs report player A's strategy first and player B's strategy second. For example, (U, R) is read, "A plays U and B plays R.")

$$U_A = \begin{cases} 5 & for \, (U, L). \\ 0 & for \, (U, R). \\ 8 & for \, (D, L). \\ 1 & for \, (D, R). \end{cases}$$

$$U_B = \begin{cases} 5 & for \, (U, L). \\ 8 & for \, (U, R). \\ 0 & for \, (D, L). \\ 1 & for \, (D, R). \end{cases}$$

All this is the same information that is conveniently presented in the simple 2×2 matrix in table 1. As mentioned above, for simple games such as this, it's often easier just to look at a table rather than to present it in a more abstract form. But as the number of players increases and as the set of strategies become larger, the tabular form becomes too unwieldy, and it's actually easier to present and understand a game in the form of N, S_i, and U_i, $i \in N$.

So far we have simply defined the elements of a "normal-form game." An *equilibrium* in a game is a set of strategies such that no player can receive a higher payoff by unilaterally changing strategies, given what the other players are playing. Several aspects of this notion of equilibrium should be underscored. First, it looks at incentives to change strategies only one player at a time. That is, to test for an equilibrium, the strategies of all the players *but one* are "frozen." You then ask whether the remaining player can do better by changing strategies, given the "frozen" strategies of the other players. If that player can do better by changing to another strategy, then the original set of strategies was not an equilibrium. This process is repeated for all the players in the game. Even if there are many players and many strategies, if only one player has an incentive to change to just one other strategy (given the other players' strategies), then the proposed set of strategies is not an equilibrium. No player in the game can do better by playing any other strategy if that set of strategies (also called a strategy combination or a strategy profile) is an equilibrium.

Second, equilibrium is defined by the absence of an incentive for any player to deviate to a different strategy. In this notion of equilibrium, players neither "converge" toward an equilibrium nor are they "close" to an equilibrium. Either they're at an equilibrium or they're not. Nash equilibrium does not tell us anything about the ability of players to converge to an equilibrium when they are playing nonequilibrium strategies. Rather, this equilibrium concept only tells us whether a proposed or conjectured set of strategies is in fact an equilibrium. (It should be stressed that the absence of notions of convergence or closesness of strategies to an equilibrium is different from the concept of off-the-equilibrium path actions, which is an important concept discussed below.)

We now apply this notion of equilibrium to the game in table 1. In as simple a game as this is, it is feasible to check all pure-strategy combinations to identify which is a Nash equilibrium.[4] In the game above, there are four pure-strategy combinations. These combinations are expressed as an ordered pair, (s_A, s_B), in which A's strategy choice is listed first and B's strategy choice is listed second. The possible strategy combinations for this game are (U, L), (U, R), (D, L), (D, R). Begin with the strategy combination (U, L). To determine whether this is a Nash equilibrium, we check whether at least one player can do better by playing a different strategy while the other player's strategy is held frozen. Begin by considering player A. The payoff to player A of playing the strategy combination (U, L) is 5. Freezing player B's strategy to L, we now ask whether player A can do better by deviating from U to D. Well, player A's payoff to the strategy combination (D, L) is 8. Because 8 > 5, player A does have an incentive to change strategies from U to D. Therefore the strategy combination (U, L) is not an equilibrium.

If one player has an incentive to change strategies in a given strategy combination, then that strategy combination is not an equilibrium We do not need to test whether any other player does or does not also want to deviate. Nonetheless, for completeness, we might note that, for the strategy combination (U, L), player B has an incentive to deviate from L to R. B's payoff from the strategy combination (U, L) is 5, while B's payoff from the strategy combination (U, R) is 8.

Next consider the strategy combination (U, R). Again, consider whether player A has any incentive to change from playing U to playing D. Player A's payoff from the strategy combination (U, R) is 0. If A instead played D, A's payoff would be 1. Because 1 > 0, player A would want to change strategies, given the strategy combination (U, R). Therefore, that strategy combination is not a Nash equilibrium. (The reader might note that in the case of (U, R), player B does *not* have an incentive to change strategies. But it doesn't make any difference. Because player A does have an incentive to change strategies, the strategy combination is not an equilibrium.) By a similar argument, it should be obvious that the strategy combination (D, L) is not an equilibrium. In this case, player B has an incentive to deviate from playing L to playing R.

Finally, consider the strategy combination (D, R). Start with player A. The payoff to this strategy combination for player A is 1. If player A changed this strategy and played strategy B (with player B's strategy frozen on R), then A's payoff would decrease to 0. Therefore, player A has no incentive to change strategies from the conjectured strategy combination. Now, let's check player B. Player B's payoff for the strategy combination (D, R) is 1. If player B were to deviate and play strategy L (with player A's strategy remaining frozen to D), then B's payoff would also decrease to 0. Since neither player has an incentive to change strategies, given what the other player is playing, then the strategy combination (D, R) is a Nash equilibrium.

Before leaving this discussion, we might also describe why the "prisoners' dilemma" has the name that it does. To do so, we need to introduce the idea of "Pareto optimality," or "Pareto efficiency." When game theorists speak of something being "efficient" or "optimal," they usually mean this concept. (If they don't, they typically specify what other definition they're using.)

An outcome is "efficient" (or "Pareto optimal," etc.), if there is no other feasible outcome in the game such that at least one player is better off without the other player(s) being worse off. Another way to think of this is that an outcome is efficient or optimal if there is not another outcome in the game such that the players in the game would *unanimously* agree to another outcome—and players would unanimously agree to move only if no player was left worse off by the move.

Consider the game in table 1. We consider the outcomes one by one, starting with the strategy combination (U, L). This is a Pareto optimal (or Pareto efficient) outcome. While it is possible for one player to be made better off by moving to (D, L) or (U. R), it is also possible if the other player is left worse off relative to playing (U, L). While one player's payoff would increase from 5 to 8, the other player's payoff would decrease from 5 to zero. So, there would *not* be unanimous agreement among the players to move away from (U, L). Therefore (U, L) is an efficient outcome.

Next consider the outcomes represented by strategy combinations (D, L) and (U, R). Again, while it's true that in each case one of the players could do better, with a payoff increasing from zero to 5, in both cases, one player's payoff will decrease from 8 to 5. That player would not consent to the move; therefore, (D, L) and (U, R) are efficient outcomes.

Finally, consider the outcome of the strategy combination (D, R). In this case, there is one outcome such that at least one player is better off and the other player is not worse off. Indeed, if they were to move from (D, R) to (U, L), both players would be better off. So, there would be unanimous consent for the move, and the strategy combination (D, R) is not efficient.

As is obvious from this example, in game theory, equilibrium outcomes are not necessarily efficient, and efficient outcomes are not necessarily equilibrium outcomes. The prisoners' dilemma illustrates this divergence with a vengeance. The single equilibrium—(D, R)—is not efficient, and all of the other (pure-strategy) combinations are efficient without being equilibria. It's this aspect of the prisoners' dilemma that draws so much attention. While it's not really a "dilemma," it is a social tragedy that even though both players want to reach the efficient outcome, they're unable to do so voluntarily because of the incentive structure of the game. So the players are trapped in an inefficient outcome.

The Significance of Actions That Occur with Zero Probability

We now turn from defining equilibrium to consider three important implications or results in game theory. These three concepts certainly don't exhaust the list of important implications, but they are useful beginning points. Further, these concepts are used in several essays in this volume. The three topics we discuss are the significance of actions that occur with zero probability, how repeating or iterating a game can produce dramati-

FIGURE 1 A simple, extensive-form game of international interaction

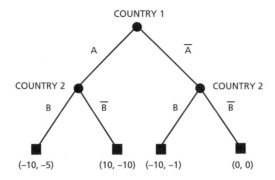

cally different outcomes than when the same game is played in a "single-shot," and how actions can signal otherwise unknown information.

We start with the significance of actions that occur in equilibrium with zero probability. This is one area in which game-theoretic reasoning helps to flesh out stories that wholly empirical studies can only partially reveal. To illustrate this idea, we will consider a subject area in which people are used to understanding the significance of actions that are not taken, namely, military deterrence. After developing the ideas in this more well-known area, we will then apply the lesson to a more controversial area in judicial politics. The simple model underscores the critical important distinction between actions that "cannot" occur and actions that "do not" occur.

Consider first the extensive-form game pictured in figure 1. The model is drawn in a game tree rather than in a table, because it's simpler to understand this way. (In fact, extensive-form games can be represented in normal-form tables and vice versa.) As stated above, we first consider military interaction between two countries, because it's one area in which most people readily perceive the significance of actions that don't occur for the actions that do occur. The model is very simple and aims only to illustrate this point.

There are two players, Country 1 and Country 2. Country 1 chooses between attacking and occupying territory it covets in Country 2 ("attack" is designated as "A") or not to attack Country 2 (designated as $\overline{A}$). In response, Country 2 chooses whether to bomb Country 1 (B) or not to bomb Country 1 ($\overline{B}$). Bombing Country 1 secures the return of its territory, albeit at the cost of this war. Country 1's strategy set is similar to those illustrated above in the normal-form game. $S_1 = \{A, \overline{A}\}$. Country 1's strategy set is simply a choice between two actions, attack or don't attack.

When Country 2 chooses its actions, however, it already knows what Country 1 has done. In identifying its strategy, then, we must stipulate actions for two contingencies—the contingency that Country 1 attacks and the contingency that Country 1 does not attack. A "strategy" in this game is not the same thing as an action (as it was in the normal-form game in table 1). Country 2's *actions* in this game are bombing or not bombing Country 1. Country 2's *strategy*, however, will state what action it will take in each of the contingencies it might face in the game.

One strategy for Country 2 is that it bombs Country 1 if it is attacked and that it bombs Country 1 even if it's not attacked. It is represented as follows, (B|A, B|$\overline{\text{A}}$). The ordered pair is read, "bomb given attack," and "bomb given no attack." Given that Country 2 has two contingencies, either one of which it might need to respond to, and given that it has two actions that it can take in either contingency, its strategy set is composed of four strategies. They are, S_2 = {(B|A, B|$\overline{\text{A}}$), (B|A, $\overline{\text{B}}$|$\overline{\text{A}}$), ($\overline{\text{B}}$|A, B|$\overline{\text{A}}$), ($\overline{\text{B}}$|A, $\overline{\text{B}}$|$\overline{\text{A}}$)}. Note that only one event will occur in equilibrium in the game— either Country 2 is attacked or Country 2 is not attacked. So, one of Country 2's contingencies will not arise even though Country 2's strategy dictated an action should that contingency have arisen. We will see below how this is very, very different from the nonexistence of that possible action.

Payoffs in the game are reported in figure 1. If Country 1 attacks Country 2 and Country 2 bombs Country 1, then Country 1 receives a payoff of −10 and Country 2 receives a payoff of −5. (The numbers, of course, are completely made up. What matters is the relationship of the payoffs to each other; not the abstract magnitude of the made-up numbers.) Country 2 gets its territory back from Country 1, but it suffers the destruction of people and materials in accomplishing that end. Country 1 does not get the territory and suffers from the bombing.

If Country 1 attacks Country 2 but Country 2 does *not* bomb in response, then Country 1 and Country 2's payoffs are (10, −10), respectively. Country 1 gets the territory it covets, while Country 2 loses that territory. If Country 1 does not attack Country 2, but Country 2 nonetheless bombs Country 1, their respective payoffs are (−10, −1). Country 1 gets bombed, Country 2, while not losing people and materials to Country 1's attack, nonetheless expends people and material in bombing Country 1. Finally, if Country 1 doesn't attack and if Country 2 doesn't bomb, then we have a continuation of the status quo, with a payoff for the respective countries of (0,0).

We solve this game by applying the concept of Nash equilibrium. As above, a Nash equilibrium exists only when no player has an incentive to deviate to another strategy, given what the other player is playing. There are eight (pure) strategy combinations in this game. Country 1's strategy is reported first, then Country 2's strategy is reported. The strategy combinations in this game are:

(A, (B|A, B|$\overline{\text{A}}$))
(A, (B|A, $\overline{\text{B}}$|$\overline{\text{A}}$))
(A, ($\overline{\text{B}}$|A, B|$\overline{\text{A}}$))
(A, ($\overline{\text{B}}$|A, $\overline{\text{B}}$|$\overline{\text{A}}$))
($\overline{\text{A}}$, (B|A, B|$\overline{\text{A}}$))
($\overline{\text{A}}$, (B|A, $\overline{\text{B}}$|$\overline{\text{A}}$))
($\overline{\text{A}}$, ($\overline{\text{B}}$|A, B|$\overline{\text{A}}$))
($\overline{\text{A}}$, ($\overline{\text{B}}$|A, $\overline{\text{B}}$|$\overline{\text{A}}$))

For example, the strategy combination,(A, (B|A, B|$\overline{\text{A}}$)), is read as "Country 1 attacks; Country 2 bombs if it is attacked and bombs if it is not attacked." The reader might ask, "Why should a strategy for Country 2 stipulate what it will do if Country A doesn't attack it, since Country 2 *has* attacked it in this strategy combination. We'll see why this is, in fact, very commonsensical (as well as analytically necessary) below.

In this game, we can apply "backward induction" to the game to determine the equilibrium outcome. Backward induction simply means that we start at the end of the game, seeing what action Country 2 will take in either contingency. Then, based on the choices it knows Country 2 will make, Country 1 will be able to choose its best strategy. The remaining equilibrium will be a Nash equilibrium. (Indeed, "backward induction" will sometimes return a smaller set of Nash equilibria that are called "subgame-perfect Nash equilibria.") Since we're reasoning backward up the game tree, we first consider Country 2's actions. If Country 2 is attacked, it has the choice of bombing or not bombing Country 1. If it bombs Country 1, then its payoff is −5; if it does not bomb Country 1, then its payoff is −10. So, if attacked, Country 2 is always better off bombing Country 1 (and getting back its territory, albeit, at the expense of military conflict). If Country 2 is not attacked, and it bombs Country 1, then its payoff is −1. If it is not attacked and it does not bomb Country 1, then its payoff is 0. So, Country 2 is better not bombing Country 1 if it is not attacked.

Applying backward induction, we've seen that Country 2 will play the following strategy, (B|A, $\overline{\text{B}}$|$\overline{\text{A}}$). Country 1 can look at Country 2's reason-

FIGURE 2 The game in figure 1 with off-equilibrium-path actions eliminated

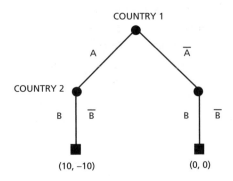

ing and deduce the outcomes of the game (and its payoffs) from whichever strategy it chooses. Given that Country 2 will bomb Country 1 if Country 1 attacks, then if Country 1 attacks, its payoff will be −10. Given that Country 2 will not bomb Country 1 if Country 1 does not attack, then if it does not attack, its payoff will be 0. Because 0 > −10, Country 1 will not attack Country 2. The (subgame-perfect) equilibrium in the game is the strategy combination, ($\overline{A}$, (B|A, $\overline{B}|\overline{A}$)).

Note, however, that the strategy combination reports an action for Country 2 for a contingency that does not occur in equilibrium. Namely, Country 2's strategy says, "bomb if attacked." But Country 1 does not attack. Why is it important for Country 2's strategy to include a response that it won't be required to take? Indeed, perhaps a peace movement arises in Country 2 and argues the following: "Look at the empirical evidence. Country 1 has never attacked us—we've had decades of peace—yet, we spend billions of dollars on bombs that we never use. We think the evidence shows that Country 1 is a peace-loving country. It's now time to reciprocate that trust and reduce our own military so we can spend the resources elsewhere."

Let's say that Country 2's peace movement succeeds in persuading the country's decision makers of Country 1's pacific nature, and Country 2 eliminates its bomber program. Now, no longer is it the case that Country 2 doesn't *choose* to bomb Country 2, now it *can't* bomb Country 2.

The new game is illustrated in figure 2. Country 2's alternative of bombing Country 1 is no longer feasible, so those actions have been dropped from the game. Consider the outcome now. If Country 1 attacks, Country 2 will not bomb it in response (indeed, Country 2 cannot bomb in response), and Country 1's payoff is 10. If Country 1 does not attack,

FIGURE 3 A simple game of institutional interaction

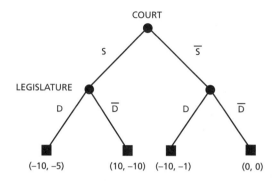

(-10, -5)   (10, -10) (-10, -1)   (0, 0)

Country 2 also does not bomb, and Country 1's payoff is 0. In this case, Country 1 is better off attacking Country 2, and does so.

Note, however, that the only thing changed in the games between figures 1 and 2 is that we dropped an action that *never* takes place in the game in figure 1. In the original game, Country 2 never bombs Country 1. But the reason that Country 2 never bombs Country 1 is that Country 1 knew that it would get bombed if it invaded. Country 2's threat deterred Country 1 from attacking. But a successful deterrent threat exists when that threat doesn't need to be carried out. Nonetheless, the action that occurs with zero probability in the original game—that is, in the original game, Country 2 bombs Country 1 with probability zero—is absolutely critical to the "no attack" outcome in the game. Eliminate the action that we don't observe in equilibrium, and the outcome of the game changes dramatically. Note that the two characterizations of Country 1's behavior are observationally equivalent. In both cases we observe "no war." This could be the result of Country 1's pacific nature, or it could be because Country 1 isn't pacific, but is deterred by Country 2's retaliatory threat. Which is truly the case is an important question that cannot be answered simply by an empirical appeal to the absence of war, and the project of that outcome into the future regardless of the strategies available to the two players.

There is a critical difference between a player *not choosing* to do something and a player not being *able* to do that same thing. This lesson is potentially important in judicial politics as well as in strategic studies. Consider a simple relabeling of the players and actions specified in the game presented in figure 3. Instead of two nations, we have a court and a legislature. Instead of attacks and bombings, we have a court that can choose to substitute its own policy preferences for those of the legislature (S) or choose not to substitute its policy preferences ($\overline{\text{S}}$). In response, the legislature may discipline the court (D) or not discipline the court ($\overline{\text{D}}$).

The payoffs remain the same. If the court substitutes its policy preferences for those of the legislature, and the legislature responds by disciplining the court, then the court is subordinated to the legislature, which the court does not like. Its payoff in that case is −10. The legislature has had to undergo a fight with a coordinate branch that has cost it in public support and time that could be devoted to other legislative needs. So, its payoff is −5. If the court usurps the legislature's policy role and the legislature does not discipline it, then the court can now realize its policy preferences (10), and the legislature has ceded some of its policy power to the court (−10). If the court does not usurp the legislature, yet the legislature still disciplines it, the court is still humbled (−10), and the legislature still must spend time and support disciplining the court (−5). Finally, if the court does not usurp the Legislature and the legislature does not usurp the court, then both players realize a payoff of 0. The (subgame-perfect) equilibrium will be ($\overline{\text{S}}$, (D|S, $\overline{\text{D}}|\overline{\text{S}}$)). The court doesn't substitute its policy preferences of those of the legislature, and the legislature is never observed disciplining the court for policy reasons.

Empirically, the U.S. Congress has never successfully impeached a Supreme Court justice for policy reasons. This observation is consistent with the problems of overcoming the supermajority requirement for impeachment. It's also consistent with the possibility that the Court never disagrees with the Congress that much, so Congress never has cause to impeach a justice. Some scholars go even farther, claiming that "Supreme Court justices *cannot* be removed from office for unpopular decisions" (Spaeth and Segal 1999, 18, emphasis added). All of these theories, however, are observationally equivalent to the outcome identified in the simple game above. In the game, the reason we've never seen a justice removed from office for policy reasons is because the threat of discipline itself deters justices from going too far in substituting their policy judgments for those of Congress.

I suspect that there is substantial empirical truth in all of the above hypotheses at one historical point or another. Nonetheless, it is incorrect to deduce a "cannot" from a "does not." That Congress, as an empirical matter, "does not" remove justices from office for policy reasons does not at all imply that they "cannot" do that. Indeed, as with the deterrence game above, if the "does not" is formally changed into a "cannot," then a completely different outcome can obtain in a game.

Actions that are never observed because they are "off the equilibrium path," nonetheless can play an absolutely critical role in the actions that we do observe. One implication of game theory is the possibility that empirical observable events are just the tip of the analytical iceberg. In political, economic, and social interaction, we often cannot explain or understand what we see unless we theorize about and model actions that we never see empirically, but nonetheless can have a critical influence on observed events.

Repeated Interaction

We now turn our attention to another concept used by writers in this book—how repeated play of a particular game can generate different outcomes. Consider again the version of the prisoners' dilemma in table 1. Recall that the equilibrium in the game was (D, R), with payoffs (1, 1) to the players. We are going to compare this result with what can happen if the game is repeated without a time horizon (i.e., is repeated infinitely).[5] We need to alter our jargon just a little bit in that table 1 now represents a "stage game," that is, a game played in a single stage of the infinite horizon game.

There is an immediate problem with repeating the game in table 1 an infinite number of times. While a payoff of 5 is greater than a payoff of 1 in the stage game, if the game is repeated an infinite number of times, then the payoffs of both outcomes would be infinity. Because neither the summation of an infinite number of 5s nor the summation of an infinite number of 1s is well defined, we can't compare the two payoffs.

But payoffs in the future are not really the same as payoffs today. Indeed, if someone were to ask you what you would pay today to have $1.00 delivered to you a year from now, you would probably be only willing to pay something less than $1.00. After all, the value of the dollar might be less next year because of inflation, or you might die between now and then and not be able to enjoy the dollar then as you would if you spent it today. And so forth. For all these reasons, most people would pay less than a dollar today for a contract that offered to deliver a dollar to them a year from today.

The amount that you would be willing to pay today for a dollar delivered to you next year is called your discount rate, δ, where $0 \leq \delta \leq 1$. The closer your discount rate is to zero, the more present oriented you are. The closer your discount rate is to one, the more future oriented you are. For example, if you think you're probably going to die within the next year, then you might pay only $0.20 today for a dollar delivered to you next year. That is, unless the return on your investment was very high, you would want to keep your dollar and spend it this year. In that case, your discount rate is $\delta = 0.2$. Conversely, if you were fairly confident that you'd be around to collect on your contract, then maybe you'd be willing to pay $.90 today for a dollar delivered a year from now. In that case, your discount rate would be $\delta = 0.9$. As your discount rate decreases, it means that you increasingly prefer consumption today to consumption in the future.

The existence of discounting also permits us to calculate the present value of an infinite stream of value. For example, what value would you place today on a stream of income that would pay you $1 every year ad infinitum? If your discount rate were δ, then the present value of a stream of payments starting today would be:

$$1 + \delta \cdot 1 + \delta^2 \cdot 1 + \delta^3 \cdot 1 + \ldots = \sum_{t=1}^{\infty} \delta^{t-1} \cdot 1 = \frac{1}{1-\delta}.$$

So, for example, if your discount rate is $\delta = 0.9$, the present value of this stream of payments for you would be $10. If your discount rate is $\delta = 0.2$, the present value of this stream of payments for you would be $1.25. The discounted value of sums different than 1 are easy enough to compute simply by multiplying the above fraction by the different value. For example, the present value of $5 is

$$\frac{5}{1-\delta},$$

and the present value of "s" dollars is

$$\frac{s}{1-\delta}.$$

A strategy for an infinite-horizon game specifies an action to be taken in each stage game. That also means that there are an infinite number of possible strategies in the game. So, listing all feasible strategies is obviously impossible. Instead, scholars often stipulate that players will play the same strategy in each stage game and then identify a rule that states when strategies played in the stage games will change. One of the best known of such rules is called "tit for tat." In this strategy, player 1 starts the game playing U (and player 2 plays L). Both players continue playing that strategy in every stage game *unless* one player changes and plays another strategy. In that case, the other player will play the other strategy in the next period, and in every subsequent period. For example, for player 1, the rule states that he will play U for all periods unless, in the previous period, player 2 plays R instead of L. If player 2 plays R in the previous period, then player 1 will play D in the next period and in all remaining periods. This is called a "trigger strategy," because player 2's change in strategy triggers a change in player 1's strategy.

So, now we consider the payoffs to playing this strategy and the incentive to deviate from this strategy. If neither player deviates from the tit-for-tat strategy, then each player will receive a payoff 5 ad infinitum. The present value (V) of this strategy is:

$$V = 5 + \delta \cdot 5 + \delta^2 \cdot 5 + \delta^3 \cdot 5 + \ldots = \frac{5}{1 - \delta}.$$

Now, we need to consider whether either player has an incentive to deviate to another strategy. Say player 1 deviates from this strategy and plays D in the current period instead of U. Player 1 then gets a payoff of 8 in the current period, but a payoff of 1 in all subsequent periods (because player 2 plays R in all subsequent periods). The present value of this action would be:

$$V = 8 + \delta \cdot 1 + \delta^2 \cdot 1 + \delta^3 \cdot 1 + \ldots = 8 + \frac{\delta}{1 - \delta}.$$

So, player 1 will not deviate from the tit-for-tat strategy as long as:

$$\frac{5}{1 - \delta} \geq 8 + \frac{\delta}{1 - \delta}.$$

Solving for δ, player 1 will not deviate from the tit-for-tat strategy as long as his discount factor is $\delta \geq {}^3/_7$. That is, as long as a player's discount factor is not "too low," then the player will play the tit-for-tat strategy defined above.

Unlike the single-shot game in which players end up at the jointly worst outcome, repeated interaction allows for future punishment for actions taken in the current period. As a result of the threat of future loss, players can sustain equilibrium strategies in each stage game that are not an equilibrium in the stage game considered by itself.

Signaling Games

Several of the essays in this volume also draw on the concept of signaling games. Signaling games can model the existence and communication of asymmetric information between the players. It is a means of modeling uncertainty regarding one or more of the players. That communication "can" occur doesn't mean that it must occur, or that it's always beneficial to the signaling player (the "sender"). Indeed, sometimes a player would prefer to communicate no information, but can't avoid it. Other times a player might want to send a message that seeks to mislead the other player. The player observing the message (the "receiver") sent by the sending player will use any information revealed to increase the receiver's expected payoff.

In the canonical form of the game discussed below, player 1 (the sender) has two "types." These "types" can reflect information external or internal to the player. They could be about the state of the world—whether there will be drought or flood this summer—or they could characterize internal disposition—whether the player is aggressive or pacific. Player 1 (the sender) knows his own type with certainty. Player 2 (the "receiver") is initially uncertain over which type player 1 is. Player 2, however, has "beliefs" about player 1's type and, critically, the strategy that player 1 chooses to play can (but not necessarily will) reveal information to player 2, allowing updating of beliefs about player 1's type.

Consider the game in figure 4. Player 1 has two types, t_1 and t_2. The probability that player 1 assumes either type is 0.5. In the parlance of these games, "nature" makes the initial selection regarding player 1's type. From this point onward, each type can effectively be considered a different player. Thus, the most basic signaling game effectively has three players, type 1 of player 1 (t_1), type 2 of player 1 (t_2), and player 2. Both types of player 1 can take one of two actions, L or R. A *strategy* for player 1 must stipulate an action that the player will take for any contingency. Thus, player 1's strategy sets includes four pure strategies. Each of these strategies are reported in this fashion: $(L|t_1, L|t_2)$. This reads that player 1 chooses left given that he is type 1 and chooses L given that he is type 2. Player 1's strategy set then is composed of the following pure strategies:

$$S_1 = \{(L|t_1, L|t_2), (L|t_1, R|t_2), (R|t_1, L|t_2), (R|t_1, R|t_2)\}.$$

Strategies $(L|t_1, L|t_2)$ and $(R|t_1, R|t_2)$ are called "pooling" strategies, because both types of player 1 take the same action. Strategies $(L|t_1, R|t_2)$ and $(R|t_1, L|t_2)$ are called "separating" strategies, because each type of player 1 takes a separate action. Whether player 1's types "pool" or "separate" in their actions critically affects the ability of player 2 to determine player 1's type.[6]

Player 2 observes only the actions that player 1 takes and does not directly observe player 1's type. From those actions, and from an initial

FIGURE 4   A simple signaling game

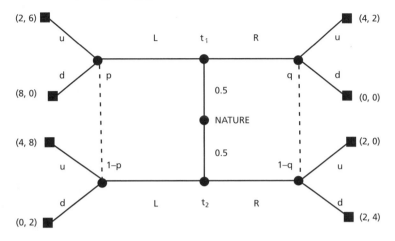

understanding of the probability distribution over player 1's types (which is common knowledge at the beginning of the game), player 2 can "update" beliefs about which type of player is playing the game. Player 2's beliefs are represented in figure 4 as p and 1-p (when player 1 chooses L), and as q and 1-q (when player 1 chooses R). These beliefs are formed by the strategy player 1 implements and by the application of a probability result known as Bayes's rule. (Because this rule is applied trivially in the canonical game, I will invoke it only intuitively below; there's no need to define it rigorously here.[7]) We will discuss these beliefs more below. As mentioned, player 2 observes only whether player 1 chose L or R. Therefore, player 2's strategy set is as follows:

S_2 = {(u|L, u|R), (u|L, d|R), (d|L, u|R), (d|L, d|R)}.

Equilibria in signaling games are typically a refinement of the regular Nash equilibrium. One of the most popular is called "perfect Bayesian equilibrium." As above, this initially includes the notion that no player or player type has any incentive to deviate to a different strategy, given the strategy of the other player. Beyond this, however, it also includes beliefs that player 2 forms based on the actions that player 1 takes. It is easiest to understand how this works in the context of a concrete example.

Consider the game in figure 4. We first consider whether there is an equilibrium in which player 1 adopts the pooling strategy of ($L|t_1$, $L|t_2$). The dotted lines on the left- and right-hand sides of figure 4 simply mean that player 2 must take the same action at the connected decision nodes (which are called "information sets"). So, if player 2 chooses u at the upper left-hand node, then player 2 must also choose u at the lower left-hand node. Given that *both* types of player 1 take the same action (L), and trivially applying Bayes's rule, it should be obvious that player 2 cannot know any more about player 1's type in observing "L" than at the beginning of the game. If both types of player 1 take the same action, then there is nothing in their behavior that allows player 2 to discriminate between the two types. Hence, at player 2's decision nodes on the left-hand side of figure 4, the belief about player 1's type is just p = 0.5. This is just what player 2 knew at the beginning of the game about the probability distribution over player 1's type.

Given that both types of player 1 play L, and given player 2's belief that p = 0.5, which action is most beneficial? If player 2 plays "u," the expected payoff will be ½(6) + ½(8) = 7. If the play is "d," the expected payoff will be ½(0) + ½(2) = 1 So, if player 2 chooses u|L, there will be no incentive to deviate to "d."

Recall, however, that a strategy in an extensive-form game must state the action a player will take in any possible contingency that might arise in the game. (And recall from above that actions along paths not taken in equilibrium can dramatically affect the outcome of the game.) So, we need to figure out what player 2 will do after observing that player 1 plays "R." The problem is that player 2 does not have any obvious belief about player 1's type after observing "R." After all, both types of player 1 are conjectured to play "L" in the strategy combination we're considering. To figure out what player 2 would be willing to play, we need to see what actions off-equilibrium-path beliefs would induce. To do this, we need to solve player 2's expected payoff for taking u and d respectively. Player 2's expected payoff for playing "u," given an observation of "R," is $2q + 0(1 - q) = 2q$. Player 2's expected payoff for playing "d," given an observation of "R," is $0q + 4(1 - q) = 4 - 4q$. So, for $2q > 4 - 4q$, player 2's best response is to play "u" (i.e., do not deviate to "d") and for $2q < 4 - 4q$, player 2's best response is to play "d." Solving for the q, we see that for any belief $q \geq \frac{2}{3}$, player 2 will play "u," and for $q \leq \frac{2}{3}$ player 2 will play "d." To identify which of player 2's actions are consistent with an equilibrium, we need to examine how player 1 would respond to each of player 2's possible choices.

First, consider t_1 of player 1. If player 1 plays L, given that player 2 is playing u|L, then t_1's payoff is 2. t_1 will have no incentive to deviate to R only if player 2 plays d|R (If player 2 plays u|R then t_1 receives a payoff of 4 from playing R. This would cause player 1 to want to deviate from L, where the payoff is only 2, given that player 2 is playing u|L.) Player 1's type 2 will never want to deviate from L to R, given that player 2 plays u|L. This payoff is 4 for playing L, and would be 2 if player 1 played R, irrespective of what player 2 chooses. Since player 1's strategy of playing $(L|t_1, L|t_2)$ can be sustained only if player 2 plays d|R then from the above paragraph, we know that player 2's "off-equilibrium-path beliefs" (i.e., the belief deduced from seeing "R" being played instead of "L") must be $q \leq \frac{2}{3}$.

Putting this altogether, then one equilibrium in this signaling game is

$$\left[(L|t_1, L|t_2), (u|L, d|R), p = 0.5, q \leq \frac{2}{3}\right].$$

The statement of the equilibrium specifies not only what action each player (and type of player) will take, but also specifies the beliefs that the receiver (player 2) will have as a result of the play of the game in order to sustain the strategy combination as an equilibrium. The reader can also confirm that another pure-strategy equilibrium exists in this game in which player 1's types separate. When that occurs, player 2 is able to deduce player 1's type from the actions player 2 observes.

Conclusion

The goal of the "primer" has not been to present an exhaustive course in game theory, but to build up the intuition of individuals who have not been exposed to much game theory in order to help them navigate some of the essays in this volume. As with any skill, such as map reading, what might seem abstract and off-putting at the beginning, with practice, can soon seem to be an almost indispensable tool with many useful applications. Part of the goal of this volume is to display the usefulness of "games" as one way to understand interaction between different parts of the government and the judiciary.

Notes

1. There are many introductory game theory texts ranging from very simple and intuitive introductions to sophisticated and technically rigorous. The following list is not exhaustive, but would be sufficient for those interested in a more-exhaustive introduction to game theory than this appendix provides. On the most intuitive level, Avinash Dixit and Barry Nalebuff's 1991 book, *Thinking Strategically: The Competitive Edge in Business, Politics and Everyday Life,* is hard to beat. Dixit also wrote (with Susan Skeath) a very accessible introductory undergraduate text, *Games of Strategy.* Robert Gibbons's *Game Theory for Applied Economists* does a very good job of introducing a more-rigorous un-

derstanding of game theory through the use of fairly simple, illustrative games. Rigorous introductions to game theory can be found in texts such as *A Course in Game Theory*, by Martin J. Osborne and Ariel Rubinstein, *Game Theory*, by Drew Fudenberg and Jean Tirole, and *Game Theory: Analysis of Conflict*, by Roger Myerson.

2. See, for example, Dixit and Nalebuff's decidedly nontechnical 1991 book, *Thinking Strategically*.

3. The name of the "prisoners' dilemma" derives from an early story used to motivate the game's incentive structure, that of a deal offered by a district attorney to two suspects in a crime to induce one or both of them to inform on the other suspect. Given the incentive structure constructed by the D.A., both suspects inform on each other, even though they would both be better off if both kept quiet.

4. A "pure strategy" is a strategy that a player plays with probability 1. It is distinguished from the play of mixed-strategy, when a player plays two or more strategies with nonzero probability. When referring to an "strategy combination" in this essay from now on, I'm referring to a pure-strategy combination unless I expressly state otherwise.

5. This can also be interpreted as a game that ends in the current period with some positive probability.

6. In games with more than two types, player 1's strategies may be pooling/separating hybrids called "semiseparating" or "partial pooling" strategies. These can permit the receiver sometimes to develop more refined beliefs about the sender's type without knowing that type with certainty, as it does in the game developed here.

7. Almost all of the texts mentioned in footnote 1 above discuss Bayes's rule more formally.

REFERENCES

Albert, James H., and Siddhartha Chib. 1993. "Bayesian Analysis of Binary and Polychotomous Response Data." *Journal of the American Statistical Association* 88 (June):669–79.

Austen-Smith, David, and Jeffrey S. Banks. 1996. "Information Aggregation, Rationality, and the Condorcet Jury Theorem." *American Political Science Review* 90 (March): 34–45.

Baker, Thomas E. 1994. *Rationing Justice on Appeal: The Problems of the U.S. Courts of Appeals.* St. Paul, MN: West Publishing Co.

Banks, Jeffrey, and Barry R. Weingast. 1992. "Political Control of Bureaucracies under Asymmetric Information." *American Journal of Political Science* 36 (May): 509–24.

Barnum, David G. 1985. "The Supreme Court and Public Opinion: Judicial Decision Making in the Post-New Deal Period." *Journal of Politics* 47 (February): 652–65.

Baum, Lawrence. 1976. "Implementation of Judicial Decisions." *American Politics Quarterly* 4 (January): 86–114.

———. 1977. "Policy Goals in Judicial Gatekeeping: A Proximity Model of Discretionary Jurisdiction." *American Journal of Political Science* 21 (February): 13–35.

———. 1978. "Lower Court Response to Supreme Court Decisions: Reconsidering a Negative Picture." *The Justice System Journal* 3 (Spring): 208–19.

———. 1981. "Comparing the Implementation of Legislative and Judicial Policies." In *Effective Policy Implementation,* edited by Daniel Mazmanian and Paul Sabatier, 39–62. Lexington, MA: Lexington Books.

———. 1995. *The Supreme Court.* 5th ed. Washington, DC: CQ Press.

———. 1997. *The Puzzle of Judicial Behavior.* Ann Arbor: University of Michigan Press.

Bennett, Robert W. 1979. "'Mere' Rationality in Constitutional Law: Judicial Review and Democratic Theory." *California Law Review* 67 (September): 1049–1103.

Bensel, Richard Franklin. 2000. *The Political Economy of American Industrialization, 1877–1900.* New York: Cambridge University Press.

Bergara, Mario, Barak Richman, and Pablo T. Spiller. 2003. "Modeling Supreme

Court Strategic Decision Making: The Congressional Constraint." *Legislative Studies Quarterly* 28 (May): 247–80.

Berger, Raoul. 1977. *Government by Judiciary: The Transformation of the Fourteenth Amendment.* Cambridge, MA: Harvard University Press.

Berry, William D., Evan J. Ringquist, Richard C. Fording, and Russell L. Hanson. 1998. "Measuring Citizen and Government Ideology in the American States, 1960–1993." *American Journal of Political Science* 42 (January): 327–48.

Bickel, Alexander. 1962. *The Least Dangerous Branch.* Indianapolis, IN: Bobbs-Merrill.

Blumm, Michael C. 2001. "Twenty Years of Environmental law: Role Reversals between Congress and the Executive, Judicial Activism Undermining the Environment, and the Proliferation of Environmental (and Anti-Environmental) Groups." *Virginia Environmental Law Journal* 20 (1): 5–15.

Boucher, Robert L., Jr., and Jeffrey A. Segal. 1995. "Supreme Court Justices as Strategic Decision Makers: Aggressive Grants and Defensive Denials on the Vinson Court." *Journal of Politics* 57 (August): 824–37.

Brams, Steven J., and Douglas Muzzio. 1977. "Unanimity in the Supreme Court: A Game-Theoretic Explanation of the Decision in the White House Tapes Case." *Public Choice* 32 (Winter): 67–83.

Brazill, Timothy J., and Bernard Grofman. 2002. "Factor Analysis versus Multidimensional Scaling: Binary Choice Roll-Call Voting and the U.S. Supreme Court." *Social Networks* 24: 201–29.

Brehm, John, and Scott Gates. 1999. *Working, Shirking and Sabotage: Bureaucratic Response to a Democratic Republic.* Ann Arbor: University Michigan Press.

Brenner, Saul. 1979. "The New Certiorari Game." *Journal of Politics* 41 (May): 649–55.

Brent, James C. 1999. "An Agent and Two Principals: U.S. Court of Appeals Responses to *Employment Division, Department of Human Resources v. Smith* and the Religious Freedom Restoration Act." *American Politics Quarterly* 27 (2): 236–66.

Caldeira, Gregory. 1986. "Neither the Purse nor the Sword: Dynamics of Public Confidence in the Supreme Court." *American Political Science Review* 80 (December): 1209–26.

Caldeira, Gregory A., and James L. Gibson. 1992. "The Etiology of Public Support for the Supreme Court." *American Journal of Political Science* 36 (August): 635–64.

Caldeira, Gregory A., and Donald J. McCrone. 1982. "Of Time and Judicial Activism: A Study of the U.S. Supreme Court, 1800–1973." In *Supreme Court Activism and Restraint,* edited by Stephen C. Halpern and Charles M. Lamb, 103–27. Lexington, MA: D. C. Heath.

Caldeira, Gregory A., John R. Wright, and Christopher Zorn. 1999. "Sophisticated Voting and Gatekeeping in the Supreme Court." *Journal of Law, Economics and Organization* 15 (3): 549–72.

Calvert, Randall. 1995. "The Rational Choice Theory of Social Institutions: Cooperation, Coordination, and Communication." In *Modern Political Economy,* edited by Jeffrey Banks and Eric Hanushek, 216–67. New York: Cambridge University Press.

Cameron, Charles M. 1993. "New Avenues for Modeling Judicial Politics." Paper presented at the Wallis Institute of Political Economy, University of Rochester, October.

Cameron, Charles M., and Lewis A. Kornhauser. 2005. "Decision Rules in a Judicial Hierarchy." *Journal of Institutional and Theoretical Economics* 161 (June): 264–92.

Cameron, Charles M., Jeffrey A. Segal and Donald Songer. 2000. "Strategic Auditing in a Political Hierarchy: An Informational Model of the Supreme Court's Certiorari Decisions." *American Political Science Review* 94 (March): 101–16.

Cameron, Colin, and Pravin K. Trivedi. 1998. *Regression Analysis of Count Data.* New York: Cambridge University Press.

Caminker, Evan H. 1994. "Why Must Inferior Courts Obey Superior Court Precedent?" *Stanford Law Review* 46 (April): 817–73.

Canon, Bradley C. and Charles A. Johnson. 1999. *Judicial Politics: Implementation and Impact.* 2nd ed. Washington, DC: CQ Press.

Carp, Robert A., and C. K. Rowland. 1983. *Politics and Policy Making in the Federal District Courts.* Knoxville: Univ. of Tennessee Press.

Carrubba, Clifford. 2002a. "An Analysis of the Evolution of Monitoring Mechanisms." [Unpublished manuscript.]

———. 2002b. "The Politics of Supranational Legal Integration: National Governments, the European Court of Justice and Development of EU Law." [Unpublished manuscript.]

———. 2005. "Courts and Compliance in International Regulatory Regimes." *Journal of Politics* 67 (August): 669–89.

Casper, Jonathan. 1976. "The Supreme Court and National Policy Making." *American Political Science Review* 70 (March): 50–63.

Cho, In-Koo, and David Kreps. 1987. "Signaling Games and Stable Equilibria," *Quarterly Journal of Economics* 102: 179–221.

Clark, Hunter R. 1995. *Justice Brennan: The Great Conciliator.* New York: Birch Lane Press.

Clinton, Robert. 1994. "Game Theory, Legal History, and the Origins of Judicial Review: A Revisionist Analysis of *Marbury vs Madison.*" *American Journal of Political Science* 38 (May): 285–302.

Cohen, Felix S. 1935. "Transcendental Nonsense and the Functional Approach," *Columbia Law Review* 35 (June): 809–49.

Cohen, Linda R., and Matthew L. Spitzer. 1994. "Solving the Chevron Puzzle." *Law and Contemporary Problems* 57 (Spring): 65–110.

———. 1996. "Judicial Deference to Agency Action: A Rational Choice Theory and an Empirical Test." *Southern California Law Review* 69 (January): 431–76.

Cox, Archibald. 1976. *The Role of the Supreme Court in American Government.* New York: Oxford University Press.

Cross, Frank R., and Emerson Tiller II. 1998. "Judicial Partisanship and Obedience to Legal Doctrine." *Yale Law Journal* 107 (May): 2155–76.

Dahl, Robert A. 1957. "Decision-Making in a Democracy: The Supreme Court as a National Policymaker." *Journal of Public Law* 6 (Spring): 279–95.

Daughety, Andrew F., and Jennifer F. Reinganum. 2000. "Appealing Judgments," *RAND Journal of Economics* 31 (3): 502–25.

DeGroot, Morris H. 1970. *Optimal Statistical Decisions.* New York: McGraw-Hill.

Dixit, Avinash, and Barry J. Nalebuff. 1991. *Thinking Strategically: The Competitive Edge in Business, Politics, and Everyday Life.* New York: W. W. Norton & Co.

Dixit, Avinash, and Susan Skeath. 2004. *Games of Strategy.* 2nd ed. New York: W. W. Norton & Co.

Eisler, Kim Isaac. 1993. *A Justice for All: William J. Brennan, Jr., and the Decisions That Transformed America.* New York: Simon & Schuster.

Ely, John Hart. 1980. *Democracy and Distrust.* Cambridge, MA: Harvard University Press.

Epp, Charles. 1998. *The Rights Revolution: Lawyers, Activists, and Supreme Courts in Comparative Perspective.* Chicago: University of Chicago Press.

Epstein, Lee, and Jack Knight. 1996. "On the Struggle for Judicial Supremacy." *Law and Society Review* 30 (1): 87–120.

———. 1998. *The Choices Justices Make.* Washington, DC: CQ Press.

Epstein, Lee, Jack Knight, and Andrew D. Martin. 2001. "The Supreme Court as a Strategic National Policymaker." *Emory Law Journal* 50 (Spring): 583–611.

Epstein, Lee, and Joseph F. Kobylka. 1992. *The Supreme Court and Legal Change: Abortion and the Death Penalty.* Chapel Hill: University of North Carolina Press.

Epstein, Lee, and Carol Mershon. 1996. "Measuring Political Preferences." *American Journal of Political Science* 40 (February): 261–95.

Epstein, Lee, and C. K. Rowland. 1991. "Debunking the Myth of Interest Group Invincibility in the Courts." *American Political Science Review* 85 (March): 205–17.

Epstein, Lee, and Jeffrey A. Segal. 2000. "Measuring Issue Salience." *American Journal of Political Science* 44 (January):66–83.

Epstein, Lee, and Thomas G. Walker. 1994. "The Role of the Supreme Court in American Society: Playing the Reconstruction Game." In *Contemplating Courts,* edited by Lee Epstein, 315–46. Washington, DC: CQ Press.

Erikson, Robert S., Gerald C. Wright, and John P. McIver. 1989. "Political Parties, Public Opinion, and State Policy in the United States." *American Political Science Review* 83 (September): 729–49.

———. 1993. *Statehouse Democracy: Public Opinion and Policy in the American States.* Cambridge, UK: Cambridge University Press.

Eskridge, William N., Jr. 1991a. "Overriding Supreme Court Statutory Interpretation Decisions." *Yale Law Journal* 101 (November): 331–417.

———. 1991b. "Reneging on History? Playing the Court/Congress/President Civil Rights Game." *California Law Review.* 79 (May): 613–648.

Eskridge, William, Jr., and Philip Frickey. 1994. "Forward: Law as Equilibrium." *Harvard Law Review* 108 (November): 26–95.

Fama, Eugene. 1980. "Agency Problems and the Theory of the Firm." *Journal of Political Economy* 88 (April): 288–307.

Farquharson, Robin. 1969. *The Theory of Voting.* London: Hodge.

Feddersen, Timothy, and Wolfgang Pesendorfer. 1999. "Elections, Information Aggregation, and Strategic Voting." *Proceedings of the National Academy of Science USA* 96 (September): 10572–74.

Fenno, Richard F. 1973. *Congressmen in Committees.* Boston: Little-Brown.

———. 1978. *Home Style.* Boston: Little-Brown.

Ferejohn, John A. 1992. "Law, Legislation, and Positive Political Theory." [Unpublished manuscript].

———. 1999. "Independent Judges, Dependent Judiciary: Explaining Judicial Independence." *Southern California Law Review* 72 (March): 353–84.

Ferejohn, John A., and Charles Shipan. 1990. "Congressional Influence on Bureaucracy." *Journal of Law, Economics and Organization* 6 (Special Issue): 1–20.

Ferejohn, John, and Barry Weingast. 1992. "A Positive Theory of Statutory Interpretation." *International Review of Law and Economics* 12 (June): 263–79.

Fisher, Louis. 1988. *Constitutional Dialogues: Interpretation as Political Process.* Princeton, NJ: Princeton University Press.

———. 1992. *Political Dynamics of Constitutional Law.* St. Paul, MN: West Publishing.

———. 1993. "The Legislative Veto: Invalidated, It Survives." *Law and Contemporary Problems* 56 (Autumn): 273–92.

———. 2001. "Congressional Checks on the Judiciary." In *Congress Confronts the Court: The Struggle for Legitimacy and Authority in Lawmaking,* edited by Colton C. Campbell and John F. Stack, 21–35. Lanham, MD: Rowman and Littlefield.

Flemming, Roy B., B. Dan Wood, and John Bohte. 1999. "Attention to Issues in a System of Separated Powers: The Macrodynamics of American Policy Agendas." *Journal of Politics* 61 (February): 76–108.

Frankfurter, Felix. 1924. "A Note on Advisory Opinions." *Harvard Law Review* 37 (June): 1002–9.

———. 1937. *The Commerce Clause.* Chapel Hill: University of North Carolina Press.

Frankfurter, Felix, and James M. Landis. 1928. *The Business of the Supreme Court.* New York: Macmillan.

Fudenberg, Drew, and Jean Tirole. 1992. *Game Theory.* Cambridge, MA: MIT Press.

Funston, Richard W. 1975. "The Supreme Court and Critical Elections." *American Political Science Review* 69 (September): 795–811.

Gates, John B. 1992. *The Supreme Court and Partisan Realignment: A Macro- and Micro-Level Perspective.* Boulder, CO: Westview.

Gely, Rafael, and Pablo T. Spiller. 1990. "A Rational Choice Theory of Supreme Court Statutory Decisions with Applications to the *State Farm* and *Grove City* Cases." *Journal of Law, Economics, and Organization* 6 (Fall): 263–300.

———. 1992. "The Political Economy of Supreme Court Constitutional Decisions: The Case of Roosevelt's Court-Packing Plan." *International Review of Law and Economics* 12 (March): 45–67.

Gibbons, Robert. 1992. *Game Theory for Applied Economists.* Princeton, NJ: Princeton University Press.

Gibson, James, Gregory Caldeira, and Vanessa Baird. 1998. "On the Legitimacy of National High Courts." *American Political Science Review* 92 (June): 343–58.

Giles, Michael W., Virginia A. Hettinger, and Todd Peppers. 2001. "Picking Federal Judges: A Note on Policy and Partisan Selection Agendas." *Political Research Quarterly* 54 (September): 623–41.

Gilligan, Thomas, and Keith Krehbiel. 1990. "Organization of Informative Committees by a Rational Legislature." *American Journal of Political Science* 34 (May): 531–64.

Goldman, Sheldon. 1975. "Voting Behavior on the U.S. Courts of Appeals Revisited." *American Political Science Review* 69 (June): 491–506.

———. 1997. *Picking Federal Judges: Lower Court Selection from Roosevelt through Reagan.* New Haven, CT: Yale University Press.

Graber, Mark A. 1998. "Establishing Judicial Review? *Schooner Peggy* and the Early Marshall Court." *Political Research Quarterly.* 51 (March): 221–39.

Grofman, Bernard, and Timothy J. Brazill. 2002. "Identifying the Median Justice on the Supreme Court through Multidimensional Scaling: Analysis of the 'Natural Courts' 1953–1991." *Public Choice.* 112: 55–79.

Grossman, Sanford, and Oliver Hart. 1983. "An Analysis of the Principal-Agent Problem." *Econometrica* 51 (January): 7–46.

Gruhl, John. 1980. "The Supreme Court's Impact on the Law of Libel: Compliance by Lower Federal Courts." *Western Political Quarterly* 33 (December): 502–19.

Hamilton, Alexander (1782/1987, 477), *Continentalist, No. 5,* 3 Papers (1782). In *The Founders' Constitution,* edited by Phillip Kurland and Ralph Lerner, 75–82. Chicago: University of Chicago Press.

———. [1787] 1961. *Federalist 78.* In *The Federalist Papers,* edited by Alexander Hamilton, James Madison, and John Jay. New York: Penguin.

Hamilton, Alexander, James Madison, and John Jay. [1787] 1999. *The Federalist Papers,* edited by Charles Kesler. New York: Mentor Publications.

———. [1788] 1961. *The Federalist Papers,* edited by Charles Kesler and Clinton Rossiter. New York. NAL Penguin.

Hammond, Thomas H., Chris W. Bonneau, and Reginald S. Sheehan. 1999. "Toward a Rational Choice Spatial Model of Supreme Court Decision-Making: Making Sense of Certiorari, the Original Vote on the Merits, Opinion Assignment, Coalition Formation and Maintenance, and the Final Vote on the Choice of Legal Doctrine." Presented at the Annual Meeting of the American Political Science Association, Atlanta.

———. 2005. *Strategic Behavior and Policy Choice on the U. S. Supreme Court.* Stanford, CA: Stanford University Press.

Hausegger, Lori, and Lawrence Baum. 1999. "Inviting Congressional Action: A Study of Supreme Court Motivations in Statutory Interpretation." *American Journal of Political Science* 43 (January): 162–85.

Hay, Peter, and Ronald D. Rotunda (1982). *The United States Federal System: Legal Integration in the American Experience.* New York: Oceana Publications.

Hellman, Arthur D. 1997. "The Shrunken Docket of the Rehnquist Court." In *The Supreme Court Review 1996,* edited by Dennis J. Hutchinson, David A. Strauss, and Geoffrey A. Stone, 403–38. Chicago: University of Chicago Press.

Hettinger, Virginia A., Stefanie A. Lindquist, and Wendy L. Martinek. 2004. "Comparing Attitudinal and Strategic Accounts of Dissenting Behavior on the U.S. Courts of Appeals." *American Journal of Political Science* 48 (January): 123–37.

Hettinger, Virginia A., and Christopher J. W. Zorn. 1999. "Signals, Models, and Congressional Overrides of the Supreme Court." Presented at the Annual Meeting of the Midwest Political Science Association, Chicago.

Holland, Kenneth, ed. 1991. *Judicial Activism in Comparative Perspective.* New York: St. Martin's.

Holmes, Oliver Wendell. 1897. "The Path of the Law." *Harvard Law Review* 10: 457–78.

Hyde, Alan. 1983. "The Concept of Legitimation in the Sociology of Law." *Wisconsin Law Review* 1983 (March–April): 379–426. 2001. "Explaining the Incidence and Timing of Congressional Responses to the U.S. Supreme Court." Working Paper, Emory University.

———. 2000. "Signals, Models, and Congressional Overrides of the Supreme Court." [Unpublished manuscript.]

Jackson, Vicki C. 1998. "Introduction: Congressional Control of Jurisdiction and the Future of the Federal Courts—Opposition, Agreement, and Hierarchy." *Georgetown Law Review* 86 (July): 2445–79.

Jensen, Michael C., and William H. Meckling. 1976. "Theory of the Firm: Managerial Behavior, Agency Costs and Ownership Structure." *Journal of Financial Economics* 3 (October): 305–60.

Johnson, Charles A. 1979. "Lower Court Reactions to Supreme Court Decisions: A Quantitative Examination." *American Journal of Political Science* 23 (November): 792–804.

Kagan, Robert, Bliss Cartwright, Lawrence M. Friedman, and Stanton Wheeler. 1978. "The Evolution of State Supreme Courts," *Michigan Law Review* 76 (6): 961–1005.

Kaplow, Louis. 1992. "Rules Versus Standards: An Economic Analysis." *Duke Law Journal* 42 (December): 557–629.

Kass, Robert E., and Adrian E. Raftery. 1995. "Bayes Factors." *Journal of the American Statistical Association* 90 (June): 773–95.

King, Gary. 1989. *Unifying Political Methodology: The Likelihood Theory of Statistical Inference.* New York: Cambridge University Press.

King, Gary, Michael Tomz, and Jason Wittenberg. 2000. "Making the Most of Statistical Analyses: Improving Interpretation and Presentation." *American Journal of Political Science.* 44 (April): 347–61.

Knight, Jack, and Lee Epstein. 1996. "The Norm of *Stare Decisis.*" *American Journal of Political Science* 40 (November): 1018–35.

———. 1998. *The Choices Justices Make.* Washington, DC: CQ Press.

Kornhauser, Lewis A. 1989. "An Economic Perspective on *Stare Decisis.*" *Chicago-Kent Law Review* 65 (1): 63–92.

————. 1992. "Modeling Collegial Courts I: Path-Dependence." *International Review of Law and Economics* 12 (June): 169–85.

————. 1995. "Adjudication of a Resource-Constrained Team: Hierarchy and Precedent in a Judicial System." *Southern California Law Review* 68 (September): 1605–29.

Kornhauser, Lewis A., and Lawrence G. Sager. 1993. "The One and the Many: Adjudication in Collegial Courts." *California Law Review* 81 (January): 1–59.

Kovacic, William E. 1991. "The Reagan Judiciary and Environmental Policy: The Impact of Appointments to the Federal Courts of Appeals." *Environmental Affairs* 18 (Summer): 669–713.

Krafka, Carol, Joseph Cecil, and Patricia Lombard. 1995. *Stalking the Increase in the Rate of Federal Civil Appeals.* Washington, DC: Federal Judicial Center.

Kraft, Michael E., and Norman J. Vig. 1990. "Environmental Policy from the 1970s to the 1990s: An Overview." In *Environmental Policy in the 1990s: Toward a New Agenda,* edited by Norman J. Vig and Michael E. Kraft, 3–31. Washington, DC: Congressional Quarterly.

Kreps, David M. 1990. *A Course in Microeconomic Theory.* Princeton, NJ: Princeton University Press.

Kuersten, Ashlyn K., Donald R. Songer, and Erin B. Kaheny. 1998. "Reexamining When and Where the Haves Come Out Ahead: The Intersection of Party Capability Theory and Political Disadvantage Theory in State Supreme Courts." Presented at the Annual Meeting of the Midwest Political Science Association, Chicago.

Kunda, Ziva. 1990. "The Case for Motivated Reasoning." *Psychological Bulletin* 108 (November): 480–98.

Landes, William, and Richard Posner. 1975. "The Independent Judiciary in an Interest Group Perspective." *Journal of Law and Economics* 18 (December): 875–902.

————. 1976. "Legal Precedent: A Theoretical and Empirical Analysis." *Journal of Law and Economics* 19 (September): 249–307.

Levinson, Sanford. 1973. "The Democratic Faith of Felix Frankfurter," *Stanford Law Review* 25 (February): 430–48.

Linde, Hans A. 1976. "Due Process of Lawmaking." *Nebraska Law Review* 55: 197–255.

Lindquist, Stefanie A., and David A. Yalof. 2001. "Congressional Responses to Federal Circuit Court Decisions." *Judicature* 85 (2): 60–68.

Llewellyn, Karl N. 1950. "Remarks on the Theory of Appellate Decision and the Rules or Canons about How Statutes Are to Be Construed." *Vanderbilt Law Review* 3: 395–406.

Lowi, Theodore. 1979. *The End of Liberalism: The Second Republic of the United States.* New York: Norton.

Lusky, Louis. 1993. *Our Nine Tribunes: The Supreme Court in Modern America.* Westport, CT: Praeger.

Macey, Jonathan R. 1989. "The Internal and External Costs and Benefits of *Stare Decisis.*" *Chicago-Kent Law Review* 65 (1): 93–113.

Madison, James [1785] 1987. *Draft of Resolutions on Foreign Trade, Virginia House of Delegates,* 12 Nov. In *The Founders' Constitution,* edited by Phillip Kurland and Ralph Lerner, 482–83. Chicago: University of Chicago Press.

———. [1787] 1987. *Records of the Federal Convention,* In *The Founders' Constitution,* edited by Phillip Kurland and Ralph Lerner, 483–86. Chicago: University of Chicago Press.

———. [1829] 1987. *Letter to Joseph C. Cabell, 13 Feb 1829,* 4 Letters. In *The Founders' Constitution,* edited by Phillip Kurland and Ralph Lerner, 52. Chicago: University of Chicago Press.

Maltz, Earl. 1980. "Some Thoughts on the Death of *Stare Decisis* in Constitutional Law." *Wisconsin Law Review* 1980: 467.

Maltzman, Forrest, James F. Spriggs II, and Paul J. Wahlbeck. 2000. *Crafting Law on the Supreme Court: The Collegial Game.* New York: Cambridge University Press.

Maltzman, Forrest, and Paul J. Wahlbeck. 1996. "Strategic Policy Considerations and Voting Fluidity on the Burger Court." *American Political Science Review* 90 (September): 581–91.

Manwaring, David R. 1972. "The Impact of *Mapp v. Ohio.*" In *The Supreme Court as Policy-maker: Three Studies of the Impact of Judicial Decisions,* 2nd ed., edited by David H. Everson, Carbondale, 1–43. IL: Public Affairs Research Bureau.

Marks, Brian A. 1989. *A Model of Judicial Influence on Congressional Policymaking: Grove City v. Bell.* PhD diss. Washington University.

Marshak, Jacob, and Roy Radner. 1972. *The Theory of Teams.* New Haven, CT: Yale University Press.

Marshall, Thomas. 1989. *Public Opinion and the Supreme Court.* Boston: Unwin Hyman.

Martin, Andrew D. 1998. *Strategic Decision Making and the Separation of Powers.* Ph.D. diss. Washington University.

———. 2001. "Congressional Decision Making and the Separation of Powers." *American Political Science Review* 95 (June): 361–78.

Martin, Andrew D., and Kevin M. Quinn. 2002. "Dynamic Ideal Point Estimation via Markov Chain Monte Carlo for the U.S. Supreme Court, 1953–1999." *Political Analysis* 10 (Spring): 134–53.

Mayhew, David R. 1974. *Congress: The Electoral Connection.* New Haven, CT: Yale University Press.

McCloskey, Robert. 1994. *The American Supreme Court,* 2nd ed. Revised by Sanford Levinson. Chicago: University of Chicago Press.

McCloskey, Robert G., and Sanford Levinson. 2000. *The American Supreme Court,* 3rd ed. Chicago: University of Chicago Press.

———. 2005. *The American Supreme Court,* 4th ed. Chicago: University of Chicago Press.

McCubbins, Matthew D., Roger G. Noll, and Barry R. Weingast. 1987. "Administrative Procedures as Instruments of Political Control." *Journal of Law, Economics, and Organization* 3 (Autumn): 243–77.

———. 1989. "Structure and Process, Politics and Policy: Administrative Arrangements and the Political Control of Agencies." *Virginia Law Review* 75 (March): 431–82.

McCubbins, Matthew D., and Thomas Schwartz. 1984. "Congressional Oversight Overlooked: Police Patrols and Fire Alarms." *American Journal of Political Science* 28 (February): 165–79.

McLean, Iain, and Arnold B. Urken, eds. 1995. *Classics of Social Choice.* Ann Arbor: University of Michigan Press.

McLennan, Andrew. 1998. "Consequences of the Condorcet Jury Theorem for Beneficial Information Aggregation by Rational Agents," *American Political Science Review* 92 (June): 413–18.

McNollgast (Mathew McCubbins, Roger Noll, and Barry Weingast). 1995. "Politics and the Courts: A Positive Theory of Judicial Doctrine and the Rule of Law." *Southern California Law Review* 68 (September): 1631–84.

McSpadden, Lettie. 1997. "Environmental Policy in the Courts," *Environmental Policy in the 1990s, 168–86,* edited by Norman J. Vig and Michael E. Kraft. Washington, DC: Congressional Quarterly Press.

Meernik, James, and Joseph Ignagni. 1997. "Judicial Review and Coordinate Construction of the Constitution." *American Journal of Political Science* 41 (April): 447–67.

Miller, Gary J. 1992. *Managerial Dilemmas: The Political Economy of Hierarchy.* New York: Cambridge University Press.

Mishler, William, and Reginald S. Sheehan. 1993. "The Supreme Court as a Counter-majoritarian Institution? The Impact of Public Opinion on Supreme Court Decisions." *American Political Science Review* 87 (March): 87–101.

———. 1994. "Response to Norpoth and Segal." *American Political Science Review* 88 (September): 716–24.

Mitnick, Barry M. 1980. *The Political Economy of Regulation: Creating, Designing, and Removing Regulatory Forms.* New York: Columbia University Press.

Moe, Terry M. 1982. "Regulatory Performance and Presidential Administration." *American Journal of Political Science* 26 (May): 197–224.

———. 1985. "Control and Feedback in Economic Regulation: The Case of the NLRB." *American Political Science Review* 79 (December): 1094–1116.

Murphy, Walter F. 1962. *Congress and the Court: A Case Study in the American Political Process.* Chicago: University of Chicago Press.

———. 1964. *Elements of Judicial Strategy.* Chicago: University of Chicago Press.

Murphy, Walter, and Joseph Tannenhaus. 1990. "Publicity, Public Opinion, and the Court." *Northwestern University Law Review* 84 (Spring/Summer): 985–1023.

Myerson, Roger B. 1991. *Game Theory: Analysis of Conflict.* Cambridge, MA. Harvard University Press.

———. 1992. "On the Value of Game Theory in Social Science." *Rationality and Society* 4 (January): 62–73.

Nelson, Caleb. 2001. "*Stare Decisis* and Demonstrably Erroneous Precedents." *Virginia Law Review* 87 (March): 1–84.

Norpoth, Helmut, and Jeffrey A. Segal. 1994. "Controversy: Popular Influence on

Supreme Court Decisions." *American Political Science Review* 88 (September): 711–16.

Note. 1956. "Advisory Opinions on the Constitutionality of Statutes." *Harvard Law Review* 69 (May): 1302–13.

Note. 1979. "State Economic Due Process: A Proposed Approach." *Yale Law Journal* 88 (June): 1487–1523.

O'Brien, David M. 1997. "Join-3 Votes, the Rule of Four, the *Cert.* Pool, and the Supreme Court's Shrinking Plenary Docket." *Journal of Law and Politics* 13 (Fall): 779–808.

O'Leary, Rosemary. 1993. *Environmental Change: Federal Courts and the EPA.* Philadelphia: Temple University Press.

Osborne, Martin J. 2004. *An Introduction to Game Theory.* New York: Oxford University Press.

Osborne, Martin J., and Ariel Rubinstein. 1994. *A Course in Game Theory.* Cambridge, MA: MIT Press.

Page, Benjamin, Robert Shapiro, and Glenn Dempsey. 1987. "What Moves Public Opinion?" *American Political Science Review* 81 (March): 23–44.

Perry, H. W. 1991. *Deciding to Decide: Agenda Setting on the U.S. Supreme Court.* Cambridge, MA: Harvard University Press.

Phelps, Glenn A., and John B. Gates. 1991. "The Myth of Jurisprudence: Interpretive Theory in the Constitutional Opinions of Justices Rehnquist and Brennan." *Santa Clara Law Review* 31 (3): 567–96.

Poole, Keith T., and Howard Rosenthal. 1997. *Congress: A Political-Economic History of Roll Call Voting.* New York: Oxford University Press.

Posner, Richard A. 1993. "What Do Judges and Justices Maximize? (The Same Thing Everybody Else Does)." *Supreme Court Economic Review* 3: 1–41.

———. 1995. *Overcoming Law.* Cambridge, MA: Harvard University Press.

Pritchett, C. Herman. 1948. *The Roosevelt Court.* New York: Macmillan.

———. 1961. *Congress versus the Supreme Court, 1957–1960.* Minneapolis: University of Minnesota Press.

Proceedings of Commissioners to Remedy Defects of the Federal Government. 1786. Annapolis, Maryland, September 11, 1786.

Radner, Roy. 1972. "Teams." In *Decision and Organization: A Volume in Honor of Jacob Marschak,* edited by C. B. McGuire and Roy Radner, 189–215. New York: American Elvesier.

Ramseyer, Mark. 1994. "The Puzzling (In)dependence of Courts: A Comparative Approach." *Journal of Legal Studies* 23 (June): 721–47.

Rasmusen, Eric. 1994. "Judicial Legitimacy as a Repeated Game." *Journal of Law, Economics, and Organization* 10 (April): 63–83.

Redish, Martin H., and Shane V. Nugent. 1987. "The Dormant Commerce Clause and the Constitutional Balance of Federalism." *Duke Law Journal* (September): 569–617.

Rehnquist, James C. 1986. "The Power That Shall be Vested in a Precedent: *Stare Decisis,* the Constitution and the Supreme Court." *Boston University Law Review* 66 (March): 345–76.

Resnik, Judith. 1998. "The Federal Courts and Congress: Additional Sources, Alternative Texts, and Altered Aspirations." *Georgetown Law Review* 86 (July): 2589–2634.

Revesz, Richard L. 1997. "Environmental Regulation, Ideology, and the D.C. Circuit." *Virginia Law Review* 83 (November): 1717–72.

———. 2001. "Congressional Influence on Judicial Behavior? An Empirical Examination of Challenges to Agency Action in the D.C. Circuit." *New York University Law Review* 76 (October): 1100–37.

Rodriguez, Daniel B. 1994. "The Positive Political Dimensions of Regulatory Reform." *Washington University Law Quarterly* 72 (Spring): 1–150.

Rogers, James R. 1999a. "Judicial Review Standards in Unicameral Legislative Systems: A Positive Theoretic and Historical Analysis." *Creighton Law Review* 33 (December): 65–120.

———. 1999b. "Legislative Incentives and Two-Tiered Judicial Review: A Game Theoretic Reading of *Carolene Products* Footnote Four." *American Journal of Political Science* 43, (4) (October): 1096–1121.

———. 2001a. "An Informational Rationale for Congruent Bicameralism." *Journal of Theoretical Politics.* 13 (2): 123–51.

———. 2001b. "Information and Judicial Review: A Signaling Game of Legislative-Judicial Interaction." *American Journal of Political Science* 45 (January): 84–99.

Rogers, James R., and Georg Vanberg. 2002. "Expedience Versus Experience: Judicial Advisory Opinions and Legislative Outcomes." *American Journal of Political Science* 46 (April): 379–97.

Rohde, David W. 1972a. "A Theory of the Formation of Opinion Coalitions in the U.S. Supreme Court." In *Probability Models of Collective Decision Making,* edited by Richard Niemi and Herbert Weisberg. Columbus, OH: Charles E. Merrill.

———. 1972b. "Policy Goals, Strategic Choice and Majority Opinion Assignments in the U.S. Supreme Court." *Midwest Journal of Political Science* 16 (November): 652–82.

———. 1979. "Risk Bearing and Progressive Ambition: The Case of Members of the United States House of Representatives." *American Journal of Political Science* 23 (February): 1–26.

Rohde, David W., and Harold J. Spaeth. 1976. *Supreme Court Decision Making.* San Francisco: W. H. Freeman.

Rosenberg, Gerald. 1991. *The Hollow Hope: Can Courts Bring about Social Change?* Chicago: University of Chicago Press.

Rosenberg, Gerald N. 1992. "Judicial Independence and the Reality of Political Power." *The Review of Politics* 54 (Summer): 369–98.

Sala, Brian R., and James F. Spriggs, II. 2004. "Designing Tests of the Supreme Court and the Separation of Powers." *Political Research Quarterly* 57 (June): 197–208.

Schauer, Frederick. 1987. "Precedent." *Stanford Law Review* 39 (February): 571–605.

Schlag, Pierre J. 1985. "Rules and Standards." *UCLA Law Review* 33 (December): 379–430.

Schlesinger, Joseph. 1966. *Ambition and Politics.* Chicago: Rand McNally.

Schubert, Glendon A. 1959. *Quantitative Analysis of Judicial Behavior.* Glencoe, IL: Free Press.

————. 1962. "Policy without Law: An Extension of the Certiorari Game." *Stanford Law Review* 14 (March): 284–327.

————. 1965. *The Judicial Mind: The Attitudes and Ideologies of Supreme Court Justices, 1946–1963.* Evanston, IL: Northwestern University Press.

————. 1974. *The Judicial Mind Revisited: A Psychometric Analysis of Supreme Court Ideology.* New York: Oxford University Press.

Schwartz, Edward P. 1992. "Policy, Precedent, and Power: A Positive Theory of Supreme Court Decision-Making." *Journal of Law, Economics and Organization* 8 (April): 219–52.

————. 1995. "A Comment on 'The Appeals Process as a Means of Error Correction,' by Steven Shavell." *Legal Theory* 1 (4): 361–63.

Segal, Jeffrey A. 1997. "Separation-of-Powers Games in the Positive Theory of Congress and Courts." *American Political Science Review* 91 (March): 28–44.

Segal, Jeffrey A., and Albert D. Cover. 1989. "Ideological Values and the Votes of U.S. Supreme Court Justices." *American Political Science Review* 83 (June): 557–65.

Segal, Jeffrey A., Lee Epstein, Charles M. Cameron, and Harold J. Spaeth. 1995. "Ideological Values and the Votes of U.S. Supreme Court Justices Revisited." *Journal of Politics* 57 (August): 812–23.

Segal, Jeffrey A., and Harold J. Spaeth. 1993. *The Supreme Court and the Attitudinal Model.* New York: Cambridge University Press.

————. 1996a. "The Influence of *Stare Decisis* on the Votes of United States Supreme Court Justices." *American Journal of Political Science* 40 (November): 971–1003.

————. 1996b. "Norms, Dragons, and *Stare Decisis:* A Response." *American Journal of Political Science* 40 (November): 1064–82.

————. 2002. *The Supreme Court and the Attitudinal Model Revisited.* New York: Cambridge University Press.

Segal, Jeffrey A., Richard J. Timpone, and Robert M. Howard. 2000. "Buyer Beware? Presidential Success through Supreme Court Appointments." *Political Research Quarterly* 53 (September): 557–73.

Shapiro, Martin. 1972. "Toward a Theory of *Stare Decisis.*" *Journal of Legal Studies* 1 (1): 125–34.

Shavell, Steven. 1995. "The Appeals Process as a Means of Error Correction," *Journal of Legal Studies* 24 (1): 379–426.

Shepsle, Kenneth A., and Mark S. Bonchek. 1996. *Analyzing Politics: Rationality, Behavior, and Institutions.* New York: W. W. Norton.

Shepsle, Kenneth A., and Barry R. Weingast. 1987. "The Institutional Foundations of Committee Power." *American Political Science Review* 81 (March): 85–104.

————. 1995. *Positive Theories of Congressional Institutions.* Ann Arbor: University of Michigan Press.

Shipan, Charles R. 1997. *Designing Judicial Review: Interest Groups, Congress and Communications Policy.* Ann Arbor: University of Michigan Press.

———. 2000. "Legislative Design of Judicial Review: A Formal Analysis." *Journal of Theoretical Politics* 12 (July): 269–304.

Simon, James F. 1980. *Independent Journey: The Life of William O. Douglas.* New York: Harper & Row.

Smith, Jean Edward. 1996. *John Marshall: Definer of a Nation.* New York: Henry Holt.

Smith, Joseph L. 1998. "An Empirical Test of Congressional Control of Judicial Review." Presented at the annual meeting of the Midwest Political Science Association, Chicago.

Songer, Donald R. 1987. "The Impact of the Supreme Court on Trends in Economic Policymaking in the United States Courts of Appeals." *Journal of Politics* 49 (August): 830–41.

Songer, Donald R., Charles M. Cameron, and Jeffrey A. Segal. 1994. "The Hierarchy of Justice: Testing a Principal-Agent Model of Supreme Court-Circuit Court Interactions." *American Journal of Political Science* 38 (August): 673–96.

Songer, Donald R., and Sue Davis. 1990. "The Impact of Party and Region on Voting Decisions in the U.S. Courts of Appeals." *Western Political Quarterly* 43 (June): 317–44.

Songer, Donald R., and Susan Haire. 1992. "Integrating Alternative Approaches to the Study of Judicial Voting: Obscenity Cases in the U.S. Courts of Appeals." *American Journal of Political Science* 36 (November): 963–82.

Songer, Donald R., and Stefanie A. Lindquist. 1996. "Not the Whole Story: The Impact of Justices' Values on Supreme Court Decision Making." *American Journal of Political Science* 40 (November): 1049–63.

Songer, Donald R., Jeffrey A. Segal, and Charles M. Cameron. 1994. "The Hierarchy of Justice: Testing a Principal-Agent Model of Supreme Court-Circuit Court Interactions." *American Journal of Political Science* 38 (August): 673–96.

Songer, Donald R., and Reginald S. Sheehan. 1990. "Supreme Court Impact on Compliance and Outcomes: *Miranda* and *New York Times* in the United States Courts of Appeals." *Western Political Quarterly* 43 (June): 297–319.

———. 1992. "Who Wins on Appeal? Upperdogs and Underdogs in the United States Courts of Appeals." 1992. *American Journal of Political Science* 36 (February): 235–58.

Songer, Donald R., Reginald S. Sheehan, and Susan B. Haire. 2000. *Continuity and Change on the United States Courts of Appeals.* Ann Arbor: University of Michigan Press.

Spaeth, Harold. 1997. "Supreme Court Judicial Database, 1953–1996 TERMS [Computer file]." 8th ICPSR version. East Lansing, MI: Michigan State University, Dept. of Political Science [producer], 1997. Ann Arbor, MI: Interuniversity Consortium for Political and Social Research [distributor], 1998.

Spaeth, Harold, and Jeffrey A. Segal. 1999. *Majority Rule or Minority Will.* New York: Cambridge University Press.

Spiller, Pablo T., and Rafael Gely. 1992. "Congressional Control or Judicial Independence: The Determinants of U.S. Supreme Court Labor Relations Decisions, 19481988." *RAND Journal of Economics* 23 (Winter): 463–92.

Spiller, Pablo T., and Matthew L. Spitzer. 1992. "Judicial Choice of Legal Doctrines." *Journal of Law, Economics and Organization* 8 (March): 9–46.

———. 1995. "Where Is the Sin in Sincere? Sophisticated Manipulation of Sincere Judicial Voters (with Applications to Other Voting Environments)." *Journal of Law, Economics and Organization* 11 (April): 32–63.

Spitzer, Matthew, and E. Talley. 1998. "Judicial Auditing." Working Paper 98–22, University of Southern California Law School, October.

Spriggs, James. 1996. "The Supreme Court and Federal Administrative Agencies: A Resource-Based Theory and Analysis of Judicial Impact." *American Journal of Political Science* 40 (November): 1122–51.

———. "Explaining Federal Bureaucratic Compliance with Supreme Court Opinions." *Political Research Quarterly* 50 (September): 567–93.

Stearns, Maxwell. 2000. *Constitutional Process: A Social Choice Analysis of Supreme Court Decision Making.* Ann Arbor: University of Michigan Press.

Stone, Alec. 1992. *The Birth of Judicial Politics in France.* New York: Oxford University Press.

Stone Sweet, Alec. 2000. *Governing with Judges.* Oxford, UK: Oxford University Press.

Stone Sweet, Alec, and Thomas Brunnel. 1998. "Constructing a Supranational Constitution: Dispute Resolution in the European Community." *American Political Science Review* 92 (March): 63–81.

Sullivan, Kathleen M. 1992. "The Justices of Rules and Standards." *Harvard Law Review* 106 (November): 22–97.

Talley, Eric. 1999. "Precedential Cascades: An Appraisal." *Southern California Law Review* 73 (November): 87–137.

Tarr, G. Alan. 1977. *Judicial Impact and State Supreme Courts.* Lexington, MA: Lexington Books.

Tate, C. Neal, and Torbjoern Vallinder. 1995. *The Global Expansion of Judicial Power.* New York: New York University Press.

Thayer, James B. 1893. "The Origin and Scope of the American Doctrine of Judicial Review," *Harvard Law Review* 7 (October): 129–85.

Tomz, Michael, Jason Wittenberg, and Gary King. 1999. CLARIFY: Software for Interpreting and Presenting Statistical Results. Version 1.2.1 Cambridge, MA: Harvard University, http://gking.harvard.edu/.

Urofsky, Melvin I. 1990. "Getting the Job Done: William O. Douglas and Collegiality in the Supreme Court." In *He Shall Not Pass This Way Again: The Legacy of Justice William O. Douglas,* edited by Stephen L. Wasby, 33–49. Pittsburgh, PA: University of Pittsburgh Press.

———. 1991. *Felix Frankfurter: Judicial Restraint and Individual Rights.* Boston: Twayne Publishers.

Vanberg, Georg. 1998. "Abstract Judicial Review, Legislative Bargaining, and Policy Compromise." *Journal of Theoretical Politics* 10 (July): 299–326.

———. 2000. "Establishing Judicial Independence in West Germany: The Impact of Opinion Leadership and the Separation of Powers." *Comparative Politics* 32 (April): 333–55.

———. 2001. "Legislative-Judicial Relations: A Game-theoretic Approach to Constitutional Review." *American Journal of Political Science* 45 (April): 346–61.

Vig, Norman J. 1997. "Presidential Leadership and the Environment: From Reagan to Clinton." In *Environmental Policy in the 1990s: Reform or Reaction,* edited by Norman J. Vig and Michael E. Kraft, 95–118. Washington, DC: CQ Press.

Weingast, Barry. 1997. "The Political Foundations of Democracy and the Rule of Law." *American Political Science Review* 91 (June): 245–63.

Weingast, Barry R., and Mark Moran. 1983. "Bureaucratic Discretion or Congressional Control? Regulatory Policymaking by the FTC." *Journal of Political Economy* 91 (October): 765–800.

Wenner, Lettie M. 1990. "Environmental Policy in the Courts." In *Environmental Policy in the 1990s: Toward a New Agenda,* edited by Norman J. Vig and Michael E. Kraft, 189–210. Washington, DC: Congressional Quarterly.

Wenner, Lettie M., and Lee E. Dutter. 1988. "Contextual Influences on Court Outcomes." *Western Political Quarterly* 41 (March): 115–34.

White, Halbert. 1980. "Heteroskedasticity-Consistent Covariance Matrix Estimator and a Direct Test for Heteroskedasticity." *Econometrica* 48 (May): 817–38.

Whittington, Keith. 2001. "The Strategic Environment of Judicial Review." Princeton University. [Unpublished manuscript.]

Wood, B. Dan, and Richard W. Waterman. 1991. "The Dynamics of Political Control of the Bureaucracy." *American Political Science Review* 85 (September): 801–28.

Zaller, John. 1992. *The Nature and Origins of Mass Opinion.* New York: Cambridge University Press.

Zeppos, Nicholas S. 1993. "Deference to Political Decision Makers and the Preferred Scope of Judicial Review," *Northwestern University Law Review* 88 (Fall): 296–335.

Cases

Bierkamp v. Rogers. 1980. 293 N.W.2d 577 (IA).
Brown v. Board of Education. 1954. 347 U.S. 483.
C & A Carbone, Inc. v. Clarkstown. 1994. 511 U.S. 383.
Chastleton Corp. v. Sinclair. 1924. 264 U.S. 543.
Chevron U.S.A. v. National Resources Defense Council. 1984 104 S.Ct. 2778.
Cohens v. Virginia. 1821. 19 U.S. 264.
Cooley v. Board of Wardens. 1851. 53 U.S. 299.
FCC v. Beach Communications, Inc. 1993. 508 U.S. 307.
Friends of the Earth v. Laidlaw. 2000. 528 U.S. 167.
Furman v. Georgia. 1972. 408 U.S. 238.
Gibbons v. Ogden. 1824. 9 Wheat 1.
Gratz v. Bollinger. 2003. 539 U.S. 244.
Greater Boston Television Corp. v. FCC. 1970 144 F.2d 841.
Gregg v. Georgia. 1976. 428 U.S. 153.

Grove City College v. Bell. 1984. 465 U.S. 555.

Grutter v. Bollinger. 2003. 539 U.S. 982.

Hopwood v. Texas. 1996. 78 F.3d 932.

Immigration and Naturalization Service v. Chadha. 1983. 462 U.S. 919.

International Harvester Co. v. Ruckelshaus. 1973. 478 F.2d 615.

Kassel v. Consolidated Freightways Corp. 1981. 450 U.S. 662.

Lujan v. Defenders of Wildlife. 1992. 504 U.S. 555.

Marbury v. Madison. 1803. 5 U.S. 137.

New York v. Miln. 1837. 36 U.S. 102.

Pacific Gas & Elec. So v. State Energy Resources Conservation & Development Comm'n. 1983. 461 U.S. 190.

Pierce v. New Hampshire. 1847. 46 U.S. (5 How.) 504.

Pike v. Bruce Church, Inc. 1970. 397 U.S. 137.

Scott v. Sandford. 1856. 60 U.S. (19 How.) 393.

Southern Pacific Co. v. Arizona. 1945. 325 U.S. 761.

Speiser v. Randall. 1958. 357 U.S. 513.

The License Cases. 1847. 46 U.S. 504.

The Passenger Cases. 1849. 48 U.S. 283.

United States v. Carolene Products. 1938. 304 U.S. 144,

United States v. Darby Lumber. 1941. 312 U.S. 100.

United States v. Lopez. 1995. 514 U.S. 549.

Vermont Yankee Nuclear Power Corp. v. Natural Resources Defense Council, Inc. 1978. 435 U.S. 519.

Worcester v. Georgia. 1832. 31 U.S. 515.

CONTRIBUTORS

LAWRENCE BAUM is a Professor of Political Science at Ohio State University. He works primarily in the field of judicial politics. His research interests include explanation of judicial behavior, selection of judges, and specialization of judges and courts. He is author of *The Supreme Court, American Courts,* and *The Puzzle of Judicial Behavior.*

JON R. BOND is Professor of Political Science at Texas A&M University. His research analyzes how the interactions of American political institutions affect policymaking and the operation of democracy in American politics. He is coauthor of *The President in the Legislative Arena* and *Promise and Performance of American Democracy* and coeditor of *Polarized Politics: Congress and the President in a Partisan Era.* He has published articles the *American Political Science Review,* the *American Journal of Political Science,* the *Journal of Politics,* the *British Journal of Political Science,* and the *Legislative Studies Quarterly.* He was an APSA Congressional Fellow, and he has served as coeditor of the *Journal of Politics.* He is currently president-elect of the Southern Political Science Association and Pi Sigma Alpha.

CHRIS W. BONNEAU is Assistant Professor of Political Science at the University of Pittsburgh. His research focuses on judicial elections as well as on theoretical studies of judicial decision making. He is coauthor of *Strategic Behavior and Policy Choice on the U.S. Supreme Court* and has published articles in several journals, including the *American Journal of Political Science, Political Research Quarterly,* and *American Politics Research.*

ETHAN BUENO DE MESQUITA is an Assistant Professor of Political Science and Resident Fellow at the Center in Political Economy at Washington University in St. Louis. His research focuses on applications of game theory to comparative politics, including terrorism, the political economy of weakly institutionalized environments, and electoral politics. His work has appeared in the *American Political Science Review, American Journal of Political Science, International Organization, Journal of Politics,* and elsewhere.

CHARLES M. CAMERON is jointly appointed in the Department of Politics and the Woodrow Wilson School of Public and International Affairs, Princeton University.

He specializes in the analysis of political institutions, particularly courts and law, the American presidency, and legislatures. His work often combines game theory and quantitative methods and sometimes historical materials. The author of numerous articles in leading journals of political science, he is also the author of *Veto Bargaining: Presidents and the Politics of Negative Power,* which won the American Political Science Association's Fenno Prize, for best book in legislative studies and the William Riker Award, as best book in political economy. A recipient of multiple grants from the National Science Foundation, he has been a Research Fellow at the Brookings Institution, a National Fellow at the Hoover Institution, a Visiting Scholar at Princeton's Center for the Study of Democratic Politics, is a scheduled fellow at the Center for Advanced Study in Behavioral Science, and has a recurrent visiting affiliation as Professor at New York University School of Law. Before joining the faculty of Princeton, he taught for 15 years at Columbia University. He holds the M.P.A. and Ph.D. (Public Affairs) from Princeton University.

CLIFFORD J. CARRUBBA is an Associate Professor of Political Science at Emory University. His research interests include theories of legislative and judicial institutional design, the European Union, and the U.S. Supreme Court. His work has appeared in the *American Journal of Political Science, Journal of Politics, International Organization, Journal of Law, Economics and Organization,* and *European Union Politics.*

ROY B. FLEMMING is Professor of Political Science at Texas A&M University. His research is centered at the intersection of law, courts, and politics. He approaches this topic from both institutional and comparative perspectives to develop an understanding of how interactions between institutions affect decisions about the law. Professor Flemming has published extensively on local criminal court processes in different communities. He has now turned his attention to higher courts in the United State and other countries. His book, *Tournament of Appeals: Granting Judicial Review in Canada,* was recently published by the University of British Columbia Press. The National Science Foundation supported this study, as it did his earlier work on criminal courts. The Canadian project originated in prior work on the effects of U.S. Supreme Court decisions on media attention to legal issues and on how interactions between the Court, Congress, and presidency affect the decision-making agendas of each branch. Articles on these and other topics have appeared in the leading journals in the discipline. He currently serves on the executive board of the Law and Courts Section of the American Political Science Association. As a Fulbright Research Scholar at the Institute of Canadian Studies in Ottawa during the spring of 2002 and a visiting fellow in 2002–2003 at the Australian National University in Canberra, he started a new project on government litigation in Australia and Canada. This project, "Governments in Courts: Judicial-Parliamentary Interactions in Australia and Canada," would be one of first explorations of the separation of powers game in Westminster parliamentary systems.

SUSAN B. HAIRE is Associate Professor of Political Science in the School of Public and International Affairs at the University of Georgia. Her research has focused on the U.S. Courts of Appeals, with particular emphasis on judicial decision making and the role of litigant resources. Haire's current projects include a study of hierarchical relationships in the federal courts and National Science Foundation-funded collaborative research to extend the Multi-User Database of decisions of the U.S. Courts of Appeals. She is the coauthor of *Continuity and Change on the United States Courts of Appeals.* Her articles have appeared in *American Journal of Political Science, Journal of Politics, Judicature, Justice System Journal,* and *Law and Society Review.*

THOMAS H. HAMMOND is Professor of Political Science at Michigan State University. He is coauthor of *Strategic Behavior and Policy Choice on the U.S. Supreme Court.* His current research involves theoretical studies of judicial decision making, the organizational design of the U.S. intelligence community, and multi-institutional explanations for the committee and leadership structures in the U.S. House of Representatives and the U.S. Senate. He has published articles in such journals as the *American Political Science Review, American Journal of Political Science, Journal of Politics, Journal of Law, Economics, and Organization, Journal of Theoretical Politics, Legislative Studies Quarterly, Public Choice, Journal of Public Administrative Research and Theory,* and *Governance.*

LEWIS A. KORNHAUSER is the Alfred B. Engelberg Professor of Law and the Director of the Institute for Law and Society at New York University. He writes generally on a wide range of topics in the area of economic analysis of law. His work has appeared in the *Journal of Law, Economics and Organization, Journal of Legal Studies,* and *Philosophy and Public Affairs.*

STEFANIE A. LINDQUIST is Associate Professor of Political Science and Law at Vanderbilt University. Her research interests include judicial behavior in the federal courts, particularly at the circuit level, and in state supreme courts. She is coauthor of *Judging on a Collegial Court: Influences on Federal Appellate Decision Making* (Virginia) and has published articles in the *American Journal of Political Science, Political Research Quarterly, Law and Society Review, American Politics Research, Social Science Quarterly,* and *Judicature,* as well as in various law reviews.

ANDREW D. MARTIN is Associate Professor of Political Science, Professor of Law (by courtesy), Resident Fellow of the Center in Political Economy, and Director of the Program in Applied Statistics and Computation at Washington University in St. Louis. His research focuses on political methodology, Bayesian statistics, statistical computing, and American political institutions. He has authored articles in the *American Political Science Review, American Journal of Political Science, Statistical Science, Political Analysis,* and other journals and law reviews.

JAMES R. ROGERS is an Associate Professor of Political Science at Texas A&M University and coeditor of the *Journal of Theoretical Politics.* His research examines how courts and other institutions in separation-of-power systems mutually construct their decision-making environment and the impact their reciprocal influence has on institutional behavior and policy outcomes. His publications include "Information and Judicial Review: A Signaling Game of Judicial-Legislative Interaction," *American Journal of Political Science,* "National Judicial Power and the Dormant Commerce Clause (with C. Carrubba), *Journal of Law, Economics, and Organization,* and "Judicial Advisory

Opinions and Legislative Outcomes" *American Journal of Political Science* (with G. Vanberg). Other articles have been published in the *American Journal of Political Science, Legislative Studies Quarterly, Journal of Theoretical Politics, Public Choice, The Tax Lawyer,* and *Creighton Law Review.*

REGINALD S. SHEEHAN is Professor of Political Science at Michigan State University. His research focuses on decision making in the United States Supreme Court and the United States Courts of Appeals. He is coauthor of *Strategic Behavior and Policy Choice on the U.S. Supreme Court.* He is currently working on a cross-national comparative project focusing on high courts in several countries. Professor Sheehan has published in the *American Political Science Review, American Journal of Political Science, Journal of Politics,* and a variety of other political science journals and law reviews. He is also coauthor of *Continuity and Change in the United States Courts of Appeals.*

KENNETH A. SHEPSLE is the George D. Markham Professor of Government at Harvard University and a founding member of its Center for Basic Research in the Social Sciences (now the Institute for Quantitative Social Science). He formerly taught at Washington University, St. Louis. He is the author or editor of a dozen books, including *The Giant Jigsaw Puzzle, Making and Breaking Governments,* and *Analyzing Politics,* and has written numerous articles on formal political theory, congressional and parliamentary politics, and political economy. He was a National Fellow at the Hoover Institution, Fellow of the Center for Advanced Study in the Behavioral Sciences, and a Guggenheim Fellow. He is a past vice president of the American Political Science Association. In 1990 he was elected to the National Academy of Sciences and to the American Academy of Arts and Sciences. He was Chair of the Department of Government at Harvard, 1995–98. His current research is at the interface of political economy and demography, focusing on formal models and empirical analysis of political institutions and intergenerational politics.

MATTHEW STEPHENSON is an Assistant Professor of Law at Harvard Law School. His research focuses on the separation of powers, judicial independence, and administrative and environmental law. His work has appeared in the *American Political Science Review, Harvard Law Review, Journal of Legal Studies, Journal of Law, Economics and Organization,* and elsewhere.

GEORG VANBERG is an Associate Professor in the Department of Political Science at the University of North Carolina at Chapel Hill. His research interests focus on comparative constitutional and judicial politics as well as on coalition theory. His work has appeared in the *American Political Science Review, American Journal of Political Science, British Journal of Political Science,* and *Comparative Politics.*

CHRISTOPHER ZORN is Associate Professor of Political Science at the University of South Carolina. He was formerly the Program Director for Law and Social Science at the National Science Foundation and the Winship Distinguished Research Professor of Political Science at Emory University. His work on judicial and legislative politics and quantitative methods has appeared in the *American Political Science Review, American Journal of Political Science, Journal of Politics,* and other journals.

INDEX

The letter t *following a page number denotes a table, while the letter* f *indicates a figure*

abstraction, and game theory, 275–78

active justices: in Court of Appeals/Supreme Court interactions models, 163–68; and minimalist and maximalist outcomes, 164f; and open-bidding model, 166–68, 172n8

add-on appeals process, theorem of desirability of, 175–76, 203n4

administrative agencies/agents: circuit court judges' deference to, 231, 240, 242–44, 258n5; congressional concerns for presidential influence over, 241; and presidential policy preferences, 258n6. *See also* executive branch, constraints on Court; presidential policy preferences

administrative policy: constraints on court in shaping, 95n5; in enforcement-power model, 95n6; evasion of judicial decisions on, 73–74; resistance to implementation of judicial decision on change in, 70. *See also* executive branch, constraints on Court; presidential policy preferences

Administrative Procedures Act, 243, 249

agency models, xviii–xix. *See also* agent(s)

agenda-control decision-making model, 142; and active justices, 164–66; versus open-bidding model, 166–68, 172n8; and passive justices, 163–64; and policy preference change among justices, 171–72n6

agent(s): in enforcement-power model, 75, 78t; and environmental law, 232–33; in multiple-principal model, 235–38; power

ranking, in perfect Bayesian equilibrium, 83; response to judicial veto weighing public support by, 96n15. *See also* litigants; principal-agent theories

agent evasion threshold, 78–79, 95n12, 96n13

agent self-censoring equilibria: comparative statics predictions, 84t, 85; judicial power in, 82; in perfect Bayesian equilibria, 79–80

agreement with other branches, measures of, 62

"almost per se unconstitutional" test: and state laws discriminating against interstate commerce, 113–14; of weak Court model and dormant Commerce Clause doctrine, 111, 114–15

anti-error-correcting appeals process, 175

anti-error-introducing appeals process, 175

anti-selective appeals process, 175

appeals court decisions: choices in, 214–15; content of, minimalist perspective and, 130–31, 170; informational benefit of maintaining precedent in, 216; legitimate versus illegitimate, 203n1. *See also* circuit court judge(s); Court(s) of Appeals; decision contexts

appeals court judge(s): between chief justice and median justice, 161f; with chief justice between median justice and, 163f; empirical evaluation of ideal point of, 170; and ideal points for Supreme Court

information (*continued*)
203n7; asymmetric, and lower courts
compliance with Supreme Court decisions, 128; bargaining model with, 7; in
game forms, xvii; hidden, judicial error in
team approach of adjudication and, 178;
in judicial hierarchies, litigant selection
and, 194; in judicial-legislative interactions model, 39–41, 42n7; from judicial review, congressional majorities and,
123n16; in long-established precedents,
224; perfect model of Court of
Appeals/Supreme Court interactions,
137–38; private, of litigants, 190–91,
203n12; requirements for legislatures,
and rationality standard, 26–27; and
stare decisis use by policy-oriented
judges, 209. *See also* communication
between high and lower courts
informational use of legal precedent model,
210–14; appellate judge's decision, 214–
16; comparative static analysis, 218–21;
limits of legal change, 221–23, 229n15;
new hypotheses, 224–26; trial judge's decision, 217–18, 229nn12–13; use of, xvii–
xviii. *See also* communication between
high and lower courts
interest groups: circuit court judges' interactions with, 231; and circuit judge decisions on environmental law, 244–45,
249–50; as competing litigants, 58; as
disruptive element in Congress-Court
interaction model, 48, 52–53, 53f, 55,
57; environmental policy influence measures, 260n15; environmental policy
preference measures, 248; as noncompliance monitors, 74; and Supreme Court
control over circuit court decisions, 236–
37. *See also* Landes-Posner interest-group
theory of judicial independence
international agencies, and exogenous enforcement, 75
interstate commerce: Articles of Confederation on, 99; model with ascendant national court, 107–9; model without a
national court, 101, 119; model with
weak national court, 103–7; punishment

path behavior model, 104–5; regulation
of, prisoner's dilemma and, 100; solutions
to model with weak national court, 104–
9; solution to model without a national
court, 102–3; state laws not discriminating against, 122n13; weak-Court equilibrium model, 105–7. *See also* Commerce
Clause; dormant Commerce Clause
issue dimensions: assumptions in Court of
Appeals/Supreme Court interactions
models, 133–34; characterization of,
171n1

Jackson, Andrew, 69
Johnson, William, 99, 111
judicial deference: and Condorcet jury theorem, 37–38; in game theory, 36; legalist
decision making and, 224, 227–28n4;
and respect for legal precedent by policy-
oriented judges, 208–9, 228n5; Supreme
Court decision making and, 223. *See also*
deferential review
judicial errors: in informational use of legal
precedent model, 210–11; in separating
equilibrium of two-tier hierarchy model,
184; sources of, 177–78. *See also* error
rate
judicial hierarchies, xiv; appellate process
and, 173–74; error sources, 177–78; flat
model, 182–83; information structures
in, 179–80; litigant selection, 181–82;
and political control of circuit court decisions, 236; proof of proposition 2D, 201;
semiseparating equilibrium proof in two-
tier game, 199–201; separating equilibrium proof in three-tier game, 201–3;
separating equilibrium proof in two-tier
game, 198–99; structural consequences
of litigant selection, 191–93; structure of,
174–76; three-tier model, 188–91; T-tier
versus T+1, 194–98; as two levels of a
team, 264; two-tier, 182–88
judicial independence: definitions of, 41n4;
and democracy, 43–44; and interdependence of federal policymaking, 262–63;
Landes-Posner on costs of, 45. *See also*
Congress-Court interaction model;

trigger strategy, in infinite-horizon games, 291

two-tier model, of judicial appellate system, 182–88; optimal, 203n5; separating equilibrium proof, 198–99

unconstrained policy advocate courts: and constraints on other policymakers, 67n12; definition of, 50; and equilibrium policy, 67n7. *See also* originalist courts

universal divinity, 203n11

upholding decision of agent: cost of, in enforcement-power model, 76–77; in enforcement-power model, 75; and pay-off for convergent court, 95n10

utility costs, of appellate judge in informational use of legal precedent model, 213–14, 228–29n11. *See also* costs

utility function: of appellate judge in informational use of legal precedent model, 212–13; in Court of Appeals/Supreme Court interactions models, 134; in enforcement-power model, 77; in normal-form game, 279; team approach of adjudication and, 178, 181–82

Vanberg, Georg, x, 263, 272n3

vetoes. *See* judicial vetoes; legislative vetoes, enforcement of invalidation of; presidential vetoes

Wayne, James, 116, 123n15

weak-Court equilibrium: in doctrinal strategy of dormant Commerce Clause, 109–15, 116–17, 119–21; and European Union–European Court of Justice, 122n9; interstate commerce model under, 105–7

weak judicial veto threshold, 78–79, 96n13

Weingast, Barry: on citizen respect for rules of the game, 73; on court position and types, 49, 50, 67n5, 67n7; multiple principle-agents theory and, 235–36; on positive power models of judicial interdependence, 47

win-set of the status quo, 135–36, 136f

Woodbury, Levi, 111–12

Worcester v. Georgia (1832), 69

workload: for Courts of Appeal, 230–31; for lower courts, decision making and, 266; as primary basis for judicial action in courts without discretionary jurisdiction, 272n6; for Supreme Court, 265. *See also* time-and-energy limits

wrongly decided cases, probability for appeal or reversal, 175

zero probability, significance of actions that occur with, 282–89, 283f, 286f–87f

Zorn, Christopher, x, 263

Constitutionalism and Democracy

Kevin T. McGuire
The Supreme Court Bar: Legal Elites in the Washington Community

Mark Tushnet, ed.
The Warren Court in Historical and Political Perspective

David N. Mayer
The Constitutional Thought of Thomas Jefferson

F. Thornton Miller
Juries and Judges versus the Law: Virginia's Provincial Legal Perspective, 1783–1828

Martin Edelman
Courts, Politics, and Culture in Israel

Tony Freyer
Producers versus Capitalists: Constitutional Conflict in Antebellum America

Amitai Etzioni, ed.
New Communitarian Thinking: Persons, Virtues, Institutions, and Communities

Gregg Ivers
To Build a Wall: American Jews and the Separation of Church and State

Eric W. Rise
The Martinsville Seven: Race, Rape, and Capital Punishment

Stephen L. Wasby
Race Relations Litigation in an Age of Complexity

Peter H. Russell and David M. O'Brien, eds.
Judicial Independence in the Age of Democracy: Critical Perspectives from around the World

Gregg Ivers and Kevin T. McGuire, eds.
Creating Constitutional Change

Stuart Streichler
Justice Curtis in the Civil War Era: At the Crossroads of American Constitutionalism

Virginia A. Hettinger, Stefanie A. Lindquist, and Wendy L. Martinek
Judging on a Collegial Court: Influences on Federal Appellate Decision Making

James R. Rogers, Roy B. Flemming, Jon R. Bond, eds.
Institutional Games and the U.S. Supreme Court